Under Crescent and Cross

Under Crescent and Cross

THE JEWS IN THE MIDDLE AGES

Mark R. Cohen

PRINCETON UNIVERSITY PRESS

PRINCETON, NEW JERSEY

Published by Princeton University Press, 41 William Street,
Princeton, New Jersey 08540
In the United Kingdom: Princeton University Press, Chichester, West Sussex

Library of Congress Cataloging-in-Publication Data

Cohen, Mark R., 1943–
Under crescent and cross : the Jews in the Middle
Ages / Mark R. Cohen.
p. cm.
Includes bibliographical references and index.
ISBN 0-691-03378-1
1. Judaism—Relations—Christianity—History.
2. Christianity and other religions—Judaism—History.
3. Judaism—Relations—Islam—History.
4. Islam—Relations—Judaism—History. 5. Judaism—
History—Medieval and early modern period, 425–1789.
6. Jews—History—70–1789. I. Title.
BM535.C6125 1994 909′.04924—dc20 93-42865 CIP

This book has been composed in Bembo

Princeton University Press books are printed on acid-free paper and meet the guidelines
for permanence and durability of the Committee on Production Guidelines for Book
Longevity of the Council on Library Resources

Printed in the United States of America

1 3 5 7 9 10 8 6 4 2

Dedicated to the memory
of my teachers

Gerson D. Cohen
Shelomo Dov Goitein

CONTENTS

PREFACE AND ACKNOWLEDGMENTS

THIS STUDY seeks to explain why Islamic-Jewish and Christian-Jewish relations followed such different courses in the Middle Ages. Its purpose is to go beyond the facile assertion that Jews lived more securely in the medieval Arab-Islamic world than under Christendom. They did.[1] My goal is to explain how and why and thereby foster deeper understanding of Jewish-gentile relations in the medieval diaspora.

I had the opportunity to test my developing views in an essay first published in 1986,[2] and I reiterated my ideas, with emphasis on the historiographical issue, in an article that appeared in 1991.[3] The mostly encouraging responses to those two forays bolstered my resolve to pursue the research to a conclusion. As I continued to work on the problem, the hypotheses I had developed in the mid-1980s became strengthened. The present book incorporates the results.

Comparative history makes heavy demands on the knowledge of the researcher. Often, in fact, it requires collaboration between experts in different subjects. Alternatively, scholars may present their work in the form of case studies, to be compared with research on other examples.[4] I should confess that, although I have been teaching courses at Princeton on the Jews in medieval Europe for two decades, and, hence, try to keep abreast of developments in this area, I am far from a specialist on Latin Christendom. Apart from two scholarly forays into seventeenth-century Venice, my research has focused on the medieval Arabic-Islamic world. Nevertheless, it was teaching medieval European and medieval Near Eastern Jewish history that awakened and sustained my interest in the comparative perspective that informs this book. Moreover, the difficulties posed by comparative research are somewhat offset in this instance. For here, the object of comparison is the same people—of the same religion, stemming from the same ancient and late antique roots in the Near East—but living in different civilizations.

The work is aimed at both scholars and general readers, the latter including college students. While Jewish historians and to a lesser extent also general medievalists will find that I go over much ground that is familiar to them, I would hope that both groups might find in this overview a useful introduction for their students to both Christian-Jewish *and* Muslim-Jewish relations in medieval times. This holds for the educated lay reader as well.[5]

For specialists, the present book offers something new in its systematic, comparative approach to Jewish-gentile relations in the Middle Ages.

Since most specialists deal either with the Islamic-Arabic or the Christian-Latin world, the synthesis of views concerning the case they are less familiar with should be useful. The book also attempts to document with original analysis hypotheses that I have not found elsewhere or have found, but without substantiation, in the research of others. In particular, the chapter on hierarchy, marginality, and ethnicity (Chapter 6), and the discussion of persecution and collective memory (in Chapter 10) offer analysis and interpretation that I have not found in print elsewhere.

I do not cite especially voluminously in my notes,[6] especially when I feel a point has become part of a scholarly consensus, and wherever feasible I have quoted from sources for which there exist English translations (provided, of course, they are representative of a broader reservoir of texts that support the argument). I have followed this procedure in the interest of the general reader who, not knowing Arabic or Hebrew or Latin, might wish to examine the text for him or herself. Fortunately, there are now a number of valuable anthologies as well as published translations of many salient primary materials. With its generous sprinkling of salient primary sources in translation, the present book, as one reader commented in his report for Princeton University Press, lets "the voices of medieval Islam, Christendom, and the Jews therein speak for themselves."

In the course of researching and writing this book I had the good sense to consult with colleagues specializing in areas outside my primary research field. Those who gave generously of their time to read part or all of the manuscript during the last stages of the writing are David Berger, Jeremy Cohen, Michael Cook, Theodore Draper, Martha Himmelfarb, William C. Jordan, Suzanne Keller, Daniel Lasker, Hava Lazarus-Yafeh, Amnon Linder, Ivan G. Marcus, Emily Rose, Claudia Setzer, and Avrom Udovitch. Each of them offered valuable criticism that helped me refine the argument and also stay on course where I might otherwise have gone astray. For the defects that remain, I alone am responsible.

Princeton University's Committee on Research in the Humanities and Social Sciences and my own Department of Near Eastern Studies Publication Fund provided support for various stages of the research and writing. I was able to exploit the research assistance services of Kenneth Halpern (Princeton) and Adi Talmon (Jerusalem), sparing me precious time to devote to final revisions to the manuscript, and also to benefit, as in the past, from Ilene Perkal Cohen's usual editorial acumen, polishing chapters as they rolled off my computer. I completed the last revisions to this book while a Fellow of The Institute for Advanced Studies at the Hebrew University of Jerusalem (1992–93), which afforded me an opportunity to work under truly favorable conditions and to tap the knowledge and profit from the criticisms of the extraordinary group of scholars assembled by

Professors Hava Lazarus-Yafeh and R. J. Zwi Werblowski in a research group on interreligious polemics in the Middle Ages.

For her wise shepherding of this book at Princeton University Press, I thank History and Classics Editor, Lauren M. Osborne, and for his editorial work, Roy A. Grisham, Jr.

March 23, 1993

NOTE ON TRANSLITERATION

In this book Arabic terms and names are transliterated as in the *Encyclopaedia of Islam,* second edition, with the exception that *dj* and *ḳ* have been replaced by *j* and *q*, respectively. Arabic place names, dynasties, certain proper names (e.g., Hijaz, Fatimid, Muhammad), and other terms (e.g., Qur'an, Sunni) are printed without diacritical marks. In the transliteration of Hebrew words, the macron signifying long vowels has been eliminated since, unlike in Arabic, it has little significance for the meaning of words.

INTRODUCTION

WHEN I began studying medieval Jewish history nearly thirty years ago, conventional wisdom held that Jews living "under the crescent" enjoyed substantially greater security and a higher level of political and cultural integration than did Jews living "under the cross." This was especially true of the persecuted Ashkenazic Jews of northern Europe. The fruitful Jewish-Muslim interfaith "symbiosis," as S. D. Goitein termed it—a more measured way of saying "Golden Age" (my mentor, Gerson D. Cohen, used to refer to an elite of a few hundred "Golden Men")—contrasted sharply with the sorrowful record of Jewish-Christian conflict in the Ashkenazic lands. The revisionist efforts of Salo W. Baron, heralded in an essay published in 1928, had been aimed solely at recasting in more accurate and less gloomy terms the somewhat exaggerated "lachrymose conception of Jewish history," as Baron called the then prevailing view of Jewish life in Christian lands during the premodern Jewish past.[1]

While Baron succeeded in modifying the "lachrymose conception" of Jewish life in medieval Christendom, until recently no great need has been felt to reassess the picture of Jewish history under Islam, even though that, too, had been exaggerated by the Central European fathers of modern Jewish historiography in the form of a "myth of an interfaith utopia." It is fair to say that the image of the Golden Age still dominates in both scholarship and popular thinking.

Recent decades have witnessed an effort to alter this picture. Toward the end of the 1960s—or, more precisely, following the Six-Day War of June 1967—factors stemming from the Arab-Israeli conflict gave birth in some quarters to a radical revision of Jewish-Arab history. The new notion first appeared mainly in the writings of nonspecialists publishing in popular Jewish forums, and of late it has begun to turn up in more oblique form in scholarly studies. According to this view, the "Golden Age" was actually an era of hardship and oppression. The very centuries when great "golden" men like Ḥasday ibn Shapruṭ, Samuel the Nagid ibn Nagrela, and Judah ha-Levi graced the corridors of Spanish-Muslim courts—integrated, it had always seemed, into Arab political and intellectual life—now came to be characterized in terms of discrimination and persecution. Some went so far as to suggest that the fate of the Jews of Islam was at times as doleful as the lot of the Jews in Europe. I have chosen to call this view "the neo-lachrymose conception of Jewish-Arab history."[2]

This revisionism did not originate out of perversity, however. It is a "countermyth" that emerged in dialectical opposition to the twin challenge of modern Arab propaganda and Arab antisemitism. In the wake of the defeat in June 1967, Arab apologists began to pick up a somewhat older theme relating the medieval "Golden Age" of Islamic tolerance to the modern Zionist menace. They embraced the "myth" (originally Jewish) that Muslims and Jews had for centuries enjoyed utopian relations. This harmony had been shattered by the Zionist movement and, in particular, by the creation of the State of Israel. Remove the Zionist-Israeli threat, so the argument implied, and the old harmony would be restored, with Jews and Arabs living side by side in an interfaith utopia under Arab-Muslim protection.

The second challenge was the new awareness, both in Israel and in the Jewish diaspora, of a rampant, virulent, Arab antisemitism—reminiscent of the worst kind of medieval Christian Jew hatred and its twentieth-century counterpart. Arabs justified their animosity by pointing the finger at the provocation of Jewish "neocolonialism" in Palestine, which ended the interfaith harmony of the past. In response, Jews tried to understand Arab antisemitism as the continuation of an old and innate Arab-Islamic hatred and persecution of the Jews reaching back to Muhammad and the Qur'an and even, perhaps, rivaling the antisemitism of medieval Christendom.

The favorite authority of the revisionists was none other than Moses Maimonides (1138–1204), the great Spanish-Jewish philosopher, physician, legal scholar, and communal leader, the acme of the so-called Golden Age. Living in Islamic Egypt, Maimonides wrote, in an epistle of comfort and consolation to the persecuted Jews of Yemen, as follows:

> You know, my brethren, that on account of our sins God has cast us into the midst of this people, the nation of Ishmael, who persecute us severely, and who devise ways to harm us and to debase us. This is as the Exalted had warned us: "Even our enemies themselves being judges" (Deuteronomy 32:31). No nation has ever done more harm to Israel. None has matched it in debasing and humiliating us.[3]

Maimonides, it would seem, is rendering a harsh judgment about Muslim-Jewish relations: that Islam has always oppressed the Jews and that Islamic hatred and persecution surpass the enmity of any other people among whom the Jews have lived. Indeed, the young Maimonides had survived the violent and terrifying persecution wrought by the fanatic Muslim Almohads in North Africa and Spain. That wave of terror, which began in the mid-1140s, took a tremendous toll in lives, forcibly created many Jewish (and Christian) converts to Islam, and sent thousands of Jews fleeing to Christian territory and to Muslim lands beyond the reach of the Almohads. The Maimon family was among the latter. After a sojourn of several years in Almohad Morocco (Fez), possibly in the guise of nominal Muslims, and a very brief stay in inhospitable Crusader-held Palestine, they relocated permanently in the 1160s to Egypt, a land of relative safety. The persecution of Jews in nearby Yemen must have confirmed Maimonides' sense that he was living in a time of unprecedented persecution. While these circumstances seem to offer sufficient explanation for Maimonides' extremely unfavorable generalization about Islamic-Jewish relations, his statement in the "Epistle to Yemen" was taken out of context and hoisted as the banner or "prooftext" of the new train of thinking.

The polarization of views that has thus dominated discussion of medieval Islamic-Jewish relations in recent years has made it increasingly difficult to write on the subject without getting involved in apologetics and polemics. I remain convinced that the "myth of the Islamic-Jewish interfaith utopia" and the "countermyth of Islamic persecution of Jews" equally distort the past. How might we address the underlying historical question in a way that avoids both extremes and, at the same time, deepens understanding of why, as most reasonable observers will agree, the Islamic-Jewish relationship bred so much less violence and persecution than relations between Christians and Jews? The comparative approach has seemed the most useful one.

A Comparative Approach

Writing about the status of the non-Muslim minorities—the *ahl al-dhimma,* the "Protected People," or *dhimmīs*—during the "classical centuries" of the Middle Ages, the distinguished Islamic historian Claude Cahen compared their treatment to the experience of the Jews in medieval Christendom: "There is nothing in mediaeval Islam which could specifically be called anti-semitism."[4]

> Objectivity requires us to attempt a *comparison* between Christian and Muslim intolerance, which have partial resemblances and partial differences. Islam has, in spite of many upsets, shown more toleration than Europe toward the Jews who remained in Muslim lands.[5]

Cahen's call for an East-West comparative approach to Islamic-Jewish relations failed to indicate what direction that comparison might take. Jewish historians themselves have often noted—although mostly casually—certain comparative facts. Haim Hillel Ben-Sasson, who was a specialist in medieval European Jewish history, properly cautioned in his book *On Jewish History in the Middle Ages* that Maimonides' condemnation of Islam in the "Epistle to Yemen" should be understood in the context of the harsh persecutions of the twelfth century, and that furthermore "one may say that he was insufficiently aware of the status of the Jews in Christian lands, or did not pay attention to this, when he wrote the letter." Ben-Sasson continued:

> The legal and security situation of the Jews in the Muslim countries was generally better than in Christendom, because in the former, Jews were not the sole "infidels," because in comparison to the Christians, Jews were less dangerous and more loyal to the Muslim regime, and because the rapidity and territorial scope of the Muslim conquests imposed upon them a reduction in persecution and a granting of greater possibility for the survival of members of other faiths in their lands.[6]

Bernard Lewis, whose *Jews of Islam* is the most balanced assessment of the position of the Jews under Islamic rule in the Middle Ages, offers his own explanation of why the Jews fared better under Islam than under Christianity.

> If we compare the Muslim attitude to Jews and treatment of Jews in medieval times with the position of Jews among their Christian neighbors in medieval Europe, we see some striking contrasts. . . . In Islamic society hostility to the Jew is nontheological. . . . It is rather the usual attitude of the dominant to the subordinate, of the majority to the minority, without that additional theological and therefore psychological dimension that gives Christian anti-Semitism its unique and special character.[7]

One important contrast, according to Lewis, is that the Jews were one of several minorities in Islam, not the sole minority, as in Europe. And, because Muslim society was "diverse and pluralistic," the minorities were "far less noticeable."[8]

This point has frequently been made. Ben-Sasson offered the explanation without elaboration. And Goitein wrote: "Unlike Europe, where Jews formed a single and exceedingly small group within a foreign environment, in Islam the detrimental effects of segregation were mitigated by the existence of two minority groups, which, during the Geniza period, were still sizable and influential even on the conduct of the state."[9] Norman Stillman expresses the same idea this way: "The fact that the Jews shared their inferior status with Christians and Zoroastrians, who were far more numerous and more conspicuous in the Middle Ages, diffused some of the specifically anti-Jewish sentiments within a broader anti-non-Muslim context. There was, in effect, an essential equality among inferiors."[10]

This book sets out to provide a broad investigation of medieval Islamic-Jewish and Christian-Jewish relations that builds on comparative insights such as the ones mentioned above. It asks new comparative questions, attempting to answer them in a way that will shed light, reciprocally, on Jewish relations with gentiles in both medieval settings. Before defining the specific parameters of this study, it will be useful to state what it is *not*. It is *not* a comparative study of tolerance. Neither for Islam, nor for Christianity prior to modern times, did tolerance, at least as we in the West have understood it since John Locke, constitute a virtue. In the introduction to a volume of papers on "Persecution and Toleration" delivered at the annual meetings of the Ecclesiastical Historical Society in 1983, the historian G. R. Elton makes this point in connection with Christianity and other monotheistic religions.

> Religions spring from faith, and faith, endeavouring to maintain its own convictions, cannot permit the existence of rivals or dissenters. Thus religions organized in powerful churches and in command of their scene persecute as a matter of course and tend to regard toleration as a sign of weakness or even wickedness towards whatever deity they worship. Among the religious, toleration is demanded by the persecuted who need it if they are ever to become triumphant, when, all too often, they start to persecute in their turn.[11]

It seems, therefore, that monotheistic religions in power throughout history have felt it proper, if not obligatory, to persecute nonconforming religions. Thus, it is not surprising that medieval Islam should have persecuted non-Muslims, just as medieval Christianity persecuted Jews (and also Muslims), and as Judaism—briefly in power during the Hasmonean period (second century B.C.E.)—should have persecuted the pagan Idumeans, forcibly converting them to Judaism. When all is said and done, however, the historical evidence indicates that the Jews of Islam, especially during the formative and classical centuries (up to the thirteenth century), experienced much less persecution than did the Jews of Christendom.[12] This begs a more thorough and nuanced explanation than has hitherto been given.

Two central questions, accordingly, underlie the present study. Why were Islamic-Jewish relations during the classical centuries less tense, less marked by intolerance and violence, than Christian-Jewish relations during the early and High Middle Ages? And what factors account for the constraints on persecution and intolerance of Jews in the Islamic world?

In attempting to answer these questions, I have looked at similar stages of development or parallel phenomena in Jewish life in the Latin West and in the Muslim East. For the study to be meaningful and to shed light reciprocally on Christian-Jewish relations, it had to consider phases of development that were closely parallel from a structural viewpoint, though not necessarily a chronological one. I have tried to achieve this kind of rigor. Part Two addresses (1) the religious factor in early interfaith relations (Chapter 2) and (2) the Jews' legal position (Chapters 3 and 4). Part Three is devoted to the economic role played by the Jews (Chapter 5). Part Four considers the place of the Jew within the social order of both Christendom and Islam (Chapters 6, 7, and 8). And Part Five, the final section, deals with interreligious polemics (Chapter 9) and persecution itself, along with Jewish responses and Jewish collective memory of life in the two dominant societies (Chapter 10). Chapter 1 traces the historiography that has made the subject at hand so controversial.

The book does not contain a chapter on intellectual life. The story of the cultural efflorescence of the Jews living in Arabic-Islamic lands in the formative and classical centuries has been told many times (often, and frequently biasedly, contrasting it with Jewish intellectual life in the Ashkenazic world). Nonetheless, I believe that that story can be better understood against the backdrop of the chapters of the present book.

For comparative purposes, I have found it fruitful to focus on the Latin West and mainly on the *northern* lands, though the study takes full cognizance of the fact that the religious and legal foundations of the Christian-Jewish relationship were Mediterranean in origin. The contrasts in the North are simply more vivid and less encumbered than in the South, hence the reciprocal light cast on Jewish-gentile relations in Islam shines more brightly. Italy, for instance—with its Gothic, Lombard, Carolingian, Byzantine, Papal, French Norman, German Imperial, and even Arab chapters of varying length and importance, as well as its late medieval patchwork of northern city-states and republics (into which Jews began to stream in meaningful numbers only in the fourteenth century)—actually is too special a case for useful comparison. Similarly, the pervasive influence of Islamic and Arabic culture on medieval Christian Spain, in general, and on Sephardic Jewry, in particular, spoils the clarity and hence the heuristic value of the comparison. In fact, before 1391, Jews in Christian Spain enjoyed a relatively secure position that sprang, in part, from many of the same factors that mitigated intolerance in Muslim Spain (and in classical Islamic civilization in general). By the end of the Middle Ages, Christian Spain had taken on most of the attitudes of the North toward Jews, sharing the leitmotif of intense persecution and, finally, exclusion.

Medieval Christian Poland, as is well known, served as a haven and land of economic opportunity for western European Jewry, especially beginning in the thirteenth century. Polish rulers—who viewed the Jews as more-or-less a subset of a class of German-speaking merchants and town-dwellers who could fill a socioeconomic gap in Polish society—welcomed the immigrants into their lands, largely ignoring the pressures of Catholic ideology, and diverging in their beneficent Jewry policy from that of most secular rulers in western Europe. The Polish-Jewish experience during the late Middle Ages and into early modern times (before the reversal of fortunes in the middle of the seventeenth century), so seemingly the inverse of the situation of their beleaguered brethren in western Latin Christendom at that time, merits comparison with the situation of the Jews in medieval Islam, though it is beyond the chronological scope of the present work and hence not pursued here.[13]

Mediterranean France (the Midi), on the other hand, affords an unusual opportunity to sharpen the focus of our comparison. Though invaded by the Arabs in the eighth century, this region (comprising Languedoc and Provence) was never held by Islam, unlike the neighboring Christian lands across the Pyrenees. Nonetheless, Christian-Jewish relations in the Midi were less marked by enmity and persecution than in the North, even after the region came under northern French domination in the thirteenth century.[14] I will periodically refer to the position of southern French Jewry because the comparison suggests that religion was only one factor, even if probably the most salient one, in determining the course of Jewish-gentile relations in the Middle Ages. Political, economic, and social realities could temper ideological (read: religious) intolerance, creating the groundwork, as happened so fundamentally in the Islamic world, for substantial security and prosperity.

Finally, a word about the parameters assigned to the other side of the comparison. *Islam,* in this book, refers to Sunni Islam. This, the orthodox and dominant form of the religion, is the source of Islamic "policy" toward the Jews and others considered infidels. Heterodox Shiism was usually harsher in its view of how the infidel should be treated; but, for most of the period considered in this study, Jews did not live under Shiite regimes. Exceptions were truly exceptional, whether under the Shiite Buyids of Iraq from the mid-tenth to mid-eleventh century or, more dramatically, under the Fatimids of Egypt and Syria-Palestine (969–1171), who were notorious for being more tolerant toward Jews and Christians than Sunnis. Sunni Islam is also the appropriate counterpoint for comparison with the Christian world, where orthodox Christianity held power.

PART ONE

Myth and Countermyth

Chapter One

MYTH AND COUNTERMYTH

THE MYTH OF AN INTERFAITH UTOPIA

Already at the end of the Middle Ages one encounters among Jews the belief that medieval Islam provided a peaceful haven for Jews, whereas Christendom relentlessly persecuted them. These Jews were aware that Muslim Turkey had granted refuge to Jewish victims of persecution from Catholic Spain and elsewhere.[1] A spate of mainly Hebrew chronicles written in the wake of the traumatic expulsion of the Jews from Spain in 1492 drove home the contrast between Christian enmity and Muslim benevolence. In the nineteenth century, the fathers of the modern, scientific study of Jewish history transformed this perception into a historical postulate.

Frustrated by the tortuous progress of their own integration into gentile society in what was supposed to be a "liberal" age of emancipation, Jewish intellectuals seeking a historical precedent for a more tolerant attitude toward Jews hit upon a time and place that met this criterion—medieval Muslim Spain. There, they believed, Jews had achieved a remarkable level of toleration, political achievement, and cultural integration. Jewish historians took the observation of a young Lutheran scholar of Hebrew poetry who had written about a literary golden age (*das goldne Zeitalter*) that lasted from 940 to 1040, and applied the epithet to the full range of political and social life of the entire Muslim-Spanish period.[2] They contrasted this with the gloomy Jewish experience of oppression under medieval Christendom. In short, the very Jewish historians who created what Salo Baron disparagingly calls "the lachrymose conception of Jewish history" in Christian Europe also invented its counterpoint: the "myth of the interfaith utopia" in Islam.

Heinrich Graetz, the leading nineteenth-century Jewish historian, makes this point at the beginning of the story of the Jews of Arab lands in his influential *History of the Jews:*

> Wearied with contemplating the miserable plight of the Jews in their ancient home and in the countries of Europe, and fatigued by the constant sight of fanatical oppression in Christendom, the eyes of the observer rest with gladness upon their situation in the Arabian Peninsula. Here the sons of Judah were free to raise their heads, and did not need to look about them with fear and humiliation, lest the ecclesiastical wrath be discharged upon them, or the

> secular power overwhelm them. Here they were not shut out from the paths of honor, nor excluded from the privileges of the state, but, untrammeled, were allowed to develop their powers in the midst of a free, simple and talented people, to show their manly courage, to compete for the gifts of fame, and with practised hand to measure swords with their antagonists.[3]

Graetz explicitly pits his romantic, utopian slant on Jewish life among Arabs (the tribes of Arabia) against his "lachrymose" conception of Jewish life under Christendom. Further on, mindful of the advanced age in which he himself lived, and reflecting German Jewry's conviction about Sephardic supremacy over Ashkenazim (for Graetz and others, represented by contemporary Polish Jewry), Graetz extends his praise for Islam to the cultural domain:

> The height of culture which the nations of modern times are striving to attain—to be imbued with knowledge, conviction, and moral strength—was reached by the Jews of Spain in their most flourishing period. . . . No wonder, then, that the Jews of Spain were looked upon as superior beings by their uncultured brethren in other lands—in France, Germany, and Italy—and that they gladly yielded them the precedence which had formerly been enjoyed by the Babylonian academies.[4]

The premise of Islamic toleration of Jews (actually an instance of a more general axiom about Islam's forbearance toward non-Muslim monotheists) rang true to Jewish Orientalists precisely because of the comparison with medieval Christianity.[5] In Europe the period beginning with the First Crusade witnessed recurrent acts of violence directed against Jews per se. Christians came to believe that Jews murdered Christian children and extracted their blood for ritual or magical purposes. The Jewish moneylender became the object of intense Christian hatred. Jewish converts to Christianity were suspect; in Spain, especially, this led to the infamous Spanish Inquisition. In addition, entire Jewish communities were expelled from medieval Christian states. None of these excesses, however, seem to have a counterpart in Islam.

In its nineteenth-century context, the myth of the interfaith utopia was used to attempt to achieve an important political end, to challenge supposedly liberal Christian Europe to make good on its promise of political equality and unfettered professional and cultural opportunities for Jews.[6] First, if medieval Muslims could have so tolerated the Jews that a Samuel ibn Nagrela (d. 1056) could rise to the vizierate of the Spanish Muslim state of Granada, or a Maimonides to a respected position among Muslim intellectuals, could not modern Europeans grant Jews the rights and privileges promised them in the aftermath of the French Revolution? Second, did not the Christian world owe this to the Jews, to compensate for its history of cruelty toward the Jews? Third, just as Jews in Spain (and elsewhere in the Muslim world), benefiting from liberal treatment, had benefited Arab society, so would the Jews of modern Europe, if treated with equality, contribute greatly to European civilization.

The Jewish myth of an Islamic interfaith utopia persisted into the twentieth century, long after the achievement of emancipation in Europe. The title of Adolph L. Wismar's 1927 book speaks for itself: *A Study in Tolerance as Practiced by Muhammad and His Immediate Successors*. From the 1940s, there is Rudolf Kayser's delightful biography of the Spanish Hebrew poet Judah Halevi, published by the Philosophical Library, in which Kayser reiterates Graetz's tone:

> It is like a historical miracle that in the very same era of history which produced these orgies of persecution [the Crusades], the people of Israel in Southern Europe enjoyed a golden age, the like of which they had not known since the days of the Bible.[7]

Eliyahu Ashtor's Hebrew history of the Jews in Muslim Spain, now popularized in an English translation, glorifies the Golden Age to the point of romance.[8]

A favorable appraisal of the fate of the Jews of Islam, compared with the sorrowful destiny of the Jews of Christendom, also appears in the writings of Jews from Arab lands. André Chouraqui, a North African Jewish intellectual and historian, writing about the Jews of his ancestral homeland, describes the Almohad persecution in the twelfth century as being "of a passing nature." He attributes most pogroms against the Jews in the oppressive later Middle Ages to "lust and envy, rather than outbursts of hate." Further,

> there was never any time in the Moslem Maghreb [North Africa, when there was] a philosophy and tradition of anti-Semitism such as existed in Europe from the Middle Ages down to modern times. . . . During most periods of history, the Jews of North Africa were happier than those in most parts of Europe, where they were the objects of unrelenting hate; such extreme sentiments did not exist in the Maghreb. The scorn that the adherents of the different faiths expressed for each other could not obliterate the strong bonds of a common source of inspiration and a way of life intimately shared.[9]

To a certain extent, the myth of the Islamic-Jewish interfaith utopia owes it tenacity to reinforcement during and since the Nazi era. The search for the roots of twentieth-century European antisemitism correlates with perpetuation of the myth of idyllic times under Islam in such books as *Jews in a Gentile World: The Problem of Anti-Semitism*.[10] In his "Anti-Semitism: Challenge to Christian Culture," Carl J. Friedrich invokes the expulsion of the Jews from Christian Spain in 1492 and the counterexample of Islam:

An interesting contrast between the religious intolerance of Western Christian culture at that time and the relative tolerance of the Mohammedan culture of the Muslims occurred: when, following the brutal persecution of the Jews in Spain, many went to the Levant, the tolerant treatment given by the Ottoman Muslims to these persecuted Jews, as well as Christians, elicited the curiosity of political writers. In his political satires the post-Machiavellian Boccalini has Bodin punished for commending the tolerance of the Turks.[11]

In *Essays on Antisemitism,* first published in 1942 (reprinted in 1946), the contributor of the only chapter dealing with Jews and Islam declares: "No study of antisemitism can be complete that does not pay some attention to the position of the Jews under Islam." Yet his conclusions highlight the "comparative tolerance" of Islam as opposed to Christianity, asserting, following de Gobineau, that the religion of Islam did not play a role in anti-Jewish incidents and attitudes in the past. Rather, these resulted from "political expediency or economic rivalry."[12] As recently as 1978, the compilers of an annotated historical catalog of antisemitic outbursts relegate the discussion of Islam to a brief section at the end of the book.[13]

The Myth of an Interfaith Utopia in Arab and Arabist Writings

The "myth of the interfaith utopia" went largely unchallenged until its adoption by Arabs as a weapon in their propaganda war against Zionism. According to this view, for centuries, Jews and Arabs lived together in peace and harmony under Islamic rule—precisely at a time when the Jews were being relentlessly persecuted by Christianity. Modern antipathy toward Israel began only when the Jews destroyed the old harmony by pressing the Zionist claim against Muslim-Arab rights to Palestine. Accordingly, Arab hatred and antisemitism would end, and the ancient harmony would be restored, when Zionism abandoned both its "colonialist" and its "neo-crusader" quest.

An early example of Arab historiographical exploitation of the Jewish interfaith-utopia myth occurs in a pioneering work on Arab nationalism by the Christian-Arab writer George Antonius. The book closes with a condemnation of Zionist usurpation of Arab rights to Palestine; in an earlier remark, Antonius states:

> Both in the Middle Ages and in modern times, and thanks mainly to the civilising influence of Islam, Arab history remained remarkably free from instances of deliberate persecution and shows that some of the greatest achievements of the Jewish race were accomplished in the days of Arab power, under the aegis of Arab rulers, and with the help of their enlightened patronage. Even to-day, in spite of the animosity aroused by the conflict in Palestine, the treatment of Jewish minorities settled in the surrounding Arab countries

continues to be not less friendly and humane than in England or the United States, and is in some ways a good deal more tolerant.[14]

This emphasis on Islamic benevolence toward the Jews was not new. Christian Arabs—like Jews, considered "infidels" by Islam—have felt a need to affirm historical Islamic tolerance of the non-Muslim for their own sake, just as many have supported Arab nationalism as a means of ensuring their continued acceptance in the Arab world.[15]

The proposition that historical Islamic tolerance gave way in the twentieth century to Arab hostility in reaction to Zionist encroachment became a theme of Arab propaganda against Israel both in politics and in writings about Jewish-Arab history, most of them appearing after the Six-Day War. Because the literature is immense, I will touch on just a few examples, from a variety of sources.

An essay by an American professor in Beirut, in 1970, is a case in point. Drawing on Jewish scholars, notably S. D. Goitein and Salo Baron, the author surveys the "new era" of tolerance for the Jews ushered in by conquering Arabs to replace Christian persecution. This tolerance led to what Jewish historians rightly called a golden age and to the "eventual integration [of the Jews] into the mainstream of life in Arab-Islamic society." In this century, by exception, he argues, anti-Jewish sentiment arose among Arabs in reaction to Zionism and its policy of usurpation. This, however, is "*strictly* a modern phenomenon, and one that runs counter to the time-honored Islamic tradition of fraternity and tolerance."[16] The first half of a book by a Pakistani scholar, published not long after the Six-Day War, extols Muslim forbearance toward religious minorities; the second half concludes with a chapter on "Muslims in Palestine" that decries Zionist and Jewish oppression of the Arabs "in spite of the fact that Arabs and Jews have lived together in peace and harmony for centuries."[17] A source of major embarrassment for many Arabs, the well-known saga in Arabic sources of Muhammad's massacre of a Jewish tribe in Medina after expelling two others, comes in for historiographical "cleansing" in many Arabist writings.[18]

Publications in Arabic give considerable prominence to the myth of the interfaith utopia. A paper read at the Fourth Conference of the Academy of Islamic Research at Al-Azhar University in 1968 (and published in both the Arabic conference proceedings and the official English translation) is entitled "Jews in the Middle Ages: Comparative Study of East and West."[19] The author summarizes:

> It may be sufficiently evident that Jews throughout history received no better or kinder treatment than that of Muslims. The egoism and greed of Jews subjected them to persecution by the Romans in early times and by various peoples of Christian Europe in the Middle Ages. They found in Muslims—*as*

> *Jewish writers themselves admit*—merciful brothers who regarded them as fellow believers and did not allow religious differences [to] affect their treatment or attitude toward them. Spain provides a clear example of the big difference in the treatment of Jews by Muslims and Christians.[20]

Arabic books on Jewish or non-Muslim life under medieval Islam overwhelmingly favor the myth of Islamic tolerance, which, of course, is directed as much at the Christian minorities as at the Jews. A scholarly legal study by a lecturer in Islamic law at Baghdad University cites the widespread employment of non-Muslim "Protected People" in Islamic government as a sign of Islam's unprecedented tolerance (*samāḥa* or *tasāmuḥ*).[21] Qāsim ʿAbduh Qāsim, a historian at Egypt's Zagazig University, published "The Jews of Egypt from the Islamic Conquest to the Ottoman Invasion."[22] The first edition (1980) credits Islamic "tolerance" for the freedom and prosperity enjoyed by Egyptian Jewry in the Middle Ages. The second edition (1987) draws to a much greater extent than the first on recent Jewish scholarship, especially that dealing with the Egyptian Jewish florescence under the Fatimids (well documented in the Cairo Geniza), to strengthen the author's case for Islam's liberal treatment of the Jews.[23]

With undisguised polemical purpose, a propagandist of secular Pan-Arabism, ʿAlī Ḥusnī al-Kharbūṭlī, traces the story of Islamic tolerance of *dhimmīs* to the early period of Islam.[24] The chapters devoted to the Jews (there are no separate chapters on the Christian *dhimmīs*) brim with antisemitic stereotypes. One chapter contrasts the political, religious, economic, and social freedom Jews enjoyed from Muslim tolerance through the ages with the gloomy plight of the Arab refugees under the Jewish-Zionist occupation of Palestine that began in 1948.[25]

These few examples represent a trend among Arab and Arabist writers: slavish devotion to the axiom of Islamic tolerance (*tasāmuḥ*) and to the myth of an interfaith utopia.[26] This version of Muslim–non-Muslim relations in history served in part to justify and excuse another trend: a virulent strain of traditional European antisemitism in Arabic garb, which came to public attention after the Israeli victory in June 1967.[27]

Arab Antisemitism Revealed

Arab antisemitism was originally fashioned in the nineteenth century by Christian Arabs using classical Christian antisemitic stereotypes.[28] It grew in intensity, and became generalized in the Arab world, with the intensification of the Arab-Jewish/Arab-Israeli conflict. Jews became aware of its prevalence and vehemence only in the late 1960s. Yehoshafat Harkabi revealed the hitherto ignored phenomenon to the public, first in newspaper articles, then in his *Arab Attitudes to Israel,* completed before the Six-Day War and published shortly afterward.[29]

Disturbing evidence of Arab antisemitism was discovered in Arabic schoolbooks and other teaching materials (including indoctrination literature for the Egyptian armed forces) found by Israeli soldiers in Arab territories occupied in June 1967.[30] Pamphlets and scholarly studies helped spread the news in Israel and abroad.[31] Just months after the war, in February 1968, *Jewish Frontier,* the labor Zionist Alliance monthly, communicated these revelations to its readers—without comment. Mentioned again and again inside and outside Israel was the wide dissemination of the *Protocols of the Elders of Zion* in Arabic translation. Similarly alarming was the warlike, anti-Israel speech of Egyptian President Sadat on April 25, 1972, on the occasion of the birthday of the Prophet Muhammad. Sadat condemned the Jews of Medina for having acted treacherously toward the Prophet, giving this as a reason for refusing to negotiate with the present-day "nation of liars and traitors, a people of plotters, a folk created for treacherous deeds," and as a reason for fighting the Israelis to the point of powerless submission.[32] The old-new theme of Jewish hostility toward the Prophet was present in the 1950s in antisemitic writings of Islamic fundamentalists, such as Sayyid Quṭb.[33] And Rivka Yadlin has recently documented the dismaying persistence of intense antisemitism in publications in Egypt even after the peace treaty with Israel.[34]

Countermyth: The Neo-Lachrymose Conception of Jewish-Arab History

Arab polemical exploitation of the myth of the interfaith utopia, coupled with Jewish awareness of the prevalence of antisemitism in the Arab world, catalyzed a reevaluation of the history of Jewish-Muslim relations which I call, interchangeably, the "countermyth of Islamic persecution of Jews" and the "neo-lachrymose conception of Jewish-Arab history."[35] It achieved prominence after the Six-Day War, beginning with publications appearing in the Diaspora, especially in popular forums.

The America-Israel Public Affairs Committee's widely circulated *Near East Report* inaugurated its "Myths and Facts" supplement shortly after the Six-Day War. In a virtually forgotten essay of 1946,[36] the Jewish historian Cecil Roth warned of a curious interpretation fashionable among Arabs and Christian anti-Zionists that would "tend in the long run to do us a great deal of harm." What Roth was speaking of specifically was the propagandistic exploitation by Arabs and Christian anti-Zionists of the nineteenth-century Jewish theme of "halcyon days under the pallid light of the Crescent [and] of purgatory in the shadow of the Cross." In closing, he insists, "The idea that the Jews lived in the Arab world in perfect peace and tranquility until the militant Zionists wantonly disturbed the even tenor of the reciprocal relations is a perversion of the truth." AIPAC's purpose in reprinting the article was to let it serve as a complement to a feature on "background to the Arab-Israel War" and to expose, in Roth's words, "a few overlooked facts" about Islamic persecution from medieval to modern times. The Muslim regime of oppression, present even during the Golden Age in Spain, "often attained what might be termed occidental virulence." Commenting on the supposed "friendliness of the Palestinian Arabs toward Jews before the arrival of the new generation of Zionists," Roth quotes from a letter by a Jewish visitor to Palestine early in the sixteenth century. The writer describes the oppression and humiliation of the local Jews as well as their general belief that life under Islam was worse than it was under Christendom. The traveler supports his assertion by quoting from the Epistle of Maimonides (the traveler erred and called it an epistle to Spain, rather than to Yemen), "in which [Maimonides] says that there is no people in the world which wishes to humiliate and to degrade the Jews as the Arabs do."

Not long after the AIPAC publication, Saul S. Friedman sounded a distress signal: "Current Arab propaganda insists that the basic cause of antagonism between Jews and Arabs is political Zionism, which is depicted as a fanaticism born of European persecution that has destroyed a Middle Eastern harmony hitherto existing for a thousand years."[37] Reacting to the "fable of Semitic brotherhood" which claims that, "while Europe denied the light of freedom to Jews shut up in ghettos, the Saadias, Maimonides, Ibn Gabirols, and Judah Halevis were free to develop and enlighten mankind under Islamic rule," Friedman proceeds to catalog the "less widely known" hatred and persecution that befell Jews in Muslim lands from the very birth of Islam: from Muhammad's violent turn against the Jews in Medina to the ritual murder accusation in Damascus, Syria, in 1840.[38]

In 1974, another contributor to the countermyth, the journalist Rose Lewis, excoriated Zionist propagandists for dwelling on the suffering of the Jews in Europe while neglecting the story of the uninterrupted Jewish presence in Palestine, as well as Arab persecution of Jews throughout history.[39] Writing in *Commentary* a year later, Lewis pointed to the failure of Israel's advocates to recognize that "in the Middle East . . . [the Jews] have endured thirteen centuries of discrimination and persecution" and also to exploit this history to argue their "right" to (as opposed to the pragmatic need for) self-determination in Israel.[40]

Tunisian-born French Jewish writer and self-proclaimed "left-wing Zionist," Albert Memmi bitterly castigates those who assert that the Arab Jews, indigenous brothers of Arab Muslims, have until Zionism had it good and that Ashkenazic Jewry holds a monopoly on suffering inflicted at the hands of the gentile:

> When it comes to Jewish misfortune, there's just enough for them: they've confiscated it for their Ashkenazim. As if there were only a Moslem East, and

> only a Western Diaspora! As if there were only an Arab-Moslem set of claims, by contrast with a West represented by the Jews! . . . Why shouldn't we too submit our reckoning to the world?[41]

Memmi rails against contemporary historians:

> Having suffered the frightful Nazi slaughter, those Jewish historians could not even imagine such a thing elsewhere. But if we leave out the crematoria and the murders committed in Russia, from Kichinev to Stalin, *the sum total of the Jewish victims of the Christian world is probably no greater than the total number of successive pogroms, both big and small, perpetrated in the Moslem countries.*[42]

Martin Gilbert, biographer of Winston Churchill and chronicler of the Holocaust, also took up the cause of debunking the myth of an interfaith utopia. His popular piece, "The Jews of Islam: Golden Age or Ghetto?" took a gloomy view of Jewish-Arab relations in the past.[43]

More extensive is the work of Bat Ye'or, a native of Egypt who, along with other Jews, suffered humiliation when exiled from that country in 1956. She has published several pamphlets and books that sound the theme of congenital, unremitting Arab-Islamic persecution of the non-Muslim religions, Judaism and Christianity. In *The Dhimmi: Jews and Christians under Islam,* her best-known work, Bat Ye'or (or "Daughter of the Nile") marshals primary sources from all periods, documenting her thesis of the "thirteen centuries of sufferings and humiliations" that Islam heaped on the Jews and Christians.[44] In a preface to the English edition, Jacques Ellul commends the author for showing that "in many ways the *dhimmi* was comparable to the European serf of the Middle Ages."[45]

Joan Peters's *From Time Immemorial* has achieved notoriety for its assault on the demographic argument for Arab claims to the land of Palestine. Peters plays up the countermyth by presenting a litany of persecutions in Jewish-Arab history and challenging Arab rhetoric about the interfaith utopia as well as the view "that the Jews were, during certain periods in the Arab lands, 'better off' than they were in the Christian lands of Europe."[46]

The Countermyth in Scholarly Writing

Journalists and other popularizers pioneered the countermyth. Some Jewish scholars have also searched for evidence of early, innate Muslim hatred of the Jews. For instance, the theme in Egyptian President Sadat's 1972 speech denouncing Jewish treachery against Muhammad in Medina seems to have found an oblique response in a scholarly article in 1974, which argues that Muhammad never planned to tolerate the Jews and Judaism. Rather, from the very outset, the intention was to reduce the Jewish tribes of Medina to a state of powerless submission.[47] At a symposium held in Israel in 1978, six papers given on "antisemitism through the ages" dealt with medieval or modern Arab or Islamic attitudes toward the Jews.[48] One Israeli participant, who delivered a paper entitled "Jew-Hatred in the Islamic Tradition and the Koranic Exegesis," concluded that, "if the oral tradition reflects the developments in early Muslim society, then the traditions about the Jews, without doubt, not only formed the ideological infrastructure of the anti-Jewish legislation [in the Pact of ʿUmar] but were also a reflection of the actual attitude toward the Jews in the first two centuries of Islam's existence."[49] Another scholar writing on the subject of Jew-hatred opens by stating that the "positive terms" in which the social and legal status of the Jews in Muslim lands in the Middle Ages have been described, as compared with the harsher condition of the Jews in Christian Europe, while correct, "has done a great injustice to the historic truth." After the "relatively good" first three generations of Islam, the "political, legal, and security positions" of the Jews "gradually grew worse." Not unexpectedly, the author invokes Maimonides' comment in the "Epistle to Yemen" that the Ishmaelite exile was the worst ever.[50]

The Countermyth and Israel's Jews from Arab Lands

The countermyth of innately persecutory Islam figures in the political thinking of certain groups in Israel's Oriental, or Sephardic, Jewish population. The World Organization of Jews from Arab Countries (WOJAC), founded in 1975, proclaimed its philosophy in its keynote publication.[51] WOJAC held to be axiomatic that Israel's Jews from Arab lands are refugees from persecution. In compensation for the wrong these Jews had suffered at the hands of the Arabs, they deserve to live peacefully in Israel. Further, their resettlement there after 1948 represents an "exchange of populations" that counterbalances the exodus of tens of thousands of Arabs from newly born Israel and thereby cancels any obligation on Israel's part to repatriate those refugees. Rather, WOJAC contends, the responsibility for absorbing them should be borne by the other Arab countries.

In a chapter entitled "The Persecution of Jews in Arab Lands,"[52] the pamphlet features the theme of the countermyth:

> Arab oppression of Jews is not, therefore, a post-1948 phenomenon. It is rooted in Islam and has been an inescapable characteristic of the relations between Arabs and Jews since Muhammad's time. 20th century Arab persecution of Jews is only a continuation and intensification of this centuries-long tradition, in which the socially and religiously inferior Jew bore the brunt of the Muslim masses' contempt and the Muslim governments' arbitrary policies and financial troubles.[53]

This analysis may not reflect the opinion of the entire constituency WOJAC was established to represent; nonetheless, it is true that Oriental Jews in Israel are purported to mistrust the Arabs as a result of their own experience of persecution in their original homelands. This is supposed to explain their intense anti-Arabism, their opposition to giving up the West Bank and Gaza, and their long-standing support for the Likud party. Some go so far as to claim that Oriental Jews, because of their hatred of the Arabs, pose a significant obstacle to peace between Israel and its Arab neighbors.

While it is true that Jews from Arab countries often voice negative views about Arabs and Islam, it is questionable to what extent this is rooted in long-term historical memory. Most Oriental Jewish voters in Israel today are children of immigrants; they never lived in Arab lands themselves or they left for Israel at a young age. The stories of hostility (and harmony) under Islam in the old country come from their elders. The animosity to Arabs reflects, in part, the desire of Oriental Jews to differentiate themselves from the Arabs, who, in an unfortunate but predictable consequence of the Arab-Israel conflict, are the object of deep prejudice among the Israeli public. Moreover, their support for Likud at the voting booth has over the years been determined in part by their political and economic experiences in Israel.

Ever since their arrival as refugees, Jews from Arab lands have been denied equal opportunities in an Israeli society founded by Ashkenazim and ruled for the first three decades of the state by a Labor party dominated by Jews of European extraction. Much of this was not explicitly discriminatory; rather, it was an unfortunate result of the overburdening task of absorbing so many immigrants in a struggling new nation. Nevertheless, many Oriental Israelis continue to hold the Labor party responsible for their low socioeconomic status.[54] Oriental Jews perceive, correctly, that the Ashkenazim stake their claim to the fruits of Jewish independence in the Jewish state as compensation for the persecution they suffered in Christian lands—persecution that culminated in the Holocaust. Consciously or unconsciously, Oriental Jews in Israel have taken to accentuating their historic persecution (and thereby contributing to the countermyth) in an attempt to justify their claim to an equal share of the Zionist dream.[55]

A similar analysis appears in an article published in *Tikkun* magazine in 1990.[56] The writer, an Israeli scholar, and himself an Oriental Jew, illustrates how Oriental Jews distort the Jewish-Arab past in order to gain "assimilation and self-identity" in the present. He describes an Israeli television documentary about the Jews of Iraq. The documentary relates little of the cultural achievement of Iraqi Jews; instead, it portrays their story as if it conformed to "an Ashkenazic history of pogroms and persecution." The film intersperses "scenes from Baghdad with scenes from Nazi concentration camps" to draw an analogy between the well-known pogrom in Baghdad in 1941 and Nazi atrocities in Europe. The writer suggests that this may have been "another desperate attempt to assimilate into Israeli society, to share in the common destiny, to take part in the Holocaust."

Indirect evidence in support of the hypothesis connecting Sephardic anti-Arabism with domestic problems in Israel comes from a small book by an American Jew of Baghdadi origin. The author writes sympathetically about what he calls the "gap" between Ashkenazic and Sephardic Jews in Israel. In a brief excursus on "the medieval history of the Jews in Moslem countries," he seems to prepare his reader for a countermyth revision:

> Although there were trying times for Jews in Moslem lands, many historians consider their lot superior to that of the Jews in European countries. However, instances of persecution did occur; Jews were killed and robbed with greater frequency than their Moslem neighbors.

Tellingly—and consistent with his unclouded understanding of the real problem of Oriental Jews in Israel—the author continues:

> Nevertheless, anti-Jewish pogroms were less common in Moslem countries than in Christian lands. The mass burnings at the stake which took place in many sections of Europe are not known to have occurred in the Moslem world. Whereas Jews in Europe were expelled many times from their homes, only one similar instance is recorded in Moslem history: in 1678, the Jews of Yemen were ordered to accept Islam or leave the country. They left, en masse, and settled at Mauzaʿ, a small Yemenite city at the shore of the Red Sea. By 1681 they were permitted to return to Yemen.[57]

This balanced view of Jewish-Arab history by one who lived through its final stage indicates that the stereotype of Sephardic Jews as rabid Arab-haters needs to be qualified, perhaps with attention to possible differences between Sephardic Jews living in Israel and those living in the Diaspora.

The past decade has seen attempts in Israel to counteract the popular stereotype that all Jews from Arab countries despise Arabs and oppose diplomatic accommodation. A case in point is the group "Ha-mizraḥ el shalom," literally, "The East for Peace," formed in 1983 and composed of Israeli intellectuals of Oriental background who advocate socioeconomic equality at home, acknowledgment of Israel's embeddedness in the Middle East, and diplomatic concessions in return for peace with Israel's Arab neighbors. "This is the guarantee of a future of coexistence, mutual respect, and cultural cross-fertilization on the model of the Golden Age in Spain," writes Shlomo Elbaz, chairman of "East for Peace."[58]

With this brief sketch of the "myth-countermyth" debate over the fate of the Jews of Arab lands in the past as background, we now turn to the task at hand: a comparative historical assessment of Islamic-Jewish and Christian-Jewish relations during the early and High Middle Ages.[59]

PART TWO

In Religion and Law

Chapter Two

RELIGIONS IN CONFLICT

ARGUABLY, religious conflict played a formative—if not pivotal—role in Christian-Jewish and Islamic-Jewish relations during the Middle Ages. Hence, I open with an inquiry into the religious factor, specifically with a description and comparison of the early encounters of Christianity and Islam with Judaism and the Jews. I wish to determine whether the differences help explain the contrasting fates of European and Near Eastern Jewries in the Middle Ages. We shall see that this comparative approach can tell us much about the long-term relationship between each of the two new religions and its Jewish precursor. In Chapter 9, we consider interreligious polemics, an important feature of Christian-Jewish and Islamic-Jewish relations that grew out of the first interreligious encounters and changed as the Middle Ages progressed.

EARLY CHRISTIANITY AND THE JEWS

Christianity arose as a radical, messianic movement within Judaism. It was one of several varieties of Judaism that coexisted before the destruction of the second temple by Rome paved the way for the ascendancy of noncultic rabbinic Judaism. This messianic group—inspired by a Jew, Jesus of Nazareth, believed to be the divinely sent savior of mankind—posed a great threat to the modus vivendi between the Jewish leadership (the Pharisees and Sadducees of the New Testament) and the Roman government. Christianity's innovative, socially subversive interpretations of some of Judaism's most fundamental tenets were particularly threatening to Jewish leaders whose authority had already been limited by the Romans. Not surprisingly, some Jews opposed, first, Jesus and his disciples, and then, the adherents of the nascent church, many of whom were Jews. The abuse heaped on the neophytes by skeptical Jews, and the collaboration of individual Jews with Roman authorities—to eliminate Jesus as a threat and to harass his followers, recounted in the tendentious Gospels but hardly worth doubting, given the state of affairs at the time—bespeak the tension in the Jewish-Christian conflict at its earliest stage.

This tension mounted during the succeeding centuries—the period of the apostles and the church fathers—as Christianity fought to survive and then grow in the face of hostile Jews and a suspicious, often belligerent, pagan Roman administration. Marcel Simon has examined this phase of the Jewish-Christian conflict.[1] Paul, the Jew cum Christian apostle, widened the doctrinal gap between Judaism and Christianity in order to attract non-Jews. His chief innovation seems to have been assertions of the worthlessness of Jewish law, at least for gentile converts.[2] Little in the corpus of sayings attributed to Jesus indicates that he himself advocated abandonment of Jewish law.[3] Early Christian thinkers, however, adamantly expounded the doctrine that Jewish law had outlived its usefulness. They inculcated the idea of the dichotomy between letter (the Law, bound up with sin) and spirit (faith, Christ, the redeemer from sin). The Law came to be viewed as "good in principle but unfortunate in its practical effects."[4] Christianity subsequently replaced Jewish law with a new nomism, that of Christ. In this schema, Mosaic law appeared as a mere step on the way to the final, spiritual, messianic perfection of the incarnation.

In the second major departure from Judaism, Christianity challenged the Jews' claim to divine election. Early Christianity failed in its attempt to attract masses of Jews, most of whom had reservations about the legitimacy of the Christian *innovatio*. Rome, for its part, viewed Christianity as an illegal association while continuing to hold to the centuries-old legal recognition of Judaism. To counter Jewish and Roman charges of revolutionary innovation, thinkers of the early church taught that there was nothing new about Christianity, that it was merely the fulfillment of Judaism. Christian theologians interpreted everything in the Old Testament as referring to Christ and the church. Thus, by means of allegorical (or "spiritual") exegesis, any passage in the Jewish Bible could be construed as a prefiguration of something Christian.[5] The wood borne by Isaac to the site where God commanded Abraham to sacrifice his son (Genesis 22:6) alludes to the cross; Simeon and Levi's hamstringing of a bull (Genesis 49:6) prefigured the nailing of Jesus' feet to the cross by the scribes and Pharisees.[6] The church's claim to represent the New (and True) Israel, fulfilling God's word in the Old Testament through a New Testament, introduced a bold credo that would eventually undermine Judaism's place in the historical scheme of things.

Success for the church did not come at once, nor was it achieved without adversity. Nearly three centuries were to pass before the Christian community would emerge from its marginal status and rise to the rank of official state religion. It would be incorrect, however, to view the road to legitimacy as one of unrelenting Roman persecution. At first, when the boundaries between Christian and Jew were not yet clearly drawn even by many Christians, Roman authorities could not easily impose widespread, continuous repression. At the end of the third century, Emperor Diocletian cracked down on the Christians with a ferocity that spawned a new breed of martyr. Some church writings accuse the Jews of wreaking their own violence against the Christians.[7] Marcel Simon argues that Jews, especially in Palestine while they still retained a semblance of power, probably did persecute Christians and also provided Roman authorities with information to aid them in their own repression. As time went on, and the Roman government assumed the leading role in persecution, Jewish participation dwindled to individual or local acts.[8]

Regardless, an indelible memory of Jewish persecution of Christians became embedded in Christian consciousness. This memory, consistent with paradigmatic Old Testament accounts of Israelite animosity toward Moses and the prophets and also New Testament stories of Jewish persecution of Jesus and his disciples, would much later nourish fantasies about Jewish violence toward Christians, in turn invoked to justify militant Christian response, both verbal and physical, to Judaism and the Jews.

If Roman persecution and Jewish hostility threatened the future of the Christian community, Judaism's continuing appeal to pagans presented another kind of challenge. Major military defeats at the hands of Roman legions in 70 C.E. and again in 135 did not weaken Jewish receptivity to converts from among the pagans. Every gain for Judaism was a loss for Christianity. For instance, Tertullian, a church father, in the second and third centuries, berates pagans attracted to Jewish rites:

> By resorting to these customs, you deliberately deviate from your religious rites to those of strangers. For the Jewish fasts are the Sabbath and the meal of purity, and Jewish also are the ceremonies of the lamps, and the feast of unleavened bread, and the open-air prayer, all of which are, of course, foreign to your gods.[9]

Jewish proselytization seems to have continued in some places into the fourth century (although this, too, is debated), when the newly Christian emperors, alert to the threat, began to legislate severely against it.[10] Jewish encouragement of pagan attraction to Judaism had stiffened Christian hostility and intensified the motivation to curb the Jews when the chance finally came.

Judaizing—the assumption by Christians of Jewish practices—was itself a major cause of hostility toward the Jews. Indeed, many specialists in early Christianity consider Judaizing among Christians and pagans to be more important than theological opposition to Judaism as a cause of anti-Judaism.[11] During the early centuries of Christianity, many believers observed such festivals as the Sabbath and Easter on Jewish dates and in a Jewish manner. Indeed, some church ideologues defended these practices. The majority opposed them, however, with many treatises taking a staunch anti-Judaizing—hence, anti-Jewish—stance. Pseudo-Cyprian, writing probably in the first half of the third century, combined uncompromising opposition to Judaizing with caustic words for the Jews: "It should never be possible for Christians to stray from the way of truth and to trail like ignorant people after the blind and stupid Jews as to the correct day for Easter."[12] In the years 386 and 387, John Chrysostom, presbyter at Antioch, railed against the Jews. More than one scholar has asserted that Chrysostom's verbal violence toward the Jews demonstrates a link between the horror of Judaizing Christians and ecclesiastical disdain for the Jews. Though directed at Christians and intended primarily to deter them from associating with Jews and observing their holidays, Chrysostom's sermons bristled with denunciation of the Jews:

> [The synagogue] is not simply a gathering place for thieves and hucksters, but also of demons; indeed, not only the synagogue, but the souls of the Jews are also the dwelling places of demons. . . .
>
> How can you gather together in a place with men possessed by demons, whose spirits are so impure, and who are nurtured on slaughters and murders —how can you do this and not shudder? Instead of exchanging greetings with them and addressing one word to them, ought one not rather avoid them as a pestilence and disease spread throughout the whole world? Haven't they been the cause of all kind of evil?[13]

In the words of Simon, Chrysostom, "the master of anti-Jewish invective . . . turns the Jews into an eternal figure, a type; and it is a monstrous, villainous figure, calculated to inspire in all who look at it a proper horror."[14] And while this churchman "represents, in respect of his anti-Semitism, an extreme case in the early Church . . . a specifically Antiochene phenomenon," he had substantial influence on both contemporaries and successors. "Every time the subject of the Jews crops up in the Christian writings of the period Chrysostom's attitude and methods reappear."[15] His influence continued posthumously, as his sermons continued to be widely circulated. One scholar who has made a careful study of John Chrysostom's writings holds that "the homilies on the Judaizers served to support and encourage the anti-Jewish attitudes that had become characteristic of the Christian tradition and to foster hatred, hostility, and persecution."[16]

The anti-Judaism of Chrysostom, so influential for later Christian thought, might have led to early elimination of Judaism had it not been for the countervailing influence of Augustine (354–430), bishop of Hippo in North Africa. In his writings, Augustine articulated the doctrine of "witness," which, over the centuries, served to justify the preservation of the Jews within Christendom. In a post-Christmas sermon on the theme of the rejection of Jesus by "unfaithful Jews," Augustine invokes the psalmist as prooftext:

> For this reason, the Jews were expelled from their own kingdom and scattered throughout the earth so that, in all places, they might be forced to become

> witnesses to the faith which they hated. In fact, even after losing their temple, their sacrifice, their priesthood, and their kingdom, they hold on to their name and race in a few ancient rites, lest, mixed indiscriminately with the Gentiles, they perish and lose the testimony of the truth. Like Cain, who in envy and pride killed his just brother, they have been marked with a sign so that no one may kill them. Indeed, this fact can be quite definitely noted in Psalm 58 [59:11–22 in the Masoretic text]; where Christ, speaking as man, says: "My God has made revelation to me concerning my enemies: do not kill them lest they forget thy law." Strangely enough, by means of this people, enemies of the Christian faith, proof has been furnished to the Gentiles as to how Christ was foretold, lest, perhaps, when the Gentiles had seen how manifestly the prophecies were fulfilled, they should think that the Scriptures were made up by the Christians, since things which they perceived as accomplished facts were read aloud as foretold by Christ. Therefore the sacred books are handed down by the Jews and thus God, in regard to our enemies, makes clear to us that He did not kill them, that is, He did not annihilate them from the face of the earth so that they might not forget His law, for by reading it and observing, though only outwardly, they keep it in mind and thus bring judgment upon themselves and furnish testimony to us.[17]

The Augustinian doctrine of witness, with its pragmatic rationale for accepting Judaism within Christendom, may have restrained Christian intolerance; but it could not efface a fundamental and potentially dangerous ambivalence in early Christianity regarding the other. In a thought-provoking paper on the scriptural roots of intolerance in early Christianity, G. Stroumsa applies insights from sociologists Troeltsch and Weber and from Freud, pointing to the ambiguous coexistence in the New Testament and other early Christian writings of "irenic" (peaceful) and "eristic" (violent) trends. Alongside the commandment to "love thine enemy" existed sentiments of hatred and hostility toward those who denied the message of salvation. The accommodation of Christianity to the imperfect, unredeemed world of the Roman Empire in the fourth century neutralized the irenic strain, while the encounter between the universal ("totalitarian") command to love and the perceived perverse refusal of the Jews to accept the Christian dispensation spelled tension. Faced daily with a refractory Jewish presence that was legitimized by Roman law—and, we may add, restrained by the Augustinian doctrine of witness—Christianity resolved the tension by turning to religious intolerance.[18]

One need not concur fully with Rosemary Ruether, a Catholic theologian, that the vehement "adversus judaeos" tradition of the church fathers reflected a characteristic flaw in earliest Christianity, that it owed little to the influence of pagan anti-Judaism[19] to agree with her contention that conflict with Judaism took on the character of an essential ideological ingredient in Christian self-definition.[20] To be Christian was (1) to refute

Judaism on the basis of Jewish Scripture; (2) to believe that the promises of the Old Testament no longer applied to the people of Israel; (3) to emphasize that the stubborn defiance of contemporary Jews stemmed from a congenital rebelliousness manifested already in the Children of Israel's backsliding into idolatry and their scoffing at their own prophets; and (4) to scorn and vigorously combat Christians who elevated Judaism by observing its commandments and customs. Thus, in this earliest encounter between Judaism and Christianity, we have religions in conflict, as the precedent is set for more friction and discord in times to come.

Early Islam and the Jews

Can a comparison between the early Christian-Jewish conflict and the first encounter between Islam and Judaism illumine the larger question of why Islamic-Jewish relations in the Middle Ages were marked by so much less violence than were Christian-Jewish relations? Superficially, one can draw a rough parallel between the rise of Islam and the rise of Christianity. The first encounter between Islam and the Jews represents a case of religions in conflict. Though not born and educated a Jew, as Jesus was, Muhammad, nonetheless, had contact with Judaism, whose teachings and reverence for a written, divine revelation made a profound impression on him. Precisely how a pagan merchant from the Arab tribe that dominated the commercial town of Mecca (home of the Kaʿba, northern Arabia's most important pagan shrine) learned so much about Judaism remains a mystery to this day.[21] True, much Christian influence can be felt in the Qur'an, and the indigenous impulse toward monotheism among some Arabs in pre-Islamic Arabia cannot be discounted. Yet even a casual reader of the Qur'an is struck by how much it rings with echoes of the Bible and, equally important, of the midrash or post-biblical homiletic commentary. There is little mystery about Muhammad's intentions: he expected his Israelite stories and the Jewish customs he adopted to endear him to the Jewish tribes of Medina; he also hoped they would join the *umma* (community) of Islam while retaining their faith. In the "Constitution of Medina," his compact with the Arab and Jewish tribes of the oasis, Muhammad stipulated that "the Jews have their religion, and the Muslims have theirs."[22] Jesus, too, expected his message to resonate in Jewish ears and win adherents among his fellow Jews.

Thus there are similarities between Muhammad's mission in Medina and the early meeting between Christianity and Judaism. There are, also, important and revealing differences, some of which suggest a more confrontational atmosphere than existed between Christians and Jews and others of which suggest a more harmonious state of affairs. Consider the Jewish reaction to Muhammad and the Prophet's response. An Arab rather than a Jew, and a prophet appearing centuries after the cessation of biblical prophecy, Muhammad could only have appeared to the Jewish tribes of Medina as an impostor whose teachings in the name of God bore but a skewed resemblance to biblical and rabbinic Judaism. Moreover, the Prophet couched his message in a verbiage foreign to Judaism both in its format and its rhetoric. Thus, Jewish distaste for Muhammad was in some ways more pronounced than Jewish antagonism toward Jesus, who did not claim to have founded a new religion and who was and remained a Jew.

Only a tiny number of the Jews of Medina converted to Islam. Jewish enmity toward Muhammad pervaded the Jewish tribal settlements there. Little wonder that Muhammad lost his patience and turned to violence, expelling two of the main Jewish tribes (one fled to the oasis of Khaybar where Muhammad later finished them off) and massacring nearly all the male members of the third. Later Islamic tradition harped on the theme of the treachery of the Jews of Medina against Muhammad and Islam, a motif reminiscent of one of the more salient themes in the Christian-Jewish conflict.[23]

For proponents of the countermyth, Muhammad's violence against the Jewish tribes of Medina exemplifies a fundamental, even congenital, Islamic persecutory posture toward the Jews. Mindful of the suffering inflicted on the Jews of Christendom in the name of avenging Jewish persecution of Christ, some champions of the countermyth, by implication and by comparison, represent Islam as inherently more anti-Jewish at its origins than even Christianity. Subsequent history, however, exhibits a much less grizzly interfaith relationship. Why?

The Birth of Islam

The circumstances of the birth of Islam in relationship to Judaism, though marked by conflict, differ fundamentally from those of Christianity's origins. Jesus, the messiah (and, to some, the son of God) was crucified. His crucifixion, blamed by Christians on the Jews, seemed at the time tantamount to nullification of the divine plan. Despite the positive redemptive interpretation assigned by Christ's disciples to his death in the concept of the vicarious atonement, the act of killing Jesus continued to be considered an unforgivable act, to be remembered in perpetuity. An early exegetical elaboration of the Gospel account of the crucifixion identified the Jew as the last tormentor of Christ. This tradition, later fleshed out in a long-lived medieval iconographic tradition and in passion plays, was symbolized in crucifixion scenes by a repulsive, evil-looking figure at the foot of the cross offering the thirsty, dying Jesus a bitter drink of vinegar and gall via a sponge affixed to the end of a pole.[24] In the twelfth century, the old charge of deicide gave birth to stories of ritual child murders, by which Jews allegedly commemorated and reenacted that first act of God-murder.

By contrast, the founder of Islam claimed neither messiahship nor divinity. While Jews ridiculed him during his lifetime, Muhammad died a natural death. Thus, unlike Christians, Muslims had no grounds for holding the Jews responsible for the demise of their progenitor. Nevertheless, biographical accounts of the Prophet and Muslim traditions (*ḥadīths*) depict Jewish attempts on the Prophet's life.[25] These stories surfaced whenever Muslims looked for reasons to mistrust contemporary Jews.[26] Without a "propheticide," however, and lacking an iconographic tradition—iconography being forbidden in Islam—that might have provided the illiterate Muslim masses with a graphic depiction of Jewish enmity toward Muhammad in Medina, the Islamic-Jewish conflict could not generate the tension and hatred that so inflamed the conflict between Christianity and the Jews.

Stroumsa's insight into the ambiguous nature of Christian attitudes toward Judaism and the Jews suggests another important contrast in the early relationship of Muslims and Jews. The comparison with Islam reciprocally reinforces Stroumsa's point about Christianity. Unlike Christianity, with its love-hate ambivalence toward the enemy—Judaism—Islam evinces no ambiguity about the infidel—Jew and Christian. The Jihad mentality, fed by scriptural injunctions, required Muslims to combat (not love) the enemy, something Islam did in the extreme during its early years. The battle lines against Christians and Zoroastrians living in the "Domain of War" were clearly drawn. As the Conquest spread, those People of the Book among them who submitted to Arab rule were guaranteed residential rights and protection inside the Domain of Islam in return for obedience and tribute. Thereafter, Muslims treated Jews with contempt, but minus the love-hate tension that so complicated Christianity's relationship with its Jewish infidels. Relieved of this ambiguity, and spared Christianity's eschatological disappointment once it had gained power, Islam was less inclined than Christendom to persecute the Jews and could more readily abide a vital Jewish presence in its midst. Indeed, to the contrary, Jews were allowed to prosper, and even participate, in the political and intellectual life of the majority society.

Another contrast between the circumstances surrounding the rise of the two new religions concerns locale. Unlike Christianity, Islam arose in an area peripheral to Judaism. The Jewish tribes of northern Arabia had dwelt there for centuries, far from the centers of rabbinic Judaism in Palestine and Babylonia. Moreover, they lacked the demographic strength and communal and institutional solidarity of the Jews living in Jesus' immediate milieu. There was little the Jews of Arabia could do to resist the progress of the new religious faith and community. Islam's easy triumph over Arabian Judaism was assured; this, in turn, obviated much of the impulse for the kind of continuous interfaith conflict that characterized the centuries of struggle by early Christianity to humble a demographically large and institutionally powerful Judaism. Even in the Fertile Crescent, the heartland of Judaism, Islam's demographic challenge came from the huge indigenous Christian and Zoroastrian populations, not from the numerically smaller communities of Jews.

Early Islam, in contrast to early Christianity, did not have to struggle for recognition against a hostile and powerful enemy like Rome. After Medina, Islam carried the day as the established religion of Arabia. Tensions such as those experienced by early Christians with Jews, pagans, and Roman authorities alike dissipated rapidly with the triumphs over the polytheists, the suppression of the brief "apostasy" (*ridda*) movement among some Arab tribes immediately after the Prophet's death in 632, and the subjugation of powerful Christian settlements in the south (especially the community of Najran).

This situation contrasts sharply with the stiff opposition Christianity's founders met from Roman authorities, even as the hostile competitor, Judaism, continued to benefit from Roman toleration. Under these circumstances, early Christian thinkers inevitably came to emphasize the superiority of Christianity over Judaism in their writings and sermons. At the same time, Roman persecution strengthened Christian resolve to weaken its religious rival. Once Christianity had achieved official toleration and then recognition under Emperor Constantine, culminating in its establishment as the Roman state religion in 391,[27] it began to implement its hitherto restrained anti-Jewish intentions.[28]

Early Christianity faced a related problem, one not experienced by early Islam. Having failed to convince all Jews that Christianity fulfilled God's messianic promises to Israel in the Bible, nascent Christianity appropriated Israel's identity—at Jewish expense. As early as Paul, the church had shifted its attention to the pagan Romans, preaching that they were the *new* Israel. Chosen by god to replace the old Israel, the gentiles were, in Paul's famous metaphor (Letter to the Romans 11), the wild olive grafted to the olive tree to replace those branches (faithless, rejected Judaism) temporarily lopped off; the New Covenant offered to the gentiles fulfilled the divine promises of the Old. It took generations of preaching to win this point, however. Until it prevailed, the young Christian church had to endure the skepticism of the Jews and the reluctance of many Christians to sever their relationship with the Israel of the Old Testament.

Islam never portrayed itself as "New Israel." Genealogically, Arabs traced their descent from Ishmael, Abraham's firstborn son, the brother of Isaac. Chronologically, Arab peoplehood paralleled the peoplehood of Israel: Arabs and Jews had the same ancestor. The Ishmaelite branch simply had been dispersed for centuries, awaiting its revival and the fulfillment of its claim to centrality in history. This came with the advent of the Prophet Muhammad. Unlike Christianity, Islam felt no need to establish its identity at the expense of the Jews.

Nature of the Religion

The important distinction between Islam and Christianity with regard to the Jews had other facets, which further elucidate Islam's fundamentally different and less confrontational posture toward the Jews. Theologically, Islam did not represent itself as the divine fulfillment of Judaism. The Qur'an harks back to Abraham—the original, pure monotheist—as its progenitor and spiritual ancestor. Abraham was the first "Muslim" by virtue of his complete, unquestioning "surrender" (*islām,* in Arabic) to God's will. In the words of the Qur'an:

> O People of the Scripture [Jews and Christians]! Why will ye argue about Abraham, when the Torah and the Gospel were not revealed till after him? . . . Abraham was not a Jew, nor yet a Christian; but he was an upright man who had surrendered [*muslim;* i.e., to God], and he was not of the idolaters. Lo! Those of mankind who have the best claim to Abraham are those who followed him, and this Prophet and those who believe [with him].[29]

In the thought of the Qur'an and of Islam, then, Abraham, who boldly rejected the polytheism dominant in his world, was the forerunner of Muhammad. Religion as it developed after Abraham, first into Judaism then into Christianity, deviated from Abraham's pristine belief in one God. In the person of Muhammad and in the form of his revealed message, Islam had arisen to revive the forgotten, pure monotheism of that ancestor, the father of Ishmael, forebear of the Arabs. In the words of one scholar: "Islam, which means 'surrender' [to the will of God], was seen not as a new covenant but as an urgently needed restoration of the old. The Koran was thought to have been sent down to re-establish a 'pure' religion that had been defiled."[30]

Because the Abraham story established the priority of Islam over both Judaism and Christianity,[31] Islam's relationship to Judaism and to Jewish Scripture differed significantly from that of Christianity. It is true that Paul had proclaimed Abraham before his circumcision the first "Christian." Abraham was bound by monotheism and by the moral law, to the exclusion of the ritual that came later on, at the time of Moses.[32] For all practical (and ideological) purposes, however, Christianity accepted its chronological posteriority vis-à-vis Judaism at face value, claiming that Christ represented the next and final stage in the fulfillment of God's message to the Jews. That meant Christians accepted the Jewish Bible as their own—the "Old Testament" had prefigured the "New"—and those Christians, like Marcion in the second century, who rejected the Hebrew Bible were branded by the church as heretics. Shared claim to Scripture laid the foundation for continual tension over the interpretation of the message of Jewish holy writ.[33]

Islam, in contrast, dismissed the existing texts of the Scriptures of the Jews and Christians as a corruption of their original, divinely inspired teaching. This approach took Islam in a different direction from that of Christianity. As we shall see, this difference in approach to the Book of the Jews—between the Islamic doctrine of *taḥrīf* (falsification) and the Christian principle of prefiguration—goes a long way toward explaining the lower level of interfaith conflict in the Islamic environment.

Another, related contrast between Christianity and Islam in relation to Judaism bears on the issue of imitation of Jewish practices. Judaizing posed a serious obstacle to the church's efforts to differentiate the rejected forerunner from the newly chosen beneficiary of God's salvation. Church fathers fought Judaizing for generations precisely because many Christians still took seriously the original Christian proposition that Christianity is an extension of Judaism. Islam approached Judaism differently. Muhammad himself originally adopted the fast of the tenth day (called *ʿāshūrāʾ*) of the first Muslim month.[34] In keeping with yet another Jewish custom, Muhammad taught his followers to face Jerusalem during prayer. Soon, however, he forsook these "Judaizing" observances, not because they posed a threat to the identity of the Muslim community but because, in Medina, he encountered fierce opposition from the Jews.

A similar pattern of initial acceptance, followed by repudiation, characterizes the attitude of early Islam toward the narrative traditions of the Jews. Initially, permission was granted to quote sayings and reports about the Banū Isrāʾīl (Children of Israel), edifying and miraculous tales called "Isrāʾīliyyāt." This approval reflected a common belief that the Holy Books of the Jews include information about the life and acts of prophets before Islam and about the Prophet himself, in particular, in the form of predictions of his advent. At the same time, Muslims were adjured not to imitate the custom of the children of Israel. Eventually, permission to transmit traditions about the children of Israel was also revoked, and Muslims were banned from learning or copying Jewish Scripture altogether.[35]

Paradoxically, because the boundaries between Islam and Judaism were clearly delineated early on, much that was basic in Judaism could ultimately take root in developed Islam. Religious law (*sharīʿa*), the most fundamental feature of Islam, corresponds directly to—and, in fact, has the same meaning (the way) as—Jewish *halakha*. The dietary laws of Islam, including not only the conspicuous prohibition of pork but also a system of ritual animal slaughter, closely resemble Jewish practice.[36]

Judaism is, in fact, often referred to in Muslim sources as *sharīʿat al-yahūd*. This contrasts with such common pejorative Latin locutions for Judaism as "the Law of the Jews" and more disparaging commonplace epithets such as "superstition of the Jews" and "perfidy of the Jews." Whereas the Christian vocabulary for the Jews and Judaism reflects animosity and hostility, Islamic parlance betrays recognition of mutually held religious concepts and values.

If Islam did not share Christianity's concern about the taint of Judaism, that is because Islam's "church"[37] originated further away psychologically from Judaism than had Christianity and because Islam was not threatened by a substantial "Judaizing phenomenon." The lure of Judaism (and Christianity) was expressed among some of the Muslim masses in a certain popular syncretism, not, as in Christianity, in loyal attachment to Jewish observances considered superior to Islam because of their priority.

Islamic opposition to imitating Judaism (as well as Christianity) had a special doctrinal expression—the principle of *khālifūhum* (be different from them). Interestingly, this opposition parallels the biblical admonition to eschew the customs of the gentiles.[38] The concept "be different from them" originated in the *ḥadīth*.[39] A major book featuring this theme was written by the theologian and jurist Ibn Taymiyya (1263–1328). He wrote:

> Differing from them is the cause of the victory of Islam, the purpose of sending prophets is that the divine faith should emerge triumphant. Thus the very act of differing from them constitutes one of the greatest prophetic offices.[40]

And:

> Granted that the Scriptuaries are permitted to practice their innovated and abrogated religions on condition that they shall not make a show of it, a Muslim cannot be permitted to practice an innovated and abrogated religion, either secretly or openly.[41]

Ibn Taymiyya fretted over Muslim saint worship, the cult of tombs, and certain unordained festivals ascribed by him to the influence of Judaism and, especially, Christianity. Although this concern seems akin to the problem of Judaizing that so vexed the church fathers, there is a revealing difference.[42] At stake for Ibn Taymiyya, writing centuries after the rise of Islam, is not differentiating Islam as a religion from Judaism or Christianity, but rather preserving the unadulterated purity and superiority of the Islamic faith. The great Hanbalite theologian worried that if Muslims failed to distinguish themselves from *dhimmīs,* the hierarchical supremacy of Islam would be diminished and the prestige of Jews and Christians enhanced. Ibn Taymiyya's rhetoric is less hateful than John Chrysostom's, for the two perceived the danger differently. The presbyter of Antioch lived at a time when Christianity, despite its recognition as the official religion of the Roman Empire, still felt insecure. He worried that Judaizing practices might weaken Christianity's exclusive claim to truth and undermine its recent and still fragile triumph over paganism. His Muslim counterpart, Ibn Taymiyya, saw imitation of non-Muslim saint worship both as religious innovation (*bidʿa*) and as detracting from the superiority of an already triumphal Islam. He did not, however, express concern that Judaizing Muslims might mistake Christianity or Judaism for a more genuine Islam.

Chapter Three

THE LEGAL POSITION OF JEWS IN CHRISTENDOM

WE CAN CONCUR that legal status is "the most deceptive of all standards of a people's well-being," as R. W. Southern writes in his *Making of the Middle Ages*.[1] Inevitably, there is a gap between theory and practice; and this was certainly true for the Jews in the Middle Ages. Nevertheless, a discussion of the legal position of Jews in a work such as this belongs near the beginning, because, alongside religion, legal status is the earliest aspect of the problem of gentile-Jewish relations that we can know with clarity. Moreover, since this book is a comparative study, the inquiry into legal position yields more useful information than might otherwise be the case.

There are many similarities between the legal status of the Jews of Islam and that of the Jews of Christendom. The most important similarity is that, in both societies, Jews enjoyed virtually complete autonomy in their practice of Judaism. In practical terms, this meant that, for most purposes of religious and personal status, such as ritual, marriage, and divorce, Jews were governed by Jewish law—the law of the Talmud—administered by Jewish judges trained and licensed by Jewish religious authorities.

Differences in legal status between Christendom and Islam reflected or helped shape the dominant society's contrasting attitudes toward the Jews. Along with differences in religious attitude between early Christianity and early Islam discussed in Chapter 2, the differences in legal approach help explain the lower incidence of persecution in the Muslim world. In Chapter 3, we review the rather complex legal status of the Jews in Western Christendom, to prepare the way for an analytical comparison with the legal position of Jews in Islam (Chapter 4).

JEWRY LAW IN CHRISTENDOM

The great legal scholar Guido Kisch has plumbed the subject of Jewish legal status.[2] He gave the useful name "Jewry law" to Christian legal material concerning the Jews. In this way, Kisch distinguished "Jewry law" from "Jewish law," the term used for the vast corpus of legal matter written by Jews themselves which pertained to inner Jewish life and to the relationship of Jews to their surroundings.

The Christian Middle Ages knew numerous and sometimes overlapping systems of law. There was surviving Roman law in the age of the

Barbarians; Germanic tribal or customary law; revived Roman law beginning in the late eleventh and twelfth centuries in Italy; canon law of the church; feudal and territorial law, which ultimately blended into the law of the state; and municipal law.[3] Just as law in medieval Christendom was complex, so Jewry law was complex. Like law in general, it, too, developed and changed over time.

Roman Jewry Law

Jewry law in Christendom had numerous sources, the earliest being Roman law. Although few pre-Christian Roman statutes concerning the Jews have survived, such nonlegal sources as Josephus's description of Roman treatment of the Jews indicate that the Romans continued the tolerant policy they had inherited from Hellenistic and Persian antiquity. Judaism was recognized as a *collegium* (association) whose adherents were permitted to congregate for religious purposes and "live by their ancestral laws."[4] *Collegium* was often applied to the Jews interchangeably with *religio licita,* or "licit religion." The latter, though not a legal term, was in use as early as the beginning of the third century.[5]

In some ways, Roman legal policy toward the Jews exceeded the tolerant stance of the earlier regimes. Faced with a religion that prescribed such distinctive (and, to Romans, peculiar) customs as circumcision, worship of a single invisible God, abstention from work one day each week (the Sabbath), and sending donations to the Patriarch in Tiberias—peculiarities which fed an anti-Jewish strain in literature that some call "pagan antisemitism"—Rome was obliged to tolerate "ancestral laws" it did not allow even its own citizens.[6]

An edict of Augustus from about 1 B.C.E. states that "Jews shall use their own customs in accordance with their ancestral law, just as they used to use them in the time of Hyrcanus, the high priest of their highest god."[7] This law aptly illustrates Roman rulers' forbearance toward the Jews, a policy practiced consistently and steadfastly for centuries. They temporarily reversed themselves on the legality of Jewish observance about the time of the Jewish revolt of 132–35 C.E., when Emperor Hadrian proscribed Sabbath observance and circumcision.[8] The decree was rescinded by Emperor Antonius Pius (r. 137–61). Moreover, in the year 212, Emperor Caracalla granted citizenship to all non-Romans in the empire. Although the edict does not mention Jews by name (or any other "foreign" group, for that matter), scholars generally agree that Caracalla's law included the Jews.[9] Hence, during the final century of pagan Roman rule, legally Jews graduated from tolerance to near parity with other Roman citizens.

The "tolerance" accorded the Jews was derived from an essential feature of Roman society: its pagan, polytheistic religion. In polytheistic societies, the gods and their respective peoples tolerate one another's existence. Polytheism breeds what the modern world would call "religious pluralism."[10] By contrast, monotheism is inherently exclusive. The unity of God has its counterpart in the desire of his adherents for all people to be united in worshiping him. Thus, in the ancient world, the monotheists par excellence—the Jews—did not reciprocate the religious toleration of pagan Rome. Indeed, they sought to make converts among the Romans. Early Christians inherited from Judaism their monotheistic intolerance for the Roman "gentile." At the same time, as the new monotheists on the scene, convinced of the veracity of their own version of God's revelation, Christians found the continuing presence of the Jews both problematic and a source of competition. When, in the fourth century, Christianity replaced paganism as the state religion of the Roman Empire, the opportunity arose to reduce the influence of paganism and Judaism alike. It is the latter to which we now turn.

Christian-Roman Jewry Law

The Theodosian Code, compiled by order of Emperor Theodosius II between 429 and 438, incorporates Roman imperial legislation dating from the beginning of the Christian period.[11] Jewry law in the Code is a mixture of tolerance (the legacy of polytheistic Rome) and the intolerance inherent in monotheistic Christianity. Because the Code had considerable influence in the Latin West during the early Middle Ages, both in its own right and in its epitomizations, it is the foundation of Jewry law in Latin Christendom.

Amnon Linder's study of Jewry law in Roman imperial legislation provides an excellent guide to this subject.[12] The Theodosian Code contains thousands of laws divided topically into "books" and "titles." Laws concerning the Jews comprise a minuscule portion of the whole.[13]

The vast majority (fifty-one out of sixty-eight) of the citations concerning Jews in the Theodosian Code occur in the final section, Book 16, which covers the relationship between the established Christian church and other religions. Not surprisingly, this book departs from the religious pluralism that underlay pagan Roman law. We find a series of ordinances which, on one hand, grant special privileges to the Christian clergy and, on the other, combat early Christianity's principal foes—heresy, paganism, and Judaism. For example, Title 5, "On Heretics," impugns Jews along with heretics as partners in anti-Catholic enmity, calling them "a pestilence and a contagion if it should spring forth and spread abroad more widely."[14] Reissued some two months later, with strengthened admonitions to Roman officials to be vigilant about such offenses, this same law couples Jews with heretics and "the gentiles, who are commonly called pagans."[15] Linder comments that, from the beginning of the fifth century, the regular association of Jews with pagans and heretics in laws "indicates a fundamental change in the Jewish policy of the imperial government" which "was bound to affect the legal status of the Jews during that period."[16]

Titles 8 and 9 of Book 16 deal exclusively with the Jews.[17] By consolidating in two consecutive titles so many texts concerning the Jews, even at the expense of repeating laws left embedded in other contexts, the Code focused attention on the Jews as a problem of special concern, for whom special regulations were needed. This consolidation marked a departure from the situation that obtained between Caracalla's law of 212 and the Christianization of the Roman state—a century during which the Jews were brought under Roman law. It also foreshadowed the later evolution of Christian Jewry law into a special law for a people living on the margins of the Christian ecumene, or even outside it.

As is generally recognized, Title 8 perpetuates the features of the old pagan-Roman toleration. At the same time, some of the phraseology reflects the new concerns of the church. Carried over from the pre-Christian period is the all-important recognition of the legitimacy of Judaism and the resulting guarantee of Jewish assembly for worship. The first law on this matter, dated 393, begins with the affirmation: "It is sufficiently established that the sect of the Jews is forbidden by no law."[18] Although this may seem a rather negative way of expressing toleration, the formulation could simply reflect an attempt by codifiers to anticipate and preempt clerical objections to the continuation of an indulgent policy deeply rooted in pre-Christian Roman tradition. Other, more specific guarantees of the freedom to practice Judaism are included—for instance, the age-old assurance of noninterference in observance of the Sabbath.[19]

Essential elements of the policy of toleration inherited from the pagan period are the provisions of the Theodosian Code that protect Jews against wanton assault on their persons and property. The earliest statute dates from 397: "All insults of persons attacking the Jews shall be averted (and . . . their synagogues shall remain in their accustomed quietude)."[20] Similarly, a law of 420 combines protection of synagogues with safeguarding Jewish lives: "No person shall be trampled upon when he is innocent, on the ground that he is a Jew, nor shall any religion cause any person to be exposed to contumely. Their synagogues and habitations shall not be burned indiscriminately."[21] The statute closes with a statement characteristic of Christian stringency to the effect that "the Jews also shall be admonished that they perchance shall not become insolent and, elated by their own security, commit any rash act in disrespect of the Christian religion."

This qualification of assurances of protection by an admonition not to take protection for granted may have been anticipated in pre-Christian Rome. In 41 C.E., following riots against the Jews in Alexandria, Egypt, for demanding new privileges, Emperor Claudius wrote to the Alexandrians, insisting that they desist from violence. In his letter, Claudius specified the limits of toleration of the Jews, ordering them to stop their demands for "more privileges."[22]

In the same spirit, the Theodosian Code frequently couches safeguards for the Jews and their property in grudging, often threatening language: "We have suppressed the spirit and audacity of the abominable pagans, of the Jews also, and of the heretics. Nevertheless . . . it is Our will . . . that those persons who commit many rash acts under the pretext of venerable Christianity shall refrain from injuring and persecuting [the Jews]."[23]

Christian animosity toward Judaism is rampant in the stipulations of Title 8, which, in turn, are consistent with the tone of Christian supremacy that characterizes Book 16.[24] The right of the Jews to send money to the Patriarch in Tiberias was rescinded. Henceforth, contributions were to be diverted to the imperial treasury.[25] Another law (of 415) demoted the patriarch Gamaliel, restricted his authority to build new synagogues, and commanded him to destroy synagogues located in deserted places.[26] The same Emperor Honorius who enacted the law of 415 reversed himself in 423, prohibiting the destruction of old synagogues.[27] In his "new law" of 438, Emperor Theodosius II extended the concession: "With an equally reasonable consideration also, We prohibit any synagogue to arise as a new building, *but license is granted to strengthen the ancient synagogues which threaten immediately to fall in* [into] *ruin*."[28] After conquering the Byzantine lands of the eastern Mediterranean, Islam adopted a more repressive policy, forbidding both new construction and the repair of existing houses of worship.

Prejudicial language about the Jews tempers the principle of Roman toleration carried over into the Theodosian Code. The extensive use of the term *superstitio* is conspicuous. A pejorative in pre-Christian Roman usage, the term designated any non-Roman religion; but Roman writers also referred to Judaism, using a neutral designation, *religio*. This duality continued after the Christianization of the empire. By the beginning of the fifth century, *religio* was reserved for Christianity, whereas *superstitio,* now restricted to Judaism, was henceforth qualified by such pejorative adjectives as "abominable" and "nefarious." Other language in the Code calls attention to the Jews' obdurate rejection of Christ, to the perversity—even to the impurity of Judaism ("a plague . . . that spreads like contagion")—and to the inveterate hostility of the Jews toward the Roman Empire.[29]

Jewish power over both Christians and potential Christians among the pagan population was a major irritant to the Catholic church. An injunction placed Jewish-Christian intermarriage on a par with adultery (though not stated, this was punishable by death).[30] A law imposed by Emperor Honorius, dated 404, barred Jews and Samaritans from employment in the imperial service.[31] Honorius repeated his prohibition in 418, this time referring to the Jews alone as "those persons who are bound to the perversity of this race who are proved to have sought armed imperial service."[32] Emperor Theodosius, in his Novella 3, of 438, repeated the ban and extended its applicability to all branches of civil administration.[33]

Over the centuries, these enactments—removing Jews from positions that allowed them to bear arms (although, as late as the twelfth century, in some places, Jews continued to carry and use weapons)—initiated a drive intended to exclude Jews from positions in which they might wield authority over Christians.

Of particular concern to church leaders was the possibility that Jews would exert undue influence over slaves in their households. This fear stemmed from the Jewish law requiring that male slaves, upon entering household service, be circumcised and converted through ritual immersion in water.[34] The codifiers of the Theodosian Code dedicated the entire Title 9 of Book 16 to the subject, "No Jew Shall Have a Christian Slave." Classical Roman law had already expressed its disapproval of circumcision because of its similarity to the forbidden custom of castration.[35] Christian-Roman law, however, refocused the issue in terms of conversion. Constantine, the first Christian emperor, ruled that "if any Jew should purchase and circumcise a Christian slave or a slave of any other sect whatever, he shall not retain in slavery such circumcised person."[36] According to a law promulgated in 417, a Jew who already owned Christian slaves could keep them but only on the condition that he not "unite them, either unwilling or willing, with the pollution of his own sect." As usual, the punishment for violation was death.[37] The focus on Jewish ownership of slaves continued over the centuries with the same disproportionate intensity in canon law. The situation represented a grave violation of the fundamental premise that no infidel should be superior to a Christian.[38]

Early Christian Jewry law is summed up by this toleration of Judaism—the legacy of Rome—qualified by intolerant language and restrictions which aimed at preserving Christian supremacy over the Jews. The Justinianic Code, compiled at the beginning of the sixth century, drew heavily upon the parent codification, carrying over entire sections intact. The code also eliminated some laws while modifying others. Some of this revision reflects a hardening of attitudes characteristic of this period of tension and enhanced fear of heresy. Thus, in the statutes, heretics are regularly linked to Jews.[39] A novella of the year 535 decrees that synagogues be turned into churches and that conventicles of pagans and heretics not be allowed.[40] Justinian's most infamous "new law" regarding the Jews interdicted *deu-*

terosis.[41] Promulgation of the law amounted to interference in the freedom to practice Judaism, which radically contradicted the age-old policy of pre-Christian and Christian-Roman law.[42]

Justinian's Code—in circulation in the eastern Roman Empire in various, shortened forms—was unknown in the West until the revival of the study of Roman law at the end of the eleventh century.[43] It was the more moderate Theodosian Code that lingered in the memories of European jurists and churchmen in the early Middle Ages. Amnon Linder notes that, apart from Visigothic Spain (where the Code was replaced in 506 by an abbreviated epitome), "in other parts of the West the Code was never formally abrogated, and its legal status was comparable to that of other legal sources."[44] Especially in southern Europe—where, in general, continuity with the Roman past was strong—memory of Roman law and the persistence of many Roman legal procedures contributed to the creation of an environment that, for Jews, was considerably more secure than it was in northern Europe.

The Church: Canon Jewry Law

Inevitably, Jewry law appeared in pronouncements by the Catholic church. Influenced by Roman law, canon law, in turn, influenced the Jewry law of the state. Book 16 of the Theodosian Code, with its mix of toleration and restriction of Judaism, was accepted by the church "as an authoritative source of canon law."[45] During the early Middle Ages, edicts of ecclesiastical councils and pontifical opinions, often in the form of letters, steadily expanded the corpus of canon Jewry law.

Nearly all the canons of diocesan and ecumenical church councils regarding the Jews—whether in Spain, Gaul, or the East—are repressive, reflecting the intolerant streak in Christianity.[46] Compared to the hard line evident in the Jewry law of church councils, Pope Gregory the Great (590–604) expressed more moderate views in concordance with the Roman traditions he knew from his aristocratic upbringing and from an earlier career in civil administration. In twenty-six pastoral letters regarding Jewish-Christian relations, Gregory adhered to the tolerationist features of the Theodosian Code, notably by opposing forced baptism and upholding the inviolability of synagogues. He set a standard on Jewish matters that guided the papacy for centuries.[47]

Most important, in one sentence of a letter, Gregory enunciated what was to become the emblem of papal policy toward the Jews: "Just as it should not be permitted the Jews [*Sicut Judeis non*] to presume to do in their synagogues anything other than what is permitted them by law, so with regard to those things which have been conceded them they ought to suffer no injury."[48] True to the spirit of equilibrium between repression and tolerance in the Theodosian Code, Gregory's formula first limits the Jews to the observance of laws and customs permitted in the past; then guarantees them protection from interference in the practice of any of those laws and customs. The pronouncement is also reminiscent of the formulation in Claudius's letter to the Alexandrians (where, however, the guarantee precedes the restrictions).[49]

The most significant pronouncement of ecclesiastical Jewry law appears as a bull that opens with Gregory's very words and is known as the papal bull *Sicut Judeis*. Another appellation attached to it in some medieval collections—"Constitutio pro judeis" (Constitution in favor of the Jews)—clearly indicates its protective intent. The earliest pope to issue this decree was apparently Calixtus II (1119–24), though the existence of his precedent-setting and influential edict is known only through reference to it in later renewals. It is believed that Calixtus issued the bull in response to a petition from Jews hoping to improve the security of a people whose vulnerability had been distressingly revealed so recently during the massacres of the First Crusade. On the other hand, the request may have sprung from concern about localized anti-Jewish violence in Rome or elsewhere in Italy.[50]

The papal bull *Sicut Judeis* elaborates on the second half of the Gregorian formula, the "guarantee" clause. It specifies what the twelfth-century church deemed to be the Jews' rights, including freedom from forced baptism, protection of persons and property from unwarranted assault, the unimpeded right to practice Judaism, and the inviolability of Jewish cemeteries. These guarantees are backed up with a commitment to punish Christians who trespass them. The bull was issued by five more popes before the end of the twelfth century, by another ten in the thirteenth, and then not again until 1348. The one promulgated by Pope Clement III (between 1187 and 1191) was incorporated into "authoritative" canon law in the *Decretals* of Pope Gregory IX (1227–41), promulgated in 1234.[51]

Papal assertion of the right of Jews and Judaism to protection and toleration, anchored in Roman law and mediated into medieval Christianity by Pope Gregory I, had already found its theological rationale in the thought of St. Augustine: God allowed the Jews to survive and live among Christians because they played the multifaceted role of "witness." In keeping with both Augustinian doctrine and the protections guaranteed in the bull *Sicut Judeis,* throughout the Middle Ages the papacy maintained staunch and fairly consistent opposition to forced conversion of the Jews as well as to unwarranted physical brutality toward them. Indeed, from time to time, a Pope might even add a clause to the "Constitutio pro Judeis" defending the Jews against some new, current threat. For example, in 1247, Innocent IV reissued his own version of the bull within a year of the first promulgation, adding a section denouncing the newly risen blood libel.[52]

I do not mean to imply that the papacy went out of its way to nurture

Jewish life among Christians. Quite the contrary; during the eleventh, twelfth, and especially the thirteenth centuries, as the papacy struggled to assert its supremacy over secular rulers, it also asserted its authority over the Jews. This was done by inculcating the complementary ideas of Jewish subservience and inferiority. Beginning with Pope Innocent III, in 1205, the idea of subservience was expressed in the revival of an old patristic doctrine about the "perpetual servitude" of the Jews, which gave ideological ballast to Innocent's newly intensified campaign to segregate and subjugate the Jews. It was Innocent III who introduced the unfriendly qualification at the end of the "Constitutio pro Judeis" when he renewed it in 1199: "We wish, however, to place under the protection of this decree only those [Jews] who have not presumed to plot against the Christian faith."[53] A disparaging preface mentioning "Jewish perfidy" was not included in subsequent papal renewals of the bull.

The Fourth Lateran Council

At the Fourth Lateran Council, in 1215, Innocent III and his prelates legislated against improper subordination of Christians to Jews. A handful of the seventy canons enacted concerned what was considered intolerable Jewish influence over Christians. For instance, "Since it is quite absurd that any who blaspheme against Christ should have power over Christians, we . . . forbid that Jews be given preferment in public office since this offers them the pretext to vent their wrath against the Christians" (Canon 69).[54] This restatement of the old law of the Theodosian Code, barring Jews from positions in the imperial service and from other public offices, had over the centuries been adopted by ecclesiastical legists.[55] I will return to this point when I take up the subject of the place of the Jews in the social order of Christendom and of Islam (Chapter 6).

Canon 68 of the Council promulgated for the first time a prescription that is perhaps the most infamous piece of ecclesiastical Jewry law during the Middle Ages. The law decrees that where normal external signs fail to differentiate Jews and Saracens (Muslims) from Christians (Spain, especially, but also, likely, the Normal Kingdom of Sicily appear to have been intended), Jews and Saracens must henceforth be distinguished from Christians by their dress (no particular form was stipulated). The Council wished to prevent "accidental" commingling of Christians with members of the two inferior, infidel religions, especially "polluting" sexual contact.[56]

The order was qualified in a subsequent letter of Innocent, in which he stated that Christians should "not force [the Jews] to wear such as would lay them open to the danger of loss of life."[57] It is difficult to imagine how this rider could have been implemented.

The same canon forbade Jews to appear in public during Eastertide or to blaspheme Christ, an old law founded on the widespread presumption—

not entirely untrue—that many Jews hated Christians and ridiculed their beliefs and practices.

Yet another canon ruled that Jewish converts to Christianity should be prevented from backsliding, consistent with church teaching on the irreversibility of baptism.[58] A fourth law prohibited Jewish moneylenders from oppressing Christians with their "heavy and immoderate usury."[59]

The canons on distinctive dress and Jewish officeholding entered authoritative canon law in the *Decretals* of Pope Gregory IX, while rulings on Eastertide came into that same code from the pronouncement of an earlier pope, Alexander III.[60] Following the lead of Innocent III, the church witnessed considerable erosion of the papacy's protective policy during the thirteenth century.[61] Beginning with Gregory IX, in 1239, the papacy, briefly and unprecedentedly, interfered with the free practice of Judaism by investigating the Talmud, and ordering that copies of it be burned. The torching of twenty-four cartloads of books of the Talmud in Paris was carried out in 1242 by order of the French king, Louis IX.[62] Gregory had learned from a Jewish apostate, Nicholas Donin, that the Talmud contained anti-gentile "heresies" and other inanities, which, as Gregory asserted in his letter to the archbishops of France ordering them to seize the Jewish books, was "the chief cause that holds them in their perfidy."[63] In 1240, Donin, the Pope's "mentor," represented the Christian side in a great public disputation on the Talmud in Paris, at which the Jewish books were formally sentenced to destruction. Pope Innocent IV (1243–54), who renewed Gregory IX's ban on the Talmud and similarly ordered it burned, justified this departure from the ecclesiastical guarantee of religious freedom to Jews in a comment on one of the *Decretals* of Pope Gregory IX. He declared that the pope had jurisdiction over Jews when it came to teachings in their own books that perverted the true meaning of the Torah—that is, as it *should* be understood, namely, christologically—if the Jewish authorities failed to act.[64] Among various likely motives (as distinguished from rationalizations) for this foray into inner Jewish life, one that stands out is the wish to assert papal sovereignty over all of Christendom in the face of the supremacist claims of monarchs, especially those of the Holy Roman Emperor.

Further erosion of the principle of *Sicut Judeis* occurred later in the thirteenth century. The papacy asserted its jurisdiction over Jews in a new way with the bull *Turbato corde* ("With a troubled heart . . ."), first issued in 1267 by Clement IV and repromulgated three more times before the end of the century. In this edict, the Inquisition established by the papacy in the 1230s to find and prosecute Christian heretics was granted extended authority to prosecute professing Jews suspected of influencing Christians (former Jews who had converted to Christianity) "to join their execrable rites"—that is, by re-Judaizing—itself an act of heresy.[65]

Modern assessments of papal pronouncements, and of ecclesiastical Jewry law in general, range from the reproachful to the apologetic. Traditionally, Jewish historians have tended to saddle the popes with a large measure of responsibility for the oppression of the Jews in medieval times, especially during the High and later Middle Ages. At the other extreme, a Catholic scholar has attempted to mitigate papal culpability by blaming their harsh policies on precedents gleaned from Christian emperors. This author cites papal fears that Jews were in league with the Muslims against Christendom and finds antecedents or parallels to papal hostility in Jewish statements inimical to Christianity.[66] Another apologetic work argues (extravagantly and unconvincingly) that antisemitism in medieval Christendom arose not from Catholic theology regarding the Jews, but, rather, from a conviction that the Jews were somehow identified with Muslims and were allied with them against Christians.[67] A Jewish historian of papal-Jewish relations maintains a sympathetic view of the popes' tough treatment of the Jews. He explains it contextually, as resulting not from "hatred of the Jews" but from the need to enhance the power and prestige of the ecclesiastical establishment ("love of the church").[68] The same scholar believes that secular governments bore far more responsibility than did the papacy for inflicting harm on medieval Jews.[69] The editor of a seven-volume collection of papal documents regarding the Jews from the end of the fifth to the mid-sixteenth century points to vacillating and sometimes contradictory policies "between protection and persecution" that must, he argues, "be judged in the light of prevailing circumstances."[70] However one judges the motives of the popes, it remains true that the papal guarantee of protection to the Jews increasingly became attenuated in the thirteenth century by hostility and a strong desire to exclude the infidel Jews from the company of Christians.

Canon Lawyers

While popes contributed to canon law with their authoritative pronouncements and epistles, law in the medieval church was, formally speaking, the province of a class of experts known as "canon lawyers" (a few of whom also became popes). The practical impact of their policy, or attitude, toward the Jews is difficult to assess, owing to their essentially theoretical concerns. In the prevailing view, canonists prior to the First Crusade held moderate views concerning the Jews.[71] A shift toward harshness is thought to have followed the escalation of popular hostility toward the Jews during the first two Crusades. This change in canonist policy is said to have first been expressed about 1094 in anti-Jewish feelings found in the legal writings of the canonist Ivo of Chartres.

Gilchrist offers a different view. He suggests that the negative attitude toward the Jews in canon law can be traced to a time well before the First

Crusade. Analyzing collections of canon lawyers from before and after 1100, Gilchrist concludes that already in the *Decretum*, or *Liber Decretorum* of Burchard, bishop of Worms (ca. 1012), an attitude of strict segregation of Jews from Christians prevailed, along with appropriately harsh language. Gilchrist intimates that this view may have influenced the violent actions against the Jews at the end of the century, rather than the other way around.[72]

"Liberal" Views among the Canonists

Walter Pakter, who devoted an entire book to the Jewish question, gives a subtler presentation of the views of canon lawyers.[73] Even as the Crusades began, during the heyday of codifying canon law (from Gratian on), Pakter finds that the most important canonists held a relatively liberal opinion of how the Jews should be treated. Indeed, even as the Jews' social and political standing deteriorated in the twelfth and thirteenth centuries, canon lawyers managed to improve their status. They avouched Jews' fundamental rights, including the binding nature of Jewish laws of marriage, divorce, and parental prerogatives.[74] Canonists from the south (the "Italian school") did not take seriously the concept—promoted by the papacy—of "servitude of the Jews," invoked by some canonists, most of whom were in northern Europe, to justify forced baptism of Jewish children.[75] In another example of leniency, one that seemed to deny the supposed servility of the Jews, canon lawyers countenanced Jews serving in public office provided they performed services not easily provided by Christians.[76]

In an ironic twist, Pakter shows that some of the greatest canon lawyers after Gratian countered papal "theological" presuppositions about the Jew as outsider by expanding ecclesiastical jurisdiction over the Jews, at least in theory. By making Jews "subjects of prejudiced courts administering prejudiced law," the canonists contributed to the erosion of Jewish status while, at the same time, offsetting the gains made in papal protection after the First Crusade.[77] The Jews welcomed these expressions of greater papal concern, insofar as they added protection at a time of growing hatred of Jews and of violence toward them. In return for this boon, however, the Jews lost whatever sanctuary from Christian prosecution they had known earlier.[78]

Impact of Canon Law on Secular Law

Just as papal decrees and conciliar edicts had a direct, if slow and uneven, impact on the content and practice of secular law, so did canon law. As Guido Kisch points out in his study of medieval Germany, "even if [papal decretals and conciliar decrees] did not immediately influence the state's Jewry legislation,

> they nevertheless seriously affected the status of the Jews; for, as a rule, medieval Christians . . . would not openly incur the ecclesiastical sanctions extending even to excommunication and interdiction. Thus the effects of canon Jewry legislation were promptly felt by the Jews. . . . Their economic and social position was adversely affected and their life made miserable.[79]

The story of the papal attempt to enforce segregation by requiring Jews to wear a distinctive sign on their outer garments provides a case in point. Some monarchs acceded to the papal directives that began in 1215, with Lateran Council IV. Others used the law as an excuse to extract money from the Jews in the form of bribes intended to obtain exemption. Jews feared that wearing such a sign would make them more vulnerable to physical attack.

The wearing of distinctive garb was first enforced in England, beginning with the reign of King Henry III. The sign was to consist of "two white tables made of white linen or parchment" worn "upon the fore part of their upper garments."[80] As its use spread to other countries in the High and late Middle Ages, the stigma assumed a variety of forms, mainly yellow in color. The Holy Roman Empire did not apply the church's law until the fifteenth century, probably because the Jews under the empire's jurisdiction wore a distinctive conical hat that already distinguished them from Christians. In the fifteenth century the custom was enforced in the form of a yellow wheel sewn on the outer garment.[81] This was the forerunner of the infamous Nazi "Jewish badge."

Movement toward Expulsion

In the thirteenth century, church leaders began to move away from their protective policy on the Jews, toward one of restriction and exclusion. Secular powers began to enforce the policy, albeit unevenly. The hardening policy of both church and state boded ill for the security of the Jews, leading to their expulsion.

Jeremy Cohen, in his *Friars and the Jews,* argues that vehement anti-Jewish preaching and writing of the mendicant orders (Dominicans and Franciscans) in the thirteenth century undermined the Augustinian tradition of preserving Jews within Christendom as witnesses.[82] With this prop removed, the way was open to ultimate exclusion of the Jews: physical removal from Christian society.

There is some question whether this thesis, focusing as it does on theology, can be upheld in its categorical form.[83] Simonshon has shown that the Augustinian formula continued to appear in papal writings down to the end of the Middle Ages.[84] Whatever the outcome of the scholarly debate about the impact of ecclesiastical thought on Jewish status in the High and late Middle Ages, the actual expulsions from Christendom were to be the work not of the church but of the medieval state.

Secular Jewry Law in the Medieval State

The legal position of the Jews in the medieval state (an anachronism commonly used for territorial entities under royal sovereignty) originally was fashioned by incorporating special privileges into charters, not by legislative codes or the law of the church. Charters (the earliest extant ones are Carolingian) consisted in grants of privileges to Jewish merchants—first to individuals and their families, later to entire Jewish communities, and eventually to all Jews in an area controlled by a monarch. These charters attest to the important function fulfilled by Jewish traders in early medieval Europe and their economic utility to governing authorities. The charters exemplify the beginning of a process whereby Jews, over time, came to belong (in the sense of nearly absolute control) to a secular ruler and thus to have special, but limiting, status under the law.

From a legal standpoint, we lack explicit evidence regarding how the Jews were viewed by the Germanic invaders of the western Roman Empire. Based on their interpretation of Germanic customary law, some scholars believe that the Jews were considered unfree aliens. That is why the Jews needed every bit of special legislation they could get from kings.[85] Most students of the period believe that, from the outset, Germanic rulers regarded the Jews as Roman citizens, hence subject to Roman Jewry law. The Barbarians had epitomes, or models, of Roman law compiled for the benefit of the Romans within their realm (Romans were much more numerous in the south, near the Mediterranean, than in the north). The most influential epitome was the *Lex Romana Visigothorum* (506 C.E.), an abridgment of the Theodosian Code intended for Romans living under Visigoth rule in Spain and southern Gaul. Also called the "Breviary of Alaric," this epitome contained nine laws from the Theodosian Code regarding the Jews, plus Theodosius II's own Novella 3 from the end of the same corpus and two more from another source, all meant to apply to the Jewish subjects of the Visigothic king.[86] Many scholars believe that the Breviary of Alaric reflects the tone of the Theodosian Code, as well as a tendency toward tolerance regarding the Jews that was characteristic of Arian Christianity, something the Visigoths professed at the outset of their Christianization.[87]

Unfortunately for Jews living in the Visigothic Kingdom, after the conversion (589) of the Visigothic royal house to "orthodox" Nicaean Catholicism, the way was open to revocation of the Breviary and, with it, Roman law as it applied in Spain. In 654, the Breviary was replaced by *Leges*

Visigothorum (Laws of the Visigoths) a new, unified code for both Visigoths and Romans."[88] The protection Jews had enjoyed by virtue of their Roman citizenship disappeared. All the Jewish provisions in the new code were restrictive and intolerant in the extreme.[89] This was one of several factors that set the stage for the rapid decline of Visigothic Spanish Jewry during the remainder of the seventh century. The Germanic Franks continued to apply the Visigothic Breviary of Alaric to Romans in parts of southern and eastern France which they conquered, mainly Burgundy.[90] The employment in Frankish courts of scribes and notaries familiar with Roman laws and legal procedures helped ensure this continuity.[91]

Very few Romans, but many different Germanic tribes, lived in northern France and Germany, the original area of Frankish settlement. There, the Franks applied Barbarian customary law, with its principle of the personality of the law—the idea that the law for an individual depended on the tribe or group to which that person belonged, rather than on the region in which he lived.[92] We have little hard data about Merovingian Frankish policy toward the Jews. The edict of King Lothar II (614), in many of its clauses echoing the church Council of Paris held a week earlier, cannot be said to provide insight into this matter on the basis of its provision prohibiting Jews from holding public office over Christians.[93] Clearer evidence issues from the legislative remains of the Carolingian king, Louis the Pious (813–40), Charlemagne's son and successor. Louis set out to induce itinerant Jewish merchants to settle permanently in his realm by issuing standard Carolingian charters of privileges, including the all-important right to live by their own laws, in addition to generous dispensations to facilitate their commercial activities.[94] This privilege conformed with the pluralistic premise underlying the principle of the personality of law, which the Franks, more than other Germanic groups, perpetuated in the early Middle Ages. As was true of the pagan Roman world, the pluralism of the tribal world of the German Barbarians carried advantages for the Jews. The relatively secure position of the Jews in northern Europe during the early Middle Ages owes much to this feature.

In the countries of northern Europe, royal and imperial charters governing and protecting Jews evolved into direct, unmediated, legal dependence on a central ruler. As enmity and physical attack became more prevalent after the First Crusade, this dependence was of considerable benefit to the Jews. An example is the charter issued by the German emperor, Frederick I, in 1157, for the Jews of Worms. The charter confirms a previous one granted by Frederick's great-grandfather, Henry IV, apparently around 1090; its date is inferred from its similarity to a charter of Henry IV for Jews in Speyer, dated February 1090.[95] Certain concepts and privileges, most of them dating from the earliest Carolingian charters, are common to many of these documents:

Inviolability of property
Freedom to travel for business and trade, without having to pay tolls
Exemption from the obligation to house and resupply soldiers on the march
Fair legal treatment if discovered with stolen goods
Protection from forced baptism
Permission to hold pagan slaves, even those baptized by Christians in order to secure their emancipation (purchasing a slave already Christian was, however, prohibited)
Permission to employ Christians as domestic servants
Fair legal treatment in mixed litigations
Judicial autonomy in internal Jewish legal disputes
The right to sell wine, dyes, and medicines to Christians[96]

Chamber Serfdom

The charter's introduction states that the Jews of Worms "belong to our chamber, or treasury" (*ad cameram nostram*). This crucial phrase, which appears to be an innovation by Frederick[97] (such a phrase is absent in Henry IV's Speyer charter of February 1090),[98] represents an important landmark along the way to developing what has come to be known as "chamber serfdom."

Much has been written about the legal concept associated with *servi camerae nostrae* (serfs of our [royal] chamber) or *servi camerae regis* (serfs of the royal chamber), Latin phrases which first appear in 1236, in a charter for the Jews of the Holy Roman Empire. In the past, historians viewed both term and status as degrading. The word *servi* implies "absence of freedom." To scholars who believe the Jews had been unfree aliens in the Barbarian kingdoms, the use of *servi* to describe the Jews after the thirteenth century was nothing more than a semantic change. James Parkes, for example, sees the concept as a station on an inexorable trajectory from the unfreedom of the Carolingian Jews to the state of "the Jew as private property"—a mix of protectionism and cavalier exploitation, all geared to ensure the financial utility of the Jews to the state.[99]

Contemporary scholarship applies a more nuanced interpretation to the terminology, as well as to its legal implications. Scholars argue, for instance, that the word *servi* need not be taken as a sign of total, and demeaning, enslavement to a feudal lord. Most people in the Middle Ages were "unfree," in the sense that they owed allegiance to, and were dependent on, some higher authority.[100] Moreover, because Jews were excluded from the feudal system, it is natural to assume that the status of *servi,* as applied to them, would have features uncharacteristic of "normative serfdom," if there were such a thing.[101] Salo Baron, forever combating the "lachrymose conception of Jewish history," has pointed to the benefits that accrued to the Jews as a result of being placed under the direct protection of secular rulers. One important advantage Jews had over unfree Christian serfs was their freedom to live wherever they wished—in most places, a freedom denied Christians. Another advantage was membership in recognized, "corporate" Jewish communities whose autonomy in matters of Jewish law effectively bestowed on them rights that, in many ways, offset their technical "unfreedom."[102] Cecil Roth argues that the status of the Jews as direct dependents of the king of England (where the phrase *servi camerae* seems not to have been used) entailed stringent, absolute proprietorship with attendant exploitation but also with "unmistakable privileges."[103]

We should avoid the temptation, when tempering the "lachrymose conception," to overstate the virtues of Jewish serfdom. Neither should we jump to apply the dismissive (similarly, anti-lachrymose) approach to the assumed degradations of Christian serfdom found in some recent revisionist work by medieval European historians. The urge to achieve freedom—even with its different set of burdensome obligations toward the seigneur—through manumission, underscores "the central substantive issue . . . the meaning and limits of freedom, that mystically vague notion embodied in a status that men and women in the thirteenth century paid dearly for; that men and women in the fourteenth century and since have often purchased with their lives."[104]

We would do well, too, to bear in mind R. W. Southern's comment on serfdom: "To nearly all men serfdom was, without qualification, a degrading thing." Men, Southern says, "well knew, however theologians might seem to turn common notions inside out, the difference between the yoke of servitude and the honour of liberty. . . . What men feared and resented in serfdom was not its subordination, but its arbitrariness."[105] According to Southern, a serf lacked two crucial things: liberty and the protection of law—liberty because he was totally dependent on the will of his overlord; and law, because the serf needed the inherent, dependable protection that could come only from law and its enforcement. "The higher one rose toward liberty, the more the area of action was covered by law, the less it was subject to will. . . . At the bottom of society was the serf, who could least appeal to law against the arbitrariness of his superiors."[106]

From Chamber Serfdom to Exclusion

Guido Kisch and Gavin Langmuir, who have analyzed Jewish serfdom, explain its evolution as well as the way in which it ultimately acquired the degrading characteristics of serfdom in general. Kisch[107] traces a regressive path in medieval Germany from the comfort and security that accompanied inclusion in evolving public law, to the insecurity and unfreedom that resulted from relegation to a special, dependent status as "serfs," with concomitant exclusion from society. Until the thirteenth century, he argues, the German monarchy followed a dual policy of protecting Jews and integrating them into the normal apparatus of secular law. For the charters issued to Jews belonged to a class of documents that served as the standard vehicle by which kings legislated in the early Middle Ages.

The massacres of the First Crusade in 1096 convinced the German emperor, Henry IV, that the Jews, along with other vulnerable groups such as merchants, clerics, and women, needed increased protection. Beginning in 1103, Henry inaugurated a secular version of the older, ecclesiastical Peace of God (or Truce of God)—the Land Peace Law, a kind of truce which stipulated no one might harm a specified person or group over a defined period of time. Though included under Henry's law, Jews as a group were no longer allowed to bear arms. This revival of a principle of Christian-Roman Jewry law thus robbed Jews of what in medieval times was an important source of honor.

As Kisch shows, Jews continued to receive charters. Christian hostility toward Jews steadily increased during the Crusades, but the German charters (for instance, that of Frederick I, in 1157) offered extra protection by placing the Jews under direct imperial control. In 1236, a year after introduction of the blood libel in Germany, the German monarchy took the final—in a sense, regressive—step. It declared Jews *servi camerae nostrae,* terminology which was inspired by the recently revived papal doctrine of *servitus Judeorum* (servitude of the Jews). Kisch believes that this church-inspired idea marked the beginning of Jewish unfreedom. From then on, he says, Jews were no longer part of the organic legal structure of the Land Peace Law, which had briefly imparted to Jews an aura of inclusion in society, albeit as members of a class especially vulnerable. Henceforth, the legal status of Jews was governed by special legislation designed specifically for them, a *jus singulare.*[108] Already diminished when they lost the right to bear arms, the honor of the Jews fell to a new low. In the view of Friedrich Lotter, German imperial law on the Jews in the mid-thirteenth century began to yield to ecclesiastical pressure, in order to eliminate the old privileges granted Jews in Carolingian and Salian times. This setback was reflected in the large-scale persecution of the Jews in the last two decades of the century.[109]

Gavin Langmuir concurs in the belief that the condition of Jewish "serfdom of the chamber" constituted an abasement of the legal status of the Jews. Actual employment of *servi camerae* was less important, however, than the practice of exclusive royal dominion over the Jews and the exploitation of them. For instance, the words *servi camerae* do not appear in English royal charters.[110] But, Langmuir observes, England by the twelfth century already had a strong central monarchy, at a time when the Jews' perceived dependency on royal whim and protection was real. Thus the terminology was superfluous. At the other extreme, in Germany and Spain, where centralization was least developed, royalty employed the terminology of *servi camerae* in asserting direct control over the Jews. In France, where Jews were never described as *servi camerae,* the appearance of *Judei nostri* (our Jews) in royal legislation as early as 1198 anticipated the growing dependency of Jews on the monarchy. Moreover, in France, barons maintained possessory rights over the Jews in their respective domains.

The concentration of authority over the Jews in the hands of the French monarch thus was a process that moved slowly yet organically. In 1230, in legislation regarding the Jews, the Capetian monarchy asserted the barons' exclusive dominion over their Jews, wherever the Jews happened to be—even as fugitives in the domain of other barons. This legislation became a milestone on the road to full, centralized royal authority and administration in France. For the first and only time in French ordinances, and strictly as an analogy, this law used the terminology of serfdom for the Jews, stating that a Jew who fled to the domain of another baron could legally be seized by his lord *tanquam proprium servum* (like his own serf). Whereas a true serf earned his freedom by living unchallenged in the territory of another lord for a year and a day, a Jew could be forcibly returned to his original lord regardless of where a Jew lived as a fugitive or how long he had lived there.[111] This law set a precedent that continued the erosion of freedom that had long privileged Jews in feudal France, compared to Christian serfs. Ultimately, the legislation confined Jews to a status more restrictive than ever before.

The very principle of possessory rights (with or without the terminology of serfdom, and regardless of whether the rights were exercised in the domain of a monarch or a baron) that were exercised by secular authorities over Jews with increasing vigor as the Middle Ages wore on included the right to tax Jews to the limit. Because of their vulnerability, Jews proved compliant prey for royal and baronial tax collectors. With variation from place to place, the tax obligations of Jews might include annual levies on households or communities, fees connected with loans, tolls, and, most vexingly, periodic "unscheduled" arbitrary exactions or confiscations to meet various pressing financial needs of an overlord.[112] Because they needed protection, Jews had no choice but to pay.

By the thirteenth century, Langmuir says, "as a result of the efforts of ecclesiastics, kings, and barons to exploit Jews, each for their own ends, Jews had been given a degraded legal status that set them apart from all others in European society and denied them even the protection usually accorded serfs."[113] To invoke Southern's perspective on medieval serfdom, it can be said that Jews came to know what medieval people called "the yoke of servitude," to experience loss of the "honour of liberty," and to fear the "arbitrariness" of absolute dependence on the will of their overlords.[114] The many arbitrary, burdensome tallages levied upon the Jews during the later Middle Ages, and, much more oppressive, their expulsion—from England in 1290; from France in 1306, 1322, and 1394; from Spain in 1492; and from dozens of German principalities and towns during the later Middle Ages—constituted for the Jews a more severe outcome of "enserfment" than any experienced by Christian serfs, namely, their effective exclusion from lands where they had dwelt for centuries.

The Legal Status of Jews in Medieval Towns

Mention should be made of the legal status of Jews in the medieval towns of Europe, which is where most Jews in northern Europe lived. For Germany, Kisch has shown that Jews were treated rather fairly by municipal authorities in, for example, legal disputes.[115] Church doctrine on Jewish usury—or, for that matter, on usury in general—did not find expression in the older medieval German lawbooks where German customary law was codified. Nor did church doctrine appear in the municipal law of Magdeburg, which achieved great popularity as a model law and was adopted by numerous German frontier cities in the High and late Middle Ages. Rather, jurisdiction over Jewish usury was turned over to the ecclesiastical courts. Kisch suggests that the secular courts did not wish to interfere with what they recognized as an essential element in the growing economy beginning in the twelfth century.[116]

The question remains: Did municipal customary law recognize Jews as citizens (burghers) of the towns in which they lived?[117] Or were Jews included among the "large number of people in all the larger towns who did not rank as members of its community?"[118] In the case of Germany, until the mid-fourteenth century, Jewish rights were "almost identical with that of Christian citizens" in such matters as domicile, protection of life and property, equitable treatment by municipal courts and by various "supreme courts" such as that in Magdeburg, and also in the acquisition of real estate, location of residence, and activity in trade or crafts.[119] In numerous cases, a royal, baronial, or ecclesiastical overlord ceded possession of Jews to a town, in which case the town applied to them its own combination of protection and exploitation.

Where Jewish townspeople continued to maintain their special legal relationship with the central authority—be it emperor, king, territorial prince, or bishop—their status was a complicated one. Insofar as this relationship meant additional privileges, such as concession of autonomy in internal Jewish affairs, local Christian townspeople doubtless resented the

Jews. Unlike the Christian urban majority, Jews, even where they boasted some form of municipal "citizenship," nonetheless suffered degradation. They were excluded from municipal political rights, including the right to hold public office, and they bore the burden of special taxes. Assessing the "meaning of citizenship" for the Jewish urban resident, Baron writes:

> It is somewhat difficult to envisage all Jews sharing with the rest of the burghers the repeated, sometimes annual, ceremony of retaking the oath of fealty to the city, wherever such reiteration was required by law, without leaving any traces in the contemporary records. The ever present social differences between Christian and Jewish burghers must also have in many ways impinged on the latter's legal status.[120]

Thus, Jews, while benefiting from fair treatment in municipal courts, and often acquiring some form of official membership in the town, continued to occupy a marginal place compared to Christians, with their full citizenship. In extreme cases, municipal authorities requested from an overlord the right not to tolerate the Jews in their midst. Increasingly as the Middle Ages wore on, towns decided to do away with the "Jewish problem" altogether by the draconian act of expulsion. In a word, marginality degenerated into exclusion.

We have revisited territory well trod by specialists in medieval European Jewish history, though the ground may be less familiar to the lay reader and the general historian. The overarching theme is the variation and changeability of the legal status of Jews in Latin Christian lands. Christianity inherited from Roman law the idea that Jews are entitled to protection from wanton violence and from interference in the practice of Judaism. Within those limits, both the church and the state manipulated Jewish status in keeping with their own needs and ideologies. In the ecclesiastical realm, popes struggled to balance their obligation to preserve the Jews as "witness" with a desire to exclude them from the company of Christians. Secular authorities at the imperial, royal, baronial, or municipal level followed the law of utility regarding the Jews.

In the early Middle Ages, when Jews performed vital commercial services not otherwise fulfilled, rulers applied the most tolerant features of the legal traditions at their disposal, sometimes to the extent of going beyond them. As the need for Jewish commerce decreased, rulers found the Jews, now heavily concentrated in moneylending, a ready source of revenue through heavy taxation and extraordinary exactions—what William Jordan, referring to France and England, has labeled "fiscal terrorism."[121] This brought with it ever-increasing direct Jewish dependency on their overlords, along with an attendant arbitrariness. Such an arrangement undermined Jewish security, for, in the absence of a corpus of Jewry law that was unified, uniformly applied, consistent, and "constitutional," the potential always lurked to revoke royal, baronial, or imperial backing for the Jews' economic activities and residential rights. This situation might arise whenever considerations of piety or political expediency outweighed those of Jewish utility. Thus, as various rulers accepted church calls for limiting Jewish excesses in moneylending and for segregating Jews from Christians, the legal position of the former declined. At best, Jewish communities managed to buy their way out of danger by meeting the persistent demands of the tax collector for money or by bribing officials to revoke or refrain from enforcing restrictions, such as the discriminatory Jewish badge. At worst, Jews were increasingly vulnerable to the general violence of medieval society, which, in their case, was intensified by the anti-Jewish hatred prevailing. When the time came that rulers saw no further use for the Jews, they confiscated whatever remained of their wealth and expelled them.

Chapter Four

THE LEGAL POSITION OF JEWS IN ISLAM

"Jewry Law"—*Dhimmī* Law in Islam

With respect to the legal status of the Jews, two fundamental distinctions between Islam and Christendom must be established at the outset. First, Islam considers Jews and other non-Muslims living under Islamic rule (while enjoying internal autonomy in religious and most civil matters) to be subject to the jurisdiction of Islamic law.[1] In contrast, the medieval church tended to waive jurisdiction over Jews. Moreover, where the medieval Christian state, for its part, progressively tightened its hold on the Jews until they constituted a special case of monarchical "property" outside the umbrella of evolving public law, Islamic law never asserted the ruler's possessory rights over the non-Muslims. They were his subjects, albeit second-class ones, not his chattel.

Second, whereas in Christendom Jews were the only infidel living continuously *within* Christian society—hence, a special and focused object of both church and state regulation—Jews were seldom singled out by Islamic law. Rather, they were subsumed under a broader category of infidels: the *dhimmīs*.[2] The *dhimmīs* were, in turn, the "People of the Book" (*ahl al-kitāb*), those non-Muslims recognized by the Prophet Muhammad as recipients of a divinely revealed scripture. Originally, this category included only Jews and Christians (plus the Sabi'ans in the Qur'an), the two monotheistic religions with which Muhammad came into contact. As Islam expanded, other religions were assimilated into the *dhimmī* category.[3]

This important (and telling) distinction is seen when we compare certain features of the legal literatures of Islam and Christendom. As already noted, the Theodosian Code of the fifth century devotes a separate section to the Jews in the book which deals with relations between the church and other religions, thereby supplementing and sometimes repeating laws dispersed elsewhere under various other, general headings. As early as the ninth century, canon lawyers were following a similar procedure. In his *Decretum* (ca. 1012), Bishop Burchard of Worms consolidated restrictive Jewry law provisions mainly toward the end of his fourth book, a section that deals with Christian baptism and confirmation. The first provision concerns a procedure for examining Jewish proselytes before admitting them to baptism.[4] It begins with the traditional, offensive Christian metaphor for the obstinate Jews, drawn from the Old Testament (Proverbs

26:11, "Like a dog returning to its vomit"): "If Jews, whose perfidy frequently returns to its vomit, wish to come to the Catholic faith. . . ."[5] Ivo of Chartres recorded an even larger number of anti-Jewish canons in his compilation (ca. 1094), concentrating most of them in Book 13, where "they formed a veritable code for the Jews."[6] By the thirteenth century, under the rubric *De judeis*, canon lawyers were regularly devoting special sections to Jewry law.[7]

Islamic lawbooks do not include a comparable synthetic subdivision, *Fi'l-yahūd*, the Arabic equivalent of the Latin *De judeis*. Not until the late Middle Ages did there appear a book that dealt comprehensively and exclusively with the more general Islamic law for *dhimmīs*: *Aḥkām ahl al-dhimma* [The Laws Pertaining to the Protected People], by the fourteenth-century jurist Ibn Qayyim al-Jawziyya.[8] I draw extensively upon this work (not yet published when Fattal wrote his book), because it provides a handy synthesis of material that is widely scattered through the earlier literature.

Like Roman law, Islamic law is organized according to subject. Typically, statutes regarding the *ahl al-dhimma* are integrated into conventional, topical schemes—consistent with the principle that *dhimmīs* are subject to Islamic law. The early but noncanonical *ḥadīth* collection, *Al-muṣannaf*, by ʿAbd al-Razzāq al-Ṣanʿānī (d. 826) does have a long section, "On the People of the Book" (*Kitāb fī ahl al-kitāb*), but this is an exception. None of the six *ḥadīth* collections considered canonical (all of them later than ʿAbd al-Razzāq)—nor the *Muṣannaf* of Ibn Abī Shayba,[9] ʿAbd al-Razzāq's contemporary (d. 849)—has such a subsection. For the most part, passages referring to *dhimmīs* and/or the People of the Book are isolated from one another in the *ḥadīth*, even within the book on Jihad. The decentralization of statements about non-Muslims in the most important books of *ḥadīth* is consistent with the diffusion of "Dhimmī law," to adapt a term, in Islamic juristic literature (*fiqh*) per se.

A few examples of the diffusion and dispersal of Dhimmī law throughout the Islamic legal corpus illustrate this point. The massive compendium of Hanafite law,[10] *Kitāb al-mabsūṭ*, by al-Sarakhsī (d. 1090), by convention collects laws pertaining to marriage in a Book on Marriage, *Kitāb al-nikāḥ*, and one of its twenty-nine chapters is devoted to *dhimmī* matrimony.[11] Sarakhsī's Book on Sale (*Kitāb al-bayʿ*) contains, as is common in Islamic law, a "Chapter on Sale by *Dhimmīs*."[12] Provisions regarding the *dhimmīs* also crop up in chapters on criminal law. The chapter on brigands (*Bab quṭṭāʿ al-ṭarīq*) in Sarakhsī's "Book on Prescribed Punishments" (*Kitāb al-ḥudūd*) begins by declaring, "If a group of Muslims or *dhimmīs* attacks a group of Muslims or *dhimmīs*, killing and stealing money, we say that the Imam shall cut off their right hands and left feet."[13]

When an Islamic legal compendium singles out one of the *dhimmī* subgroups by name, it is usually the Christians, who were immeasurably more prominent than the Jews during the centuries when Islamic law was in the process of formation. Some discussions single out Zoroastrians, *majūs* in Arabic, for they presented the special problem that they appeared to engage in the idolatrous worship of fire and to lack a revealed book. These observations about Islamic ways of conceptualizing the legal status of non-Muslims further explicate what I mean when I say that Islamic law lacked a special focus on the Jews. The effacement of "Jewry law" behind the category of "Dhimmī law" constitutes an important distinction between Islamic and Christian approaches to the legal status of the Jews. Islam does not single out the Jews as a group requiring a special set of laws.

Another important contrast with Christendom is that traditional Islam knows no distinction between secular and religious law, between the law of the state and the law of the "church." This goes back to the very foundations of the Islamic polity. Muhammad began his mission as a man of religion, a prophet preaching a revealed message. But he rapidly turned founder of a religiopolitical community, which he called the *umma*. "Muhammad's role as a prophet (*nabi*) within a community that he himself had summoned into being necessarily included the functions of legislator, executive, and military commander of the *umma*."[14] In theory, the regulations governing the conduct and treatment of Jews (and of Christians) rested in readily identifiable, fairly circumscribed laws inscribed in the *sharīʿa*—the Holy Law of Islam—and administered by a single authority, whether the caliph, a sultan, or an amir (governor), through his appointed judges.

Jewry law in Christendom—with its inherent duality, secular and ecclesiastical, and its frequently arbitrary application—offers a study in contrast with the uniformity and relative constancy of the Islamic law of the *dhimma*. True, zealous Muslim religious leaders and scholars often exerted pressure on sultans, the official guardians of the law of the *dhimma*, especially in the later Middle Ages. But the goal of the clerics was primarily to enforce the time-honored, though all too often neglected, restrictions rather than devise new, stricter ones. These factors, whose significance can be appreciated when contrasted with secular law in the Christian West, made for greater predictability and, accordingly, a greater feeling of security for religious minorities living within the orbit of Islam.

The Pact of ʿUmar

The law of the *dhimma* has its most characteristic form in a document known as the Pact of ʿUmar, a kind of bilateral contract in which the non-Muslims agree to a host of discriminatory regulations in return for protection.[15] Though attributed to the second caliph—ʿUmar ibn al-Khaṭṭāb, who ruled from 634 to 644, during the first wave of Muslim conquests outside the Arabian Peninsula—no text of the document can be dated earlier than the tenth or eleventh century.[16] But the stipulations themselves evolved out of principles of pre-Islamic tribal custom, precedents established by the Prophet in Arabia, the specific circumstances of the early Islamic conquests, and influences of law in the eastern Roman and Sassanian empires. In particular, as the first wave of expansion outside the Arabian Peninsula incorporated much of the eastern Roman Empire, Byzantine Christian-Roman Jewry law had a marked influence on the content of the Islamic law of the *dhimma*.[17]

Islam adopted the Persian-Greek-Roman and Christian-Roman recognition of Judaism as a licit religion. Indeed, Islam in a way carried this principle even further. Already the Qur'an stipulates "there is no compulsion in religion."[18] While it may be true that the verse was meant only descriptively—that it was unrealistic to expect naturally obdurate unbelievers to convert to Islam—later Muslims took the text as a prescription for religious tolerance and pluralism.[19]

Muhammad established another precedent for religious toleration in the Constitution of Medina, his compact with the Arabs and some of the Jews of Medina, which granted religious autonomy to the latter.[20] True, Muhammad later fiercely repressed the Jews in reaction to their enmity and ridicule, but this kind of conduct was not the norm in Muhammad's treatment of non-Muslims. His treaties with the Jewish or Christian inhabitants of various other oases and towns in Arabia guaranteed them safety in return for tribute, called *jizya* (payment), a policy that endured.[21]

Following the Prophet's death, treaties granted during the conquests in southwest Asia and along the southern shore of the Mediterranean offered assurances of protection for persons and property, including houses of worship and freedom of religious observance. The religious duty to protect the defeated *dhimmīs* reverberates in *ḥadīth*. Not atypical is an utterance attributed to the dying Caliph ʿUmar (d. 644) speaking to his successor about the *ahl al-dhimma:* "I charge him with [upholding] the protection of God [*dhimmat allāh*] and the protection of His Messenger [*dhimmat rasūlihi*], that he should observe the compact [*ʿahd*] made with them and fight those that attack them and not overburden them [with taxes] beyond their capacity."[22]

Such fundamental assurances of security conform with the law already in force for those Jews living in the Byzantine domains before the Muslim conquests. The Justinianic Code, the repository of law for the eastern Roman Empire, had incorporated them from the Code of Theodosius.[23] Following the Arab conquests and for decades thereafter, most administrators continued to be local Christians familiar (as the Muslims were not) with administrative practice. During the Umayyad period (661–750), when the capital of the caliphate generally stood in Damascus, it would have been in the interest of Christians in the Muslim bureaucracy to champion protective features of Christian-Roman Jewry law in the interests of their own, suddenly disenfranchised, Christian brethren.

The privileges of the conquest treaties depended on payment of *jizya*, now conceived of as an annual poll tax, that is, a tax on persons rather than collective tribute. *Jizya* is the *only* non-Muslim disability mentioned explicitly—and only once—in the Qur'an. "Fight against those who have been given the Scripture . . . until they pay the *jizya ʿan yadin wa-hum ṣāghirūn*" (Sura 9:29). Exegetical and juristic literature reveal that no one knew for sure what the last four words meant.[24] Most interpretations take the words *wa-hum ṣāghirūn* to refer to the humiliated state of the non-Muslims, in keeping with the basic meaning of the root *ṣ-gh-r*, "to be, to make little, to belittle." From this came the term *ṣaghār*, summarizing the entire regimen of humiliating restrictions in Islamic Dhimmī law, regularly associated with the less-legalistic synonym, *dhull*, or "lowliness."

The more problematic *ʿan yadin*, literally, "out of hand," gave rise to both stringent and lenient interpretations in commentaries, *ḥadīth*, and juristic books. Stringent exegesis holds, for instance, that a non-Muslim must place his hand beneath that of the Muslim tax collector, ceremonially acknowledging his inferiority and subordination, or that the tax collector is to slap the nape of the *dhimmī*'s neck with his hand at the time of payment. A more lenient approach "translates" *ʿan yadin* as "according to his financial ability," a considerate interpretation implemented in some parts of the Islamic empire in the form of a graduated scale keyed to the *dhimmī*'s financial capacity. A *ḥadīth* regarding the *dhimmī* who cannot pay his *jizya* makes the charitable statement (doubtless, rarely heeded):

> One should be patient with him until he finds the means to pay, and [meanwhile] nothing should be held against him. If he should become rich, it should be taken from him when he comes. If he is unable to comply with any part of the peace settlement to which he agreed, the burden should be lifted from him if his inability is confirmed, and the Imam shall assume the burden on his behalf.[25]

If medieval Islamic opinions on this text are correct, we must conclude that the Qur'an itself does not prescribe humiliating treatment for the *dhimmī* when paying *jizya*.[26] In the eyes of Muslims later on, however, the verse contained an unequivocal warrant for debasing the *dhimmī* through a degrading method of remission. For Jews, who assuredly were subject to such an impost in pre-Islamic times,[27] that fact removed some of the sting of the *jizya*. For Christians living in the Byzantine (and Zoroastrians in the Sassanian) lands who had been exempt, the Islamic fiscal exaction must have been a jolting blow.

In the conquest treaties, the Arabs demanded that the vanquished inhabitants be helpful and loyal to their new rulers. This stipulation, incorporated in the Pact of ʿUmar, is explained by the strategic needs of the conquerors. The Arab armies, making their way through unfamiliar territory, badly needed the goodwill and cooperation of the natives and could not tolerate their collusion with the enemy.[28]

The Form of the Pact

The Pact of ʿUmar, itself a product of cumulative development based on Muhammad's practice, the exigencies of conquest, and the influence of Christian-Roman Jewry law, has at first glance at least a puzzling form.[29] It takes the form of a letter to Caliph ʿUmar from vanquished Christians, who obligate themselves to a regimen of disabilities in exchange for a promise of security.[30] ʿUmar grants the request ("confirm what they asked") but adds two amendments. Most scholars continue to share Tritton's skepticism, published more than sixty years ago, about ascribing the text to the time and person of the second caliph. The principal reason for Tritton's skepticism is, however, less compelling than the considerations mentioned at the beginning of this paragraph.[31]

Recently, the German scholar Albrecht Noth reopened discussion of the Pact. Noth argues that much of the *shurūṭ ʿumariyya* (ʿUmarian stipulations) either has its source in the conquest treaties or reflects the reality of Muslim–non-Muslim relations at the time of the conquest.[32] He contends that the terms originally did not have the restrictive, discriminatory purpose so blatant in the text of the Pact as it existed later on. Rather, many of the stipulations were devised to protect the fragile identity of the Arab conquerors. Faced with a massive majority of non-Muslims, the conquerors instituted measures designed to distance themselves from their subjects.[33]

To this we may add the following: The literary form of the Pact—a letter to the caliph by the conquered subjects, which made Tritton and then others so skeptical about its ascribed origins—becomes less mysterious if we view the document as a kind of petition from the losers promising submission in return for a decree of protection (*amān, dhimma*). Normally, administrative enactments in Islamic government originated in response to petitions, either for redress of grievances or for confirmation of privileges.[34] Thus, the Pact of ʿUmar may be seen as an outgrowth of the conquest treaties (Noth's view) but transformed into the mold of a petition. Its epistolary style, probably the very form of the primitive Arabic petition, was then embellished with details of the cumulative practice of the first centuries of Muslim-*dhimmī* encounter.[35]

Virtually all versions of the Pact of ʿUmar mention Christians, and several of the religious restrictions refer *only* to Christian ritual. Doubtless, this is because, at the time of the conquests, Christians represented both the majority population and the ruling authority in the eastern Roman Empire, where the first Arab ruling dynasty, the Umayyad, established its capital. Nonetheless, the Pact's stipulations extended in practice to the Jews as well.

Houses of Worship

In its first stipulation, the Pact of ʿUmar echoes Christian-Roman Jewry law, ruling that non-Muslims may not build new houses of worship or even make repairs to existing buildings that had fallen into ruin.[36] If vigorously enforced, this restriction would have severely limited the growth of the non-Muslim communities.

The categorical stipulation in the Pact of ʿUmar seems to have evolved toward this stringency over time. Regulation of houses of worship does not appear to have concerned the early caliphs at all, and some of them actually permitted *dhimmīs* to construct new ones.[37] The presence of synagogues and churches in "new" post-conquest Islamic cities such as Kufa or Cairo strongly indicates that Jews and Christians were successful in circumventing the law. The pious Umayyad caliph, ʿUmar II (717–20), may have been the first to forbid construction of new houses of worship. Thereafter, historical sources report instances of churches or synagogues ordered destroyed or converted into mosques, of mobs incited by clerics to attack religious buildings (especially in the late Middle Ages), but also episodes in which the authorities allowed the restoration of buildings.[38]

With only intermittent interest on the part of Islamic authorities in enforcing the letter of the law regarding *dhimmī* houses of worship, Islamic law annotated around the categorical prohibition in complex ways. Exemptions arose. The criterion for deciding whether to permit a house of worship became the status of its town at the time of the conquest. Minor differences of opinion characterized each of the four orthodox schools of Sunni law.[39] A pair of treatises written in the mid-fourteenth century by the jurist al-Subkī discusses construction and repair of houses of worship in great detail.[40] And there are many more of this genre from the late Middle Ages. It is not surprising that we find a separate juristic literature on the status of *dhimmī* houses of worship, for these constituted the most conspicuous aspect of non-Muslim religious life and therefore a natural target for complaint.

The various views on the topic were summarized in the eighteenth century by the Egyptian scholar Shaykh Damanhūrī, responding to a question about the status of the churches of Cairo. He explained that the Hanafi school allowed houses of worship to be erected in towns taken from non-Muslims by peace treaty provided the treaty stipulated that the land belonged to the indigenous inhabitants and they paid *kharāj* (land tax). If the terms of the surrender considered the land Muslim and imposed the poll tax on the native inhabitants, their places of worship were not allowed.[41] Reconstruction of a permitted building after it had been destroyed or upon its impending collapse was strictly regulated so as not to seem to be "new." Its building materials had to be identical to those of the original structure.[42] By the letter of Islamic law, the churches of Cairo should not have been allowed to stand; characteristically, however, Damanhūrī's treatise did not lead to their destruction.[43]

Al-Subkī insists that claims against houses of worship must meet the test of Islamic laws of property and evidence.[44] Historical and documentary sources bear this out. In the year 1038, for example, the Jews of Old Cairo (Fustat) were accused of possessing a synagogue that was "modern, built only recently." The leader of the Jewish community was summoned before a Muslim tribunal, where he testified to the antiquity of the building. To support the claim, he brought with him a large contingent of Muslim witnesses who confirmed that the "synagogue was of ancient construction and not recently built." The judge "gave judgment in accordance with the facts and findings and made his decision compulsory." The synagogue was saved. Fortunately for the historian, the Jewish community of Cairo also saved the judicial decision in its archives, to be produced as proof of the antiquity of the synagogue should the question arise again.[45]

The second example, from the later Middle Ages in Egypt, reveals the predictable, though potentially uneasy, modus vivendi between *dhimmīs* and Islamic religious and legal authorities over the status of houses of worship. A chance conjuncture of Islamic historical and Jewish documentary (Geniza) sources regarding a Cairo synagogue in 1442 tells an interesting story. Looking for signs of illegal repairs during a routine inspection of a synagogue, a delegation of Muslim religious authorities discovered an almost obliterated Arabic inscription carved on the *minbar,* or "preacher's platform." They read the words *Aḥmad* and *Muḥammad,* two names for the Prophet, and concluded that they had come upon a case of the capital crime of blasphemy—Jews treading on the name of the founder of Islam. Even in this late period of increasing oppression of the non-Muslim population, the judges and the *muḥtasib* (market inspector) pursued their investigation and prosecution of three alleged Jewish perpetrators with relative judicial objectivity. Eventually, satisfied that the community as a whole had had nothing to do with the alleged misdeed, the judges ordered only that the *minbar* be destroyed; and no additional harm to the structure occurred. Nor was the episode accompanied by the kind of collective punishment that likely would have occurred in a German town of the period had a real or alleged Jewish anti-Christian act been so "discovered." Only the confessed perpetrators were punished and publicly beaten.[46]

The Jewish community of the time was deeply concerned about an internal crisis: the misrule of its Head. In their petition (the Geniza document) to the Mamluk sultan, asking him to oust the man from office and replace him with a "venerable" former holder of the office, the Jews buttressed their argument with an allusion to the evil-doing Head, suggesting that he had some culpability in the blasphemy of the *minbar*!

Even when controlled in their anti-*dhimmī* violence, such violations of the contract between the *dhimmī* and his Muslim overlord could spell danger. The discovery in one Cairo synagogue in 1442 prompted the Muslim authorities to investigate other non-Muslim houses of worship. This aroused much fear within the protected communities. Several churches came under suspicion, as did a Karaite Jewish house converted into a house of prayer. In the end, Jewish (Rabbanite and Karaite), Samaritan, and various Christian leaders were summoned before a Muslim judge and compelled to renew their allegiance to the venerable Pact of ʿUmar.[47]

The Public Display of Religion

Related stipulations in the Pact of ʿUmar have to do with the public display of religion. In order to protect its own superiority, Islam intended primarily to minimize the visibility of *dhimmī* religion. Christianity rather than Judaism was the main concern, for Oriental Christianity conducted many of its ceremonies outdoors. These form the backdrop for such proscriptions as the one forbidding the display of crosses and sacred books in the roads or markets, the prohibition against beating the clappers outside the walls of a church, and the stipulation forbidding *dhimmīs* from raising their voices too loudly during church services or when participating in funeral processions. Christians had to forgo public processions on Palm Sunday and Easter. Because Islam considered Christianity idolatrous, Muslims could become quite exercised over this issue.[48]

These limitations seem to have had little effect on the Jews. Where Arabic historical sources record numerous incidents in which Christians celebrating a ritual within view of Muslims are ordered to desist, Jews are rarely singled out.[49] In part, this was because most Jewish ritual took place indoors and contained nothing that Islam could easily construe as idolatrous. Moreover, centuries of care not to offend Christians by praying too loudly within earshot, or by appearing in public at Eastertide, had prepared the Jews to accept the Muslim restriction with equanimity. (The one outdoor religious practice that caused problems for Jews was the one that could not be avoided—funeral processions.)[50]

Early Christian-Roman Jewry law contains a rough parallel to this stipulation in the Pact of ʿUmar, forbidding Jews from hanging Haman in effigy on the festival of Purim.[51] Similarly, ecclesiastical law from as early as the sixth century imposed on the Jews a curfew during Eastertide, lest, as Pope Innocent III wrote, "the Jews, contrary to ancient custom, publicly run about streets and public places and everywhere deride as they are wont Christians because they adore the crucified on the Cross, and attempt, through their improprieties, to dissuade them from their worship."[52]

Comparison with the Pact of ʿUmar underscores an important difference between Muslim and Christian attitudes toward Judaism. Christianity legislated against the public display of infidel blasphemy. The latter represented a challenge to the truth of the Christian religion. Islam, much less dialectical than Christianity in its relationship to prior monotheistic religions, concerned itself with the public exhibition of Jewish and especially Christian ritual, not on account of blasphemy but because it wished to keep Jews and Christians and their religions in their deserved humble position. Hence, hierarchy, more than theology, motivated Islamic law in this matter.[53]

Proselytization and *Dhimmī* Conversion to Islam

Alongside the ban on public celebration of religious rituals, the Pact of ʿUmar commands non-Muslims not to proselytize or place obstacles in the path of coreligionists who wished to convert to Islam. This last stipulation recalls the Christian-Roman Jewry law: "Jews shall not be permitted to disturb any man who has been converted from Judaism to Christianity or to assail him with any outrage."[54] But the context is different. Christianity fought hard to prevent neophytes from backsliding to Judaism, which had an unsettling effect on Christian self-assurance. Conversion or relapse from Christianity to Judaism represented an ideological blow to Christianity's fundamental tenet that Judaism had "died" at the hour of Christendom's birth. The stipulation in the Pact of ʿUmar does not suggest concern with relapse. Asserting its superiority, Islam simply prohibits conversion to *any* religion other than itself.

Symbols of Separation and Humiliation

As part of the humiliation of the *dhimmīs,* the Pact of ʿUmar requires them to rise in the presence of Muslims when the latter sit down. The *dhimmīs* also have to demonstrate their low station by refraining from mounting on saddles and by not bearing arms.[55] The Pact further admonishes *dhimmīs* to construct their houses at a lower elevation than those belonging to Muslims.

Another group of conditions *dhimmīs* had to accept were those meant to distinguish them from the dominant group. They must speak differently from Muslims (the exact meaning of this is uncertain), avoid the use of honorific names (names beginning with "Abū") and of Arabic inscriptions on their seals, and dress in distinctive garb. The requirement to dress differently from Muslims apparently is the source of the Christian prescription that first made its appearance in the canons of the Fourth Lateran Council in 1215.[56] In Christendom, the original purpose was to bar sexual relations between Christians and Jews. Enforcement of the canon by secular rulers proceeded gradually and unevenly. Where the "Jewish badge" was not commuted into cash payment, it served to underline the alien, outsider status of the Jews and render them more vulnerable to violence from the populace.

The circumstances surrounding the origin of the law requiring non-Muslims to distinguish themselves in dress are revealingly different.[57] As Tritton has observed, in the beginning, non-Muslim inhabitants of the conquered lands would have been readily distinguishable by their clothing from the rugged, desert Arabs of the conquests.[58] Later on, when non-Muslims sought to evade the oppression that attended their political condition, and as Arabs themselves adopted a more "civilized" garb, often imitating the habit of the indigenous people, the motive to dress like the Muslim ruling class, and hence to interdict this, would have increased.[59] This reasoning underlies Tritton's skepticism about the overall authenticity of the Pact of ʿUmar.

Tritton and other scholars after him believe that the pious Umayyad caliph ʿUmar ibn ʿAbd al-ʿAzīz (ʿUmar II) was the first to impose the dress restrictions on the non-Muslims, including the famous *zunnār* (girdle or belt).[60] In his article on the Pact, however, Albrecht Noth suggests that the *zunnār* regulation (and, by extension, other external signs of non-Muslim status) could have originated earlier, even as early as the time of ʿUmar I himself, products of the circumstances of the conquests. Noth speculates that *zunnār* (which, he notes, derives from a Greek loanword, *zōnarion*)[61] originally was part of the normal garb of Christians, which the Arabs insisted they retain as a distinctive identifying mark. The language in the Pact of ʿUmar, he argues, proves this: The *zunnār* regulation begins with the Christian promise, "*We shall always dress in our traditional fashion* and we shall bind the *zunnārs* around our waists.[62]

As Tritton had noted but apparently without seeing the implications, the belt (called a *zonara,* perhaps pronounced *zonnara,* in Syriac) was worn by Christians well before the advent of Islam.[63] It was even employed as a distinguishing mark of clothing. According to a passage in the Nestorian Chronicle of Seért, Nestorian Catholicos (head of the Church of Iraq and Iran) Mar Emmeh (Maramma), who died after a three-year reign during the caliphate of ʿUthman (644–56), decreed that schoolboys must wear the *zunnār* as a kind of uniform to distinguish them from others: "He was the first to order schoolboys to fasten the *zunnārs* around their waists so that they would be distinguished from others."[64] The *zunnār,* therefore, was an article of clothing worn by indigenous Christians in the conquered territories. Far from being a stigma, however, and continuing a tradition from pre-Islamic times, it was an insignia of high status. In an episode from the second century, under the Roman emperor Tiberius, reported by the sixth-century Monophysite churchman John, bishop of Ephesus (d. 586), we read that the emperor, wishing to demonstrate his fear of God, summoned Roman officials to hear a recitation of acts committed by the pagans ("whether in the East or the West"): "And whosoever was not present he gave orders that his girdle (Syriac: *zonin*) should be cut, and he should lose his office."[65] Even if this passage stems from an early, non-Christian Roman source, it nonetheless indicates that in the sixth century, Syriac Christians considered this belt an item of clothing that signified status, one whose removal was a sign of degradation.

Taken together, these and other passages confirm Noth's speculation that the *zunnār* was not invented by the Arabs to discriminate against non-Muslims but, rather, was intended to perpetuate a distinction in external appearance in place at the time of the conquest. (Jews also, it turns out, sometimes wore the *zonara* belt in pre-Islamic Palestine.)[66] The goal, Noth maintains, was to sharpen the boundaries between the massive indigenous, conquered populace and the insecure Arab ruling minority.[67]

The regimen of special clothing for non-Muslims did not arise from discriminatory or stigmatizing motives, let alone those intended to prevent accidental defilement through sexual intercourse, as was the case with the imposition of the "Jewish badge" in the Christian West. The Arab conquerors insisted that the Christians continue to wear their traditional garb lest the Arabs be unable to distinguish them. Simultaneously, Muslim tradition implored Arabs not to imitate non-Muslim mores.[68] But Muslims observed the so-called *khālifūhum* rule largely in the breach; the gradual adoption of the many dress habits of indigenous non-Muslims in the Islamic empire constitutes one example.

Only secondarily, and later—perhaps already by the time of ʿUmar II—did the Islamic dress code serve to reinforce the humiliating laws of the *dhimma,* and even then, the code was enforced unevenly and sporadically. From Abbasid caliph al-Mutawakkil, in the year 850, comes the first extant edict spelling out the type of distinctive dress required of the *dhimmī,* including the *zunnār.*[69] Jews in early Abbasid Babylonia seem to have honored the requirement to don the distinctive *dhimmī* belt.[70]

In succeeding centuries, the dress laws, often in tandem with the prohibition of riding horses, were renewed sporadically, long after Islam had achieved demographic superiority, an indication of how often the rules fell into disuse.[71] There are abundant references in the Geniza to clothing and other passing evidence in the documents, indicating no differences between the attire of Jews and Muslims during Fatimid and early Ayyubid times (mid-tenth to the late twelfth century). To the contrary, it seems that it was often difficult to tell them apart. Only later on was the discriminatory measure regularly enforced.[72] Even then, in contrast to Europe, there is no indicating that Muslims—at least, Sunni Muslims—feared contracting impurity through intimacy with Jews and Christians; they could marry their women and eat their meat. Shiism considers *dhimmīs* to carry ritual impurity, *najāsa,* based on a broad interpretation of the Qur'anic pronouncement (immediately preceding the *jizya* verse), "O ye who believe! The idolaters only are unclean (*najas*). So let them not come near the Inviolable Place" (that is, the holy mosque in Mecca) (Sura 9:28). Shiites took this to apply to all infidels without distinction, but even some of them agreed with the Sunnites that the meat of Jews and Christians was permitted.[73] It seems, therefore, that the concern of Islam in requiring distinctive dress of non-Muslims was not simply to discriminate but to demonstrate unambiguously who were the rulers and who the ruled, to delineate boundaries, and to facilitate the proper functioning of an interethnic etiquette in an inherently hierarchical society.[74] In Christendom, by way of contrast, the distinctive garb regulation, motivated in the first instance by fear of physical contamination through sexual contact, was designed to segregate and exclude.

The Slaves of *Dhimmīs*

The Pact also deals, albeit briefly and unclearly, with *dhimmī* possession of slaves, a question that occupies considerable prominence in Christian-Roman Jewry law.[75] The non-Muslims promise that they would not "take slaves who have been allotted to the Muslims." A clause in one of the earliest conquest treaties stipulates that any slave wishing to become Muslim must be sold to a Muslim.[76] This parallels the determination of Christian-Roman Jewry law and subsequent church councils, canon law books, and papal missives to prevent Jewish ownership of Christian slaves.[77]

The motive for the slave clause is not stated in the Pact. In his commentary, Ibn Qayyim al-Jawziyya, citing classical Muslim jurists, states that the clause refers to slaves taken captive by Muslims, who must not be sold to Jews or Christians.[78] This circumstance is discussed in *ḥadīth,* where attention is paid to "young" pagan captives, who were ripe candidates for conversion to Islam, as well as to Judaism and Christianity.[79] If the (pagan) slave is still young, Ibn al-Qayyim explains, his sale to an unbeliever is forbidden on the grounds that if the youthful pagan remains in Muslim hands, he is a ready and willing candidate for conversion to Islam. One authority dissents, claiming that there is no assurance that the slave will accept Islam. If the captive is an adult and presumably unlikely to change his religion, a Muslim *may* sell him to a non-Muslim, provided the buyer is not a native of a land outside the Domain of Islam, lest he return there and the former captive give information that is helpful to the enemies of Islam.[80]

There is a noteworthy distinction between Muslim concern with slaves owned by *dhimmīs* and Christian concern about slaves possessed by Jews. Christian-Roman Jewry law (and, later, canon law) make the Jewish-Christian conflict the central issue.[81] Christian sources simmer with deep-seated fear of Jewish power over Christians and of the Judaization of pagans or Christians come into the service of Jews. As the theological concept of the "perpetual servitude" of the Jews took hold in the thirteenth century, it became taboo for Jews to have even *free* Christians for domestic service.[82] The guiding principle behind the rulings on slaves is revulsion at the thought that a Jewish slaveowner might convert his servant to the "pollution of his own sect," in which case the slave would be damned. The concern that Jews would convert their slaves was not unfounded, however; Jewish law required owners to convert slaves in their households. Canon law heaped up canons on the subject, with conversion to Judaism the main worry.

Islam differed in this matter in one significant respect. The language of discourse on *dhimmī* possession of slaves suggests that Islamic authorities were driven more by fear of violating the hierarchy than by fear of the nefarious influence of Judaism. In actuality, the Geniza proves that Jews commonly possessed slaves, mainly as domestics. Goitein speculates that, in the case of slaves, the Islamic law forbidding conversion to any religion other than Islam "was largely disregarded."[83]

Exclusion from Public Office

Two other legal disabilities, which do not figure in the formal texts of the Pact of ʿUmar themselves, had a major impact on non-Muslim communities: exclusion of Jews and Christians from public office, and payment of the *jizya,* or poll tax. The ban on service in state administration recalls a similar prohibition in Christian legal texts, introduced as early as the fifth century and reiterated by church councils, canonists, and the papacy. Historically, the phenomenon was far more pervasive and enduring in Islam. Employment of non-Muslims in Islamic administration begin in earnest with the conquest itself and with the approval of Muslim rulers. It was expedient to allow natives to continue to administer the conquered territories rather than replace them with inexperienced Arabs who, anyway, found honor in fighting rather than in state service.[84] But eventually this placed power over Muslims in the hands of non-Muslims, and this became problematic. Non-Muslims, it was believed, were inherently hostile toward Muslims and would unhesitatingly cheat them. It was feared that *dhimmīs* in high places might betray their Muslim overlords to foreign rulers who shared their own religious persuasion (the main concern, of course, was with Christian *dhimmīs*). Jurists found an abundance of statements in the Qur'an and *ḥadīth* literature warning of *dhimmī* enmity and treachery.[85] Qur'anic verses specifically understood to forbid employment of non-Muslims in civil office include Sura 5:51: "O ye who believe! Take not the Jews and Christians for friends. They are friends one to another. He among you who taketh them for friends is [one] of them. Lo! Allah guideth not wrongdoing folk."[86]

Apparently, the first Muslim ruler to order non-Muslims expelled from government office was Umayyad caliph ʿUmar ibn ʿAbd al-ʿAzīz. The practice did not end there, however.[87] In his decree of 850, Abbasid caliph al-Mutawakkil had to reiterate the ban on *dhimmī* state service. "He forbade their employment in government office and on official business where they would have authority over the Muslims."[88] As rationale for the ouster, the caliph's decree stated that the *dhimmīs* "oppress them [the Muslims] and stretch out their hands against them in tyranny, deceit, and enmity."[89] The justification recalls the one cited by Christian legists for excluding Jews from public offices. The allegation was substantiated by Qur'anic and post-Qur'anic stories of Jewish treachery toward the Prophet in Medina.

Nonetheless, over the centuries, al-Mutawakkil's decree, and many others like it, were only sporadically enforced. Complaints that non-Muslims exploited the power and wealth that often came with government office recur time and time again in Muslim sources. For centuries throughout the Muslim world, even during the period of decline after the twelfth century, effective administration continued to depend on Christian, Jewish, and in Persia, Zoroastrian bureaucrats.[90]

The *dhimmīs'* ubiquitous presence in Arab ruling circles involved them in the business of state in ways unimaginable for Jews in Christian northern Europe. It gave them influence and honor and imparted to the minority communities to which they belonged a feeling of embeddedness in the larger society. To some extent, this diminished the marginalization imposed on the non-Muslims by law and religion.

This was certainly the case with the illustrious Jewish courtiers of Muslim Spain. Ḥasday ibn Shapruṭ played a very important role in the diplomacy of the Andalusian caliphate in tenth-century Cordova, and his importance to the Muslim ruler, which Arab writers acknowledged, certainly bestowed on his Jewish community pride and self-esteem.[91] A century later, the Jews of the Berber kingdom of Granada derived similar gratification and honor from the knowledge that their rabbinic and communal leader, Samuel ibn Nagrela, served as vizier and head of the army. To be sure, there were limits to Jewish empowerment. More than one Jewish courtier lost his life when he was perceived as lording it over Muslims. Both Arab and Jewish sources attest that the vicious assassination of Joseph, Samuel's son and successor, in 1066 came about because the Jewish courtier had become haughty in his position.

A few examples of the opposition to *dhimmī* officials will illustrate the pervasive phenomenon of non-Muslim involvement in the political life of medieval Islam. The Fatimid dynasty in Egypt (969–1171) was notorious for condoning *dhimmī* participation in state service. Geniza documents provide evidence of the widespread professional involvement of non-Muslims in Fatimid government.[92] A fragment from an Arabic epistolographic manual for chancery secretaries (*kātibs*), transcribed into Hebrew letters (presumably for easier reading), was certainly meant to be read by Jews destined for that profession.[93] A famous satirical Arabic poem decrying what the poet viewed as an intolerable abuse refers (though not by name) to a powerful Jew in the Fatimid court in the mid-eleventh century, Abū Saʿd al-Tustarī:

> The Jews of this time have attained their uttermost hopes, and have come to rule.
>
> Glory is upon them, money is with them, and from among them come the counsellor and the ruler.
>
> O People of Egypt, I advise you, turn Jew, for the heavens have turned Jew![94]

A Coptic Christian "monk" in the Fatimid civil service during the twelfth century, infamous for his fiscal extortions affecting all classes of the population, comes in for condemnation both in Islamic literary sources and in incidental comments in contemporary Jewish correspondence preserved in the Geniza.[95]

Inevitably, discomfort with *dhimmī* service in government became more pronounced as the relative leniency of the classical Islamic period gave way to the harsher, more intolerant late Middle Ages. Citing Qur'anic texts which speak of the enmity non-Muslims held for Muslims, a *fatwā* (responsum) of the thirteenth century rules that a Jew may not be engaged as inspector of coins in the state mint.[96] A dignitary from Morocco visited Egypt at the beginning of the fourteenth century, at a time when the disabilities of the *dhimma,* including the exclusion from public office, were rigorously enforced in his home country. Indignant at what he observed of non-Muslim evasion of the ban on office-holding as well as of the sumptuary laws in general, the visitor prevailed on the Mamluk authorities to order the enforcement of the relevant provisions of the Pact of ʿUmar.[97] We are told that the Christians and Jews offered large sums of money, albeit unsuccessfully, to avert the severe decree. This tactic, identical to the common strategy of bribery employed by Jews of Europe to stave off oppression and violence, may have come into greater use by Jews (and Christians) in the late Islamic Middle Ages, when the comparative security of the earlier age had diminished.[98]

Conversion to Islam by non-Muslim courtiers suspected of desire to retain office accelerated in the post-classical period. The allegedly insincere neophytes in Egypt were given the diminutive, hence pejorative, name of *muslimānī* (plural *musālima*) instead of *muslim*.[99] To deal with heterodoxy and blasphemy, Islam had its own version of the Inquisition, which usually took the form of investigation by a regular court of Muslim judges. *Musālima* suspected of loyalty to their original religion also came under judicial scrutiny.[100]

Treatises dedicated wholly or in part to exposing, bemoaning, or calling for the elimination of the evil practice of non-Muslim service in government abound after the twelfth century.[101] The most common accusations were corruption, fiscal oppression of the populace, unbelief (*kufr*), the spread of moral laxity, dishonesty, favoritism toward coreligionists, anti-Muslim plotting, and treachery. Thus, in the Islamic world the issue was the improper subordination of Muslims to non-Muslims and the intolerable non-Muslim oppression of Muslims that might ensue. One charge that appears not to figure in the various campaigns to remove *dhimmīs* from positions of authority is that they will blaspheme the Prophet. This notwithstanding the fact that, in Islam, blasphemy is one of the gravest sins, and despite that it is the first cause for revocation of the Pact of ʿUmar discussed by Ibn Qayyim al-Jawziyya.[102] We have already seen how a case of alleged blasphemy affected the Jews of Cairo in 1442. Apparently, however, fear of blasphemy was not offered as justification for excluding non-Muslims from the government bureaucracy.

The Poll Tax

Earlier in this chapter we discussed the Qur'anic basis for the poll tax, or *jizya,* and the system of tribute that evolved during the early Islamic conquests.[103] Since *jizya* is the only one of the *dhimmī* disabilities mentioned in the Qur'an, detailed discussion of the legal status of the non-Muslims often appears in Muslim juristic literature under the *jizya* rubric. Thus, for example, Abū Yūsuf's *Kitāb al-kharāj* (Book on Taxation), commissioned by Caliph Hārūn al-Rashīd at the end of the eighth century,[104] includes, immediately following the expected chapter on *jizya,* another one on the distinctive dress of non-Muslims, and, a bit further on, a third, entitled "Churches, Synagogues (*biyaʿ*), and Crosses." Characteristic of the centrality of the poll tax in Dhimmī law, that chapter contains a summary of all the *dhimmī* obligations, mentioning the attendant peace settlement (*ṣulḥ*), which, in Abū Yūsuf's words, was given "in return for payment of the *jizya*."[105]

Kitāb al-umm, the great compilation of Islamic law by the jurist al-Shāfiʿī (d. 820), contains several chapters on the *dhimmīs* in its *Kitāb al-jizya* (Book on the Poll Tax). Shāfiʿī discusses the various groups that belong to the "People of the Book" (hence were privileged to pay the *jizya*). A key chapter opens, "If the Imam wishes to write a document for the poll tax of non-Muslims, he should write. . . ." There follows a much amplified, juridical description of all the stipulations found in the later texts of the Pact of ʿUmar, plus the poll tax itself, along with several other items.[106] Another chapter in Shāfiʿī's *Kitāb al-jizya* lists the obligations the Imam should impose on *dhimmīs* living in garrison towns. They were more or less the same as the disabilities in the Pact of ʿUmar. The next chapter catalogs the types of protection the Imam owes the *dhimmīs* in return for their submission.[107] At the beginning of his *Aḥkām ahl al-dhimma,* Ibn Qayyim al-Jawziyya declares that he had composed his comprehensive treatise on the laws of the *dhimma* in response to a request for a detailed explanation of the poll tax.[108]

Jurists debated whether the *jizya* mandated by the Qur'an constituted a penalty (*ʿuqūba;* that is, a means of debasement) or a fee (*ujra*), paid to secure physical protection and residential rights. Most authorities held that it was a penalty.[109]

Islamic jurists discussed the amount of the *jizya*. Some schools of law set it at a fixed rate; others made it a graduated impost (12, 24, or 48 *dirhems*), depending on the financial means of the *dhimmī* and consistent with a widespread interpretation of *ʿan yadin* in the Qur'anic *jizya* verse. The latter method had been the practice of the Sassanians and remained in force in Islamic Iraq.[110] The poor did not escape the poll tax obligation, though certain other categories did. According to most jurists, since the poll tax represented a monetary payment in lieu of military service, logically those disqualified for army service did not have to pay. This category included women, the prepubescent young, slaves, and the infirm.

As mentioned, the poll tax was supposed to be collected in a manner that emphasized the *dhimmī*'s "lowliness." Numerous humiliating ceremonies were employed, such as the hand-slap on the neck. Sometimes, the humiliating ritual was omitted. The *ḥadīth* literature preserves an oft-quoted tradition counseling moderation when collecting the *jizya,* which may have been intended to justify such a departure from the norm:

> Hishām b. Ḥakīm b. Hizām found a man who was the governor of Hims making some Copts [*nās min al-qibṭ*] stand in the sun for the payment of *jizya*. He said: What is this? I heard the Apostle of Allah [may peace be upon him] as

> saying: Allah Most High will torment those who torment the people in this world.[111]

In addition, there are statements in the Islamic literature that seek to restrain public degradation of the non-Muslim poll taxpayer once he had remitted his annual "penalty":

> If you take the poll tax from them, you have no claim on them or rights over them. . . . [D]o not enslave them and do not let the Muslims oppress them or harm them or devour their property except as permitted, but faithfully observe the conditions which you have accorded to them and all that you have allowed to them.[112]

And:

> The Prophet said: "He who robs a *dhimmī* or imposes on him more than he can bear will have me as his opponents."[113]

According to Islamic law, *dhimmīs* paid twice the commercial taxes levied upon Muslims, usually 5 percent. *Tujjār ahl al-ḥarb,* "merchants from the Domain of War," paid ten.[114] Geniza documents reveal that Jewish communities, like those in Christian Europe, periodically endured other huge tax levies in connection with one or another governmental fiscal need.[115]

Payment of the poll tax is the one disability imposed upon the non-Muslims about which we hear frequent, mainly financial complaints in the Geniza correspondence.[116] For the poor and those with modest incomes, it constituted a burden, and Jewish communal or private charity often had to defray the expense for those who could not afford it. The *dhimmī* had to produce proof of payment. In certain periods, the humiliating seal stamped on the neck served as receipt for payment of the *jizya*.[117] The Geniza indicates that the receipt took the form of a piece of paper called *barā'a,* "quittance." Anyone caught by the revenue authorities without it might have to remit his poll tax a second time that year.[118] A ruler might on occasion raise the amount of the poll tax to extortionate levels.[119] The real-life evidence of the Geniza correspondence regarding the burden of the poll tax belies the conclusions of many modern devotees of the myth of the interfaith utopia who claim that, historically, the *jizya* had no humiliating connotation and that Muslims collected it only with compassion.[120]

Conceived as "protection money," however, *jizya* played a constructive role, exactly as was intended by the Qur'anic commandment. It guaranteed non-Muslims protection at an annual price ("Fight against [them] . . . until they pay the *jizya*"). The very regularity of the *jizya* assured *dhimmīs* of regular and continuous security.[121] Here, again, a story preserved among the Geniza fragments offers contemporary evidence.

The tale, apparently told by Jews of Iraq in the tenth century, indicates how valuable a protection they considered the annual capitation to be. The manuscript fragment containing the narrative apparently belongs to an account of the exploits of wealthy Jewish court bankers in early tenth-century Abbasid Baghdad, whom we will meet again in Chapter 5.[122] The protagonist, Neṭira, was the son-in-law of the merchant-banker Joseph b. Phineas. Combining motifs found in other Jewish stories, the anecdote relates how the caliph al-Muʿtaḍid (Abbasid caliph from 892 to 902), encouraged by a Haman-like adviser, issues a decree to harm the Jews. But the prophet Elijah appears to the caliph in his dreams and warns him that dire consequences will ensue should he carry out his malevolent plan. The caliph thence summons Neṭira, who comes, somewhat like Joseph before Pharaoh or Esther before King Ahasuerus, fearing for his life and clothed in a shroud. When Neṭira identifies Elijah as the divinely appointed guardian of the helpless Jews, the caliph relents. Among the rewards he offers the Jewish notable is cancellation of the *jizya* payment of the Jews. Neṭira rejects the offer. His rationale reflects the ambivalent feelings Jews had about the poll tax:

> O my lord, by the *jizya* the Jew spares his life. If they are exempted from it, their lives will surely become forfeit. Moreover, those who come after them will not be safe in the future, because [payment of] what they had previously been excused from will be demanded from them, and they will be obligated to pay it all at one time, thereby becoming ruined and impoverished. The kindest thing [to do] for them is to have them pay the *jizya* according to the will of the Commander of the Faithful [i.e., the caliph], may God lengthen your life, with maximum compassion, and to impose it mercifully. Thereupon [the caliph] said: "You collect it from them in accordance with the custom of the Prophet, peace be upon him, as was done in his day." [Neṭira] complied, and the Jews lived in peace and tranquility for the nine and a half remaining years of al-Muʿtaḍid's reign without enduring harm or affliction.[123]

Underlying this tale is the ambivalent attitude of tenth-century Iraqi Jews toward the poll tax. Indeed, the levy was normally collected with harshness (hence, Neṭira's plea that it be collected in the future "with maximum compassion"). But the Jews relied on it to guarantee the protection promised by Islamic law, consistent, as it were, with the Muslim juristic opinion, mentioned above, that the *jizya* payment represented a fee in return for physical protection and residential rights. Underscoring this, the story relates that the caliph severely punished some Muslim Sufis who later on tried to disturb the Jews' peace.[124]

A story about a persecution of the Jews in Baghdad in the first half of the twelfth century related in another Geniza fragment states quite explicitly that payment of *jizya* benefited the Jews (*kānat ḥasana lahum*) whereas exemption from it could lead to trouble (*ʿiqāb,* lit. "punishment").[125] A harsh (albeit minority) legal opinion of the fifteenth-century North African anti-Jewish *qāḍī* al-Maghīlī cites lax enforcement by the Muslims of the *jizya* collectable from the Jews as a rationale for canceling their Pact and for wreaking physical violence against them.[126]

For a greater appreciation of the perception of security that the Jews of Islam associated with payment of the *jizya,* consider the more unstable situation of the Jews of Europe. The Jews there paid numerous and often unreasonably high and arbitrary taxes to the ruling authority, but—until 1342 in the Holy Roman Empire—no regular poll tax in return for official protection.[127] Safety constituted a unilateral gift of the state, tendered because Jews were useful to the economy and/or dependable (because increasingly vulnerable, hence dependent) taxpayers. When physically threatened (which happened much more frequently than in the Islamic world) the Jews of Europe routinely resorted to bribery to purchase or restore protection. This reliance on bribery created uncertainty, instability, and collective anxiety, for one never knew when a payoff might be required or whether the sum offered would be sufficient.

A sign of the widespread utilization of bribery in Jewish life in Latin Christendom is the regular use of the verb *le-shaḥed* (from the biblical noun *shoḥad,* "bribery"), rare in mishnaic Hebrew, to express the action.[128] In Islam, as in Christendom, many a ruler discovered that the threat to enforce the sumptuary laws among the *dhimmīs* was a convenient ploy to raise cash as a substitute. But by contrast, I know of little evidence from the classical Islamic period that bribing officials to prevent violence against persons became a regular Jewish practice. Carrying the comparison further, in the Latin West, Jewish residential security was often linked to their economic utility. Thus, in England in 1290, when tallages had ceased to yield significant sums from the increasingly impoverished Jews, King Edward I canceled their right of residence and expelled them, confiscating what little remained of their property.

Despite the humiliating connotation and the financial burden, the Jews of Islam had in the *jizya* a surer guarantee of protection from non-Jewish hostility than their distant brethren had in the Latin West. The "testament" of Caliph ʿUmar, the purported originator of the Pact bearing his name, stipulates regarding the Protected People, that Muslims must "do battle to guard them, and put no burden on them greater than they can bear, provided they pay what is due from them to the Muslims, willingly or under subjection, being humbled."[129] This principle was not always upheld, but it remained a steadfast cornerstone of Islamic policy toward the non-Muslims even into late medieval and early modern times.

The Pact of ʿUmar and the European Charters

The Pact of ʿUmar operated differently from the charters of privileges granted to the Jews in Europe. The Latin charter constituted the normal instrument by means of which lords expressed the obligations and privileges of groups within their domain: churches, monasteries, towns, and vulnerable dependents like the Jews. It was normal for each ruler to renew the patent upon his accession. This created a certain amount of insecurity for the Jews, for the new king or emperor might arbitrarily opt not to renew their guarantee of security. Or as often happened, the ruler might alter the privileges by removing former protections or adding new restrictions (or, for that matter, new privileges—another sign of arbitrariness). Similarly, the *Constitutio pro Judeis* of the papacy had to be reissued by each new pope, placing on the shoulders of Jewish intercessors the burden of periodically petitioning to have Jewish rights renewed.

Islamic jurists debated whether the stipulations (*shurūṭ*) of the Pact of ʿUmar needed to be renewed by an Imam if, for some misdeed of the *dhimmīs,* the Pact had been annulled. Conservative jurist Ibn Taymiyya, Ibn Qayyim al-Jawziyya's mentor, opined that it was not necessary—in fact, it was to no avail legally—to promulgate the compact anew: the original Pact issued by Caliph ʿUmar and carried out after him "by caliphs of excellent repute" sufficed for all later generations. By the same token, a ruler could not grant relief to the *dhimmīs* from any of the Pact's restrictions.[130] Muslim abhorrence of unacceptable "innovation" (*bidʿa* in Arabic) assured non-Muslims that the authorities would neither arbitrarily add to nor detract from the canon of disabilities and protection that regulated their relations with the majority society. Similarly, Latin Christendom, with its more complex and diffuse legal system, abhorred *innovatio* (the word is Latin, of course). But it seems to have been able to sustain changes in the legal status of the Jews by relying on appropriate ancient precedents or rationales. In a clear-cut example of this, the authors of German law codes in the thirteenth century were able to justify the German emperor's overlordship over the Jews as "serfs of his imperial chamber" and also of their servile status on the basis of an ancient story told by Josephus, according to which the Jews who survived the Roman siege of Jerusalem were sold into slavery to the victorious Roman emperor Vespasian (or, alternately, Titus).[131]

When, on occasion, it became necessary to enforce some neglected restriction or restrictions in the Pact of ʿUmar, authorities might repromulgate the entire Pact as a reminder to the violators, who, we read, might actually disclaim direct knowledge of the compact. In the late Middle Ages, for example, we find Mamluk sultans reissuing the Pact, incorporating the demand that *dhimmīs* be excluded from the service of the state.[132] This latter clause did not constitute an innovation, for, as we have seen, the regulation had been part of the restrictive regimen since as early as the eighth century, and it was frequently invoked when a ruler or religious scholar wished to remove non-Muslim secretaries from the administrative apparatus.

The most eccentric departure from the traditional stipulations came during the indiscriminate persecution in Egypt and Syria by Fatimid caliph al-Ḥākim (996–1021). Among other innovations, he made Jews and Christians wear a humiliating symbol around their necks in the public bath (the Jews, a heavy wooden image of the golden calf "which their ancestors had worshipped," and the Christians, a long wooden cross). Muslim chroniclers recognized these and other outrageous impositions by the "mad" caliph as going far beyond the law of the Pact of Caliph ʿUmar ibn al-Khaṭṭāb—"the stipulations which al-Ḥākim *added* to the ʿUmariyyan ones," as one medieval Arab historian put it dryly.[133]

For non-Muslims, therefore, the relative stability over time of the basic law regarding their legal status assured them a considerable degree of continuity in this important matter. Further, Islamic judges remained faithful to the principle of noninterference in the adjudication of intra-Jewish issues unless brought before them voluntarily by the parties. Even when this occurred, as it did quite frequently, *qāḍīs* especially observed the rule of nonintervention when the matter related to personal status, as evidenced, for example, in the phrase *la nataʿarraḍ fī dhalika (*or: *lahum) li-makān ʿaqd al-dhimma,* "we do not interfere in this matter (or: with them) on account of the *dhimma* pact," sprinkled through a discussion of *dhimmī* marital law.[134]

Finally, as is well known, in Christian lands the Jews often endured collective punishment for the alleged or real transgressions of individuals. The view of one of the stricter Islamic schools of law, the Malikite, is that Islam should not impose collective retribution for one person's violation of the Pact if the other non-Muslims repudiate the act or are found to have transgressed under compulsion.[135] Instances of mob assault on an entire Jewish community because one Jew violated the Pact are, in fact, extremely rare. They include the pogrom in 1066 in Granada, a favorite of the countermyth revisionists but, nonetheless, an exception to the rule in the classical period of Islam.

PART THREE

In the Economy

Chapter Five

THE ECONOMIC FACTOR

IN ACCOUNTING FOR the fate of the Jews, Jewish historiography has traditionally placed considerable emphasis on their economic role in society. Similarly, prejudice about the economic ethic (or alleged lack of ethic) of the Jews, still prevalent in modern society, has sparked interest in the economic dimension of Jewish history. Prejudice aside, it cannot be denied that economic factors figured prominently in determining the position of the Jews in any given society, as well as helping to shape their relations with the non-Jewish majority, for the economic realm straddled the boundaries that otherwise separated Jews from non-Jews. It was the locus of their most frequent interaction. Hence, any meaningful understanding of the status and fate of medieval Jews in Islam and in Christendom requires careful attention to the economic factor, including the attitudes of the respective majority cultures toward economic activity in general.

IN THE CHRISTIAN WORLD

Christianity and the Mercantile Life

Early Christianity disapproved of the accumulation of wealth, especially of wealth generated by profit gained through commerce. This was not new; it had its antecedents in pagan Greek society. As John W. Baldwin explains, Plato "decried the characteristic temptation towards exorbitant profits in commercial transactions . . . [and] was pessimistic about the possibility of many men maintaining a moderate course in trade." His student, Aristotle, "maintained that this 'business' for the sake of wealth had no limits and was an *appetitus divitiarum infinitus* [endless appetite for riches], as it was later formulated. Such excess contradicted Aristotle's basic ethical principle of moderation."[1]

It seems likely that Aristotle had no direct influence on the economic thought of the church fathers, who were guided instead by Scripture.[2] Jesus' dictums, which stress the priority of spiritual over material matters, seem also to attack excessive accumulation of material goods. Paul likewise condemned this evil, and Christianity esteemed poverty. Wealth seemed coterminous with materialistic delight in mundane, earthly preoccupations. "It is easier for a poor man to get into heaven than a rich man to go through the eye of a needle"—so said Jesus in a phrase whose very fame affirms the saliency of its message in nascent Christian thinking.

Baldwin cites three reasons for patristic misgivings about merchants: (1) greed was believed to be the basis of trade; (2) people believed that merchants employed immoral means in the pursuit of gain; (3) merchants had control over many of the necessities of life. "In large measure the thinkers of the Middle Ages inherited this uneasy conscience of the church fathers about riches and their acquisition through trade."[3] By contrast, rural pursuits were viewed with favor by the church, which itself owned huge tracts of agricultural land.

The merchant's very way of life gave offense to those living the stable, sedentary existence of the dominant rural economy. A "hierarchy of dignity" in medieval Christendom ranked intellectual, agricultural, and industrial occupations higher than that of the merchant, who, Norman Zacour writes,

> grew nothing, added nothing to the general store, but only bought something to sell it unchanged for a higher price. The desire for profit had all the earmarks of the sin of avarice. Was money not the root of all evil? The acts of buying and selling, even if neither good nor bad in themselves, presented so many temptations for fraud as to make the merchant's occupation extremely hazardous for the soul. . . . No merchant, it seemed, could please God. No one could buy or sell without cheating. . . . In sum, merchants were an abomination.[4]

Alienation from the trader is summed up by the sociologist Georg Simmel, who finds in the Jews of Europe the historical example par excellence of "the stranger":

> Throughout the history of economics the stranger everywhere appears as the trader, or the trader as stranger. As long as economy is essentially self-sufficient, or products are exchanged within a spatially narrow group, it needs no middleman: a trader is only required for products that originate outside the group. Insofar as members do not leave the circle in order to buy these necessities—in which case *they* are the "strange" merchants in that outside territory—the trader *must* be a stranger, since nobody else has a chance to make a living. . . . Trade can always absorb more people than primary production; it is, therefore, the sphere indicated for the stranger, who intrudes as a supernumerary, so to speak, into a group in which the economic positions are actually occupied—*the classical example is the history of European Jews*. The stranger is by nature no "owner of soil"—soil not only in the physical, but also in the figurative sense of a life-substance which is fixed, if not in a point in space, at least in an ideal point of the social environment. Although in more intimate relations, he may develop all kinds of charm and significance, as long

> as he is considered a stranger in the eyes of the other, he is not an "owner of soil." Restriction to intermediary trade, and often (as though sublimated from it) to pure finance, gives him the specific character of *mobility*. If mobility takes place within a closed group it embodies that synthesis of nearness and distance which constitutes the formal position of the stranger. For, the fundamentally mobile person comes in contact, at one time or another, with every individual, but is not organically connected, through established ties of kinship, locality, and occupation, with any single one.[5]

The Jew as Merchant

For the earliest Jewish settlers in Western Europe, the prevalence of these negative beliefs among churchmen, aristocrats, and peasants alike was singularly unfortunate. These first Jews to cross the horizon of the indigenous inhabitants of the Latin Christian world were predominantly long-distance merchants. They originated mainly in the Near East, arriving on northern European soil via trade routes that linked first the pre-Islamic and then the Islamized Orient with Italy, southern France, and the eastern Germanic regions. Some traversed Latin Christendom between Spain and the Slavic lands, where they procured pagan slaves (the name comes from *Slav*) for marketing in the slave emporium at Verdun and ultimately for resale in Muslim Spain.

Emblematic of the roving—hence, alien—Jewish merchant in early medieval Europe are the Radhanite Jewish merchants. Arabic sources of the ninth century describe them as international traders exchanging goods between Europe and the Near and Far East. From the East they brought mainly spices, doubtless for avid consumers among the Christian nobility and royal circles. They were long thought to have had their home base in Europe. Moshe Gil, however, has shown that the Radhanites originated in Iraq, in a region east of the Tigris River fanning out from Baghdad and called in Arabic "the land of Radhan."[6] These Radhanites would have seemed alien to Christians on three counts: their Jewish religion, their vocation, and their foreign provenance.

Thus, to the theological disdain of the Jews, long-rooted in Christianity, was added a general suspicion of the Jew-as-merchant. The disdain intensified after the Islamic conquest of the Near East, when "Syrian" traders, who once shared the East-West international trade with the Jews, faded from the European scene. Now nearly every long-distance trader traveling the roads of Latin Europe was either an itinerant foreign Jew or a Jew whose ancestors had originated outside the domain of Christendom.[7]

Carolingian thinkers subscribed to the Christian belief that cupidity was inherent in economic endeavors, which therefore led inevitably to "shameful gain" (*turpe lucrum*).[8] This did not deter rulers from encouraging Jewish long-distance traders to settle permanently in their domain. The desire on the part of the monarchy to exploit the professional skills of Jewish merchants for the good of the primitive Frankish economy, or at least to satisfy the aristocracy's lust for spices and luxury items from the East, overrode religious scruples. The ninth-century charters of the Carolingian king Louis the Pious granted itinerant Jewish trading families substantial privileges designed to induce them to establish a permanent base of operations on Christian territory.

We may imagine that the expansive privileges, many of which exceeded those enjoyed by Christians, were necessary to overcome the Jews' fear of the hostility that the Christian populace harbored toward them, both as Jews and as traders. The dispensations included exemption from certain tolls, freedom from interference in mercantile affairs, the absolute right to live according to their Jewish laws, and protection from discrimination in cases of mixed litigation in a Christian court. Particularly surprising is that Louis permitted the Jews to retain slaves who wished (or were induced by others) to become Christians in order to qualify for emancipation and escape from bondage to their Jewish owners.

Encouraged by civil authorities, Jews specializing in long-distance trade continued to settle permanently in northern Europe during and after the Carolingian period. Duly conscious of the close relations between the Carolingian dynasty and early Jewish mercantile settlement, Ashkenazic Jews in northern Europe in the twelfth century (and doubtless earlier) cherished a folk memory that "King Charles" (Charlemagne) had personally brought the first Jewish settlers from Italy to the Rhineland.[9]

Latin sources for the "dark" centuries of the early Middle Ages portray the Jews almost exclusively as merchants, who typically frequented and furnished goods to royal and episcopal courts. Bernhard Blumenkranz, in his lifetime the leading historian of medieval Jewry in Latin Christendom, thought this to be an illusion: merchants were precisely those Jews who would have attracted the attention of Christian chroniclers, who maintained close ties to royal courts. Blumenkranz contends that modern antisemites, fixated on the Jews' alleged innate and covetous bent for profiteering and commerce, exaggerated Jewish ardor for this walk of life in the early Middle Ages. Moreover, he argues apologetically on the basis of Latin and Hebrew sources, Jews engaged in diverse occupations during the Barbarian period. These included medicine, agriculture (with Jewish landowners even employing slaves and Christian laborers), and various crafts.[10] Blumenkranz notwithstanding, it is nonetheless evident that Jews preponderated in commerce, and for that reason their Christian neighbors thought of them coterminously with merchants.[11] This doubtless contributed to their alienation within a predominantly sedentary, rural society deeply suspicious of the roving stranger-merchant.

Thus an ambivalent attitude toward the Jews reigned during the early European Middle Ages. Jews were derided for their predominant profession, for Christian society had inherited the ancient Roman and early patristic disdain for the merchant. This negative sentiment went hand in hand with the traditional religious antipathy toward the Jews engraved in the minds of the leaders of the church. Since "Jew" and "merchant" were nearly synonomous, the aversion was compounded. At the same time, Jews who settled in Europe prospered from trade precisely because Christians still eschewed commercial life and because some secular rulers recognized the utility of a mercantile presence, necessarily Jewish. Their ambivalent reception in the Latin West during the early Middle Ages was sufficient cause for worry among the Jews. But, protected by secular rulers at a time when the religion of Christianity had not yet gained wide acceptance in society at large, at a time when the church was still too weak to influence the policy of practical-minded temporal monarchs, the economic gain seems to have offset the risks.

Because of their identification with a despised, shunned profession, on the one hand, and because of the stigma of their religion, on the other, Jews operated at the economic margins of what Christianity considered proper. When, later on, the church's opinion of trade became more friendly, it was the Jews' unfortunate lot to be denied the opportunity to move from the margin into the mainstream of European economic life.

With the revival of urban life in the late tenth and eleventh centuries, a Christian commercial class emerged in Europe.[12] This was bound to have a deleterious effect on the Jews, although they retained some of their prominence in trade as late as the second half of the eleventh century. Bishop Rudiger, the temporal ruler of the Rhenish town of Speyer, wished to establish his town as a prosperous commercial center. To this end, in 1084, he invited Jewish merchants to settle there, promising privileges so expansive as to constitute, in his words, "a legal status more generous than any which the Jewish people have in any city of the German kingdom."[13]

Official Christian prejudice against commerce and the trader mellowed beginning in the twelfth century, when rapid urban growth and attendant commercial expansion drew Christians into the profitable vocation in ever-increasing numbers. Nevertheless, the old view persists in the work of Gratian, the greatest of the early compilers of canon law. His *Decretum* (ca. 1140) seems to consider commercial profits condemnable and declares certain forms of investment to be the equivalent of usury. But subsequent authorities "softened the rigours of the earlier doctrine" in keeping with the reality of the commercial revolution and of Christian involvement in mercantile pursuits. They "distinguished the profits of sale from those of usury. . . . [They] distinguished between profits made without and those made with some expenditure of time and labour and money." Only the former were considered shameful gain. If the merchant's intention was to earn a livelihood for himself and his family rather than turn a profit for its own sake, his commercial activity met with approval.[14]

Gilchrist, building on the work of predecessors such as John Baldwin and Raymond De Roover, counters the view (represented by Weber and Tawney) that the economic doctrines of the medieval church impeded the growth of a monetary, market economy in the Middle Ages. True, many theologians in their pronouncements on economic activity reiterated the early Christian condemnation of excessive profits. Everything had its "just price," which was set to prevent profiteering. But, explains Gilchrist (following Baldwin), far from crippling economic growth by fixing prices at a level that would limit a return amounting to no more than the cost of production plus a moderate profit, in canon law the doctrine of the "just price" was made equivalent to the current free market price, based on the utility of an item—"its capacity to satisfy needs." Thus, "economic growth was not impeded by bad teaching or price regulation."[15] Responding to the growth of the commercial economy with its need for loans, canonists and theologians of the High Middle Ages relaxed the older Christian sanctions against all forms of usury. Those views had been propagated in an earlier age when the need for credit was small. Now, in light of the new economic reality, the church began to tolerate "moderate" interest charges.[16]

Jewish merchants gained nothing from the more favorable view of commerce that came into vogue during the twelfth century. The rise of a Christian urban commercial class for whose benefit the church modified its opposition to commercial profiteering created difficulties for the veteran Jewish long-distance trader. Formerly monopolizing this function in a backward, predominantly rural environment, he was now seen as a competitor.[17] Gradually, Christian traders in northern Europe squeezed their Jewish counterparts out of the commercial market economy. Jews were excluded from the developing commercial guilds; unwanted, they were, for all practical purposes, barred from membership because of their inability to swear the required Christian oath of initiation. Already accustomed to dealing partly in loans with surplus capital generated by commercial transactions, Jews were now compelled to transfer their main energies to moneylending. Other Jews, who for various reasons were pushed out of productive occupations, found their only means of livelihood in making loans to Christians as well.

The Jew as Moneylender

Grounded in biblical precepts, Judaism forbade loans at interest to coreligionists but not to foreigners. Deuteronomy, Exodus, and Leviticus are explicit about this. The Deuteronomic statement (23:20–21) commands:

"You shall not deduct interest from loans to your brother . . . but you may deduct interest from loans to foreigners." Paradoxically, these Old Testament verses, coupled with one in the Gospel of Luke ("Lend, hoping for nothing in return" 6:35), formed the basis of the original ban on usury between Christians ("brothers"); in this case, the Old Testament law given to biblical Israel was declared to apply equally to "New Israel."

The rabbis of talmudic Babylonia discouraged Jews from taking interest from gentiles, either on the grounds that the contact might lead to imitation of gentile ways or because it was unethical. In Babylonia, most Jews continued to till the soil and lived in predominantly Jewish settlements, removed, by and large, from economic intercourse with non-Jews.[18] Beginning in the twelfth century, however, rabbis in medieval Europe justified exacting usury from Christians for various local economic and social reasons, such as hard times, the exclusion of Jews from landed occupations, their heavy tax burden, and the need to amass funds to bribe Christians when Jews came under threat of persecution.[19] In his *Dialogue of a Philosopher with a Jew and a Christian,* the Christian philosopher Peter Abelard put into the mouth of his Jew the most typical of Jewish rationales for engaging in moneylending:

> Confined and constricted in this way as if the whole world had conspired against us alone, it is a wonder that we are allowed to live. We are allowed to possess neither fields nor vineyards nor any landed estates because there is no one who can protect them for us from open or occult attack. Consequently the principal gain that is left for us is that we sustain our miserable lives here by lending money at interest to strangers; but this just makes us most hateful to them who think they are being oppressed by it.[20]

To ensure that the Jews maintained a regular flow of taxable income, secular rulers condoned and supported moneylending to Christians—for instance, by using Christian courts to enforce payment of Christian debts to Jews. Not surprisingly, this increased hatred of the Jew on the part of Christians, who understood that governmental encouragement of Jewish moneylending was simply an indirect way of filling royal treasuries with monies that originated in Christian pockets.

This observation applies mostly to the more affluent borrowers from the new Christian bourgeoisie, who actually could be expected to repay their debts in cash. The Christian poor usually borrowed in distress by pawning an item from their meager possessions (often an article of clothing), which they forfeited upon failure to repay the loan on time. Naturally, they, too, had no great affection for the Jewish pawnbroker, upon whom they were so dependent. As Guido Kisch put it: "There is some truth to the remark that usury secured for the Jews official protection at the price of public detestation."[21]

Christian dependence upon Jewish moneylenders constituted a major irritant in Jewish-Christian relations in the High and later Middle Ages. As we have seen, the cardinal principle of Christian teaching—that no Jew should have power over any Christian—underlay laws in early Christian times forbidding Jews to possess Christian slaves or to hold public office, both of which put Jews in positions of authority over Christians. The principle also precipitated the decrees of the Fourth Lateran Council, in 1215, banning employment of Jews in public office and limiting Jewish usury.

Dependence on the Jewish moneylender created an improper inversion of the appropriate hierarchical relationship between Christian and Jew. William C. Jordan considers the impact of this impropriety at the level of popular culture in his study of Jewish moneylending in Picardy, a region of northern France, in the thirteenth century. Jordan speculates that this dependence on what was considered an unsavory source of credit fostered anti-Jewish hostility among the lower classes. His evidence shows that the Christian borrowers included a high proportion of women. These women were constrained to leave their homes in a Christian sector of town and go into the forbidding Jewish neighborhood to secure the loans or make payments. Jordan assumes that

> if they had children they took their children with them. A pattern of behaviour of this sort—given the general context of Christian-Jewish relations and the unnatural aspect of dependency which coloured the act of borrowing from a Jew—was an important factor in perpetuating, perhaps intensifying, hostility between the two communities or certain elements of them.[22]

More detailed research on the relationship between Jewish moneylending and persecution would be necessary to substantiate the thesis that "usury begets hatred." Stuart Jenks has tested this theory by applying statistical analysis to complaints about Christian debtors and Jewish moneylenders in Franconia (Würzburg) in the Holy Roman Empire during a period when several violent anti-Jewish persecutions took place (1298, 1336–37, 1348–49). He found no correlation between the credit transactions and these outbursts of Jew hatred.[23] However, this is not conclusive. The borrowers studied were predominantly Christian landed gentry and other upper-class rural dwellers who borrowed in distress, whereas the sources describe the persecutors of the Jews as urban and poor. Such individuals might well have been clients of Jewish pawnbrokers, their pledges subject to lawful seizure for default, who therefore would not have shown up as litigants in the district court.[24]

There is other evidence connecting indebtedness to the Jews with persecution. An example are the reports of the massacre of Jews in York, England, in 1190. It was during a time of heightened religious tension fueled by calls for another crusade to the Holy Land. In 1189, a riot against the Jews of

London was touched off by an incident that occurred during the coronation of Richard I. After the king's departure for the Continent, to prepare an army for the assault on the Holy Land, other English cities witnessed violent assaults on the Jews. The worst occurred in York, where scores of Jews died, after which the community temporarily disappeared from historical records. Accounts of the events in York in 1190 by Christian chroniclers state that a primary motive for the attack was the wish of some baronial families to wipe out their debts to Jewish moneylenders. They accomplished this by massacring Jews, moneylenders, and others and by destroying the bonds of their indebtedness where they had been deposited.[25] R. B. Dobson has suggested that the massacre in York was part of the growing baronial revolt against the encroachment of royal authority, a revolt that culminated in the signing of the Magna Carta in 1215.[26]

For other reasons, moneylending proved a risky business for Jews. Beginning in the thirteenth century, the economic florescence of northern Europe during the High Middle Ages attracted Christian moneylenders to the credit business. These provided stiff competition for Jewish pawnbrokers. As foreigners originating in southern France (the town of Cahors) or in Italy (lumped together under the name *Lombard*), Christian pawnbrokers were disliked as much as Jewish usurers. They were condemned by the church for violating the ecclesiastical ban on loans at interest between Christians. Despite the antipathy toward the Lombards and Cahorsins, Christians in need of cash turned to them out of necessity. They were very active during the thirteenth and fourteenth centuries; as a source of loans free of the stigma of borrowing from religious inferiors, they eroded Jewish income eked out from the only significant walk of life left open to them in the later Middle Ages.[27]

To make matters worse, the church's opposition to the open, embarrassing flaunting of usury among Christians spilled over into an ecclesiastical assault on Jewish usury. Popes beseeched secular rulers to compel Jewish moneylenders to remit usury collected from Christian borrowers.[28] The famous anti-usury canon promulgated at the Fourth Lateran Council explicitly maligned Jewish moneylenders for "exhaust[ing] the financial strength of the Christians" and restricted them to moderate interest rates, a concession to the need for credit in Europe's ever-expanding economy.[29]

The papal campaign against usury—first Christian, then, with particular intensity, Jewish—won only sporadic acceptance at the courts of Europe's secular rulers, who alone had the authority to enforce the ecclesiastical order. Where the papal call fell on receptive ears, Jewish economic well-being was devastated. In England in 1275, King Edward I and Parliament put an end to Jewish usury altogether by ruling that Jews henceforth would apply themselves to more productive occupations. This reform failed, however, because it was not accompanied by a relaxation of discriminatory restrictions, such as the exclusion of Jews from merchant and craft guilds (which made it impossible for Jews to succeed in commerce and artisanry).[30] Moreover, heavy tallages continued to be imposed on the Jews despite their ever-shrinking income from loans—until, finally, outright confiscation of Jewish property and outstanding debt bonds remained the only method of extracting additional money from the Jews. This set the stage for the general expulsion and spoliation of the Jews of England in 1290.[31]

Dire, too, were the consequences for French Jewry of the ecclesiastical anti-usury crusade. King Louis IX (1226–70) determined to extend royal authority in order to achieve his ideal of a kingdom ruled by a pious Catholic monarch. Mindful of the papacy's strong opposition to usury, whether practiced by Christians or Jews, the king exceeded Rome's call for the elimination of the "heavy and immoderate usury" charged by Jews. He zealously pursued an economic policy aimed at undermining the livelihood of Jewish moneylenders in his realm.[32]

The economic crackdown on the Jews in France was part of a general policy of reducing Jewish resistance to conversion to Christianity. The policy included an attack on the Talmud, enforcement of the church ruling that Jews wear distinctive garb, and heavy taxation. Louis's policy of making life for the Jews intolerable to the point of conversion continued under his son, Philip III (1270–85). Philip's son, Philip IV "the Fair" (1285–1314), escalated the Capetian dynasty's anti-Jewish policy. Wishing to purify France for Christianity, in need of money, and convinced that Louis IX's policy of burdening the Jews while tolerating their presence had failed, Philip the Fair resolved to expel them after taking the draconic measure of confiscating their possessions.[33]

Christian debt to Jewish moneylenders was a deleterious factor in the Jewish-Christian relationship during the Middle Ages. Though important for the growth of the economy and the relief of distress, and grudgingly tolerated for those reasons, moneylending contributed mightily to anti-Jewish feelings and even to violence. By the end of the twelfth century, the word *Jew* had come to mean "moneylender." A Latin neologism of the early Middle Ages, *judaizare,* originally applied to Christian imitation of Jewish ritual, now came to mean lending at interest. Hatred of the Jew intensified as a result of the association of usury in Christian minds with the twin evils of heresy and the Devil; and the subject of Jewish usury came to occupy an important place in both disputations and Jewish apologetical and exegetical works.[34]

The dangers inherent in this state of affairs are summarized by Joseph Shatzmiller:

> [The] Jews' involvement in moneylending made them subject to restrictive legislation and to hostile political actions, not to mention social opprobrium and physical violence. Things went from bad to worse in the thirteenth century. But medieval people were never absolutely clear about what they wanted to do in the matter of usury. The Christian ideology of economic modesty was well and alive, indeed; and the wish to relieve those oppressed by usurers was no doubt genuine. But at the turn of the fourteenth century, individuals probably could not have imagined a world without a widespread and well-entrenched credit system.[35]

This assessment of the general trend of hatred generated by Jewish moneylending is not undermined by Shatzmiller's own new findings. Based on a study of the trial of a Jewish moneylender early in the fourteenth century, Shatzmiller concludes that there could be a "relaxed, cordial relationship between the moneylender and his client."[36] Shatzmiller's evidence comes from Marseilles, in the south of France, where Jewish-Christian relations were better than in the north and more similar to the improved situation of the Jews of Islam.

This review of the economic factor in Christian-Jewish relations suggests that Jewish security in northern Latin Christendom followed a course inversely proportional to the general economic well-being of society at that time. The early Middle Ages saw a dimming of the last vestiges of the economic florescence of urbanized Roman civilization and its replacement by a predominantly rural economy, soon to be restructured into the web of socioeconomic relations we call feudalism. Also in turn, this retarded economic progress. In the same early Middle Ages, Jewish economic fortunes were in ascendance, as Jewish merchants played a dominant role in international trade. Though despised and feared by most because of their profession and their religion, Jews nonetheless were protected by pragmatic kings and barons.

With the economic rise of Europe in the twelfth and thirteenth centuries, Jews, displaced by Christian mercantile competitors, were increasingly relegated to the hated profession of moneylending while, at the same time, being squeezed economically by the rogue Christian usurer. There is evidence that Jews continued to prosper from moneylending, although they may have expended larger and larger portions of their income on taxes, confiscations, or bribes. More important, the support temporal rulers accorded Jewish moneylending angered Christian debtors of the Jews, which only increased the hostility of Christians toward the Jews. As the economy expanded, secular rulers, responding to church objections to Jewish usury, withdrew their support for Jewish credit transactions. This, too, had an adverse effect on the Jews—efforts at routing them into other occupations having failed to alter their economic plight.

The inverse relationship between Jewish security and general economic well-being in Latin Christendom contrasts sharply with Jewish life under Islam. There, Jewish economic well-being and physical security correlate directly with economic trends in society as a whole. This was only one symptom among many of the extent to which the Jews were embedded in the economic and social order of the larger Muslim world in which they lived.

In the Islamic World

Islam and the Mercantile Life

In the thirteenth century, Jacob b. Elijah of Venice, a Jew, left his home in France for Venice and settled later in the Muslim East. Blaming Christians for the concentration of Jews in moneylending, Jacob compared the Jewish plight in Christian lands to their more favorable economic situation in Muslim countries. In a well-known polemical letter to Pablo Christiani, a Jewish apostate, Jacob wrote:

> Among the Orientals, each person makes his livelihood from whatever is his occupation. And, while Arab rulers may be wicked and sinful, they do possess reason and understanding. They take a prescribed tax each year, from the older ones each according to his seniority and from the young ones each according to his youthfulness. It is not this way in our lands nor is it done in our place that way. Our kings and princes think only how to assail and fall upon us, in order to take away our gold and silver.[37]

Jacob thus tells us that Jews living in Muslim lands enjoyed occupational diversification and that the taxes Oriental Jews paid were fair rather than arbitrary and exorbitant. Though simplistic, his comparison is accurate, and it shows that, even in the Middle Ages, Jews sensed that the contrast between Jewish well-being in East and West had much to do with economics.

A brighter picture emerges from an examination of the economic factor in Jewish-gentile relations in the Islamic world during the early and High Middle Ages. In contrast to their coreligionists in Christendom, the Jews of Islam were well integrated into the economic life of the larger society. Measured against the European standard, the relative absence of economic discrimination against Jews in the Muslim world during the classical centuries makes a vivid impression. What circumstances determined this reality? How did they affect other aspects of Muslim-Jewish relations?

In the Christian West, the Barbarian invasions had snuffed out what remained of the dwindling long-distance trade of late Roman antiquity. Islam, by contrast, appeared on the scene at a time when commercial exchange over considerable distances was entrenched in the conquered areas of southwest Asia and North Africa. Pre-Islamic Arabians had participated in the caravan trade linking spice-rich southern Arabia with the markets of Egypt, Byzantium, and Syria. Muhammad was born and reared in Mecca, a wealthy trading emporium in northern Arabia. The city was home to a pilgrimage shrine, the Kaʿba, symbol of the city's importance as a way station and marketplace for merchants traversing the north-south trade axis. Muhammad's tribe, the Quraysh, played a central role in the mercantile economy of pre-Islamic Arabia. The young Prophet-to-be frequented Syria on trading journeys with his uncle. He married a wealthy merchant (named Khadīja), who enabled him to trade on his own account, in partnership with a nephew of her former husband.[38] Thus, it is not surprising that nascent Islam, in contrast to Christianity, asserted a positive attitude toward commerce.

In the Qur'an, God praises gain through commerce. For example, "It is no sin for you that ye seek the bounty of your lord [by trading]" (Sura 2:198). In the following utterance, usury (disapproved) and commerce (approved) are contrasted: "Those who swallow usury cannot rise up save as he ariseth whom the devil hath prostrated by [his] touch. That is because they say: Trade is just like usury; *whereas Allah permitteth trading and forbiddeth usury*" (Sura 2:275). In the words of Maxime Rodinson, the Qur'an "looks with favour upon commercial activity, confining itself to condemning fraudulent practices and requiring abstention from trade during certain religious festivals. The Koran . . . says that it is proper to combine the practice of religion and material life, carrying on trade even during pilgrimages, and goes so far as to mention commercial profit under the name of 'God's bounty.'"[39]

Similarly, Muslim traditions encourage profitable commercial activity. For example,

> The best of gain is from honorable trade and from a man's work with his own hands.
>
> The honest, truthful Muslim merchant will stand with the martyrs on the Day of Judgment.
>
> I commend the merchants to you, for they are the couriers of the horizons and God's trusted servants on earth.
>
> Nine-tenths of livelihood is trade; the tenth is livestock.[40]

The ideological encouragement of trade, firmly established in both the Qur'an and the *ḥadīth,* carried over into the realm of Islamic law as it gradually took shape during the early Islamic period. Most important, the jurists who compiled Islamic law were themselves merchant-scholars.[41]

They took into account the needs of the merchant as they formulated the laws relating to commerce. Even Ibn Taymiyya, the conservative Muslim theologian of the late thirteenth, early fourteenth century, attached "very great importance to individual freedom in economic behaviour." In a *fatwā* (responsum) he wrote: "We believe that Allah has permitted earnings (*makāsib*), trades (*tijārāt*), and industries (*ṣināʿāt*) and He has prohibited fraud and injury."[42] Unlike medieval Christian religious thinkers who extolled the virtues of poverty, in keeping with Jesus' teachings, Ibn Taymiyya does not praise indigence. He believed, rather, that "man should seek prosperity and independence, since these are necessary for the fulfillment of a number of obligations and religious duties."[43]

It is an overstatement to claim that Islam is innately compatible with capitalism, as Weber, Tawney, and others argue for Protestantism and as Sombart, with antisemitic overtones, asserts about Judaism. But Maxime Rodinson's *Islam and Capitalism* speaks a large measure of truth about Islam's positive disposition toward profit-making enterprises. Rodinson points out that, in the Muslim milieu, there was less ideological resistance to the constant striving for profit than in the Christian West. Whereas both classical Christianity and classical Islam condemned lucre, there were "subtle and significant divergences." Christianity condemns avarice—namely, the striving for anything beyond one's needs. "For Islam the stress is laid rather upon the good use to be made of one's possessions, the merit that lies in expending them intelligently and distributing them with generosity—an attitude more favourable to economic expansion than that of the Christian theologians."[44]

The compatibility of Islamic law and theology with profitable economic activity both resulted from and contributed to what Goitein calls the "rise of the Near Eastern bourgeoisie."[45] The advent of a middle class occurred centuries before a similar development in Europe. The enterprising trade of early Islam resulted primarily from the rapid creation of a vast, unified empire with considerable resources and a great demand for goods. By the ninth century, the Islamic world possessed a flourishing trade and was employing sophisticated instruments of credit for converting capital into profit—something the medieval West did not achieve until the High Middle Ages.

The Jew as Merchant

It is difficult, if not impossible, to overstate the significance of Islam's positive attitude to urban life and trade for the predominantly urban-dwelling Jews. Such a viewpoint gave them, by association, more status and a higher degree of integration than they could achieve in northern Europe, where the prejudice against merchants (and against the towns, in which they lived) relegated the urbanized, Jewish trader to the status of an alien, marginal character—the model of "the stranger" sketched by the sociologist Georg Simmel. The Arab world saw many people constantly "on the move," also in contrast to the sedentary West. Hence, Muslims did not view the long-distance trader as an alien. With so much access to world markets, Islamic merchants had no reason to consider Jews competitors. In the period of economic florescence (through the twelfth century), Jew and Muslim shared the fruits of commerce without the fear—prevalent among Christian merchants of the European "commercial revolution"—that one might diminish the other's profits.

One finds evidence of Jewish integration into the international trade of early Islam in sources describing Jewish merchants from "the land of Radhan" in Iraq, the center of the Islamic empire, beginning in the middle of the eighth century. By the beginning of the tenth century, a Jewish consortium in Baghdad had accumulated great wealth. Headed by two merchant-bankers—Joseph b. Phineas and Aaron b. Amram—whose origins seem to have been in the province of Ahwaz in southern Iraq, the consortium became attached to the Abbasid caliphate at Baghdad as a provider of loans and other banking and mercantile services. The vital services of the merchant-bankers are described in Arabic chronicles and other sources. (We met Joseph's son-in-law Neṭira at the court of the Abbasid caliph in Chapter 4.) These individuals represented a significant class of Jews from the eastern Islamic lands; along with their Muslim counterparts, they fueled the commercial revolution of the early Islamic centuries.[46]

Before, but especially after the Abbasid Empire began to disintegrate (ninth century), commercial opportunities in the expansive Islamic empire drew countless merchants from the eastern provinces to the new Mediterranean "frontiers." From the time of the conquest of the Mediterranean lands and of Spain, great numbers of traders from Iran and Iraq, Jews among them, migrated westward and established themselves in the multitude of Islamic cities and towns that dotted the Mediterranean. This migration of Jewish traders must be distinguished from the migration of Jewish merchants from the domain of Islam to the western European orbit during the early Middle Ages. The movement within the Islamic world was, first, part of a general phenomenon in which Muslim merchants transferred their commercial operations from East to West.[47] Second, Jewish merchants were not viewed as aliens, as they were in Europe; for one thing, indigenous to the Near East, they were largely indistinguishable physically from their Arab-Muslim neighbors. Jewish immigrants enlarged the Jewish population of Palestine, Egypt, North Africa, and Spain and laid the foundations for prosperous communities that culminated in the establishment of independent religious institutions and a devotion to scholarship that paralleled and eventually superseded ancient sources of Jewish authority in Palestine and Babylonia.

One of the most famous Jews to come from the East and flourish in the Islamic frontier lands of the West was Yaʿqūb ibn Killis. Born in Baghdad in 930, he accompanied his father to the busy commercial town of Ramla, in Palestine. There, Ibn Killis served as a representative of merchants. This important, officially recognized post in the Islamic world of commerce involved legal representation of foreign merchants, storage and marketing of goods of absent traders, and related functions. Goitein, who likens this functionary to the consul of the Italian merchant colonies in the Levant in later centuries, speculates that there was a connection between the Islamic institution and its European counterpart.[48]

Apparently, Ibn Killis had to flee to Egypt to escape charges that he had mismanaged funds belonging to merchants. In Egypt, he became an economic official in the service of Kāfūr al-Ikhshīdī, a quasi-independent ruler. After converting to Islam, Ibn Killis went to North Africa, where he joined the Fatimid court. He accompanied the Fatimid ruler al-Muʿizz on his triumphal march to Egypt following the Fatimid conquest of 969. In Egypt, Ibn Killis served as a principal builder of the Fatimid financial administration, finally attaining the coveted post of vizier, which he retained almost continuously until his death in 991. The former Jewish vizier maintained relationships with his erstwhile coreligionists, some of whom attended the weekly intellectual salon he hosted in his personal court.[49]

The Tustarī family is another example of the spread of Jewish commerce from East to West. The family originated in Tustar in southwestern Iran, then the center of a flourishing textile industry. Arabic sources refer to them as the Banū Sahl al-Tustarī ("sons of Sahl the Tustarite"). By the third decade of the eleventh century, we find three brothers from this family settled in Old Cairo, where they were active in the jewel trade. Of the three, Abū Saʿd and Abū Naṣr, like Ibn Killis a century earlier, rose to positions of political influence at the Fatimid court. They had commercial dealings with merchants far beyond Egypt's borders, including merchants of Iraq and people in their Persian homeland. Abū Saʿd reached the pinnacle of his influence at court during the regency of the mother of the caliph al-Mustanṣir, which began in 1036. A wielder of considerable power by virtue of his relationship with the queen mother (originally a slave girl whom he had sold to al-Mustanṣir's father), Abū Saʿd fell victim to political intrigue and was assassinated in 1047. Unlike Ibn Killis, Abū Saʿd remained Jewish. It was long debated whether the family were Rabbanites or Karaites. In a monograph on the family, Moshe Gil presents new evidence of their Karaite adherence.[50]

The Tustarīs were merchants whose fame and proximity to the corridors of power earned them a place in Arabic chronicles. In the Geniza they appear both as merchants and as leaders of the Jewish community. The Geniza's value, however, lies equally in the detailed picture it provides of the working lives of hundreds of Jewish merchants who flourished in the relatively open, nonexclusive economy of Egypt and other Mediterranean countries during the High Middle Ages of Islam. After studying these documents, Goitein came to the conclusion that the Jewish merchants of the Geniza papers pursued economic activities in complete conformity with the mercantile practices of the time. This view has been fleshed out by A. L. Udovitch, who studied the classical Islamic law of partnership and the commercial instrument known as the *commenda* (the Latin name by which it was known in Europe). The *commenda* was a mutual loan whereby one party put up capital and the other contributed his time and work as agent, trafficking with the investor's contribution. Udovitch proved that what seems theoretical in Muslim juristic sources of the eighth century was practiced in real life by eleventh- and twelfth-century Jewish merchants represented in the business correspondence and related documents of the Geniza. He concludes that Muslim merchants in the early centuries of Islam followed customs tailored to their professional needs and analogous to the law merchant of medieval Europe. This customary law of the merchants was absorbed into Islamic law at the time of its classical development.[51] The same phenomenon occurred among the Jews.

The case of the *suftaja* well exemplifies a parallel development in Islam and in Judaism. The *suftaja* was a letter of credit issued by one party to be used by the bearer to collect payment from a party in another city who had an obligation toward or who held funds belonging to the issuer. Muslim merchants followed this custom extensively to avoid the risks of transporting specie. Because the *suftaja* had no basis in Islamic law, it needed official sanction, lest Muslim merchants feel they were transgressing. Some authorities disallowed it, but the otherwise conservative jurist Ibn Taymiyya accepted it, saying "the Prophet never prohibited the thing which is useful and beneficial and people need it."[52]

Jewish legal opinion shows similar awareness of the "law of the merchants" and the indispensability of the *suftaja*. Witness this Geonic responsum in Judaeo-Arabic:

> There is no basis in our law for sending the *suftaja,* since our rabbis have stated [in the Talmud, Bava Kamma 104b]: "One may not send money in the form of a letter of credit [*diyokne* (from Greek), used in the geonic period to designate a document for transfer of money] even if witnesses have signed it." However, having seen that people do business with one another using it, we began ruling on its basis [i.e., admitting it in court], lest trade among people cease. We rule on its basis, neither adding to it nor subtracting from it [i.e., "exactly"], in accordance with "the law of the merchants" [*ḥukm al-tujjār*].[53]

This remarkable congruence between Muslim and Jewish economic practice, as well as the shared judgment of Muslim and Jewish legal experts regarding the necessity for flexible response to "the law of the merchants," could occur only in a market atmosphere that knew no confessional boundaries and did not exclude minorities. Samuel Stern argues persuasively that commercial and craft guilds of the European variety—corporate and limited to members of the majority faith—did not exist in the early Islamic period, for corporate groups in general were absent.[54]

The easy interaction between Jews and Muslims in day-to-day economic undertakings led to a new leniency regarding Jews who preferred drawing up business agreements and settling disputes in the Muslim religious courts, in violation of the ancient talmudic prohibition against "going to the gentiles' court." To accommodate this reality, legal documents drawn up and witnessed in Muslim courts were routinely admitted as evidence in Jewish tribunals. Resort to Muslim courts was so commonplace that the standard formulary for a power of attorney secured in a Jewish court "indicates whether the attorney is allowed to approach a non-Jewish court in addition or in lieu of the Jewish."[55] He usually was.

A responsum of one of the Babylonian Geonim indicates the extent of the practice of using the Muslim courts among Jews. It further indicates that the practice was tacitly validated by the Jewish judiciary out of a genuine trust in the court of the *qāḍī*.

> This is our opinion: In the city in which we live, Baghdad, the Muslim courts accept only witnesses that are wise, great, and rich, who have never been charged with theft or lying or dishonesty, and who are expert in their law. They are called *al-muʿaddilīn,* "honest" [the technical Arabic term for professional witnesses in an Islamic court]. If these kinds of people acted as witnesses on a deed of sale or loan, and the testimony was set out in their court and was accepted by their judge, we also adjudicate according to that legal document and consider it valid. This is our custom at this time, and it happens daily.[56]

The illustrious Hay Gaon (d. 1038), chief justice, so to speak, of the entire Jewish population of the Islamic world, writes in his "Book on Buying and Selling": "These Muslims treat us with great solicitude and protection."[57]

This attitude contrasts sharply with Ashkenazic policy on litigating intra-Jewish suits before Christian courts. Ashkenazic rabbis insisted on strict adherence to the talmudic prohibition, for fear of prejudicial or dishonest treatment and other indignities.[58] They also worried that embittered Jews would use the Christian authorities to inform against their brethren.[59] In principle, the Geonim and later halakhic authorities in the medieval Arab world frowned on Jews applying to Muslim courts, and they regularly repeated the talmudic ban. However, realism about the autonomous dynamics of the law of the marketplace, coupled with a certain confidence in the quality of justice in Islamic tribunals, made them flexible in economic matters. In matters of personal status, especially family law, where the need to maintain boundaries between Jews and Muslims was understandably greater, *qāḍīs* often referred litigants back to the Jewish judiciary. At the same time, as Gideon Libson has begun to show, in matters of personal status, the Geonim endeavored to keep Jews loyal to the Jewish courts by consciously absorbing into Jewish law in the form of binding "custom" many procedures and standards of Islamic law perceived to be advantageous—yet another means of accommodation.[60]

The traversibility of boundaries in daily economic affairs echoes throughout Jewish sources for our period. Both the letters of Jewish traders in the Geniza and the rabbinic responsa are filled with casual references to Muslim and Jewish merchants as part of the same, unified, nonsectarian economic community. The relatively relaxed ambience of interfaith relations in the Islamic marketplace created trust, which in turn encouraged partnerships for profit between members of the Jewish minority and their friends among the Muslim majority. Rabbinic authorities often received queries about partnerships between Jews and Muslims, because these dealings frequently gave rise to questions of Jewish law, such as whether the Muslim partner's working on the Jewish Sabbath required special arrangements for distributing profits from transactions concluded on that day.

Louis Ginzberg published some leaves from a collection of Geonic responsa containing several that deal with interdenominational partnerships. One concerns "a Jew who made a partnership with a gentile [i.e., a Muslim] who manned the store and made sales on Saturday."[61] The ruling in such cases, following the Talmud, was that Saturday's profits belong to the non-Jew alone (with some kind of compensatory assignment of another day's profits to the Jew) and that the method of distribution had to have been agreed upon by the partners in advance.[62] An interdenominational partnership in agriculture raised questions about possible transgression of biblical precepts should the Muslim plow on the Sabbath using the jointly owned animal or muzzle the beast or couple an ox with an ass. The ruling, which Ginzberg labels "lenient," disqualifies the arrangement only with respect to Sabbath plowing, because an animal possessed by a Jew must be allowed to rest on the Sabbath as commanded in the Torah.[63]

A responsum of Maimonides presents yet another variant.

> Some people who are partners in a workshop are engaged in the same craft, some of them being Jews and some of them gentiles [i.e., Muslims]. The partners agreed that the Friday [proceeds] would belong to the Jew and Satur-

> day's to the gentile. The tools of the workshop are pooled, and the craft is either silversmithing or glasswork. Is it permitted to him [the Jewish partner] that they divide the profit even though they [the tools] have been put to work on Saturday? Or, should they render account for the days on which work was completed and deduct the portion [of Saturday] when he [the Jewish partner] leaves it [the workshop] to the gentile?

Maimonides sustained the arrangement agreed upon by the partners. The profits of Saturday and Friday would belong to the Muslim and the Jew, respectively, and the agreement did not disqualify the partnership on the grounds that jointly owned implements might be used on the Sabbath.[64]

Reciprocally, Islamic law discusses the case of partnership, or *commenda,* with a non-Muslim. The dominant view permits it provided the Muslim retains control over what is bought and sold. In other words, the Muslim must be the agent and active partner. The legists reason that the non-Muslim, as agent, might traffic in items forbidden to Muslims, like pork (a Christian partner, obviously) or wine, or employ a contract that is invalid according to Islamic law. Another concern stemmed from the fact that non-Muslims practiced usury, and a Muslim should not be a party to such a violation of Islamic law. A more stringent opinion condemns interfaith partnerships as reprehensible, since they lead to friendship.[65] This last opinion shows that sociability between Muslim and infidel partners was a common by-product of interdenominational business dealings.

A query to Maimonides about a case involving a Jew and his Muslim business partner indicates that Muslims who engaged in interdenominational partnerships did not necessarily observe the Islamic requirement that they serve as the trafficking agent. Here, the *Muslim* acted as investor and the Jew, as his agent.

> Concerning a Jew in whose hands was money of a gentile [i.e., a Muslim] as a *commenda.* He [the Jewish agent] bought some merchandise and wished to sell it for a *dīnār* [this means: as a cash sale], the buyer being Jewish. The [Muslim] investor would not allow a cash sale, but rather [wanted] deferred payment [*al-ṣabr*] at a higher price. Is it permissible for the Jewish agent to accept the additional money or not?

The issue before the Jewish legal authority was not the interdenominational partnership per se but the matter of usury between Jews ("interest" consisted of the difference between the price of the moment and the higher figure charged for the convenience of deferring payment). The Jewish agent might be seen as taking interest from another Jew, in violation of the law of the Torah. Maimonides permitted the transaction, using the rationale that the real vendor was the Muslim investor, not the Jewish agent.[66]

Credit in the Economy

Credit transactions struck deep roots in the interdenominational monetary economy of the Near Eastern marketplace. In keeping with the practice of merchants, both Muslims and Jews engaged extensively in credit transactions, in spite of the appearance of usury.

This situation begs comparison with the Latin West. At first glance, it seems similar to its analog in Christendom. Islam's view of usury compares favorably with that of Christianity. *Ribā,* as it is called in Arabic, is forbidden already in the Qur'an. "O ye who believe, devour not usury, doubling and quadrupling" (Sura 1:130). Elsewhere (4:161), even interest taken by Jews is specifically condemned, the verse apparently referring to the biblical injunction against usury between Jews. Yet, Islamic law, originating as it did during the Middle Eastern commercial revolution and compiled by merchant-scholars necessarily au courant with the "law of the merchants," allowed the *ribā* ban to be circumvented by various legal fictions. A favorite method involved disguising loans as capital investment. The *commenda* often served this purpose. In practice, the agent earned his share of the profits because he invested time and work. The portion of the proceeds he returned to the investor along with the original capital looked very much like interest on a loan, but it was sufficiently indirect to be excluded from the Islamic prohibition of overt usury.

Characteristic of the accommodation of law to economics in Islam, jurists recognized that without such credit arrangements, including deferred payment at a higher price, the economy would be stifled.[67] In the words of an eleventh-century Muslim jurist:

> We hold that selling for credit is part of the practice of merchants, and that it is the most conducive means for the achievement of the investor's goal which is profit. And in most cases, profit can only be achieved by selling for credit and not selling for cash.[68]

Almost echoing the Muslim jurist, the great Maimonides upheld a case of deferred payment at an increased price in a transaction between Jews: "Such is the custom in business dealings of people with one another, and were it not for this, most means of livelihood would cease."[69]

Among themselves, Jews regularly adopted the Islamic *commenda* for long-term commercial enterprises because it was more flexible than a similar instrument in the Talmud for circumventing usury between Jews called *'isqa*. The Jewish religious courts recognized the "gentile *commenda*" as valid. Like the Islamic legists, they, too, regularly condoned the deferral of payment for goods sold to another Jew in return for a higher price, a way around the prohibition of loans at interest between Jews.

The Jew as Moneylender and Debtor

As they did in Europe, Jews in the orbit of Islam also engaged in moneylending. In a revealing contrast with Europe, however, the main arena for Jewish credit transactions in the Islamic world during the period was *within* the Jewish community. Like Muslim merchants, Jews involved in trade needed to have access to capital, and Jews with capital were reluctant to supply it unless they could make money on it. There was, to be sure, some lending on interest to the non-Jew, which biblical law expressly permitted (even though it was discouraged by the Geonim, like their rabbinical counterparts in Europe).[70] But the reverse was also true: Jews regularly borrowed on interest from Muslim moneylenders.[71] Far from exceptional is the instance recorded in a Maimonidean responsum of a Jew who "owed money to gentiles [Muslims] and fled from them" with the result that the Muslim creditor demanded payment from the fugitive's brother and guarantor.[72]

Differing again from the practice in Christian lands, Jewish moneylending activities were diverse and not concentrated in consumption loans to strapped gentiles. The prominent bankers to the Abbasid court described earlier performed myriad banking functions for their Muslim lords, not just loans. Even their loans showed variety: some stipulated actual interest while others took the form of advances in cash to be recouped through tax-farming.[73] Loans on interest to Muslims, despite their permissibility in Jewish law, are rarely mentioned in the Geniza documents. Goitein notes the obvious contrast with Europe:

> Moneylending to Gentiles has found hardly any mention in the mass of private and business letters, court records, and accounts preserved in the Geniza. Instructive in this respect is also a comparison of the responsa and other legalistic literatures of the medieval rabbis of France and Germany with those of their Near Eastern predecessors and partial contemporaries. . . . While the legal and moral questions created through usurious lending to Gentiles occupy enormous space in the works of the former they play no role in the writings of the latter.[74]

The theme of the malevolent Jewish moneylender is, nonetheless, not absent from Arabic literature. One of the arguments of a thirteenth-century Muslim polemicist against *dhimmī* service in government is based on the fact that they "hold that interest may be taken from those who are not of their religion." Significantly, this hostile writer does not object to the principle in Islamic religious terms (as was the case in Christendom) but rather to the resulting financial exploitation of Muslims.[75]

Economic Diversification

We have devoted most of this discussion of economic activity of the Jews of Islam to trade, paying some attention to its adjunct, moneylending, because of the stark contrast with the Christian West, where Jews found themselves out of conformity with their surroundings. They played an alien role as traders in the early European Middle Ages, as unwanted competitors in commerce later on, and finally, most damagingly, as detested moneylenders. But another major difference between the economic profile of eastern and western Jewry also adds to our understanding of the improved lot of the Jews of Islam. I refer to their broad economic diversification. Neither the Islamic economy nor the attitude of Muslims toward Jews restricted the latter to a narrow range of occupations. Our main source, the Geniza, probably gives disproportionate weight to merchants because it is they, more than others, who wrote letters filled with or soliciting information needed to conduct business affairs.

At the same time, the Geniza proves that Jews made a living from industrial crafts. An appendix to Goitein's *Mediterranean Society* shows Jews involved in dyeing, metalworking, weaving, bread-baking, winemaking, manufacture of glass vessels, tailoring, tanning, production of cheese, sugar manufacture, and silkwork.[76] Where financially possible, Jews owned agricultural land, and many raised crops in the arable Egyptian countryside. Jews owned and worked orchards and date groves. Some assigned gentile sharecroppers to work their fields, vineyards, and orchards.[77] In short, far from occupying predominantly one economic niche, Jews in the Islamic world during our period were broadly distributed throughout the various sectors of the economy. The more differentiated they were, the more they appeared like others around them, including the Muslim majority. This variegated economic profile, much more diverse and much more widespread than Blumenkranz claims for early medieval Jewry in the Latin West,[78] militated against the social abuse that Jews in Christian lands had to endure in part on account of their identification with a limited and problematic set of occupations.

The Anthropological Study of the Traditional Islamic Marketplace

Anthropologists studying the position of Jews in the economy of the traditional Arab marketplace in our own time have sketched a picture that can easily be imposed on the historical evidence for the Islamic High Middle Ages. Clifford Geertz's classic study of the marketplace of Sefrou, Morocco, in which Jews figured prominently, is a case in point. Geertz observes, for instance, that "Jews mixed with Muslims under uniform ground rules, which, to an extent difficult to credit for those whose ideas about Jews in traditional trade are based on the role they played in premodern Europe, were indifferent to religious status."[79] Further, "the distribution of Jewish merchants and artisans across the economic class structure was, to the degree one can measure it, very similar to that of the Muslim."[80] Regarding the same market of Sefrou, Lawrence Rosen writes that Jews did not occupy a set of distinctive trades or crafts,

> as has been the case in many other instances of Jewish economic organization in the non-Jewish world. Rather, the Jews of Sefrou, with a few exceptions, were engaged in most of the same crafts and businesses as the Muslims, almost always side by side with them in the part of the bazaar where such practitioners were located. . . . To the Muslim the Jew in Sefrou society was, therefore, both an individual who could be dealt with in terms of many of the same concepts and negotiated ties employed in relationships with a fellow Muslim and a member of an inferior religious community with whom full ties of reciprocity were inapplicable.

This, concludes Rosen, was the key to Jewish security in the Sefrou environment.[81]

Writing about "trade as a mediator in Muslim-Jewish relations" in the Moroccan port city of Essaouira (Mogador) in the nineteenth century, Daniel Schroeter applies to a historical case the observations and analysis of such anthropologists as Rosen and Geertz. In spite of the many boundaries dividing Jews from Muslims, most notably the residential segregation of Jews in the mellah (a kind of ghetto), "on a business level Jews interacted with Muslims in the wide open spaces of the urban market. . . . [N]either penetrated into the other's private sector, but both were free to trade and even interact socially in the business sector."[82]

> In the urban markets, ethnic barriers were broken down. Jewish traders were subject to the same administration as were their Muslim counterparts. In the town of Essaouira, Jewish commercial activities in the bazaar came under the surveillance of the *muḥtasib* just as did Muslim activities. Jews were free to rent shops from the *habous,* the Muslim religious endowments. The requirements of business overrode religious differences.[83]

The conclusions of Geertz, Rosen, Schroeter, and others resonate with evidence from the medieval Jewish-Arab world. The embeddedness of Jewish commercial activity in the Islamic lands depicted in the Geniza, the relative absence of boundaries between Jew and Muslim in the marketplace, the considerable occupational diversification of the Jews, and their detachment from the detested role of usurious moneylender allowed for decent human relations between Jewish and Muslim merchants. This transcended confessional differences and prevented the emergence of an irrational stereotype of the type that captured the popular imagination in northern Europe, where most Jews occupied an economic niche that put them at odds with the Christian population.

Letters from Jewish Traders

Some excerpts from the commercial correspondence of medieval Jewish traders, as translated by Goitein in his collection, *Letters of Medieval Jewish Traders,* round out our description of the Jewish place in the vibrant trade of the Islamic High Middle Ages.

The first excerpt comes from a letter of about 1010, addressed to the head of the Tustarī family firm of merchants, Sahl, the father of Abū Saʿd and Abū Naṣr. The writer was head of another family partnership, the Tahertī brothers of Qayrawan, Tunisia, who had two more brothers in Old Cairo, where the Tustarīs lived. The passages speak of trade in expensive textiles and of interplay with Muslim merchants.

> The cloaks sent by you have arrived, and I wish to thank you for your kindness and exertion in the matter. You noted also that the rest of the order had been carried out. All you have sent, my lord, is fine, but I wish to ask you to buy everything all over again, for the three robes striped with curved lines, as well as the white robe which I wanted to have for me as a mantle, were taken from me by a man who imposed on me. . . .
>
> I would like the robe to be deep red, as red as possible, and the white and yellow also to be of excellent color. I did not like the color of the yellow which arrived. . . . The best robes manufactured are the old ones. . . .
>
> I have another wish, my lord. Should a caravan set out in which trustworthy Muslims, who have given you sureties, will travel, let the merchandise of my brothers be sent with them as if it were yours. They would profit from this in many respects.[84]

The next letter comes from a Jew involved in India trade. He "mailed" his missive from the African port of ʿAydhab (in modern Sudan), a stage on the India route, to his son in Alexandria, Egypt. He relates that he has forwarded for sale in Egypt Indian goods acquired in the market of ʿAydhab. The proceeds were to be distributed to various partners before the remainder was dispatched to his family in Alexandria. The writer also mentions his Muslim traveling companions. His emphasis on the importance of rendering accounts is typical. In one sentence, he refers anxiously to "profit," which was *the* goal of all commercial enterprises. Goitein surmises that he had had discouraging news while in ʿAydhab about the current state of the India trade.

> Please take notice that I acquired 330 pounds of lac out of the pepper, brazilwood, and lac available here in ʿAydhab, for they sold the brazilwood and pepper to the Muslims and took the price, but assigned to the Jews the lac and some cash ["gold"]. I have not left cash for other shipments. Two dinars went for packing, canvas, and ropes, . . . one third for a sari, as a gift, and two-thirds . . . [word omitted by mistake]. One dinar was taken by the elder Abū 'l-Faḍl b. Abū 'l-Faraj al-Dimyāṭī for the expenses for the lac. He carries the lac, a copy of the account, and the list of the distribution [to the partners]. He will deliver all this to my lord, the illustrious elder Abū Zikrī Judah, the Kohen—may God make his honored position permanent. He will kindly sell everything and deliver his share to everyone; he will send the balance to you, and you will also deliver his share to everyone. He also will send you the account. . . .
>
> Know, my son, that this voyage will not bring much profit, unless God, the exalted, ordains otherwise.[85]

The Jews of the Midi

Reciprocal comparison of the economic factor in Jewish-gentile relations in northern Christendom and in Islam supports the hypothesis that a vibrant commercial economy contributed directly to the relatively greater security of the Jews of Islam and inversely to the deterioration of interfaith relations in the northern European world. A useful comparison, which provides additional confirmation of these findings, brings in yet another element, namely, the case of the Jews of southern France (the Midi).

Mediterranean Christendom, most agree, offered a much more hospitable environment to Jews than the northern reaches of Europe.[86] Jewish communities of the South experienced much less persecution and over all lived in more placid, integrated fashion with their surroundings than their northern European brethren. They were less segregated from Christians, and their economic activities varied, from moneylending to small- and large-scale trade, including long-distance commerce. Jews also worked as toll-gatherers in association with Christians and in land-transfer brokerage.[87] Though moneylending was the dominant profession, in Languedoc Jews also engaged in many other occupations, such as agriculture (either as landowners or as tenant farmers), artisanry, commerce (butchery, cereals), peddling, brokerage, medicine, public offices. And they owned immovable property, whether in the form of agricultural land, houses, or artisan or commercial establishments.[88]

Jewish moneylending seems to have had less dire consequences for Christian-Jewish relations in the Midi than in the North, Joseph Shatzmiller argues in *Shylock Reconsidered*. As mentioned, documentation about the trial of a Jewish moneylender from Marseilles at the beginning of the fourteenth century evidences cordial relations between Christians and Jewish usurers, according to Shatzmiller. He points to the favorable character testimony by twenty-four Christians from a wide variety of classes in defense of the Jewish moneylender Bondavid de Draguignano, whose adversary in litigation was a Christian debtor who claimed, probably falsely, that he had repaid his debt.[89]

The good relations between many Jewish moneylenders and their Christian clients to which, according to Shatzmiller, the testimony of the character witnesses in this trial attest probably did little to counteract the negative stereotype of the evil Jewish moneylender to which most Christians subscribed, even in the South.[90] But the findings of his "micro"-study of Jewish economic life in the Midi, viewed together with other findings of our comparative analysis of Jewish-Christian and Jewish-Muslim relations in the economic sphere, suggest that heterogenity in Jewish economic life was a crucial agent tempering anti-Jewish feeling. Other features peculiar to southern Europe similarly seem to have made Jewish life there less frightful than in the North and more akin to Jewish life in the lands of Islam. In southern Europe, as mentioned in Chapter 3, continuity with the Roman past and a sharper memory of Roman legal traditions contributed to the relative security of the Jews as compared with their status in the northern communities. So, too, the antiquity of Jewish settlement in the South—bordering on indigenous habitation and resembling the native status of Jewry in Arab lands—contributed to a more tolerant atmosphere. As we turn now in Part Four to "the social order," deepening the comparative analysis of how Jewish-gentile relations worked in Christian and Muslim lands during the Middle Ages, we shall again return briefly to the case of southern France to support the argument that factors outside of religion could both exacerbate and moderate the innate religious intolerance of the societies in which Jews lived.

PART FOUR

In the Social Order

Chapter Six

HIERARCHY, MARGINALITY, AND ETHNICITY

Hierarchy and Marginality

Hierarchy

In *Homo Hierarchicus,* the French social anthropologist Louis Dumont, studying the caste system in India, draws some important implications for the social order of premodern societies.[1] Dumont argues that the fundamental idea unifying societies composed of a multiplicity of groups and statuses is *hierarchy,* that hierarchy, more than power, determines how the elements of such a society interact. Hierarchy is "the principle by which the elements of a whole are ranked in relation to the whole, it being understood that in the majority of societies it is religion which provides the view of the whole, and that the ranking will thus be religious in nature."[2] The hierarchical relationship is that "between encompassing and encompassed or between ensemble and element."[3] Paradoxically, the elements of caste systems—and, by extension, the components of any stratified society—manage to coexist more or less harmoniously precisely because each knows that it and all the other subgroups of the population are part of a totality. Differences are accepted as natural in a fully formed, or "ideal-type" hierarchical society, of which the Indian caste system is the best-known example. This, Dumont says, explains the tolerance toward others often noticed among Indians or Hindus.

> It is easy to see what this feature corresponds to in social life. Many castes, who may differ in their customs and habits, live side by side, agreed on the code which ranks them and separates them. They will assign a rank, where we in the West would approve or exclude. . . . In the hierarchical scheme a group's acknowledged differentness whereby it is contrasted with other groups becomes the very principle whereby it is integrated into society.[4]

Medieval Christians had ways of talking about the social order and the place, if any, of the infidel or nonconforming Christian in that order. They were conscious of *status* rather than *class.* Thinkers spoke in terms of hierarchies—who was above whom. At the beginning of his history of the hierarchical concept of the "three orders" (those who pray, fight, and labor) in medieval Christendom, Georges Duby quotes the words of Pope Gregory the Great to describe the "necessary inequality" of the social order:

> Providence has established various degrees and distinct orders [*ordines*] so that, if the lesser show deference to the greater, and if the greater bestow love on the lesser, then true concord and conjunction will arise out of diversity. Indeed, the community could not subsist at all if the total order of disparity did not preserve it. That creation cannot be governed in equality is taught us by the example of the heavenly hosts; there are angels and there are archangels, which are clearly not equals, differing from one another in power and order.[5]

Jeffrey Burton Russell's description of the principle of "right order" in medieval Christian society complements Dumont's formulation:

> There were three social hierarchies, the feudal-manorial, the urban, and the ecclesiastical. Within this ordered society, every institution and every person had *libertas*. The meaning of *libertas* was quite different from the meaning of "liberty" now. It meant the right—and the duty—of an individual to occupy his proper place in society.[6]

In terms of its social structure, medieval Islam is less easy to define than Christendom. A considerable body of modern scholarship has endeavored to show how analogies with the West frequently do not work. Feudalism and corporation are fundamental characteristics of European society now generally believed to have been absent in Islam, at least in the form known in the West, and in the classical medieval centuries. On the other hand, the notion of hierarchy—while neglected—can aptly be applied to Islam. At the beginning of a discussion of "Islam and the social order," a leading Islamic historian regrets that "the problem of the hierarchies is one of those rarely touched on by orientalists except from the slightly different angle of 'social classes.'"[7] Few orientalists, however, would dispute the notion of hierarchy as appropriate in an analysis of the position of non-Muslims in Muslim society.

Marginality

To hierarchy, which marked the social order of the two societies in which the Jews lived during the Middle Ages, must be added the element of *marginality*. As refined by certain sociologists, "marginality theory" describes a type of hierarchy in which members of a group "(1) do not ordinarily qualify for admission into another group with which, over varying lengths of time, it is more or less closely associated; (2) when these groups differ significantly in the nature of their cultural or racial heritage; and (3) between which there is limited cultural interchange or social interaction."[8] In a "marginal situation"—unlike caste systems with their ideal of permanent or total group exclusiveness—there is some permeability of the barriers (or boundaries) separating elements in the hierarchy.[9] While both marginality and exclusion engender or reflect intergroup tensions, marginality expresses a less alienated relationship between the subordinate group and the larger society.[10]

Hierarchy, Marginality, and Medieval Jews

The concept of marginality that best describes the position of the Jews in the Middle Ages is one that "refers to the fairly long-lasting, large-scale hierarchical situation in which two or more groups or even nations exist together."

> The groups vary in degree of privilege and power and there is inequality of status and opportunity. The barriers between the groups are sufficient to prevent the enjoyment by the subordinate group, or groups, of the privileges of the dominant, non-marginal group, but do not prevent the absorption by the former of the latter's culture.[11]

Not infrequently, subordinate strata resist the absorption of some feature of the dominant group's culture that is incompatible with their own value system.[12] This, too, fits the Jewish condition in the medieval diaspora.

Hierarchy, Marginality, and the Jews of Medieval Christendom

The Jews can be said to have begun at the bottom of the hierarchy in Christendom, but in a marginal situation. As the historian Bernhard Blumenkranz has shown,[13] there was considerable social interchange between Jews and Christians during the centuries between the Barbarian invasions and the rise of the crusading spirit in Latin Europe. Spatially, the Jews were not excluded; they lived relatively close to and peacefully with their Christian neighbors. The Jews probably engaged in amicable debate about religion with learned Christians. Here and there, Jews held public office. In time of warfare, they could be found standing side by side with Christian comrades in armed defense of their towns. The Jews maintained their own cultural identity by resisting attempts to convert them and by rigorously enforcing Judaism's ancient taboo against marriage outside the Jewish community.

Even in this relatively tranquil period in Christian-Jewish relations, however, the idea of excluding Jews from Christendom was not absent. In an oft-cited letter of Pope Leo VII (r. 936–39), appointing a certain Frederick archbishop of Mainz, the pope responds to Frederick's query "whether it is better to subjugate [the Jews] to the holy religion or expel them from your towns." The pope responds by urging his vicar to strive to convert the Jews through preaching (though not by force). If, however, they refuse to accept baptism, the archbishop possesses delegated authority to expel them, "for we ought not to associate with the Lord's enemies."[14]

Until the eleventh century, Pope Leo's view had little practical import. The church retained only limited influence over mundane, or even spiritual, affairs in the world at large, and Jews enjoyed substantial support from secular rulers interested in exploiting their economic utility. True, a Latin source relates that the German emperor Henry II expelled the Jews from the town of Mainz in the year 1012. They were allowed to return several weeks later, though, and there is no evidence that Henry's act was more than a local affair.[15] It is thought that he was retaliating for the apostasy earlier that year of a deacon and cleric named Wecelin.[16] Nonetheless, the event of 1012 was a harbinger of the more definitive and traumatic expulsions to come during the High and late Middle Ages. It underscored the tenuous dependability of the Jews' presumptive right to reside among Christians.

With the rise of the crusading spirit and the deepening of Christian consciousness and piety in the population at large beginning in the eleventh century, Jews were gradually excluded from society. As infidels, they were considered "outside the church" (*extra ecclesiam*); practically speaking, this meant they were not subject to ecclesiastical jurisdiction. In his *Decretum,* Gratian, the great canonist of the twelfth century, reinterpreted a Pauline saying in the New Testament to support this position:

> Their [the infidels'] punishment, however, is left for divine judgment alone, when we cannot exercise discipline over them, either because they are not subject to our law or because their crimes, although known to us, nevertheless cannot be proven by clear evidence. As for those who are not of our law, the Apostle says in the First Epistle to the Corinthians; For what does it concern me to judge those who are *outside* [*his qui foris sunt*]? God will judge them.[17]

Canon law grouped Jews together with other peoples, especially pagans and heretics, with whom contact was discouraged. As we have seen, this clustering of Jews with other subordinate groups, implying guilt by association, was already present in Christian-Roman Jewry law. Medieval canon law included precepts excluding these outsiders from the rights held by Christians in courts of law. Gratian's *Decretum* declares that "pagans, heretics or Jews cannot sue Christians."[18] Probably influenced by Roman and canon law, Germanic law disqualified Jews, along with heretics and unbelievers, from "being spokesmen of a man and of standing in court against a Christian."[19]

Common, too, was the tendency to lump Jews together with lepers, an association that reinforced their status as outsiders.[20] At about the middle of the thirteenth century, as we have seen, the ecclesiastical decree of the Fourth Lateran Council, requiring that Jews exhibit an identifying sign on their clothing, began to be implemented. Secular rulers responded, albeit unevenly, to the church's call, ruling that Jews must sew different distinguishing marks on their outergarments. Because special attire was prescribed for abhorrent groups such as prostitutes, Christians could not help but consider the Jews' special sign as also a mark of degradation and exclusion.[21] Symbolically, too, descriptions of the role of the Jews in the ceremony of welcoming a king or bishop upon his entry into his city turn from integrative—with "the Jews as part of the community like any other, and often dispersed among it"—to exclusionary beginning in the twelfth century, "a change in the welcoming ritual, whose effect was to exclude them from the political community."[22]

We may conclude that, over time, Jews, as they came to be excluded from the hierarchy of the Christian social order, lost the benefits of their marginal situation. By the thirteenth century, Jews in the Latin West no longer conformed to Dumont's model of hierarchy based on relations "between encompassing and encompassed or between ensemble and element." Neither Christians nor Jews felt that the latter were integral to society, that they were an encompassed element of the encompassing whole. By that time, the universalism of the encompassing whole had been tempered by a "Christian particularism, the primitive solidarity of the group and the policy of apartheid with regard to outside groups." None of the complex models subdividing Christendom into socioprofessional "estates" which increasingly came to characterize the social order from the beginning of the thirteenth century had any place for the Jews.[23]

True, the centuries-old Augustinian tradition that Jews have a role to play in Christian soteriology (as witness to the superiority and chosenness of the Christian faith) continued to assure the Jews of their low rank in the hierarchy of Christian society. The Augustinian theology, however, faced powerful countervailing political, economic, and social forces. The Augustinian tradition did not protect the Jews of the late Middle Ages from exclusion. Once they were no longer tolerated on even the lowest rung of the Christian hierarchy, the groundwork was laid for the widespread explusionary policy of the thirteenth to fifteenth centuries.

Hierarchy, Marginality, and the Jews of Medieval Islam

Turning now to medieval Islam, the question can be asked: What of hierarchy and marginality there? Did the Jews (and other non-Muslims) occupy an organic place in the hierarchy of the Muslim social order? Or did they, like their counterparts in the Christian world, come to be excluded from the prevailing society? It is possible to read the Pact of ʿUmar as a document that imposed exclusion on the *dhimmīs,* since it required that they distinguish themselves from Muslims by special garb and certain behavior. In reality, the regulations of the Pact were intended not so much to exclude as to reinforce the *hierarchical* distinction between Muslims and non-Muslims within a single social order. Non-Muslims were to remain "in their place." They were to avoid any act, particularly any religious act, that might challenge the superior rank of the Muslims or of Islam. The *dhimmī,* however, occupied a definite slot in Islamic society—a low rank but a rank, nevertheless. Like Hinduism, Islam recognized and accepted difference as a natural concomitant of the hierarchical order of social relationships.

The inclusion of non-Muslims within the Muslim hierarchy is affirmed in the most fundamental distinction between insiders and outsiders in Islamic thinking—the division of the world into two parts: the House, or Domain, of Islam [*dār al-islām*]; and the House, or Domain, of War [*dār al-ḥarb*]. The Domain of War borders on the Domain of Islam, and Muslims are commanded to wage *jihād* (holy war) against unbelievers living outside Islamic territory, forcing them to choose between Islam and the sword. A non-Muslim native of the Domain of War may enter Islamic territory—for instance, on business—under a guarantee of safe conduct.[24] But this is a temporary protected status only. Ranking above these *musta'mins* are the permanent non-Muslim inhabitants of the Domain of Islam, the *ahl al-dhimma* (the Protected People) who benefit from a third option: the privilege of paying tribute in return for security and the more or less free exercise of religion, without compulsion to convert.[25] Thus, marginal though they were, the Jewish and Christian *dhimmīs* occupied a recognized, fixed, safeguarded niche within the hierarchy of the Islamic social order.

Hanafite law—one of the four canonical, or orthodox (Sunni) schools of Islamic jurisprudence—expresses this well. A chapter comparing the juridical status in Muslim courts of legal documents of non-Muslim *musta'mins* and *dhimmīs* states the following regarding inheritance law:

> The position of the *ahl al-dhimma* vis-à-vis the *musta'mins* is the same as that of the Muslims vis-à-vis the *ahl al-dhimma, for they belong to our Domain* [*li'annahum min ahli dārinā*] in contrast to the *musta'mins*. For this reason, too, a *dhimmī* slave shall not be left in the possession of a *musta'min* so long as he stays among us. Rather, he shall be compelled to sell him, just as a Muslim shall not be left in the possession of a *dhimmī*.[26]

The position is asserted more explicitly, though in passing, in another Hanafite compendium: the punishment for brigands is said to apply equally to Muslims and *dhimmīs,* "because they belong to our Domain permanently" [*ʿalā al-ta'bīd*].[27]

The concept of a hierarchy that encompasses *dhimmī*-Muslim relations can be inferred from terminology used in medieval Islamic discussions of the *dhimma*.[28] The most common descriptive for the *dhimma* system is *ṣaghār,* derived from the final word in the Qur'anic verse prescribing the *jizya* payment, *ṣāghirūn*. As we have seen, many commentators on the Qur'an, as well as other medieval scholars, understand this to prescribe a symbolically humiliating act. An authority as important as Ibn Qayyim al-Jawziyya, however, rejected all those meanings, favoring, instead, the more fundamental notion that *ṣaqhār* refers to non-Muslim submission to the authority (laws) of Islam [*iltizāmuhum li-jiryān aḥkām al-milla ʿalayhim*], symbolized each time he rendered payment of the poll tax.[29] Ibn Ḥazm, the eleventh-century Spanish-Muslim litterateur and jurist, spelled this out three centuries earlier:

> The *ṣaghār* means that they are subject to the authority of Islam [*yajrī ḥukm al-islām ʿalayhim*] and that they shall not expose publicly anything of their unbelief [*kufr*] nor anything that is forbidden in the Islamic religion. . . . The *ṣaghār* is summed up by the "Stipulations of ʿUmar," may God be pleased with him because of these.[30]

Clear hierarchical ranking of groups within the one totality underlies these characterizations of the fundamental relationship between non-Muslims and Muslims.

The people subjected to *ṣaghār* are marginal but not excluded, for the *dhimmī* may cross boundaries to participate in a wide range of activities along with the dominant Muslim group so long as he behaves according to his lowly rank. Though manifest in economic activities, it extended to cultural interchange, service in the government bureaucracy, and the medical profession. In other words, the presence of Jews and Christians in a marginal situation *within* the hierarchy of Islam constitutes a structural feature of its social order.

Conventionally interchangeable with the term *ṣaghār,* another cluster of Arabic words used to describe the relationship between Muslims and *dhimmīs* seems to soften the impact of their lowly rank. The most common such term is *ghiyār*.[31] Sometimes the synonym *tamyīz,* signifying differentiation or distinction, occurs. In the first instance, *ghiyār* stands for the distinctive dress required of non-Muslims, but by extension the term also connotes the entire system of differentiation between Muslim and non-Muslim.[32] Less imperious than *ṣaghār,* a word straight from the pugilistic Qur'anic *jizya* verse, *ghiyār*/*tamyīz* suggests the possibility of "horizontal" relationships between differentiated ethnoreligious groups, separated yet parallel, coexisting with Muslims who have shared interests, despite the hierarchical sense conveyed by *ṣaghār.*

Indeed, actual social relations, shaped by the marginal situation of the *dhimmīs,* somewhat alleviated the discriminatory intent of the regime of *ṣaghār.* On the basis of sources for tenth- and eleventh-century Iraq, Roy

Mottahedeh describes how clerks, soldiers, and merchants (as well as physicians) formed recognizable groups manifesting loyalties that bound them to one another in the pursuit of common interests.[33] These "categories," as Mottahedeh calls them, were not guilds of the European variety with strict confessional criteria for admission. Indeed, the Muslim world had nothing like the guilds of the medieval West.

Dhimmīs, it is crucial to state, could be found in nearly all categories of Islamic society, working alongside Muslims who outranked them by virtue of their religion. They appear as merchants, artisans, agriculturalists, physicians, government clerks (*kātibs*), and in any one of a number of other categories identified by their professions (excluding the army, with the notable exception of Samuel ibn Nagrela, head of the Berber army of Muslim Granada in the mid-eleventh century, who was also vizier, a post hardly ever granted to a non-Muslim). In such situations, *ghiyār* let everyone know who was a non-Muslim and who was a Muslim. The "loyalties of category," to use Mottahedeh's terminology, extending across the Muslim–non-Muslim distinction, doubtless softened the discrimination incorporated in the concept of *ṣaghār.* Being a Jew (or a Christian) in these usually prestigious categories somewhat offset their low status in the overall hierarchical scheme.

Arabic sources often refer to the Jews as *ṭā'ifat al-yahūd* or even *sharīʿat al-yahūd. Ṭā'ifa,* a term common in medieval Arabic, stands for some sort of social category.[34] It usually connotes a subgroup of Muslim society, individuals bound together by a common interest, and is often translatable in political contexts as "faction."[35] The petty rulers who divided up the Umayyad caliphate of Cordova when it collapsed at the beginning of the eleventh century are called *mulūk al-ṭawā'if* (party-kings).[36] Among the Jews, in classical Islamic times, the two main factions, the Rabbanites and the Karaites, are regularly referred to as "the two *ṭā'ifas*" [*al-ṭā'ifatayn*] in Judaeo-Arabic Geniza texts and elsewhere. Alternatively, the term might designate an entire Jewish community, as when a record of testimony in an Islamic court refers to the leader as *al-rayyis ʿalā ṭā'ifat al-yahūd,* "head of the Jewish community," meaning, from the Muslims' perspective, head of the subgroup of society known as the Jews.[37] The use of such a nonpejorative, generic term to designate the Jews seems to temper the hierarchical relationship encompassed in such terms as *ṣaghār.*

A more striking term used to refer to the Jews of Islam is *sharīʿat al-yahūd,* "the *sharīʿa* of the Jews." *Sharīʿa* means "way" or "path." The equivalent of the Hebrew *halakha,* it stands for the holy religious law of Islam (*sharīʿat al-islām*). Its use in Muslim texts, referring to Judaism, reflects recognition of a certain religious parity between Judaism and Islam. This, in turn, conforms to the idea of the Prophet himself, that Judaism—and Christianity—have parity with Islam as divinely inspired religions.

A similar blurring of qualitative distinctions between Judaism and Islam is perceptible in Jewish texts. Jewish scholars readily employed Islamic religious terminology in their Judaeo-Arabic writings. Saadya Gaon, the first great rabbinic figure to write in Arabic, could refer unself-consciously to the Torah as *sharīʿa,* the Hebrew Bible as *Qur'an,* the direction facing Jerusalem while praying as the *qibla,* and the prayer-leader (*ḥazzan*) as *imām.*[38] As Andrew Rippin shows with reference to a chapter in Saadya's Arabic translation of the Bible, the Gaon employed the target language in a way that displayed an attitude of integration toward the surrounding Arabic-Islamic culture.[39]

Exchanges of halakhic questions and responsa employed Arabic phraseology similar to that found in Islamic *fatwās.* A question would open with *mā yuftīnā* (what is your answer to us . . .), using the verbal form of the noun *fatwā;* the Judaeo-Arabic responsum itself would include formulaic phraseology (even if in Hebrew translation—a conspicuous sign of assimilation) characteristic of Islamic responsa.[40] On the basis of Geniza evidence, Goitein suggests that the Jews recognized the institution of jurisconsult (*muftī*), separate from that of the judge (*dayyan*) and paralleling the distinction in function between the *muftī* and the *qāḍī* in Islam.[41] We may imagine that the considerable similarity between Jewish and Islamic law, the analogous way in which each legal system operated in daily life, and the shared universe of linguistic discourse in such fundamental religious and social domains—all enhanced the potential for decent human relations when Jews drew on the possibilities inherent in their marginal situation to associate with Muslims of similar professional category.

I have applied considerations of hierarchy and marginality to our subject to arrive at a new theoretical approach to conceptualizing the place of the Jews in the social order of the two societies in which they lived in the Middle Ages. Summarizing and evaluating the discussion so far, the following can be stated. Within the "natural" hierarchical social orders of medieval Christendom and Islam, Jews had a recognized place, albeit at a very low rank. Egalitarian assimilation was not a possibility, but neither the ruling group nor the subordinate Jews wanted integration. The former perceived it as contrary to "right order," while the latter viewed it as a threat to communal and religious solidarity. Nevertheless, the marginal situation associated with hierarchy offered numerous opportunities for positive interaction. Whereas Jews as a group occupied a recognized, low rank in the medieval hierarchy, individuals were capable of crossing barriers.

For Jews in Christendom, marginality degenerated into exclusion during the long period from the early to the High and especially late Middle Ages, as they were increasingly restricted to residential quarters (not yet ghettos), physically assaulted, forced to abandon Judaism, murdered individually or in groups, and expelled. Islamic society allowed Jews and Christians the benefits of living in a marginal situation within its hierarchical social order, but the marginal situation had greater staying power there. And, it did not degenerate into exclusion via expulsion.

Ethnicity

Light can be shed, I believe, on the reasons for the more favorable position of the Jews of Islam by examining the Jewish-gentile relationship through yet another sociological lens, that of ethnicity. Historically, ethnic heterogeneity has been much more characteristic of the medieval Orient than of the medieval Occident. Arabs, Iranians, Turks, Kurds, Berbers, Jews, Christians, Zoroastrians, and others populated the social landscape, giving society a richly hued human and cultural texture. Further, the *dhimmī* group exhibited heterogeneity within its own ranks, with two (in some places, three) nonconforming religions coexisting in the same area. Discrimination and theological contempt by the dominant group were thus more widely distributed, hence somewhat more diffused among these, which made intolerance less onerous for each group. Ethnic differentiation—a counterforce to the exclusivism inherent in "national" homogeneity of whatever kind—was a major factor in preserving the embeddedness of the Jews and Christians in the Arab world and preventing them from being totally excluded from the social order.

Ethnic depiction of the medieval Islamic social order comes from the anthropological study of contemporary traditional Muslim societies. Carleton S. Coon, one of the early anthropologists to write about the Middle East, recognized and characterized the ethnic nature of Middle Eastern society with the metaphor of "mosaic."[42] Most contemporary anthropologists consider this terminology inadequate, finding that the mosaic model fails to take into account the dynamic nature of intergroup relations, that it oversimplifies reality, and that it offers little insight into the historical processes that led to ethnic group formation.[43] Many would, nonetheless, agree that some of the core insights in Coon's analysis remain useful for depicting the operation of the ethnic factor in traditional Arab-Islamic society.

Discounting the inappropriate reference to race, we can learn much about the medieval relationship between Muslims and Jews (or Christians) from Coon's description:

> In the old Middle Eastern culture . . . the ideal was to emphasize not the uniformity of the citizens of a country as a whole but a uniformity within each special segment, and the greatest possible contrast between segments. The

> members of each ethnic unit feel the need to identify themselves by some configuration of symbols. If by virtue of their history they possess some racial peculiarity, this they will enhance by special haircuts and the like; in any case they will wear distinctive garments and behave in a distinctive fashion. Walking through the bazaar you have no trouble identifying everyone you meet, once you have learned the sets of symbols. These people want to be identified. If you know who they are, you will know what to expect of them and how to deal with them, and human relations will operate smoothly in a crowded space. . . . This exaggeration of symbolic devices greatly facilitates business and social intercourse in a segmented society. It saves people from embarrassing questions, from "breaks," from anger, and from violence. It is an essential part of the mechanism which makes the mosaic function.[44]

Fredrik Barth's work on ethnicity adds an important nuance that clarifies the role of ethnicity in modulating hostile intergroup behavior in the Middle Eastern context:

> Ethnic distinctions do not depend on an absence of mobility, contact and information, but do entail social processes of exclusion and incorporation whereby discrete categories are maintained *despite* changing participation and membership in the course of individual life histories. Secondly, one finds that stable, persisting, and often vitally important social relations are maintained across such boundaries, and are frequently based precisely on the dichotomized ethnic status.

And:

> The persistence of ethnic groups in contact implies not only criteria and signals for identification, but also a structuring of interaction which allows the persistence of cultural differences. . . . Stable inter-ethnic relations presuppose such a structuring of interaction: a set of prescriptions governing situations of contact, and allowing for articulation in some sectors or domains of activity, and a set of proscriptions on social situations preventing inter-ethnic interactions in other sectors, and thus insulating parts of the cultures from confrontation and modification. . . . Where social identities are organized and allocated by such principles, there will thus be a tendency towards canalization and standardization of interaction and the emergence of boundaries which maintain and generate ethnic diversity within larger, encompassing social systems.[45]

Barth's formulation fits well the situation of the medieval Middle East. In the Islamic social order, people belonged to groups characterized by distinguishable ethnic traits. They lived alongside other ethnic groups. For Muslims of different ethnic origins, membership in the Islamic *umma* complemented ethnic identity. Creating and maintaining boundaries that reinforced ethnicity and regulated relations with other ethnic groups was a goal or mechanism of the social order, and this included the *dhimma* system. In their religious and ethnic particularity, Jews conformed to a basic norm of the social order: they defined themselves vis-à-vis others just as others defined themselves vis-à-vis the Jews and other dissimilar groups.

Udovitch and Valensi have illustrated this culture of differences in traditional Islamic society through field work among a modern vestige of classical Jewish-Arab interethnic coexistence. They write that "the paradox of a community which was at once so intensely and completely Jewish and at the same time culturally so thoroughly embedded in its Muslim, North African environment promised to tell us something important about both Jews and Muslims and about their interaction in the present and in the past."[46]

Through external signs such as distinctive clothing, dialect of Arabic, choice of personal names, innovation in the architecture of domestic space, and adherence to the Jewish calendar, to give a few examples, the traditional Jews of Jerba ensured their differentiation from Muslims. This, in turn, reinforced their ethnic and religious identity and secured their position as a community paralleling and successfully interacting with the dominant group. Social differentiation extended to the marketplace, where Jews interacted most frequently with Muslims. "Although the ethnic and religious boundaries separating Muslims and Jews are by no means absent or obliterated in the marketplace, it is here that the lines of demarcation are most fluid and permeable," write Udovitch and Valensi.[47] In the economic transactions between Jews and Muslims, a certain measure of trust and familiarity were presumed, as well as a common respect for "the Law"—that is, religious law, a property that reinforced Muslim confidence in Jewish honesty in economic affairs. Udovitch and Valensi maintain that this image of the "honest Jew," embodied in the Arabic notion of *ḥaqq al-yahūd* (the law, the justice, the honesty of Jews) underlies the entire realm of Jewish-Muslim interethnic intercourse: "It expresses a vision of organic integration into a system of life in which the fact of their Jewishness becomes a paramount element even in the mundane pursuit of their daily bread *and the basis for their relations with Muslims*."[48]

In his study of economic life in Sefrou, Morocco, Clifford Geertz lists as one of the basic givens, or "characteristic ideas," of the "mosaic" pattern of social organization in Middle Eastern society the fact "that non-Muslim groups are not outside Muslim society but have a scripturally allocated place within it." On the question of diversity,

> Middle Eastern Society . . . does not cope with diversity by sealing it into castes, isolating it into tribes, or covering it over with some common denomi-

nator concept of nationality. . . . It copes . . . by distinguishing with elaborate precision the contexts (marriage, diet, worship, education) within which men are separated by their dissimilitudes and those (work, friendship, politics, trade) where, however warily and however conditionally, men are connected by their differences."[49]

With specific reference to Sefrou, he says: "The Jews were at once Sefrouis like any others and resoundingly themselves." Not "a set-apart pariah community, deviant and self-contained, though they were as certainly that too. Moroccan to the core and Jewish to the same core, they were heritors of a tradition double and indivisible and in no way marginal."[50]

Complementing the model of hierarchy and marginality, these anthropological findings can be applied to medieval Muslim society. In part, they explain what appears to be a tolerant, intergroup relationship between Muslims and non-Muslims. This becomes clearer when we again turn to the Latin Christian West for comparison and contrast.

In the early European Middle Ages, ethnicity was an important factor in what, compared to the later period, was a time of substantial acceptance of the Jews. Considerable ethnic heterogeneity characterized the Barbarian period. Visigoths, Franks, Lombards, Burgundians, and other Germanic tribes coexisted, each tolerating ethnic diversity and distinctive customary law while, at the same time, recognizing the ethnic distinctiveness and separate legal tradition of the native Roman populations. As in Islam, such ethnic heterogeneity, coupled with the existence of large areas of still unchristianized pagan peoples in the Slavic lands of central and eastern Europe, created an environment in which the Jews could be somewhat "tolerated" despite their religious nonconformity and cultural and legal distinctiveness. Here again, ethnicity was an integral part of the social order.[51]

By the eleventh century, ethnic diversity had receded as a significant factor in Christian-Jewish relations. With the completion of the conversion of the last pagans living in western and central Europe, and the concomitant spread of the notion of a unified, universal, Catholic social order, the Jews, already alien on account of their religion, came even more to be viewed as outsiders. As the ethnic diversity of the Barbarian period gave way (to be sure, in England more so than in France) to a somewhat more homogeneous society bound together by Christianity, the exclusivistic imperative implicit at all times in Christian religious theory rose to the fore and pushed the Jews further toward exclusion. In many cases, exclusion turned out to be a way station on the path to the elimination of Judaism through conversion of the Jews or through their expulsion. This did not happen in Islam.

Hierarchy, marginality, and ethnicity belong to the realm of social scientific theory. They do explain, however, some basic differences in Jewish-gentile relations in Christendom and in Islam. But where shall we turn to view Jewish-gentile relations in action (apart from the marketplace)? In the next two chapters, I attempt to do this in a preliminary way, discussing life in the medieval town and interpersonal sociability.

Chapter Seven

THE JEW AS TOWNSMAN

SOME JEWS lived in rural areas, where they engaged in agricultural pursuits, both in Islamic lands and in Europe. The vast majority, however, inhabited towns. A comparison of the Jew as townsman in Christendom and in Islam yields insights into why the Jewish-Muslim relationship generated less hatred and persecution than the encounter between Christian and Jew.

IN THE CHRISTIAN WORLD

Scholars no longer believe that the Barbarian invasions destroyed the urban life of the Roman Empire. Although a decline had indeed begun by the period of the late empire, towns continued to exist in attenuated form. The legacy of Roman urbanism was an underlying element of urban growth during the Middle Ages.

On the whole, life was predominantly rural and agricultural. By the early Middle Ages, "the former Roman centres [had] turned into islands amidst a world which [had] become predominantly rural." Although the "town as a residential centre had survived the age of tribal migrations in some particularly important sites of the Rhine, Meuse and Moselle valleys, . . . the distinctively urban way of life with its special contribution to civilization had not survived." The trading centers (called *wiks*) that appeared for a period of two centuries during the Merovingian and Carolingian periods "constituted alien enclaves within the Carolingian world rather than organically belonging to it."[1]

Oriental long-distance traders (Jews and Syrians; later, Jews alone) could be found living in settlements that were much diminished in area and population, as well as political and cultural importance. Traders were an alien, mercantile presence within a social environment itself considered alien by the larger society.

Only as trade began to revive in the tenth century, and as the commercial revolution took hold in the eleventh, did commercial urban centers sprout anew (or expand on old foundations). Most of the Christian inhabitants of these settlements were traders accustomed to considerable freedom, which was fundamental to their profession. They were also equipped with a body of customs—the "Law Merchant." Hence, in many places, merchants petitioned the monarch or feudal seigneur for urban liberties exceeding those granted most others in society. Later, organized burghers demanded formalization of self-government in the form of charters. Many central authorities—be they royal, aristocratic, or ecclesiastical—opposed the evolution of towns into independent "corporations," legal bodies with their own laws and customs and a judiciary separate from the court of the overlord.[2] The struggle to achieve emancipation from the lord of the town had some successes beginning in the twelfth century, a process that complicated the normal feudal arrangement.[3] In England, the pattern of town origin and growth in the early Middle Ages may have differed somewhat from that on the Continent.[4] There were no Jews in England, however, before the Norman Conquest of 1066. By that time, the process of evolution (toward some measure of formal corporate independence and self-government) resembled social developments in northern Europe—often to the dismay of society as a whole and against the trend toward centralized feudal authority which, in England, was the monarchy.

A stigma attached to the innovation represented by the town. Towns "were new things in the scandalous sense which was given to this adjective in the middle ages" and "a centre of what feudal lords detested: shameful, economic activity."[5] As Ennen observes, the town of northern Europe did not fit into the classic social order of medieval society based on an agrarian relationship between noble and peasant. Urban autonomy, codified in town charters, placed the town outside feudal law. The sworn assemblies of traders that took control of urban affairs throughout Europe beginning in the twelfth century and demanded rights from royal or episcopal overlords represented a revolutionary force.[6]

Presumably, the presence of settled Jews in the suspect, emergent towns of Europe added to the religious and economic background of anti-Jewish sentiment. Moreover, within the urban settlement itself, the Jew was something of an anomaly. While other townsmen fought for and took pride in achieving independence from the lord of the town, Jews continued to hold charters from their overlords and, in some places, to be exempt from municipal jurisdiction.[7] Direct dependence on the king, a baron or duke, or some other authority, reinforced the image of Jew-as-outsider. Moreover, their charters included concessions of self-government, which exacerbated differences between the urban Christian bourgeosie and the semi-autonomous Jews in their midst. True, as some believe, Jews in some of the towns held rights roughly equivalent to those of Christian burgesses. As we have seen, however, even in places where Jews appear to have experienced technical "citizenship," they were excluded from municipal offices and subjected to special taxes—handicaps which diminished their honor in a society in which honor mattered very much.

Yet another anomaly contributed to the exclusion of Jews from the normal social order. They could not partake in that fundamental ritual of urban self-identity, the oath Christian burghers swore, promising obedience to municipal authority and adherence to obligations designed to ensure urban peace.[8] Similarly barred from receiving homage, the Jew had no firm place in either the feudal system or the urban commune.[9]

By and large, Jews in European cities lived separate from Christians, usually in a street or section called a "Jewry," "Jüdengasse," or "rue des Juifs." They chose to live this way for convenience and for the greater sense of security it conferred. Residential seclusion began to impinge on Christian-Jewish relations when the church, wishing to prevent contact between Christians and Jews, especially after the thirteenth century, legislated restrictions on where Jews were allowed to live.[10] Especially during the later Middle Ages, when popular fear and hatred of the Jews grew in intensity and popular antisemitic stereotypes proliferated, the Jewish quarter became a mysterious, frightful place, increasingly the target of terrified, antisemitic Christian mobs. As a sign of the estrangement of Jews from Christian burghers, some towns in the High and later Middle Ages sought from their overlords—and were granted—the privilege of not tolerating Jews. In short, Christian townspeople were allowed to exclude or expel Jews.

Were the Jewish communities themselves—with their charters, leaders, charitable works, and rabbinic law courts—corporations, a kind of town within a town? If they were, how did this fact affect their status? Baron has articulated the view (part of his anti-lachrymose conception of Jewish history) that the Jewish community "was recognized by law as a corporate body apart, entitled not only to regulate its purely religious activities, but also to adjust many civil and political affairs to suit its own needs and traditions."[11] This, Baron believes, offset some of the disadvantages Jews suffered at the hands of Christians. At the same time, Baron recognizes that the peculiar position of the Jews—caught, as they were, in the complexity of overlapping and sometimes arbitrary and self-interested application of the different "laws" to which they were subject—detracted from the "normalization" that corporate status might otherwise have bestowed on them:

> Like the other corporate groups, it lived on the basis of specific privileges which regulated its basic rights and duties, leaving amplification and implementation to local customs. As a rule, the Jewish community enjoyed even fuller self-government than most other corporations. At the same time its rights were often less clearly defined, or willfully disregarded, while its duties were arbitrarily expanded to suit the wishes of rulers. . . . In short, the late

> medieval Jewish community simultaneously appeared as one of the many corporations *within* the European corporate system and as a corporation of its own kind in many ways placed *outside* the framework of general society.[12]

Kenneth Stow argues that the Jewish community in the Middle Ages did *not* constitute a corporation. It was not, he says, integrated into the normal structure of medieval corporate society in the sense of having freedom, independence from outside control, autonomy, and security.[13] However, even Baron does not make such an extravagant claim, nor does Kisch, whose formulation is more to the point. "Developmentally," Kisch asserts, "the Jewish 'corporate bodies' do not represent phenomena analogous to the craftsmen's guilds or other medieval corporations. Rather, did their legal and political status develop from that sum total of basic rights, privileges, and duties accorded them or imposed on them by the holders of political power."[14]

Corporate identity did not extend to the privilege of bringing actions as a community against wrongdoers.[15] In many ways, corporate identity worked in reverse: corporate appearance often encouraged Christian ruling authorities to assign collective responsibility, and even collective punishment, to an entire Jewish community for the real or imagined hostile acts of individuals.[16] More commonly, Jewish corporate status enabled rulers to amass considerable sums of money from their Jewish subjects, money exacted from the community as a whole.[17] Finally, the aspect of corporation dovetailed with the desire of the Catholic church to segregate Jews and thereby reinforce their status as inferior.

The Jews of the Midi

A few words are in order about southern Europe, specifically the Midi (Languedoc and Provence). There, Jews fared better in an urban environment than they did in the north. The contrast anticipates distinctions to be noted for the Islamic world in the next section.

Urban society never quite disappeared from the Mediterranean provinces of the Roman Empire. Unlike their counterparts in northern Europe, the nobility of southern Europe were not cut off from city life.[18] Continuity of urban life, the absence of rigid social boundaries between city and countryside, and an aristocracy receptive to the customs of the town seem to correlate with a greater openness toward the Jew in the south. There, urbanism fit more organically into the social order. In the north, where the town represented a disruption of the traditional pattern of social life and organization, the quintessential Jewish townsman may have seemed more threatening.

Because urban society in the Mediterranean Roman Empire did not suffer the radical break in continuity that befell the north, Jews, similarly rooted in the south since the early Roman imperial period, comprised a more organic part of the urban landscape. In the cities of Languedoc in the twelfth to fourteenth centuries, residential segregation was minimal. Evidence of contiguity of houses in Toulouse shows that Jews lived densely in one particular zone, but Christians were not excluded; this was typical of other towns in the region as well.[19] As Noël Coulet has shown, Jews in the cities of Provence held genuine citizenship, which included the liberties, honors, privileges, and customs accorded Christians.[20] Jewish communities in the Midi reaped more of the benefits and experienced fewer of the liabilities of corporate status than did the Jewish communities of England and royal France.[21] The economic diversification of the Jews of the Midi went hand in hand with the organic embeddedness of the Jew in the southern city, and thus served to temper anti-Judaism there.[22]

In the Islamic World

Resembling more the southern European towns than those of the Christian north, the Islamic city was an original, organic component of Islamic civilization. Whereas the presence of towns in Latin Europe (in the north) resulted for the most part from a process of rejuvenation following several centuries of, at best, attenuated survival, Islamic urbanization accompanied the rise and early spread of Islam. The early Islamic town was either an annexed pre-Islamic settlement or a new foundation. The latter, called *amṣār,* were military outposts that were rapidly converted into proper cities.[23]

The Islamic city was fully integrated into the broader political system—again, differing from its north European counterpart. This harks back to Muhammad's own origins as a townsman in Mecca and as ruler of Medina, the first Islamic city. From the beginning of Islam, there existed an intimate relationship between the ruler and the city. Caliphs always chose a city as their capital; several of Islam's greatest cities owe their origins to royal foundation. Other cities housed military governors and their entourages, who represented the caliph and exercised authority on his behalf.

The historical and political embeddedness of the Islamic town in its surroundings—contrasting boldly with the situation in the northern Christian Occident, where the commune often existed in tension with feudal overlords—bears deep significance for understanding the relatively more comfortable pattern of Muslim-Jewish relations. To be a Jewish townsman in the Muslim world meant to be part of an institution originally a component of the social order rather than part of an organism considered an innovation and encroachment on the power of traditional authority.

In addition (and quite the antithesis of the northern European city), the topography of residence in a Muslim town lent the Jew an aura of inclusion, of normalcy. As a matter of course, residential patterns in a Muslim town set religious and ethnic groups apart. This had already begun with the new garrison towns, in which tribal constituents of the Arab armies lived in separate quarters. Eventually, the division of the Muslim town into quarters became more complex. One historian of urban Islam describes it as follows:

> Almost universally, Muslim cities contained socially homogeneous quarters. Such quarters were found in cities created by a coalescence of villagers, by the settlement of different tribes, or by the founding of new ethnic or governmental districts. Quarters based on the clienteles of important political or religious leaders, religious sects, Muslim and non-Muslim ethnic minorities, and specialized crafts, were also found in cities throughout the Muslim world.[24]

It was no aberration, then, if a town in the Arab world of the Middle Ages had a separate street or quarter inhabited primarily by Jews. In that world, residential separation of ethnic and religious groups was normal—voluntary and generalized throughout society. Thus, no stigma attached to neighborhoods housing predominantly Jews.[25] This contrasts with the Christian town of the north. There, segregation of Jews into separate streets, or "Jewries," accorded with theological and social concerns expressed with renewed vigor during the thirteenth century by instilling suspicion and dread in the popular imagination.

The Geniza provides an even more impressive indicator of Jewish inclusion in Islamic society. In most cities of the Islamic Mediterranean represented in the Geniza, Jewish quarters, in the sense of exclusive Jewish districts, hardly existed. Rather, as Goitein has discovered, most Jews lived in their towns in noncontiguous clusters, such that "there were many neighborhoods predominantly Jewish, but hardly any that were exclusively so."[26] Christians or Muslims often dwelled in apartments in the same compound as Jews, and Jews, Muslims, and Christians sometimes held properties in partnership. Islamic law, for its part, permits *dhimmīs* to dwell among Muslims, the rationale being that the latter might thereby reveal the beauties of Islam to their non-Muslim neighbors.[27] The related issue of whether a Muslim may rent or sell a dwelling to *dhimmīs* (lest they perform acts of idolatry, eat pork, drink wine, and so forth therein) is frowned upon but not prohibited outright.[28]

Propinquity of residence frequently led to friction between Jews and their Muslim neighbors on account of divergent customs and mores.[29] Sometimes the presence of Muslims in a Jewish house interfered with the full halakhic observance of the Sabbath (or the more open presence of women in male society in Judaism clashed with the seclusion of women in Islam). These should not, however, be taken as signs of blatant interfaith hostility. Rather, they are indicative of the easygoing social intercourse between Jews and Muslims in the Islamic Middle Ages—so different from the xenophobia that accompanied social relations between Christians and Jews in the contemporaneous Christian town.

It is clear that the mixing of Jews and Muslims in their residential environment was an extension of intermingling in the marketplace, where "relations of mutual trust and cooperation between members of different denominations were by no means exceptional."[30] While, in Christian lands, Jews often employed an economic double standard in their business dealing with non-Jews (against which responsible rabbis, fearing adverse consequences, preached),[31] the Geniza offers little indication of such discrimination on the part of Jews.

Jewish urban dwellers in the Middle East had a less problematic legal status than did the Jews of Christian northern Europe. Unlike the cities of Christendom, those of Islam did not develop municipal autonomy detached from the universal law of Islam. The debate over whether Islamic cities achieved self-government along European lines seems to have been resolved—in the negative. Perhaps the clearest case for the absence of municipal autonomy in Islam has been made by S. M. Stern, who argues that, at the time of the Islamic conquest, the municipal institutions of Greco-Roman antiquity had already declined, offering nothing for the Arabs to imitate, and that the later gropings toward urban autonomy in some localities fell far short of full autonomy on the western model and never lasted.[32] Stern concluded that the absence of municipal institutions in Islam was simply part of a larger phenomenon: the absence of corporations in general. Characterizing the functioning of Islamic urban society in the absence of such binding force, Stern speaks of the "looseness of its structure." In recent years, the words *informality* and *fluidity* have entered scholarly parlance to describe what is now recognized as the special nature of the Islamic social order.

An ethnic and religious minority group like the Jews could only benefit from this state of affairs. In northern Europe, the Jewish townsman lacked full citizenship according to the system of urban law that bound the Christians burghers into a corporate unity. Thus, he found himself in a marginal situation. In addition, his special tie to royal or baronial authority, through the charter which protected him by defining his rights and obligations, placed him in an anomalous category that did not conform with the social order of the Christian commune. For many Jewish communities in Latin Christendom, this marginality ultimately deteriorated into exclusion. By way of contrast, in the Islamic city there was neither urban law nor corporate autonomy with which the Jew could be out of conformity. Regardless of where Jews lived, one unified law—the obligations and rights of the *dhimma,* itself a part of the universal *sharīʿa*—determined their status. Marginal within the hierarchy of Islamic society, he was; excluded, hence expelled, he was not, nor did he become.

Chapter Eight

SOCIABILITY

DESPITE segregated residence, medieval Jews and non-Jews socialized in both the Christian and the Islamic milieu. It is illuminating to compare the working of sociability in each majority society, as well as how Christians and Muslims reacted to real or potential fraternization with Jews.

IN THE CHRISTIAN WORLD

During the early Middle Ages, Jews and Christians mingled quite freely in Europe. Church councils as late as the eleventh century inveighed against eating or drinking with Jews or staying with them in the same house—sure signs that such sociability occurred regularly.[1] In letters written during the reign of King Louis the Pious, Bishop Agobard of Lyons complains about excesses in Jewish-Christian fraternization. Bemoaning the fact that Christians eat with Jews on Christian fast days, the bishop said that Jews, encouraged by the king, were preaching to Christians about the superiority of Judaism, even blaspheming Christ in the presence of Christians. Many Christians, he added, thought the Jews worthy of respect because of their ancestors. No one, however, should imagine that the Jews were superior to Christians. Rather than being granted such respect, the Jews should be despised and shunned.[2]

As we saw in Chapter 3, the Fourth Lateran Council, under Pope Innocent III, expressed concern about sociability between Christians and Jews. Sexual relations between Jews and Christians are cited as the reason for instituting the requirement that Jews (and Muslims) wear distinguishing clothing. "[I]t sometimes happens that by mistake Christians have intercourse with Jewish or Saracen women, and Jews or Saracens with Christian women."[3] From the combination "Jews and Saracens" it appears that the prelates had Christian Spain (and to a lesser extent, perhaps, Norman Sicily) in mind. In Spain, indeed, Muslims and Jews mingled freely with Christians, continuing the centuries-old habit of interfaith sociability under Muslim rule before the Christian reconquests.

The Lateran Council strictly forbade intermarriage. This restriction had long since been expressed in Christian-Roman Jewry law.[4] The "crime" was treated on a par with adultery, for which the punishment was execution. With the taboo against sexual mixing regularly ignored, legal texts repeated the prohibition.[5] James A. Brundage explains the intensity of concern over sexuality and intermarriage with Jews in medieval Christianity:

> At the center of the vagaries of medieval law concerning Jewish-Christian relations lurked a persistent concern about sexual relations between Christians and Jews. A horror of sexuality haunted much of the canon law of marriage, and the canonists' loathing was particularly acute when they dealt with non-marital sex. . . . The taboo . . . seems also to have been related to a need to assure ritual purity. . . . Contact with Jews not only endangered religious faith, but also blemished the soul and grievously displeased God.[6]

Not surprisingly, Christian aversion to socialization with Jews is prominent in the chapter on the Jews in the thirteenth-century *Siete Partidas,* the seven-part law code of King Alfonso X of Castile. The code was not immediately promulgated, nor did it achieve full application until the mid-fourteenth century. Its twelve statutes on the Jews, however, which were heavily dependent on Roman and canon law, mirror the "checkered relationship between Christians and Jews."[7] In the absence of medieval codes from the northern European kingdoms, the *Siete Partidas* offers the best glimpse we have of consolidated Jewry law as it was envisioned by a learned Christian monarch at the height of the Middle Ages.[8]

On the question of sociability resulting from residence in Jewish homes, the *Siete Partidas* echoes early church councils: "We order that no Jew shall dare to have in his house Christian servants. . . . Furthermore, we forbid any Christian, male or female, to invite a Jew, male or female, nor may a Christian receive an invitation from Jews, to eat and drink together or partake of wine made by Jews. In addition, we order that no Jew shall dare to bathe together with Christians."[9] This sweeping prohibition reflects the concern of official Christianity that Jews might seduce Christians to their religion, blaspheme Christianity, or intermingle sexually with Christians. The mention of Christian-Jewish conviviality over wine reacts against an implicit disparagement of Christianity, for Jewish law required that Jews drink only wine produced by coreligionists and that it be served only by brethren in the faith. Combined bathing glossed over differences in social status and religious affiliation, since all were naked—the infidel disrobed from his outer garments, affixed with their discriminatory sign—and friendships could grow out of the casual conversation carried on in the neutral atmosphere of the bath.[10]

The *Siete Partidas* reiterates the requirement that Jews wear distinguishing marks as a safeguard against inadvertent sexual mingling.[11] Further, Jews are permitted by church and state to live among Christians, but only "that they might live forever as in captivity and serve as a reminder to mankind that they are descended from those who Crucified Our Lord

Jesus Christ."[12] Ultimately, this traditional statement defined the highly circumscribed sociability that could officially be tolerated in medieval Christian society.

William Jordan, followed by R. I. Moore, put it well when observing that the lack of ties created over time by sociability—whether via marriage, conviviality, or the sharing of worship and ritual—deprived the Jews of popular sympathy and even a measure of support against tyranny and extortion sometimes bestowed on other victims of persecution, such as the Christian heretics harassed by the Dominican inquisition.[13]

In the Islamic World

Like Christendom, Islam preferred that its adherents avoid socializing with the inferior infidel *dhimmī.* Nonetheless, Islam—at least, orthodox Sunni Islam—had no comparable ideological or theological rationale for shunning Jews and Christians. For instance, Islamic legal pronouncements link social avoidance of Jews to their historical enmity toward the Prophet. When Ibn Qayyim al-Jawziyya deals with socialization between Jews and *dhimmīs,* he warns Muslims to be on their guard when greeting a *dhimmī.* The non-Muslim infidel is notorious for muttering "may poison afflict you" (*al-samm ʿalayka*) in place of the standard Arabic greeting "peace be upon you" (*al-salām ʿalayka*). The safest reply was, "may it be upon you, too" (*wa-ʿalayka*).[14] The *ḥadīth* literature contains numerous stories in which Muhammad encounters this contemptuous greeting as well as other manifestations of enmity when meeting Jews and Christians.[15] In the main, though, these accounts lack the damaging theological overtones of Christian stories relating Jewish alleged involvement in the death of Jesus.

Largely unfettered by ideological impediments, Muslims socialized with Jews (and other *dhimmīs*) more or less freely, thus establishing bonds.[16] As in the economic realm, so in daily life, ample opportunity arose for Jews, living in a "marginal situation," to cross barriers erected in Islamic society. Jews and Muslims met in the public baths, an important locus for fraternization outside the family. Periodically, measures were enacted regulating *dhimmī* use of the baths—for instance, by requiring that they abstain from visiting the bath on Friday until after prayer time, or, as mentioned briefly earlier in connection with the al-Ḥākim persecutions, forcing them to wear something distinctive around their necks while sitting unclothed in the bath.[17] Noteworthy in these instances, mixed bathing itself was not banned. Christian rulings forbidding Jews and Christians from visiting public baths on the same days aimed at exclusion, and a thirteenth-century Latin decretist (commentator) on Gratian's *Decretum,* reinforced the ban by raising the specter of defilement by the Jews' filth.[18] Muslim regulations were intended to underscore and reinforce the social hierarchy, of which non-Muslims were an accepted part, albeit marginally, and at a low rank.

In his discussion of the pros and cons of this fraternization, Ibn Qayyim al-Jawziyya assumes that Muslims visit sick *dhimmī* neighbors or relatives.[19] Muslims, he says, may convey condolences to non-Muslims or congratulate them on the occasion of a marriage, birth, good health, or the arrival of a person who has been absent. One may not, however, congratulate *dhimmīs* regarding religious matters touching their unbelief—for instance, on the occasion of their holidays. This dictum resembles rules in the Mishnah regulating Jewish encounters with polytheist pagans, later applied to Christians.[20]

Formal and informal business partnerships between Jews and Muslims afforded ample opportunity for people of different religions to associate with one another. The business correspondence of the Cairo Geniza attests to relaxed socialization between members of the two faiths in the marketplace, one of the two primary locuses (the other being the mosque) of public life in the Muslim world. Indeed, the very texture of bazaar life lent itself to sociability of an intense nature among Jews and their gentile counterparts.[21]

This does not mean that differences between Jews and Muslims vanished behind the hectic exchange of goods and money. The mutually recognized hierarchy held sway: Muslim on top and Jew (or Christian) on the bottom. The Islamic law of partnership, for instance, required that the Muslim partner should always act as the agent, lest the non-Muslim, be he Christian or Jew, carry out a transaction forbidden by Islam.[22] Ibn Qayyim al-Jawziyya states that some authorities frowned on partnership with *dhimmīs* altogether, either for the reason stated or "because becoming partners with them leads to intermingling [*mukhālaṭa*] and that, in turn, to friendship [*mawadda*]."[23]

Long-distance commerce required that partners correspond with one another to convey information about business dealings. Not surprisingly, Ibn Taymiyya quotes a saying attributed to the second caliph, ʿUmar: "Do not exchange letters with the *dhimmīs,* lest amity should be generated between you and them, nor call them by their surnames; you must humiliate them [*adhillūhum*] but do not wrong them [*lā taẓlumūhum*]."[24]

Islamic (Sunni) law took a permissive position on the eating of animals slaughtered by People of the Book (as sanctioned by a Qur'anic verse). This meant that Muslims could dine in Jewish homes. Even the Prophet Muhammad was said to have "eaten of their [the Jews'] food."[25] Eating in Christian homes was more problematic: pork might be served. The permissibility of Jewish slaughtering facilitated congenial relations between Muslims and Jews in one of the most important settings for sociability in Middle Eastern culture. It must have gone on regularly.

Intermarriage between Jews and non-Jews existed as a theoretical possibility in both Islamic and European Christian society. Judaism and Christianity forbade this ultimate form of sociability. Islam handled the matter more indulgently. With Qur'anic sanction, it allows the marriage of a Muslim man to a *dhimmī* woman, on the presumption that, as master in the relationship, the Muslim husband would not be susceptible to the lure of his wife's religion.[26] Remarkably, Islamic law requires the husband to permit his non-Muslim wife to observe her religious rituals and to pray inside their house, and it admonishes him not to prompt her (if she is Jewish) to break the Sabbath or to eat forbidden foods. Nor may he prevent her from reading her own Scriptures, provided she does so without raising her voice (as required in the Pact of ʿUmar), nor from fasting on fast days prescribed by her religion.[27] She might not, however, attend her house of worship—according to one authority, lest her Muslim husband forfeit his conjugal right at the time; according to another, lest he seem to be abetting her in her unbelief.[28]

Islamic lawyers debated whether a Muslim husband might demand that his non-Muslim wife perform Islamic ablutions prescribed for cleansing impurities, including menstrual contamination.[29] The aspect of pollution through sexual relations—which, Brundage asserts, strengthened Christian abhorrence of intermarriage and rendered any kind of intermarriage illegal, even between a Christian man and a Jewish woman—appears not to have been a factor in the Muslim world, at least among the Sunnis. The Shiites, however, stressed the opposition of Muslim purity versus non-Muslim impurity (*najāsa*) as a central tenet of their teaching. This affected Jews in the late Middle Ages. According to the Iranian source, around 1656, in Iran under the Safavids—the dynasty that made Shiism the state religion of Iran—a great persecution ensued after two Jews were found to be ignoring the law requiring distinguishing clothing, with the consequence "that the Muslims could not avoid being infected by impurity."[30]

Just as the Islamic marketplace furnished more opportunities than in the Latin West for Jews to meet non-Jews on neutral ground and develop friendly relationships, so did the community of the learned provide a forum for congenial interfaith encounter. This existed to a much greater extent than in northern Christian Europe. To be sure, some Christian scholars turned to Jews for explanations of passages in the Hebrew Bible, and it is certain that educated Christians and Jews established friendships on an intellectual plane even as late as the fourteenth century.[31] But in most encounters there was a polemical agenda—debate over the meaning of Jewish Scripture.

In the Islamic world, sociability between Jewish and gentile intellectuals was more regular and less fraught with conflict. Arabic, the language of high culture, was by the tenth century the shared vernacular of Muslims and Jews. Although Arabic served as the language of the dominant religion, it carried few of the negative associations that Latin, the language of the hostile church, had for Jews in Europe. Arabic was employed for writings that were religiously neutral, what might be called secular. Knowledge of philosophy, the sciences, medicine—all part of the unified, secular, Hellenistic-Arab curriculum—could be and frequently was acquired by Muslims and Jews from the same nonconfessional sources, whether written or oral. The description by the twelfth-century Jewish savant Joseph ben Judah ibn ʿAqnīn of the ideal curriculum for Jews substantially parallels the course of study of the tenth- and eleventh-century Muslim philosopher Avicenna, with the exception that Ibn ʿAqnīn's course of study required religious texts specific to Judaism.[32]

Ashkenazic Jews shared little in the way of curricular interest with Christians. No intellectual enterprise that assumed Latin as the language of discourse could easily attract them. When scholastic theology, in considerable part adapted from the philosophy of Maimonides,[33] came into vogue among Christian thinkers in the twelfth century, Jews in the Ashkenazic milieu did not follow suit. They remained aloof, as well, from the large body of Hebrew translations of philosophical texts produced in southern France, texts that played an important intermediary role in introducing the Arabo-Greek philosophical tradition into Latin.

Dhimmīs enjoyed substantial acceptance when participating in the intellectual circles of the dominant culture, exemplified in such illuminating detail by Joel L. Kraemer with respect to the "Renaissance of Islam" in cosmopolitan, tenth-century Baghdad.[34] These and other manifestations of Jewish immersion in the cultural world of Arab savants flowed naturally from what Louis Gardet, in his study of the Islamic *mentalité,* calls the "intellectual tolerance" of medieval Muslim society during its classical period, which showed "no ethnic discrimination."[35]

Jewish physicians were found in Arab society in numbers disproportionate to the Jewish presence in the population at large; they acquired their medical training as part of the standard Hellenistic-Arabic curriculum, often studying with Muslims and Christians. They formed part of the interdenominational circle of physicians working in state hospitals and adorning Muslim courts. Muslim admiration for Jewish men of medicine abounds in Arabic biographical dictionaries. Ibn Abī Uṣaybiʿa's dictionary of physicians, for example, lauds numerous Jewish (and Christian) representatives of the medical profession, including Maimonides and his son, Abraham; the author was personally acquainted with the latter from their work together as attending physicians at the government-endowed hospital in Cairo.[36] Jewish physicians had private patients who were Muslim, both dignitaries at court and ordinary people.[37] At least in the classical period, these encounters, which provided considerable opportunity for

Jewish-Muslim sociability, seem not to have been accompanied by suspicion of the inimical intentions of Jewish doctors that had its roots in late antique Christianity and became so common in medieval Europe.[38]

An aspect of Jewish-gentile sociability under Islam that seems to lack a counterpart in the Jewish-Christian world is the world of shared popular religious practices. Anthropological study of Jewish-Muslim relations in modern times reveals the existence and extent of this spectacle, particularly the joint worship of saints. Here, interdenominational religiosity has its basis in the fact that the Qur'an honors biblical figures as prophets. Their grave sites attracted both Muslims and Jews. Another example is the now famous post-Passover Mimuna festivities of Moroccan Jewry, during which Muslims played the intriguing role of presenting the first "leaven" to the Jews, a demonstration of Muslim "relief" at the Jews' return to the marketplace.[39] The phenomenon of Muslim participation in non-Muslim religious celebrations did not begin in modern times, however. In the Middle Ages, far from separating themselves from *dhimmī* religious holidays, Muslims in Egypt often partook enthusiastically of Christian and Jewish religious celebrations.[40]

Two famous European Jewish travelers of the twelfth century, Benjamin of Tudela and Petaḥiah of Regensburg, noted this interfaith phenomenon with amazement, so uncharacteristic was it of the Christian milieu from which they hailed (Christian Spain and Germany, respectively). Benjamin found Muslims and Jews sharing in the veneration of Ezekiel, the biblical prophet of the Babylonian Exile, at the site of his tomb and at the synagogue named after him, which was tended by Muslim and Jewish keepers.

> People come from a distance to pray there from the time of the New Year until the Day of Atonement. The Jews have great rejoicings on these occasions. Thither also come the Head of the Diaspora and the Heads of the Academies from Baghdad. Their camp occupies a space of about two miles, and Arab merchants come there as well. . . . Distinguished Muslims also come there to pray, so great is their love for Ezekiel the Prophet.[41]

The Jews maintained a synagogue at the sepulcher of Ezra. "And at the side thereof the Muslims erected a house of prayer out of their great love and veneration for him, and they like the Jews on that account."[42]

Petaḥiah, who made his journey shortly after Benjamin, obtained from the head of the yeshiva in Baghdad a document instructing Jews to conduct him to grave sites of Jewish scholars and righteous men (*tzaddiqim*). The first place he visited was the grave of Ezekiel. Petaḥiah relates: "On the holiday of Sukkot, people come there from all lands . . . about sixty or eighty thousand Jews, in addition to Muslims." Huts (*sukkot*) were erected in the courtyard of the prophet's tomb, and people made vows and gave donations in hopes of gaining a favor. Petaḥiah heard a story about a Muslim notable (*sar*) who vowed that if his barren mare bore an offspring, he would give the foal to Ezekiel.

> [E]very Muslim who goes to the place of Muhammad [i.e., on the pilgrimage to Mecca and Medina], travels via the grave of Ezekiel, where he gives a gift and a donation to Ezekiel and vows in prayer: "Our lord Ezekiel, if I return I shall give you such-and-such."[43]

Muslims even made donations and prayed at the tomb of the Mishnaic sage Rabbi Meir and bowed in prayer at the burial site of Ezra the Scribe.[44]

In the late fifteenth century, the Italian Jewish traveler Meshullam of Volterra gazed in wonderment at the phenomenon of Jewish-Muslim popular religion.[45] Like his two twelfth-century precursors, Meshullam hailed from a Christian environment where Jews and Christians were mutually repelled by each other's religion. Meshullam could only find this kind of interaction between Jews and gentiles astonishing.

Interfaith sociability, far more extensive in Islam than in Christendom, did not overcome the religious opposition between Judaism and Islam. Conflict, endemic between monotheistic faiths throughout most of history, persisted even as Jews and Muslims formed partnerships in business, ate at each other's tables, joined in religious festivals, and exchanged ideas. Perhaps even on the fundamental level of religious rivalry, some nuanced differences between the Judaeo-Christian and Judaeo-Muslim conflict can be detected, and so we turn our attention to interreligious polemics, looking for subtle shadings that add to our understanding of the contrasting fate of Jewry in each milieu.

PART FIVE

Polemics and Persecution

Chapter Nine

INTERRELIGIOUS POLEMICS

Christianity versus Judaism

The factors involved in the progressive exclusion of the Jews from the Christian social order might have led to their total extirpation but for the contingent religious toleration stipulated by Augustine in his doctrine of witness. That contingency was implicit in the organic connection between Old Israel and New Israel; the latter needed the former to prop up its own legitimacy. By preserving the Old Testament, the Jews—though blinded to its spiritual, christological meaning—bore witness to the gospel of the New. In so doing, they buttressed the faith of Christians and confounded those among the pagans who accused them of inventing prophecies of the advent of Christ after the fact. Living dispersed among the Christians in a state of abject defeat, Jews testified daily to the triumph of Christianity. At the Second Coming, their blindness removed, the Jews would, through conversion, crown their role as witness and thus testify to the veracity of Jesus' messiahood.[1]

Nonetheless, Christianity could not remain passive until the Redemption. It felt compelled to combat Judaism, which stubbornly insisted on its own exclusive claim to divine election. Disputing the Jewish claim to religious truth was, therefore, actively pursued by church thinkers. Polemics against Judaism were part of the fabric of Christianity from its earliest days: anti-Judaism was, from the outset, an essential ingredient of Christian self-definition.[2]

The anti-Jewish polemic is scattered throughout Christian writings as well as appearing in separate treatises devoted to the subject. A. Lukyn Williams summarized examples of this "adversus judaeos" literature.[3] More recently, Heinz Schreckenberg has assembled an impressive, chronological, descriptive bibliographical survey of Christian polemical literature against Judaism. This material, dating from the first through the thirteenth century, includes not only anti-Jewish tracts but also material in papal pronouncements, conciliar decrees, canonist texts, royal documents, historical chronicles, poetry and drama, iconography, and even comments on Christianity and its relations with the Jews in Jewish literature from Rashi to Maimonides. In size and scope alone, this enormous compilation demonstrates the fundamental, continuous struggle in Christian history to affirm Christianity at the expense of the Jews and Judaism.[4]

An early type of polemical literature in Christianity took the form of citations of biblical testimonies, perhaps even whole "Books of Testimonies," manuals of Old Testament verses with their "correct" christological meaning, usually featuring veiled foretellings of Jesus and his mission. A corollary of the conviction that the Jewish Bible contains God's authentic word about the mission of Christ, this method of interpretating the "Old Testament"—essentially Jewish hermeneutics turned against the Jews—lay at the heart of the Christian-Jewish argument. Such "testimony" served to bolster the faith of Jewish converts to Christianity.[5] The majority of Jews—those who failed to see the light—were considered "sick" or "blind" to the real meaning of their own Scripture. "Testimonies," wrote Augustine, "are to be selected from sacred Scripture, which has great authority among the Jews, and if they do not want to be cured by means of this advantage offered them, they can at least be convicted by its evident truth."[6]

A leading authority on Jewish-Christian polemics has written that "every major Christian doctrine could be supported by several verses in the Hebrew Bible."[7] For example, exegetes found support for the fundamental dogma of the divine rejection of the Jews and of God's election of the Christian "New Israel" in two famous Old Testament "testimonies" that illustrate the issue lying at the heart of the Jewish-Christian conflict. The first testimony is found in Genesis, at the close of Jacob's blessing to his twelve sons. To his fourth son, Judah, Jacob prophesies: "The scepter shall not depart from Judah nor the ruler's staff from between his legs until Shiloh comes" (Genesis 49:10). Already in ancient Jewish exegesis, the enigmatic "Shiloh" was given a messianic twist. The Targum, or Aramaic translation of the Torah, takes the verse eschatologically, rendering the final, puzzling words, "until the messiah comes, to whom belongs kingship [or, the kingdom; *malkhuta*]." Christianity adopted this Jewish interpretation. Looking back at Rome's destruction of the Second Temple, in 70 C.E., and to the dissolution of the Jewish state, Christian commentators found that Genesis 49:10 had predicted everything. With Rome's victory, the scepter departed from Judah, God having rejected the Jews. Hence, Shiloh must have come. Shiloh could be none other than Jesus himself.

Another crux, Genesis 25:23, presents God's poetic promise to Rebecca that she will bear twins, each representing a "nation," of which "one people shall be mightier than the other, and the older shall serve the younger." In context, the older child was firstborn Esau, who solidified his prophesied subservience to his younger brother Jacob when he sold the latter his birthright in return for a helping of lentil stew (Genesis 25:30–34). Later, their father, Isaac, misled on his deathbed into thinking that Jacob was Esau, bestowed on the "younger" the blessing, "Be master over your brothers" (Genesis 27:29), and upon the "older" the famous words,

"You shall serve your brother" (Genesis 27:40). Christian readers of the prophecy to Rebecca made *older* and *younger* refer, respectively, to Judaism, the "older" religion, and Christianity, the "younger" faith. Thus, God's prophecy tells of the eventual submission of Judaism to Christianity. This Christian midrash countered the standard Jewish exegesis, which identified Esau, also known as Edom in the Bible, with Rome and Roman Christendom and used the Jacob-Esau motif to shore up the Jewish conviction about God's eternal election of Israel (Jacob) and of its ultimate redemption.[8] These and numerous other Old Testament testimonies about the true Israel were used by Christian thinkers to challenge Judaism and strengthen Christian faith.

The Jewish Polemical Response to Christianity

To appreciate the intensity of the challenge that Old Testament "proofs" of the authenticity of Christianity (as well as face-to-face polemics against Judaism) posed to Jews, one need only consider the Jewish response. The early midrash includes many veiled answers to Christianity, intended to bolster Jewish self-confidence in the face of an aggressive Christian "adversus judaeos" tradition.[9] In addition, mishnaic and talmudic literature contain explicitly disparaging references to Jesus, although, by the time of printing, these were mostly excised as a result of Christian or self-imposed Jewish censorship. There was also the early medieval Hebrew biography of Jesus, *Toledot yeshu,* with its derogatory, blasphemous parody of the life and acts of Jesus. Medieval Hebrew chronicles of Jewish suffering at the hands of Christians, especially during the Crusades, heaped opprobrium on Jesus and Christianity. Jesus was called by such names as "the crucified one, a rotting corpse that cannot avail and cannot save," and Christianity was regularly classified, at least in theory, as idolatry.[10]

Christians, early on, encountered Jewish invective toward Christianity. In the ninth century, Bishop Agobard of Lyons was familiar with *Toledot yeshu.*[11] In later centuries, Christians became acquainted with alleged and real anti-Christian comments in talmudic literature, either through personal study or thanks to the good offices of such apostates as Nicholas Donin.[12] Medieval Jewish Bible commentary is filled with anti-Christian polemic. One scholar observes that rebuttal of christological interpretations of Old Testament verses was not a mere by-product of the activity of the Jewish commentators, but "an integral part of their work. . . . The whole body of medieval exegesis is an eloquent witness to the relentless struggle between a powerful Church and a Jewry at bay."[13]

Rashi (R. Solomon b. Isaac of Troyes, France, 1040–1105) used his commentary on the Bible to stress the Jewish interpretation of passages that Christianity applied to Jesus. He emphasized the eternality of the Law, the chosenness of Israel, and other Jewish claims disputed by Christianity.[14] For a time after Rashi's death, Jewish exegetes in France, notably, Rashi's own grandson, Samuel b. Meir (Rashbam), but also Joseph Qara, Rashi's student and older contemporary of Rashbam, focused their energies on the simple, literal meaning of the biblical text in order to outmaneuver Christian spiritual exegesis, with its propensity for finding christological prefigurations throughout the text.

The defense of Judaism against Christian polemics intensified in the twelfth century. This was the period of the Crusades, a time of increasing anti-Jewish hostility in Europe. Daniel Lasker divides into six categories the strategies in the literature that began to emerge in the twelfth century: exegesis of the Hebrew Bible, exegesis of rabbinic literature, attacks on Christianity, comparisons of Christian doctrines with the New Testament, attacks on the articles of Christianity, and comparisons of Christianity with the principles of philosophy.[15] Jewish philosophical polemicists, particularly studied by Lasker, strove to expose the logical impossibility of key Christian doctrines, mainly the trinity, incarnation, transubstantiation, and virgin birth.

Joseph Kimḥi (1105?–1170?), a Jewish refugee from Almohad persecution in Muslim Spain, wrote what is probably the first full Jewish treatise against Christianity. He wrote in Provence, where he regularly came in contact with Christians and may have felt impelled by what would have seemed to him a more intense anti-Jewish polemic than the type he had known in his native milieu. His *Book of the Covenant* upholds the eternal election of the Jews against Christian insistence that God had abandoned them. He responds to the christological interpretation of Jacob's blessing for his son Judah in Genesis 49:10 on historical grounds. Shiloh, he says, alludes to King David, the descendant of Judah. The Davidic line of monarchy ended with the Babylonian captivity—more than four hundred years before Jesus.[16]

Kimḥi derides the Christian dogma of the incarnation: "How shall I believe that this great inaccessible *Deus absconditus* needlessly entered the womb of a woman, the filthy, foul bowels of a female, compelling the living God to be born of a woman?"[17] He turns the tables on the Christian critique of Jewish usury, demonstrating that Jews scrupulously obey the Torah, which forbids taking usury only from one's "brother," whereas Christian moneylenders engage in usury even with their brethren.[18]

A close contemporary of Joseph Kimḥi, Jacob b. Reuven, compiled (probably in 1170) a Hebrew polemical treatise in the form of a debate between a Christian *mekhaḥed* (denier of God's unity), said to represent an actual interlocutor of the author, and the author himself, *ha-meyaḥed* (proclaimer of God's unity). The book's combative title, "The Wars of the Lord" (*Milḥamot ha-shem*), signals its polemical purpose. It begins with a philosophical, logical discussion of the trinity and incarnation; following that, it takes up and refutes alleged biblical proofs of the truth of Christianity. In an exchange about the trinity and its alleged attestation in the story of Abraham's encounter with the three visitors (Genesis 18), a story that alternates between three and one, the Jewish disputant responds, paraphrasing Isaiah (33:15), *ʿatzamta me-reʾot ʿeinekha,* "You have shut your eyes so that you cannot see." This jibe turns against the Christian the classic New Testament theme of Jewish blindness to the truth of their own Scripture. Taking the offensive against Christianity, Jacob's "Wars of the Lord" includes a daring, informed critique of the Gospel account of Jesus, about which the Jewish disputant declares: "Of this section, God knows, I did not intend to mention anything, but my friends compelled me. . . . Therefore, I have mentioned a few of the errors and distortions in their book, and a hundredth I have not revealed out of fear."[19]

A major summa of Jewish responses to Christian polemics against Judaism was compiled in the late thirteenth or early fourteenth century. Its title, again alluding to the bellicose nature of interreligious polemics, is *Sefer nitztzaḥon yashan,* "The Old Book of Polemic." The author presents Christian "testimonies" from the Bible, followed by Jewish rejoinders. The organization follows the order of the books of the Old Testament, a useful arrangement for Jews potentially finding themselves locked in debate with Christians over Scripture. David Berger, who edited and translated the treatise, notes that "the array of arguments in the *Niẓẓaḥon Vetus* is almost encyclopedic, and the book is therefore an excellent vehicle for an analysis of virtually all the central issues in the Jewish-Christian debate during the twelfth and thirteenth centuries."[20] One example from this vast anthology of anti-Judaism and Jewish response concerns the controversial issue of the status of Jewish law. Jeremiah's verse (31:31), "And I will make a new covenant with Israel and with the house of Judah," a favorite among Christians, offered proof from God Himself of the cardinal doctrine that His new covenant with the Christians had replaced Jewish law. The Jewish voice in *Nitztzaḥon yashan* produces counterevidence from the New Testament: "They contradict their own Torah, for it is written in the book of their error that Jesus himself said, 'I have not come to destroy the law of Moses or the words of the prophets, but to fulfill them.'"[21]

The Polemic over Rabbinic Judaism

Books like *Nitztzaḥon yashan* were valuable resources for Jews engaged in religious disputation with Christians. This disputation took different forms. Especially before the era of the Crusades, some could hardly be called disputations at all. They arose from more or less friendly conversation between Jewish and Christian intellectuals eager for firsthand knowledge of each other's faith and, indirectly, to convince the opposite number of his error.[22] Many Christian exegetes satisfied a yearning to know the original Hebrew of the Bible by befriending Jewish teachers. Jewish intellectuals, for their part, obtained sufficient knowledge of Latin to respond from a position of strength.[23] Blumenkranz summarizes the issues debated in the early Middle Ages under three broad headings: the lapsed nature of the Mosaic Law; the messiahood of Jesus; and the rejection of the Jews and the election of the gentiles, the True Israel.[24]

Respectful exchange of this sort, even collaboration between Jewish and Christian intellectuals, did not disappear, as Gerard Dahan has recently shown for the twelfth to fourteenth centuries.[25] By and large, however, the Christian-Jewish debate heated up in the twelfth and especially the thirteenth century, in tandem with the worsening of Jewish-Christian relations on all other levels.[26] During this period, Christians went beyond the Jewish Bible for their material, exploiting rabbinic literature, only sketchily known to them before the twelfth century. For some, the Talmud and its kindred literature provided proof of Jewish anti-Christian enmity. For others, rabbinic texts contained affirmation of Christianity's messianic claim. For still others, familiarity with rabbinic literature begot a revision of the Christian theory of Jewish history. Postbiblical Judaism—the Judaism of contemporary Jews—was no longer viewed as the fossilized bearer of a misunderstood scriptural prefiguration of the new, Christian dispensation but as a heretical departure from biblical religion. Postbiblical rabbis—the authors of the Talmud and their medieval successors—were now seen as enemies of Christendom, perversely preventing the Jews, by their inane midrashim, from ever grasping the true, christological message of their own divinely revealed book.[27]

Three great, "formal" interfaith disputations on the merits of rabbinic Judaism stand out boldly.[28] The first took place in France, the second and third in Spain. The disputation over the Talmud in Paris, in 1240, functioned more as a "trial" than a genuine debate, and the outcome—the Talmud condemned for blasphemy and then burned in Paris in 1242—was a foregone conclusion. Most scholars agree that the Disputation at Barcelona of 1263 was conducted on a higher intellectual plane than the Paris confrontation and turned out to be more open-ended. The Christian side here focused on rabbinic literature not to vilify it, as in Paris, but to exploit it to verify that the messiah (Jesus) had come. The less vituperative tone of the Barcelona confrontation reflected the relatively more secure position of the Jews in Spain at that time. They were less detested than were the Jews of northern Europe, more integrated economically and culturally into their surroundings, and still-valued servants of Aragon state interests during the *Reconquista*. In brief, Jews benefited from the more accepting, economically and politically more favorable setting of Mediterranean Christendom that we have noted with reference to the Jews of the Midi, as well as from the legacy of Muslim Spain. The last of the three, the Disputation at Tortosa, in 1414–15, came after the Jewish situation in Spain had taken a radical turn for the worse following the massive and widespread anti-Jewish pogroms of 1391. It served as a terror tactic to induce Jews to convert to Christianity, and in this it had considerable success. Many other, smaller confrontations between Jews and Christians, as well as an abundance of literary polemics on both sides, dotted the landscape during the difficult centuries of the High and late Middle Ages in the West, as the debate with Judaism, so essential to Christian self-definition from earliest times, expanded outward from biblical "testimonies" to a broader and more intensely critical evaluation of Jews and their religion, with ominous implications for the continued toleration of the Jews as an essential ingredient in Christian society and soteriology.

Islam versus Judaism

A comparison between Islamic and Christian polemics with Judaism should yield substantial insight into the attitude toward and treatment of the Jews of Islam.[29] To anticipate our conclusion: neither the Christian preoccupation with the intellectual struggle against Judaism nor the bellicose Jewish response to Christian polemics has a counterpart of similar intensity in the Judaeo-Islamic context. Combating Judaism and Jewish interpretations of Scripture was essential in Christianity; it was incidental in Islam.

At first glance, to be sure, the Islamic conflict with the Jews (and Christians) seems quite fundamental. Scriptural polemics, as in Christianity, play a major role. In many places, the Qur'an is decidedly antagonistic toward the Jews, more so even than the Gospels (especially in verses revealed in Medina, where Muhammad encountered stiff Jewish opposition). A frequently cited example likens the Jews to idolaters while holding forth with praise for the Christians: "Thou wilt find the most vehement of mankind in hostility to those who believe [to be] the Jews and the idolaters. And thou wilt find the nearest to them in affection to those who believe [to be] those who say: Lo! We are Christians. That is because there are among them priests and monks, and because they are not proud."[30] But, in the long run, this Qur'anic hostility—the product of Muhammad's head-on conflict with the Jews of his time—failed to make its stamp on the Muslim-Jewish polemic, which differed fundamentally from its counterpart in Christendom.

The Attitude toward Jewish and Christian Scriptures

Already in the Qur'an, the People of the Book are said to have corrupted their Scriptures (e.g., Sura 3:78).[31] The Torah in the possession of contemporary Jews was said to be a massive, willful falsification of the original revealed book, lost to the Jews through their sins and the vicissitudes of their history.[32] Eventually, Ezra came along and composed a new Torah, which strayed far from the original.[33] The Qur'anic theme of *taḥrīf* found its first detailed elaboration in the influential writings of the eleventh-century Andalusian savant Ibn Ḥazm, who singled out chronological and geographical inaccuracies, theological impossibilities (especially anthropomorphic descriptions of God), and instances of preposterous behavior (such as the incident of sexual intercourse between Lot and his two daughters).[34]

Islamic censure of the text of the Bible accompanies a related doctrine, *naskh,* or "abrogation." Originally applied to verses in the Qur'an said to nullify earlier revelations to the Prophet, *naskh,* as applied to the Jewish Bible, designates the abrogation of the law of Moses by the Qur'an. By expansion and extension, *naskh* characterized the supersession by Islam of both Judaism and Christianity. This recalls the Christian anti-Jewish doctrine of the divine rejection of the Jews, but it does not have quite the same salience in the Muslim-Jewish debate. A third major theme of Islamic polemics takes issue with anthropomorphic portrayal of God (*tajsīm*) in the Bible, a charge that called Jewish monotheism into question.

In matters relating to Jewish Scripture, Islam, with its doctrine of *taḥrīf,* takes the opposite approach. For Christians, the text of the Old Testament is wholly authentic; the words are divine, not open to challenge. The disagreement with the Jews concerns primarily the correct *interpretation* of the revealed text. Hence, the relentless drive by Christians century after century to press their own interpretation against that of the Jews. Muslims lack this obsession since they judge the Old Testament to be textually corrupt.[35]

To make the contrast sharper—and, thereby, differentiate more clearly between Islamic and Christian attitudes toward Judaism—it is useful to note that early Christian thinkers actually experimented with a notion of Jewish falsification of Scripture.[36] The Septuagint, the first Greek translation of the Bible, which was prepared for Greek-speaking Jews in the Hellenistic diaspora, was soon recognized by Christians as the authoritative text. As new, rival Greek translations by Jews or Jewish converts to Christianity appeared in the second century, minor variants to the Septuagint were introduced which challenged its accuracy. In an effort to uphold the official Greek Bible, certain fathers of the church, as early as Justin Martyr in the second century, accused the Jews of deliberately tampering with these versions or even the underlying Hebrew itself for the purpose of confounding Christians by denying them access to textual readings supportive of Christian doctrine. As William Adler has shown, however, this theory could not be upheld for long. Origen, Jerome, and

Augustine rejected the premise as ultimately self-defeating. "[B]y indiscriminately raising the charge of Jewish tampering with their own Scriptures, Christian polemicists were shaking one of the very foundations of their own canon, namely the Bible of the Jews."[37] Unimpeded by any such dependency on either "testament," old or new, Muslims could freely brandish their indictment of the Jews and Christians for falsifying (*taḥrīf*) Scripture.

Paradoxically, the conflict between Islam and Judaism over the meaning of Jewish Scripture generated less acrimony and tension than did the Jewish-Christian debate.[38] While Christianity uncovered (in its own perception) Old Testament verses substantiating every important Christian doctrine—whether the trinity, virgin birth, incarnation, or messiahship and divinity of Christ—Islam mostly restricted itself to locating alleged foretellings in Christian and in Jewish Scriptures of the advent of Muhammad and his divinely ordained prophethood.

Foretellings of Muhammad

The Jewish Bible provided Muslim polemicists with the lion's share of the good tidings, not because Muslims were fundamentally or ideologically more hostile toward Judaism or because Judaism posed more of a threat than Christianity. The Hebrew Bible simply contained much more usable material than the New Testament. Moreover, Muslims had the Christian example of "testimonies" drawn from the Book of the Jews as a model.

The most popular New Testament foretelling of Muhammad was "discovered" in John (14:15–16), where Jesus discourses during the last supper about an advent to come. "If you love me you will obey my commands; and I will ask the Father, *and he will give you another to be your Advocate* [in Greek, *paraklētos*], who will be with you forever—the Spirit of truth."[39] Some Muslim writers claimed that the Paraclete verse foretold the mission of Muhammad, because, they said, the word means "praised," which derives from the same root, *ḥ-m-d,* as the name Muhammad.[40]

The Jewish Bible, however, provided the richest, most abundant material. The Torah contains the patriarchal narratives—especially the Abraham-Ishmael saga—which Arabs readily adopted as part of their own ancestral history. Also, by their nature, the prophetic books of the Jewish Bible presented oracles that could be interpreted as heralding Islam. There may be yet another explanation for the prominence given to Old Testament material. One of the earliest Muslim religious polemicists was ʿAlī ibn Rabban al-Ṭabarī. At the request of Abbasid caliph al-Mutawakkil, about 855, ʿAlī ibn Rabban wrote *The Book of Religion and Empire.* The book claims that Christian and Jewish falsification of their respective Scriptures had all but obliterated forecasts of Muhammad's future mission. ʿAlī ibn Rabban's professed goal was to recover these prophecies from each holy book, to "disclose its secret, and withdraw the veil from it, in order that the reader may see it clearly and increase his conviction and his joy in the religion of Islam."[41] He wished not only to bolster belief in Islam, but also (and, probably, principally) to justify his own conversion and convince other Christians to follow his lead. ʿAlī ibn Rabban tells us that Christians who abjured belief in the Prophet Muhammad said: "We do not see that a prophet has prophesied about him prior to his coming" and "the Christ has told us that no prophet will rise after Him."[42]

Originally a Christian, ʿAlī ibn Rabban naturally had firsthand knowledge of the essentialist Christian exegetical strategy of authenticating the advent of Christ and the truth of Christian teachings with prooftexts from the Old Testament. He seems to have decided that, to authenticate Islam for Christians, he needed to focus his efforts on retrieving foretellings of the prophethood of Muhammad from the Jewish Bible.[43] The flow of anti-Jewish polemic from Christianity to Islam via converts is one of the chief conclusions arrived at by Moshe Perlmann, the most dedicated student of Islamic-Jewish polemics in the twentieth century.[44]

A brief look at some of the most popular biblical predictions about Muhammad highlights the contrast with the more essentialist Christian use of the Old Testament. For the most part, the Muslim technique relies on the literal meaning of texts, rather than on the typological-allegorical understanding so common in Christian exegesis.

The Genesis cycle of stories about Hagar and Ishmael served as grist for the Muslim exegetical mill. In chapter 16 the angel speaks to Hagar during her flight from Sarah: "I will greatly increase your offspring, and they shall be too many to count. . . . You shall call him Ishmael, for the Lord has paid heed to your suffering. He shall be a wild man [*pere' adam*]; his hand against everyone, and everyone's hand against him" (Genesis 16:9–12). Since, by universal agreement, Ishmael was the ancestor of the Arabs, the Muslims happily took this passage literally as heralding Muhammad's future absolute power.[45] On this understanding, Islam descended directly from one of the two sons of Abraham—the first Muslim—just like Judaism. Moreover, Abraham, acting at Sarah's behest and with God's blessing, did not reject Ishmael, as the biblical narrative has it. Post-Qur'anic sources beginning in the ninth century preserve a story, probably Jewish in origin, according to which Abraham twice visited Ishmael in his desert exile at Mecca, exhibiting fatherly concern and, by implication, ensuring that the patrimony of Islam would be transmitted through the long line of his first son.[46]

The relationship in Islamic exegesis between Isaac and Ishmael, the brotherly progenitors of Judaism and Islam, contrasts with the Jacob-Esau antinomy in the Christian allegory on Genesis 23. It reveals a fundamental difference between Islamic and Christian conceptions of the Jews' place in the divine historical plan. As noted, Christian exegetes took God's prophecy to Rebecca—"and the older shall serve the younger"—to prefigure the triumphal subjugation of the "older" *religion,* Judaism, to the "younger" one, Christianity. In its more characteristic form, Christianity completely supersedes Judaism: the New Israel is superimposed over the Old Israel and claims its history.

Islamic historical theory, by contrast, posits for itself a linear, "national" existence beginning with Ishmael and a history that parallels rather than assimilates the annals of both the Jewish and Christian peoples. ʿAlī ibn Rabban, for example, explains that the descendants of Abraham, through Ishmael, became dispersed among the nations of the earth, including Egypt, the Hijaz (northern Arabia), and Syria:

> Then after a long time all the prophecies were realized and the messages fulfilled, and the children of Ishmael triumphed over those who were around them. . . . They spread in all the regions of the earth like young locusts. . . . [t]hey reigned, too, in East and West. . . . The name of Abraham appeared then in the mouth of all nations. . . . As to Judaism, it had appeared only in one section [*ṭāʾifa*] of mankind. As to Christianity, although it appeared in a great and glorious nation, yet in the land of Abraham and his wife Sarah, and their forefathers, and in the land of Hagar and her fathers, it had not wielded the sceptre and held absolute power and sway such as those vouchsafed by God to their inhabitants through the Prophet.[47]

This description of the Islamic scheme of the past presumes that the Islamic people had a continuous history from the time of the biblical patriarchs. For ages the descendants of Ishmael survived among other people in a dispersion not unlike that of the Jews. With Muhammad's appearance in history, fulfilling the prophecies of his advent, the Ishmaelite people arose, united, to a position of great power and geographical dominion. The Jewish and Christian peoples had inherent limitations—ethnic exclusivity, in one case, and geographical narrowness, in the other. Only Islam achieved true universality and globality. Noticeably absent from this scheme is the suggestion that the people of Islam were anchored historically in either Jewish or Christian society, let alone that Islam constituted a New Israel or New Christendom. Following this understanding, Islam need not deny to either the Jews or the Christians their continuous history alongside Islam. They are *ahl al-dhimma* and *ahl al-kitāb*—but still an *ahl,* a "people" living out their own histories dispersed among the Muslims, and still living.

Other popular passages in the biblical patriarchal cycle foretell the coming of Muhammad. God announces the birth of Isaac to Abraham while at the same time promising to "bless [Ishmael]. I will make him fertile and exceedingly numerous. He shall be the father of twelve chieftains, and I will make of him a great nation" (Genesis 17:15–21). It is hardly surprising that the Muslims took this passage as a direct reference to the great Islamic *umma* to come.[48] Another prophecy derived from the same passage is based on the numerical value of words rather than literalism and is strikingly "Jewish" in technique. The Hebrew expression for "exceedingly," *bi-me'od me'od,* computed mathematically (each letter of the Hebrew alphabet having a numerical value), yields the numerical equivalent of the name of the Prophet (the consonants *M Ḥ M D* add up to 92, the same total as the letters *B M ' D M ' D*).[49] This exegetical method, called "gematria" in the Talmud, might be a Jewish import into Islamic polemics, for this and other "gematrias" appear in anti-Jewish polemical works written by Jewish converts to Islam.[50] It entered Islam early, however. ʿAlī ibn Rabban al-Ṭabarī employs a gematria on the "Paraclete verse" in the Gospel of John, where the words "He shall teach you everything," in what ʿAlī Ṭabarī calls a "wonderful mystery" (*sirr ʿajīb*), have the numerical value of *Muḥammad bin Abdallāh al-nabī al-hādī* (Muhammad the rightly guiding Prophet, son of ʿAbdallah).[51]

Deuteronomy 18:15ff. contains an extremely popular passage predicting Muhammad's advent. Moses speaks: "The Lord your God will raise up for you a prophet from among your own people [*me-aḥekha*] like me" (verse 15), and continuing, quotes God, "I will raise up a prophet for them from among their own people [*mi-qerev aḥeihem*], like yourself" (verse 18). Muslim exegetes understood the Arabic translation of the Hebrew words *mi-qerev aḥeihem* (literally, *min ikhwātihim,* "from among their *brothers*"), hence an allusion to the descendants of Ishmael. Jewish attempts to understand the verse differently (incorporated into the Jewish Publication Society translation just cited) constituted *taḥrīf.*[52]

Yet another prognostication widely used in Islamic polemics derives from a literal-historical reading of the opening line of Moses' blessing for Israel just before his death (Deuteronomy 33:2–3): "The Lord came from Sinai, He shone upon them from Seir, He appeared from Mount Paran." This was taken to be a prophecy of the rise of Judaism, Christianity, and Islam, in three successive divine revelations. Al-Qarāfī (d. 1285) explains: Sinai was the mountain from which God spoke to Moses; Seir, the mountain al-Khalil in Syria, where the messiah (Jesus) practiced his pieties; and Paran, the mountain of Banu Hisham, where Muhammad practiced his own pious devotions and which was identical with Mecca according to the agreed opinion of the People of the Book.[53] Thus, the verse served to proclaim that a future revelation would come to Ishmael's most famous descendant, the Prophet Muhammad. In the words of ʿAlī ibn Rabban a propos the portent in question, "If this is not as we have mentioned, let them show us 'a lord' who appeared from Mount Paran; and they will never be able to do so. The name 'lord' refers here to the Prophet. . . . [I]t is a word applied by Arabs and non-Arabs to the Most High God."[54]

Recent research on the Islamic approach to Jewish material reinforces from a different angle the distinction I am suggesting between Muslim and Christian exegetical strategies. In an illuminating study of "the evolution of the Abraham-Ishmael legends in Islamic exegesis," Reuven Firestone shows that Muhammad and the early Muslims inherited a large body of monotheistic oral traditions about the lives of this important father and son, much of it acquired from the storytelling of "Biblicists" in Arabia before and during the lifetime of the Prophet. As Islam crystallized, Muhammad, in the Qur'an, and his successors who compiled post-Qur'anic exegetical literature adopted versions that fit best with conceptions of Islam and with Arab notions of their ancient past. Muslims believed that Qur'anic and extra-Qur'anic stories about Abraham and Ishmael—such as the conviction held by some that Ishmael, not Isaac, was Abraham's intended sacrifice—were authentic originals that the Jews had simply distorted.[55]

Following Firestone's thesis, Muslim presentations of legends found in the Bible would have been distilled from oral adaptations that were already current before the rise of Islam. They preexisted—or, at least, paralleled—Jewish renderings; they did not, as in Christianity, exegetically supersede them. The challenge presented by the existence of such divergent exegetical traditions was, accordingly, far less threatening to Judaism than the one presented by Christian understanding of the Jewish Bible. Christological exegesis of the Old Testament stretched and pulled the sacred Hebrew text in new ways and put the Jewish keepers of the Bible to a severe test. In the short run, as well as the long, Jews living within the orbit of Islam found it easier to dismiss or ignore Muslim interpretations simply by holding fast to their own, "truer," literal understanding.

Islam versus Christianity

Before discussing the Jewish response to Islamic polemics, we will briefly examine the Islamic-Christian debate. The Islamic polemic against Christianity expended most of its effort denouncing doctrines that fundamentally conflicted with the religion of Islam rather than seeking foretellings of Muhammad in the New Testament. To exemplify the difference in tone and substance between anti-Christian and anti-Jewish polemic in Islam, I take the case of Ibn Qayyim al-Jawziyya's treatise, "Guide of the Perplexed in Reply to the Jews and the Christians."[56]

The Muslim author addresses the standard themes of Islamic polemic, alternating between Judaism and Christianity for his examples. He pays considerable attention to predictions in both the Old and New Testaments. Near the end of the book, however, he devotes separate chapters to each of the two other Scriptural faiths. A comparison of these sections permits us to gauge the relative opinions of this Muslim intellectual concerning Judaism and Christianity. The chapter on Judaism occupies a quarter of the space devoted to Christianity.[57] In the main, it discusses Jewish practices and beliefs considered absurd, such as rigid dietary restrictions, levirate marriage, and the Jewish claim to "chosenness." Some of the complaints about Judaism are not original with Ibn al-Qayyim; he borrows much from "Silencing the Jews" by the Jewish apostate to Islam Samau'al al-Maghribī.[58] Ibn al-Qayyim has even harsher words for Christianity, including a diatribe on the virgin birth, as well as beliefs and practices (especially intercession) regarding Mary and Jesus. He refers to the Christians as "the nation of those who go astray and of worshipers of the cross and of images on walls and ceilings."[59] Idolatry in the form of the trinity rankles him more than any belief of Judaism. "If the monotheists were to commit every sin . . . it would not reach the weight [*mithqāl*] of the sin of this immense unbelief [*al-kufr al-ʿaẓīm*] regarding the Master of the Universe."[60]

Faced with Islam's critique of the doctrines and practices of Christianity from early in the Islamic period, Christians of the Islamic world responded with numerous specifically anti-Islamic polemical works, outdoing the Jews by far in this respect, as well as ensuring a larger return of anti-Christian invective.[61] The Melkite bishop of Harran (in Mesopotamia), Theodore Abū Qurrah (bishop 795–812), wrote in Arabic a tract justifying Christian veneration of images against the critique of both Jews and Muslims, which apparently had instilled something resembling iconophobia among some Christians.[62] In the ninth century, a Muslim and a Christian conducted a "correspondence" in Arabic on the issue of Christian belief. The Muslim writer (al-Hāshimī) invited the Christian to convert to Islam, citing the unacceptability of the trinity and asserting the superiority of Islam, its doctrine of the prophethood of Muhammad, its religious law and practices, and its this-worldly rewards. The Christian (al-Kindī) responded with an emphatic defense of Christianity, especially its trinitarian theology, and with a critique of Islam's inferior laws and of the prophethood of Muhammad.[63]

Around 1150, the bishop of Sidon (Ṣaidā), Paul of Antioch, penned an "Epistle to One of the Muslims" which, in turn, elicited the apologetic treatise of al-Qarāfī. Later enlarged, this "Epistle" provoked the theologian Ibn Taymiyya to write "The Correct Answer to Those Who Changed the Religion of Christ." His theme was that "the false religion of Christians is nothing but an innovated religion which they invented after the time of Christ and by which they changed the religion of Christ." Comparing the two Religions of the Book, Ibn Taymiyya asserts that

"Christians' unbelief is more profound than that of the Jews, although they have gone to great lengths to pronounce the Jews unbelievers. They are far more deserving of being declared unbelievers than the Jews. The Jews claimed that Christ was a lying magician. . . . The Christians claim that he is God."[64]

Although Muslims occasionally challenged Christians and Jews to participate in disputation, we have written accounts mainly for Christians.[65] Timothy I, a Nestorian patriarch in the ninth century, committed to writing his version of a dialogue he had held with the Abbasid caliph al-Mahdī. Among the issues debated are the trinity, foretellings, and circumcision (the Christian abandonment of which roused much criticism among Muslims).[66]

Bernard Lewis comments on why Christianity was on the receiving end of more intensive religious polemics than Judaism:

> In general, Muslim polemicists pay little attention to the relatively insignificant Jew. . . . [T]hey are far more concerned with the Christians who, as the bearers of a competing proselytizing religion and the masters of a rival universal empire, offered a serious alternative and therefore a potential threat to the Muslim dispensation and the Islamic oecumene.[67]

To this, it should be added that the essential doctrinal congruence between Islam and Judaism regarding the unitary nature of God eliminated an important stimulus to interreligious polemics always present in the Islamic-Christian encounter.

To be sure, during the Islamic Middle Ages, members of all three monotheistic faiths often met in relative amity to discuss a wide range of issues. These learned study sessions, however, treated religion and religions in a nonparochial manner. Reason rather than revelation served as the common denominator of the interchanges. Joel Kraemer summarizes this phenomenon for the tenth-century "Renaissance of Islam": "Cosmopolitanism, tolerance, reason, and friendship made possible the convocation of these societies, devoted to a common pursuit of the truth and preservation of ancient wisdom, by surmounting particular religious ties in favor of a shared human experience."[68]

Opportunities for Jews and Christians to discuss matters of mutual concern in a neutral setting existed to a much lesser extent in Ashkenazic northern Europe. Such gatherings of Christian and Jewish scholars as existed served the former as a means of learning the allegedly "true" Jewish understanding of the Old Testament and the latter as a forum for understanding Christian exegetical methods.[69] It is doubtful, however, that the kind of open-minded discussions of religious questions characteristic of the *majlis* in Islam had a significant counterpart in northern Christian Europe. There, by way of contrast, the penetration of reason into the thinking of Christian savants, like Albertus Magnus and Thomas Aquinas, did not extend to the Jewish intelligentsia. Moreover, no winds of religious relativism blew to soften the exclusivism of either Judaism or Christianity. And there, the polemic between Christianity and Judaism often played itself out in the street in popular prejudice and violence.[70]

The Jewish Polemical Response to Islam

Commensurate with Islam's relatively mild assault on Judaism, compared with its heated polemic against Christianity, the Jewish response to Islam was similarly bland, especially when compared with the vigor of the Jewish anti-Christian polemic in Europe.

Negative Jewish Attitudes

Though far from absent in Jewish writings, hostility toward Islam had little of the acerbic tone that its counterpart in the Christian world had. Moreover, while Jesus and the symbols of Christianity evoked unbridled contempt among the Jews of Christendom,[71] a similar pattern of stimulus and response appears not to have existed among the Jews of Islam. By the time of the Islamic conquest, anti-Christian themes, whether overt or veiled, had become so engrained in the Jewish mentality that they continued to appear even in Jewish writings in the Arab world.[72] The Jews of Islam, further, continued to confront Latin Christianity in debate in the tridenominational marketplaces of the Mediterranean littoral, in such ports as Ceuta (Morocco) and Alexandria.[73]

Only two derogatory epithets describing the Prophet Muhammad are known to have been in use among Jews of the Islamic world. The first was "madman" (*meshuggaʿ*). Evidently inspired by the adjective "crazed" (*majnūn*) hurled at Muhammad by some of his unbelieving Arab contemporaries, Jews connected the word with a verse in Hosea (9:7): *evil ha-naviʾ meshuggaʿ ish ha-ruaḥ*, "The prophet was distraught, the inspired man driven mad by constant harassment."[74] The other epithet was "defective" (*pasul*), a Hebrew pun on *rasūl* (messenger). According to Islamic law, such blasphemies were punishable by death. There is little indication, however, that the Jewish characterization of Muhammad as "madman" or "the defective one" became known to Muslims, or that Jews secreted a more elaborate, irreverent jargon about Muhammad that expanded on the hostile utterances of the Jews of Medina during the Prophet's lifetime.[75]

The Response to Muslim Polemics

A comparison of anti-Islamic material in Jewish Bible commentary written in the Muslim world with interreligious polemic in European Jewish biblical exegesis yields meager results. One might expect, for example, to find a Jewish rejoinder to purported biblical foretellings of Muhammad in the commentary of the Spaniard, Abraham ibn Ezra (1089–1164). Though born in Christian Tudela and a wanderer in Italy, France, and England during a large part of his adult life, Ibn Ezra had been educated in the culture of Muslim Spain, in the Jewish courtier society of Andalusia. His treatment of the crux verses shows rather little concern with the refutation of Islam. In Genesis 17, for instance, Ibn Ezra skips over the section containing God's blessing for Ishmael, though at another occurrence of *bi-me'od me'od* in the Bible (Exodus 1:7; regarding Pharaoh's fear of Israelite overpopulation), in one edition of his commentary, Ibn Ezra dismisses the numerical forecast of Muhammad's advent Muslim out of hand.[76] For the passage in Deuteronomy 18 beginning "The Lord your God will raise up for you a prophet from among your own people, like me," he gives the simple historical explanation that the prophet whom "God will raise up" refers to Joshua, Moses' successor, and that this prophet will be sent from God, and not be a diviner. Commenting on Hosea 13:5, "I am the Lord God who have shepherded thee in the wilderness"—which, according to Muslim interpretation, alludes to Muhammad—Ibn Ezra states simply that it contains God's review of the favors he had wrought for the Israelites when they came out of the desert. Evidently, Ibn Ezra sees no significant challenge in Muslim biblical exegesis. Muslim explanations merely represent tendentious readings of the literal text, easily countered by plausible Jewish literal readings of the verses.

More complex is the treatment of the story in Genesis 16. During Hagar's flight with her son, Ishmael, the angel comforts Hagar with the prophecy that the boy will spawn a large, powerful people. Long before the rise of Islam, in a midrash on the "Sinai-Seir-Paran verse" in Deuteronomy 33:2–3,[77] the rabbis had connected the description of Ishmael in Genesis 16 with the tradition that God had offered the Torah to the gentile nations before Israel. The characterization of Ishmael as a "wild man" (*pere' adam*) whose "hand [is] against everyone" (Genesis 16) was understood by the Jewish homilist to mean that Ishmael and his descendants were all thieves, hence unworthy of receiving the Torah.[78]

For medieval Jewish commentators writing in the Muslim milieu, there was room for development of this hostile theme, but the opportunity seems, for the most part, to have been waived.[79] Ibn Ezra's remarks on Ishmael as a "wild man" illustrate this:

> Insofar as he was "wild," "his hand was against everyone," and insofar as he was a "man," "everyone's hand will be against him." The correct meaning, in my opinion, is that he will be among men like a wild person and will be victorious over everyone, but later on "everyone's hand will be against him," and this is how it is explained in Daniel, namely, that he [Ishmael] is the fourth beast.

The fourth beast of the Book of Daniel had traditionally been understood in Jewish exegesis as a symbol of Rome and Christendom, the final kingdom before the messianic Redemption. In his lifetime, Ibn Ezra experienced the exiles of both Christendom and Islam, and in his own commentary on Daniel, written after the Almohad persecution, he, like his tenth-century forerunner Saadya Gaon, "updated" the prophecy to take into account the kingdom of Ishmael.[80]

Ibn Ezra knew the old rabbinic midrash on the Sinai-Seir-Paran verse. For Deuteronomy 33:2–3, he quoted Saadya's apparently apologetic treatment of the passage. "The Gaon of blessed memory stated that Mount Sinai, Seir, and Paran in the biblical verse are near one another and that this verse tells about the revelation at Mount Sinai."[81]

Saadya's "geographical" interpretation seems aimed at the Muslim prophecy derived from that passage. Some Jews may have found the Muslim claim compelling, since the old rabbinic midrash distinguishes between the three place names and identifies the third, "from Paran," with the Ishmaelites. Possibly the inclination of Jews to believe the Muslim interpretation of the Paran passage was strengthened by another, related old midrash on the same verse, which states that God revealed himself in four languages, including Arabic.[82] Where a Muslim portent like the "Paran verse" seems to have drawn support from Jewish sources, Saadya (followed by Ibn Ezra) felt compelled to respond.

Not enough of Saadya's commentary on the Torah has been preserved for us to know how seriously he addressed Islamic polemics. There is a veiled reaction to the standard Muslim interpretation of God's blessing for Ishmael, "I hereby bless him. I will make him fertile and exceedingly numerous" (Genesis 17:20). Evidently, Saadya is responding to the Islamic interpretation when he notes that in the next verse God says he will maintain his covenant with Isaac, while later, after Isaac's birth, God exhorts Abraham to follow Sarah's advice and send Ishmael away, "for it is through Isaac that offspring shall be continued for you."[83]

In his philosophical treatise, *The Book of Beliefs and Opinions,* Saadya incorporates what may be a refutation of Islamic arguments against Judaism. In Book 3, Saadya refutes the charge of abrogation of the law (*naskh*), although he does not attribute it to Islam by name. This may not be accidental, since Christianity also preaches the abrogation of Jewish law, and Saadya challenges Christianity in several places in his *Beliefs and Opinions.*[84] Daniel Lasker contends that Saadya's polemic is concerned less with Islam than with Christianity.[85] It seems reasonable, however, that, in refuting such a central Islamic tenet as *naskh,* Saadya meant his argument to be applied principally to the dominant religion of his surroundings.[86]

Saadya brings biblical prooftexts for the eternity of the Torah, then turns to arguments drawn from reason, which he anthologizes from earlier, unnamed Jewish defenders of Judaism against *naskh*. After that, the Gaon discusses (and refutes) the contention of "proponents of the theory of abrogation" that certain biblical verses actually state that the Torah would be replaced. It is in this context that he cites the Paran verse, using geographical data culled from the Bible to show that the ostensible prophecy about three successive revelations refers to one and the same event—the theophany at Sinai. Finally, the Gaon takes up a number of biblical verses that seem to be contradicted by other verses and shows that they do *not* constitute abrogation.[87]

Karaite writers reacted more vigorously to Islam than Rabbanites such as Saadya. There were complaints about the hardship of "the Exile of Ishmael" combined with derogatory nicknames for the ruling institution, negative generalizations about Islam, and rationalistic theological arguments. Al-Qirqisānī, for instance, a tenth-century Karaite intellectual, discusses the abrogation of the law, foretellings of the prophethood of Muhammad, prophethood itself and miracles, and the lack of credibility of Muslim oral tradition.[88] In some of its practices, Karaism was closer to Islam than Rabbanite Judaism.[89] Karaite thinkers may have responded more aggressively to Islamic claims against Judaism than their Rabbanite counterparts, in order to dissuade Karaites from taking the similarity too far.

Two centuries after Saadya, the Spanish Hebrew poet and philosopher Judah ha-Levi wrote his "Book of Refutation and Proof on the Despised (or, Lowly) Faith," popularly known as *The Kuzari*. The book's very title proclaims its polemical purpose. In a Christian milieu, such a book would be devoted exclusively to refuting Christian arguments against Judaism. Characteristic of a Jew living in the Muslim milieu, however, ha-Levi finds in Islam only one of several challenges. In an effort to prove the superiority of rabbinic Judaism, he confronts Karaism and philosophical relativism. Written in Muslim Spain, where Reconquista Christianity was a factor in politics, *The Kuzari* confronts Christian polemics, as well.

Against the Islamic critique that Judaism's Scripture is filled with anthropomorphisms, ha-Levi details a doctrine of divine attributes in the *Kuzari,* which explains away Scriptural adjectives ascribing human activity to God. In answer to the Islamic prooftext of Muhammad's prophethood ("I hereby bless him [Ishmael]. I will make him fertile and exceedingly numerous), ha-Levi, like Saadya before him, points to the next verse ("But my covenant I will maintain with Isaac") as proof that God rejected Ishmael in favor of the ancestor of Israel.[90] In the same breath, he combines response to Islam with refutation of Christianity, saying: "Neither Ishmael nor Esau had a covenant," for Esau, too, was rejected, as indicated by the story of the sale of his birthright to Jacob.

Similarly, Maimonides battles Islamic arguments in his writings, though, characteristically, in works that are not devoted specifically to the defense of Judaism against Islam. In the commentary on the Mishnah, Maimonides entitles one of his thirteen compulsory articles of Jewish faith *naskh,* stating "the Torah of Moses cannot be abrogated and no other Torah but this shall come from God."[91]

Anticipated chronologically by the defensive, anti-Islamic polemical chapter 6 in the theological work, *Bustān al-ʿuqūl* [Garden of Wisdom], by the twelfth-century Yemenite Nethanel ibn Fayyūmī—written against the background of the particularly oppressive, Shiite regime of that country—Maimonides addressed to the latter's son, Jacob, his famous "Epistle to Yemen" (*Iggeret teiman*), in which he consoles a community oppressed by an Islamic regime and attracted to a local messianic pretender who had converted from Judaism to Islam.[92] Though not exclusively a polemic against Islam, the epistle contains the necessary ingredients. Maimonides responds to a report that the apostate in Yemen had adduced biblical verses announcing the future appearance of Muhammad. Before discussing them individually, he scoffs at the Muslims, saying even they realize how fallacious the foretellings are. For that reason, "they are compelled to accuse us, saying 'You have altered [*baddaltum*] the text of the Torah and expunged every trace of the name of Muhammad therefrom.'" While singling out some of the most popular Muslim portent verses in the Bible, Maimonides' response is characteristically mild and unperturbed. "I will make of him a great nation" in the blessing for Ishmael (Genesis 17:20) "implies neither prophecy nor a Law, but merely large numbers and no more." In the same vein as Saadya, Maimonides asserts that God made it clear to Abraham that all his blessings were meant only for the seed of Isaac, Ishmael being an adjunct. The Paran verse, Deuteronomy 33:2, describes only the unique revelation to Israel, which came in stages, first "coming," then "shining," and finally, "appearing." Maimonides discusses the Islamic interpretation of Deuteronomy 18:15, God's promise to designate "a prophet from among your own people," which, he says, some Jews in Yemen found compelling. "Remember that it is not right to take a passage out of its context and argue from it." The context is the divine command not to engage in occult acts, and "the prophet alluded to here will not be a person who will produce a new Law [*sharīʿa*] or found a new religion." "Our disbelief in the prophecies of ʿAmr and Zeid is not due to the fact that they are non-Jews, as the unlettered folk imagine, and in consequence of it are compelled to establish their stand from the biblical phrase 'from among your own people.'" Rather, Maimonides explains, we disbelieve a prophet who comes to alter even one precept of the Torah, which Moses told us was final and eternal.[93]

Elsewhere in the Epistle to Yemen, Maimonides responds to the report that a certain Jew in Yemen had proclaimed himself messiah. He is fully aware of the Christian polemical challenge to Judaism, citing the example of Jesus, to whom the Christians "falsely ascribe marvelous powers," which can be refuted with "a thousand proofs from Scripture." Living in the environment of Islam, in which messianism played but a minor role in (at least Sunni) religious thinking, Maimonides must address the challenge of Christianity to make his point that the Yemenite pretender is a false messiah.[94]

Maimonides' son Abraham, known for his admiration of the Muslim Sufis in his "Complete Guide for the Servants of God" (*Kifāyat al-ʿābidīn*), has some unambiguous jibes for Islam in his commentary on Genesis. His notes on chapter 21, which contains the story of the expulsion of Hagar and Ishmael, are a case in point.[95] Sarah's words, "the son of that slave shall not share in the inheritance [*lo yirash*] with my son Isaac" (verse 10), give Abraham Maimuni the opportunity to present an interpretation unfavorable to Islam. It means, he says, that the seed of Ishmael is destined not to inherit and share with Isaac the perfection (the Torah) promised his seed, "for even though they believed in it, they negated it [*abṭalūhā*] with the claim that it had been abrogated [*naskh*] and cast it away with the claim that it had been changed [*taghyīr*] and subjected to alterations [*tabdīl*]." Literally understood, he adds, the passage refers simply to Sarah's desire to remove Isaac from Ishmael's bad influence.[96] Abraham Maimonides takes the words "As for the son of the slave-woman, I will make a nation of him, too, for he is your seed" (verse 14) to be "an allusion to the appearance of the religion of Islam, of the believers in the unity of the Creator, who will descend from him . . . after the appearance of the religion of Israel, at a time of obscurity for them on account of their sins."[97] This comment, remarkably consistent with Muslim understanding of the passage, suggests that Abraham Maimuni was not greatly exercised over Muslim foretellings based on Jewish Scripture.

Most interestingly—and, again, characteristic of Jewish exegetes living under Islam—Abraham Maimuni devotes attention to Christian exegesis. He knows that Christians adduce proofs of the dominance of Christianity over lowly Judaism from such biblical passages as Genesis 25, the prophecy of the birth of Rebecca's twins, in which it is promised that "the older shall serve the younger." In Abraham Maimuni's literal understanding, the "older" must be Esau, who, indeed, served his "younger" brother Jacob "during the period of the first temple and most of the years of the second temple, and [will so] eternally in the messianic future."[98] Further, Maimuni considers the popular christological interpretation of Genesis 49:10, the "Shilo" verse, exploited in Christian exegesis to link the end of Jewish dominion with the advent of Jesus. Abraham Maimuni brings several Jewish explanations, including one in the name of Abraham ibn Ezra, which refute the polemical Christian interpretation.[99]

All of the Jewish polemical responses to Islam discussed thus far appear incidentally in works devoted to other topics. In contrast to the Jews of Christendom, with their numerous treatises dedicated to the defense of Judaism against Christianity—and differing, too, from Oriental Christians—the Jews of Islam produced no polemical text aimed exclusively and entirely at Islam. In fact, their comments in biblical commentaries, philosophical, or halakhic works often combined response to Christianity with rejoinder to Islam.

We should not forget that Rabbanite Jews had, in the Karaites, an adversary closer to home. Especially in the early Islamic period, most prominently in the person of Saadya Gaon, then, later on, in the work of Judah ha-Levi, the intra-Jewish debate with Karaism occupied an important place in Rabbanite polemics.[100] This multiplicity of polemical targets—Islam, Christianity, Karaism, and skepticism—resembles the diffusion of polemical energy in Muslim polemics against the *dhimmīs,* which diminished the intensity of specific anti-Jewish belligerency.

The only two Jewish polemical works against Islam that have come down to us were written by Jews from the Christian West, where Jewish-gentile interreligious polemics were widespread and more heated. The thirteenth-century rabbi Samuel ibn Aderet of Barcelona (Rashba) compiled a Hebrew refutation of the Islamic doctrine of *taḥrīf* (*shibbush* in his Hebrew), responding to the allegations of a Muslim, whom he calls the *meshuggaʿ* like Muhammad.[101] The other work occurs alongside a refutation of Christianity in an extract from a philosophical treatise by Rabbi Simon b. Tzemaḥ Duran (Rashbatz), a Majorcan rabbi and scholar who fled the anti-Jewish pogroms of 1391 and took refuge in Muslim Algiers. His dual polemic, given the bellicose title *Qeshet u-magen,* "Bow and Shield" in its separately printed form, affords an excellent opportunity to compare Jewish responses to the two enemy religions.

Duran begins with Christianity. He defends the eternality of the Law: the Christians perverted (*heḥeti'u*) the intention of Jesus by saying that he meant to abolish the Law.[102] He presents the Jewish version of Jesus' life and death and contradicts Christian interpretations of verses in the Bible said to herald the coming of Jesus as messiah. Christians ascribe fault to the Torah, so Duran counters with examples of the inferiority of the Gospels "which is their Torah." "Even though this be scoffing [*letzanut*], and scoffing is forbidden, this is not the case with scoffing about idolatry."[103]

Turning to Islam, Duran concentrates on the common allegations of distortion and abrogation but omits entirely a discussion of verses in Jewish Scripture claimed as foretellings of the mission of Muhammad. As a Jew reared among Christians, and accustomed to their relentless anti-Jewish polemics over the Bible, he may have perceived that the Islamic version of the Christian technique paled by comparison. Rather, Duran dwells on things in the Qur'an that are cause for ridicule, employing a Jewish strategy dating back to the Jewish encounter with Muhammad in Medina. He argues against Muhammad's prophethood, downplaying Muslim claims that the Qur'an is a miracle sufficient to confirm Muhammad's divinely ordained mission. To the contrary, Muslim interpretation of the Qur'an is filled with confusion (*bilbul*).[104] What appear in the Qur'an to be perfect acts and beliefs, including the all-important belief in the unity of God, are nothing more than Muslim imitations of the Torah and of Moses. All were slightly altered in order to maintain a distinction from the Jews. Yet many Muslim practices, notably the pilgrimage to Mecca, are paganlike and, indeed, originated as pagan rites.

Polemics and Persecution

Interreligious polemics represented one of the chief modes of discourse that sustained throughout the course of the Middle Ages the religious conflict that marked the first encounter between Judaism and each of its rival claimants to religious truth. For both Christianity and Islam, polemics was a medium for expressing their intrinsic intolerance of Judaism; for Judaism, polemics afforded a way of asserting an unflagging conviction that the Jews retained God's undivided love as well as the original religious verity.

There was a significant difference, however, between the Judaeo-Christian and Judaeo-Islamic debates. In Christianity, anti-Jewish polemic was an essential component of religious self-definition. For Islam, anti-Jewish argument was incidental, not essential; hence, both in tone and in frequency, it was more temperate than its analogue in Christianity. Judaism reciprocated with corresponding moderation, if not apathy. This important contrast reflected and helped determine the characteristically lower level of persecution that distinguished Islam from Christendom in its relations with the Jews.[105]

Chapter Ten

PERSECUTION, RESPONSE, AND COLLECTIVE MEMORY

IN THIS, the last stage in my effort to assess Muslim-Jewish and Christian-Jewish relations during the Middle Ages, let us recall G. R. Elton's assertion about monotheistic religion: "Religions organized in powerful churches . . . persecute as a matter of course and tend to regard toleration as a sign of weakness or even wickedness towards whatever deity they worship."[1]

It is not necessary to prove the existence of that which was as much a feature of medieval Islam as it was of Christianity as Christianity was practiced at the time. Rather, in addressing the issue of persecution, I wish to uncover other differences, other nuances that lay in the relations between Muslims and Jews, on the one hand, and Christians and Jews, on the other. In both contexts, the inquiry encompasses the Jewish response to persecution. Finally, this investigation climaxes with an examination of Jewish history and collective memory as they relate to the experience of persecution in Islamic and Christian societies. As I shall argue, this contrast has deep significance for the large questions about Jewish life in the gentile world in the Middle Ages.

Let me extend Elton's caveat. We say that a person or group is "persecuting" another person or group when the "persecutor" is acting outside the law or against prevailing moral standards. This view is relative, however. For example, what Americans consider persecution might, by the legal and moral standards of another country, merely be enforcement of a law, moral code, or political ideology. In the Middle Ages, the persecutor rarely considered violent assault on members of another faith "persecution." The persecutor believed that he was implementing the law—usually a law said to have divine origins—or that he was fulfilling the unspoken wish of God. In monotheistic religions—which, by nature, are exclusive—persecution overwhelmingly was justified by the claim that the persecutor was doing the work of a supreme being who demanded unquestioning belief and the absolute punishment of unbelievers.

Finally, it is important to state what is meant by *persecution*. As employed in the following discussion, the word means unwarranted violence against persons or property, including individual and mass murder. It means unlawful compulsion in matters of religion, such as forced conversion, and it includes physical expulsion. Other forms of mistreatment—what we would call discrimination, be it bias, sumptuary laws, negative attitudes, or false statements—may and do lead to persecution.[2] In and of itself, however, such intolerance was considered "normal" by medieval societies in which Jews lived.

Persecution in Christendom and Islam

In Christendom

Not even Salo Baron's anti-lachrymose revision of Jewish history in the Middle Ages managed to gloss over the fact that the Jews in Christendom suffered greatly, especially from the twelfth century on.[3] Well known are instances of large-scale massacre that began during the Crusades. Jews charged with killing Christian children were tortured and, in many cases, executed. Others were persecuted for allegedly poisoning wells or stealing and "torturing" the eucharist wafer (the "host desecration libel"). Jews experienced economic persecution (for instance, through official limitation of occupational opportunities and assaults on their property). The Talmud was burned, and Jews were forced to attend conversionary sermons—measures intended to weaken the hold of Judaism on its adherents. And Jews were expelled from towns, counties, and kingdoms.

In Islam

Claude Cahen's statement, that "one single persecution of the *dhimmīs* has been recorded in the classical centuries of Islam, that of the Fatimid al-Ḥākim," does not accord with the evidence.[4] Similarly far off the mark is Tritton's contention that persecution of the Jews was "mostly financial."[5] Islam's classical centuries were punctuated by anti-*dhimmī* persecution, some of it quite violent, especially for Christians. For Jews, it was different—less frequent and less brutal than anti-Jewish persecution in Christendom.

The first encounter between Muslims and Jews, at the dawn of Islam, resulted in persecution when Muhammad expelled or massacred the Jewish tribes of Medina. This encounter turned out to be the exception rather than the rule. Islam's triumphant expansion into southwest Asia, North Africa, and Spain saw the institutionalization of Muhammad's policy of tribute in exchange for protection. Subsequently, Islamic persecution of the Jews arose during periods of rigorous enforcement of the disabilities for *all* non-Muslim protected peoples as prescribed in the Pact of ʿUmar.

In nearly every recorded persecution involving the Jews, they were treated as *dhimmīs,* not as Jews. Geniza correspondence mentions the existence of specifically anti-Jewish feeling and oppression, called by a Hebrew neologism, *sin'ut,* or hatred. In Goitein's words, this antisemitism was "local and sporadic, rather than general and endemic."[6] This differs from European persecutions, which, by definition, were anti-Jewish and, from the time of the First Crusade, were widespread and characteristic.

Bernard Lewis sketches what he calls "possibly a typology" of the causes of Islamic repression.[7] Focusing on the essence of Islamic persecution, he summarizes: "The commonest reason by far for such outbreaks in premodern times was that the *dhimmīs* were not keeping their place, that they were acting arrogantly, that they were getting above themselves."[8] Generalizing, with Louis Dumont's insight: in any hierarchical society, groups with different status coexist more or less harmoniously, integrated into the same whole, as long as they are "agreed on the code which ranks them and separates them."

Caliph al-Mutawakkil

Muslim sources report that in the year 850, Abbasid Caliph al-Mutawakkil cracked down on the *dhimmīs:*

> In that year al-Mutawakkil ordered that the Christians and all the rest of the *Ahl al-dhimma* [Protected People] be made to wear honey-colored *ṭaylasāns* and the *zunnār* belts. . . . that any of their houses of worship built after the advent of Islam were to be destroyed and that one-tenth of their houses be confiscated. . . . He forbade their being employed in the government offices or in any official business whereby they might have authority over Muslims. . . . He forbade them to display crosses on their Palm Sundays, and he prohibited any Jewish chanting in the streets.[9]

It is generally believed that al-Mutawakkil's stringent decree, restating the *dhimmī* restrictions, correlated with his repression of the Muslim Muʿtazilites, whose unorthodox doctrines about the Qur'an had gained official recognition under Abbasid Caliph al-Ma'mūn (813–33). With the return to orthodox teaching under al-Mutawakkil came a return to orthodox policy regarding the non-Muslims, the unbelievers par excellence, which took the form of a renewal of the severe ʿUmariyyan stipulations.[10] But, Lewis notes, "there is no evidence of any violent persecution of non-Muslims under al-Mutawakkil, nor is it clear how far, how wide, and how long those restrictions were enforced."[11]

Caliph al-Ḥākim

The persecution of Christians and Jews in Egypt and Palestine during the reign of the allegedly mad Fatimid caliph al-Ḥākim (996–1021) has aroused considerable interest because of its bizarre nature. The episode is so bizarre, in fact, that it cannot easily be accommodated within Lewis's taxonomy. Al-Ḥākim punctuated his reign with arbitrary, erratic, and outlandish acts—he once ordered all dogs to be killed; but he also abolished taxes from time to time and bestowed gifts on unexpectant beneficiaries—and instilled terror in the entire Egyptian population. According to chroniclers, his persecution of Christians and Jews began as early as the year 1004, with an order to wear belts (the *zunnār*) around the waists, plus "distinguishing badges on their clothes." The oppression recurred intermittently until nearly the end of his reign. It was particularly notable for the widespread destruction of synagogues and churches (including the Church of the Holy Sepulchre in Jerusalem, an event often represented by modern historians as a long-range cause of the First Crusade).[12] Contrary to Islamic law, al-Ḥākim forced *dhimmīs* to choose between Islam and expulsion. Many fled the country, while many converted. Among his numerous unpredictable and contradictory actions, al-Ḥākim is reported to have permitted any convert who requested it of him to return to his original religion—thus violating another Islamic law that prohibited apostasy from Islam. Even medieval chroniclers question al-Ḥākim's sanity.[13]

The Pogrom in Granada

Regularly mentioned is the persecution that struck the Jews of the Spanish-Muslim Berber kingdom of Granada in 1066. Joseph ibn Nagrela, the Jewish vizier who succeeded his father, Samuel the Nagid ibn Nagrela, was assassinated by his enemies at court on December 31, 1066.[14] Enraged by his "high-handed behavior," a mob massacred the entire Jew community. The "memoirs" of Abdallah—grandson of Joseph's patron, Sultan Bādīs, who later became sultan—contain a graphic, eyewitness description of the background to the events of the massacre itself. Abdallah writes:

> Both the common people and the nobles were disgusted by the cunning of the Jews, the notorious changes which they had brought about in the order of things, and the positions which they occupied, in violation of their pact. God decreed their destruction on Saturday, Ṣafar 10 [459 A.H./December 31, 1066]. . . . The Jew fled into the interior of the palace, but the mob pursued him there, seized him, and killed him. They then put every Jew in the city to the sword and took vast quantities of their property.[15]

A polemical Arabic poem by a contemporary Muslim that apparently played a role in inciting the mob against the Jews, serves as a favorite "prooftext" of the rabid Arab antisemitism that, in the increasingly common view, tarnished the Golden Age.[16] The verses refer to the Jews as "apes" and "outcast dogs" and encourage people to "hasten to slaughter [Joseph] as an offering" and not to "spare his people," for "they have violated our covenant with them."

The pogrom of 1066 was clearly anti-Jewish. As Lewis explains, however, the poet's threat—which, indeed, was carried out—derives from the contractual nature of the *dhimma*. By lording it over the Muslims, Joseph, the Jewish vizier, violated the agreement of the subject peoples to maintain a humble—indeed, humiliated—posture vis-à-vis Islam.[17] In addition, the persecution itself needs to be placed in perspective. It fits the paradigm of the debacle of non-Muslim government officials in general. King Abdallah's complaint about the "notorious changes which [the Jews] had brought in the order of things, and the positions they occupied, in violation of their pact" also correlates with and reinforces the proposition I argue in Chapter 6—namely, that both Islam and Christendom, hierarchical societies, objected to any alteration in the "right order" of society, especially when perpetrated by infidels.

Lesser-known Persecutions

Other examples of mob attack on Jewish property, and even the lives of Jews, crop up here and there in medieval Islamic sources for the early and High Middle Ages. In 1032, for instance, the Jewish quarter of Fez came under attack along with the rest of the city, when it was taken over by a Berber chief. More than six thousand Jews are said to have been slain, alongside other barbarisms.[18]

In 1177–78, in Mada'in (near Baghdad), Muslims, offended by Jewish attempts to have the intrusive call of the muezzin in a nearby mosque toned down, complained to Baghdad. Unrequited—and, indeed, thwarted by the authorities—they were joined by a local mob and went on a rampage against Jewish shops, destroying a synagogue and burning a Torah scroll.[19] It is likely that a careful search of Arabic chronicles would turn up additional instances of this kind of specifically anti-Jewish violence during the Golden Age centuries of Islam.[20]

Persecutions in North Africa, Spain, and Yemen

The most serious persecution experienced by Jews during this period was that of the Berber Almohads, beginning in the mid-1140s, during and after the Almohad conquests in North Africa and Spain.[21] The militant preaching of this puritanical sect turned all resistors, Muslim and non-Muslim alike, into enemies.[22] To both Jews and Christians, the Almohads presented the choice of death or conversion; most chose conversion. The effort by one modern scholar to minimize the severity and persistence of the Almohad persecution seems more a by-product of his favorable appraisal of Muslim-Jewish relations in his native Morocco than the result of compelling revisionist analysis of the evidence.[23]

The Almohad terror was followed (apparently in 1172) by fierce persecution in Yemen. A zealous rebel regime forced the *dhimmīs* to convert to Islam. A great number of Jews apostatized; some were attracted to the proselytizing message of a Jewish convert to Islam who preached about the predictions of Muhammad in the Torah. Still others joined the followers of a local Jewish messianic pretender who proclaimed to receptive ears that the persecution heralded the imminent, long-awaited redemption. Our main knowledge of this persecution comes from the famous "epistle" that Maimonides, himself a refugee from Almohad oppression, wrote to counsel and console the Jews of Yemen.[24] This is the source that includes Maimonides' bitter condemnation of Islam for its unparalleled oppression of the Jews.

Earlier in the epistle, Maimonides addresses his correspondent, the head of the Jewish community in Yemen, lamenting the heavy blows Islam had inflicted on his people during his own lifetime.[25] The concatenation of calamities during Maimonides' lifetime almost certainly justified his sense that he was living in an era of unprecedented victimization. As Bernard Lewis represents the severe strictures of Maimonides, however, they "cannot be accepted as an accurate general picture [of Jewish life in the Islamic diaspora, although] his observations certainly contain a proportion of truth."[26]

Surely the Jews of Yemen and the Jews of Spain and North Africa under the Almohads were little comforted that the persecutions were aimed at the *dhimmīs,* or that the Jews were brutalized because of their generic status rather than because they were Jews. In particular, in Yemen, where there were no longer any Christians, forced conversion would have seemed essentially an anti-Jewish affair.[27] Nonetheless, the Jewish response to this and other calamities typified a perception of Jewish fate that differed from that of their cousins living in Christendom.

Expulsion

Jews did not suffer the anguish of expulsion under Islamic rule in the classical centuries. The Fatimid caliph al-Ḥākim ordered banished those *dhimmīs* who refused to accept Islam. This was the exception that proves the rule: Many Jews *fled* North Africa or Muslim Spain in order to escape persecution by the Almohads; I know of no evidence suggesting that Almohads included expulsion among the choices offered the non-Muslim victims of their oppressive policy.[28]

Neglect of expulsion as a solution to the "Jewish problem" is all the more striking when we consider that Islamic jurists discussed the option. Muhammad's expulsion of two Jewish tribes from Medina, and Caliph ʿUmar's reported banishment of those Jews still living in the Hijaz (the region encompassing the holy cities of Mecca and Medina) gave rise to the *ḥadīth,* under which "two religions shall not exist together in Arabia." The precedent provided an opportunity for jurists to consider the issue under the rubric, "On Exiling the Jews from Arabia [or the Hijaz]." Legists debated the boundaries of the Hijaz for purposes of applying ʿUmar's precedent. Some maintained that the borders extended to the northern edge of the Arabian peninsula. The tenth-century historian al-Ṭabarī, followed by a few jurists of the Mamluk period, was of the opinion that Muslims could cancel the Pact of ʿUmar and expel Jews or Christians from *any* predominantly Muslim area once Muslims no longer needed them. The majority view of the jurists over time, however, is that the *dhimmīs* had a presumptive right to reside in Islamic lands—without residential segregation—and that their property had to be protected.[29]

Disregard of expulsion as an expedient can perhaps be explained in part by reference to Baron's thesis concerning the role of "medieval nationalism in the fate of the Jews."[30] Expulsion of the Jews from England, France, and Spain, between 1290 and 1492, was the result of religious, economic, and social factors that came into play when other efforts—principally, conversion to Christianity—failed to achieve the same exclusionary end. Baron contends that expulsion occurred where there was ethnic amalgamation, or when rulers strove for "national unity."[31] In England this "nationalism" grew steadily from the time of the Norman conquest in 1066. In France from the twelfth century on, it took the form of royal centralization at the expense of English and baronial sovereignty. In Spain, it was not to occur until the aggressive national unification policy of King Ferdinand and Queen Isabella at the end of the fifteenth century. In Germany, where any striving for national unity was canceled by universalist (imperial) aspirations or by tribal, regional, or municipal solidarity, no general expulsion of Jews occurred—only wholesale banishment from cities and some principalities during the fifteenth century. Similarly, in Italy, political atomization and ecumenical pretensions in the Papal states prevented large-scale expulsion. The role of nationalism in the exclusion of minorities from society has been pointed out by social scientists working on ethnicity.[32]

Baron's theory has met with resistance in Jewish historiography.[33] The very existence of nationalism in the Middle Ages is questionable.[34] For my purposes, the hypothesis has heuristic value; comparison with the Islamic world might even refine and substantiate Baron's insight into the Christian West. The Islamic world, where expulsion did not occur, lacked even primitive nationalistic tendencies during the Middle Ages. Rather, Islamic civilization retained its deep-rooted ethnically pluralistic character far longer than did most of Christian Europe. Thus there would have been no impulse to expel Jews or Christians on those grounds. Something akin to expulsion-as-an-expedient occurred in later Islamic times but was unrelated to the forces of nationalism. After the conquest of Constantinople in 1453, the Ottomans forcibly relocated large numbers of Jews to the new capital (renamed Istanbul). Called *sürgün* (exile or deportation) in Turkish, this policy of compulsory migration in the interests of the state was applied to numerous proples in the Ottoman empire, although the Byzantine Jews—the so-called Romaniotes—felt it to be an "expulsion."[35] Similar deportations of Christians—and, probably, of Jews—to a newly conquered region occurred under the Safavid Shah ʿAbbās I of Iran at the beginning of the seventeenth century.[36] In a genuinely anti-Jewish persecution, the Jews of Yemen were temporarily banished to the desert of Mawzaʿ, on the shore of the Red Sea, from 1678 to 1681, and the Jewish quarter of Ṣanʿāʾ was destroyed and its synagogue converted to a mosque. The "Mawzaʿ Exile" (*galut mawzaʿ*), in which many lives were lost and much destruction of property was wrought, entered the literary collective memory of the Jews of Yemen as a great tragedy.[37]

"Persecuting Society"

Whether their persecution is measured in terms of expulsion, murder, assault on property, or forced conversion, the Jews of Islam did not experience physical violence on a scale remotely approaching Jewish suffering in Western Christendom. By and large, even when *dhimmīs* as a group experienced growing oppression and persecution in the postclassical period, the grim conditions found in Europe were not matched. The Black Death, which raged through Europe between 1348 and 1350, witnessed massive pogroms against the Jews, who were believed to have poisoned wells in an attempt to destroy Christian civilization.[38] The Black Death ravaged the Islamic world as well, but nowhere did people there blame the Jews, let alone try to eliminate them. In his study of the Black Death in the Middle East, Michael Dols discusses the contrasting responses of Christian and Muslim so^ieties to their respective infidels during the pandemic. The Christian concepts of "millennialism, militancy toward alien communities, [and] punishment and guilt" that contributed to persecution of the Jews during the plague were not operative in Muslim society.[39] "Compared with the contemporary massacres in Christian Europe," Baron writes of the Mamluk empire in the period 1250–1517, "anti-Jewish riots were both less frequent and less bloody. As a rule they were limited to certain localities and did not assume the epidemic proportions of the assaults by Crusaders or by the frenzied European mobs of 1348–1349 or

1391." He is pinpointing a distinction that applies even more sharply to earlier centuries, the period that is the focus of my book.[40]

How can one explain this difference? The historian R. I. Moore has called medieval Christianity, especially as of the twelfth century, a "persecuting society." The characteristics and historical circumstances that this scholar evidences in support of his conclusion help explain the relatively better condition of the Jews of Islam. According to Moore, beginning in the twelfth century, European Christendom showed increasing hostility to three groups—Jews, heretics, and lepers. The assumed connection between the Devil and both Jews and heretics (linkage between Jews and heretics, of course, went back to early Christian times), and the ascription to Jews and lepers alike of filth, stench, and putrefaction and of menace to Christian wives and children numbered among the factors that led to the deadly interchangeability of the three groups, particularly in popular thinking. "The assimilation of Jews, heretics and lepers into a single rhetoric . . . depicted them as a single though many-headed threat to the security of the Christian order."[41] Perhaps the most devastating consequence of the Jew-leper nexus occurred during the ferocious persecution in France in 1321, which was aimed at lepers accused of plotting to poison the entire population, but calamitously targeted the Jews as well.[42]

The Jew and Heresy

These criteria—linkage among Jews, heretics, and lepers—for designating Christendom a persecuting society cannot easily be applied to Islam. For one thing, heresy in Islam is quite a different matter from its counterpart in Christianity. Islam, like Judaism, places heavy emphasis on practice and allows great latitude in belief. "Heresy was persecuted only when it was seen to offer a substantial threat to the social or political order," writes Bernard Lewis. This, he says, parallels the attitude toward non-Muslims, who were oppressed when they breached the law [of the *dhimma*] or violated the "maintenance of the social or political order."[43] The "recurrent tendency" in Islam—to attribute subversive doctrines such as Shiism to the malevolent designs of a Jewish convert—was not accompanied by a generalized suspicion of Jewry's ambition to undermine the regnant religion, as happened in the West.[44]

The contrast can be carried further. The Christian definition of heresy included "Judaizing"—imitation of Judaism—which was viewed as a repudiation of the Christian dispensation. For this reason, the stigma of heresy frequently extended to professing Jews themselves because they were suspected of abetting Christians to Judaize, including Jews—"rejudaizers"—who had converted to Christianity, whether voluntarily or by coercion. The Inquisition, established at the beginning of the thirteenth century to ferret out and prosecute heretics, often extended its scrutiny and coercive power over individual Jews and Jewish writings.[45]

Unlike their counterparts in Christian Europe, Jews living under Islam did not bear the burden of suspicion of heresy or of encouraging Muslims to follow Jewish custom. As explained in Chapter 2, "Judaizing" among Muslims was expressed mainly in terms of a cleavage to popular Jewish (or Christian) practices—for example, worship of saints. This constituted a violation of the rule, *khālifūhum,* "be different from them," rather than a heretical deviation. For religious thinkers like Ibn Taymiyya, it was a blow to the prestige of Islam as well as an "innovation" in practice more than a theological affront. Thus, in his vigorous campaign to suppress Muslim indulgence in cults involving the tombs of saints, Ibn Taymiyya did not hold non-Muslims responsible for Muslim infraction of the *khālifūhum* principle.

The Devil and the Jew

The theme of the Jew-heretic, foreign to Islam, blended in Christianity with the motif of the Jew as intimate of the Devil, the arch-seducer of men to heresy. Satan, the enemy of Jesus and embodiment of all dark forces arrayed against God, appears in his inimical role in the New Testament. Further, the Devil had a continuous and pervasive presence in medieval Christendom, nourished by popular beliefs about demons rooted in the pagan past and reinforced by the exorcistic skills of local Catholic clerics.[46] The widespread belief during the High and late Middle Ages, that the Jews were intimately allied with the Devil, was inspired by New Testament passages linking the Jew with Satan.[47] This belief drew additional support from numerous Christian writers. Thus, for example, the fourth-century father Gregory of Nyssa said of the Jews: "They are confederates of the devil, offspring of vipers, scandal-mongers, slanderers, darkened in mind, leaven of the Pharisees, Sanhedrin of demons, accursed, utterly vile, quick to abuse, enemies of all that is good."[48] Eusebius of Alexandria, in the "Sermon on the Resurrection" attributed to him, addresses the Jews as follows: "Woe to you wretches, for you follow evil counsels, for you were called sons and became dogs. . . . And Hell shall revenge itself upon you for the defeat it received from the Lord, and it shall imprison you with your father the Devil."[49] The contemporary Merovingian authors of the *Life of Caesarius of Arles* depict the Jews of Arles as "perfidiously" allied with the heretical Arian Goths against the city and its Bishop Caesarius, with "the Devil rejoicing" at their evildoing.[50] When Archbishop Agobard wrote to inform the Carolingian king Louis the Pious how much damage his favoritism toward the Jews had done to the faithful of Christianity, he underscored their venality by calling them *vasa diaboli,* "vessels of the

Devil," and also, in keeping with the Gospel of John (8:44), *filii diaboli,* "sons of the Devil."[51]

Eventually the stereotyped identification of the Jew with the Devil blossomed in legend, art, drama, and sermons; and the old idea that the Devil was bent on the destruction of all of Christendom carried over to the Devil's malevolent companion—the Jew. Many irrational convictions about Jews in the High and late Middle Ages found an "explanation" in the partnership of the Jew and the Devil.[52]

In *The Devil and the Jews,* Joshua Trachtenberg argues that, while the official church adhered to its original conviction that Jews were infidels whose rejection of Christianity might someday be reversed with the removal of the veil of blindness that kept them from seeing the truth, the Christian masses, deeply fearful of both Satan and the Jew, merged the two. As Satan was the father of heresy, Jews came to be thought of as heretics, more evil even than infidels because, despite their knowledge of Christian truth, they perversely rejected and battled against it.[53] The Jews' "deliberate unbelief," as Cecil Roth called this widespread Christian conviction about the Jews in an essay published more than five decades ago, made them seem "less than human . . . [and] . . . capable of any crime imaginable or unimaginable."[54]

Medieval Antisemitism—Applying Langmuir's Theory

It is this "irrational thinking about the Jews" that Langmuir, a historian of Jew-hatred in Christendom, isolates as the fundamental cause of antisemitism from the Middle Ages to modern times.[55] Anti-Judaism, the predecessor of antisemitism, emerged when early Christians began to engage in "nonrational thinking" about the Jews after the death of Jesus—namely, that Jewish understanding was deficient, that the Jews had killed Christ, that God was punishing the Jews for deicide. Antisemitism proper emerged in Christendom beginning in the twelfth century, when Christians adopted "irrational" fantasies "that Jews ritually crucified Christian children, used human blood and flesh in their rituals, tortured the wafers of the Eucharist, and sought to destroy Christendom by sowing the Black Death." These, Langmuir says, are the "clearest examples of irrational efforts by Christians to use Jews to repress doubts about their beliefs and strengthen their faith in their Christian identity."[56] This doubt—a new, rational-empirical skepticism about such fundamental Catholic beliefs as the incarnation and the eucharist—had arisen in the eleventh century, progressing in the twelfth with the rise of scholasticism. It was all the more vexing in the face of "that incarnation of disbelief, the dispersed minority of Jews." Projection on the Jews of irrational fantasies of evil, inhumanity, and murderous intent served as a mechanism for dispelling Christian doubt while at the same time justifying physical persecution.[57]

Classical Islam did not display such irrational thinking about the Jews. Like Christians, Muslims during the Middle Ages feared Satan.[58] The Devil has an evil, rebellious, deceiving, even inimical role to play in the Qur'an and in later Arabic literature. But he is not the quintessential enemy of the founder of the Islamic religion. Nor, by extension, is he a dark force working to destroy all of society. Thus, when Jews and Satan are occasionally associated with one another in Islamic writings, as in the phrase "party of Satan," the connection does not carry the same weight.[59] As is usual with negative statements about Jews or Christians in Islam, the Devil relationship appears generically in connection with both non-Muslim peoples in discussions of the *dhimma*. Thus, the calumny, "party of Satan," is applied in a market inspection (*ḥisba*) treatise from eleventh-century Spain to both Jews and Christians, as well as in a statement of Caliph ʿUmar II to *dhimmī* (the source says *polytheist*) government clerks.[60] A source describing how non-Muslims should wear their turbans admonishes them to avoid letting the turban drape below the shoulders, as Muslims do; rather, they should follow the custom of the "turban of the Devil."[61]

Medieval Islam did not portray the Jew or the Christian irrationally, as collaborating with Satan to undermine society.[62] The increase in Islamic hostility toward Christians and Jews during the period of the Crusades and the Mongol conquest, which Lewis and others explain as stemming from a fear of fifth-columnist collaboration with the enemy, provides a striking contrast with the situation in Christendom. The suspicion that *dhimmīs* collaborated with the external enemy is decidedly not "irrational thinking about the Jews." It relied, instead, on the empirical knowledge that many non-Muslims favored Christian or pagan Mongol rule in the hope of escaping the humiliating aspects of the *dhimma*. Ibn Qayyim al-Jawziyya exemplifies the believable charge of *dhimmī* treachery in this regard with a story about a Christian clerk in Mamluk Egypt who was discovered writing letters to the European Christians (*firanj*) conveying intelligence (*akhbār*) about the Muslims.[63]

The absence of the irrational element of diabolical Jewish enmity in Islamic thinking must be considered a salient reason for the dearth of anti-Jewish persecution in Islam. Applying the contrast reciprocally, one could point out that beliefs about Jewish betrayal could only be irrational in Christendom, since Jews could not readily—hence, empirically—be identified with a militant external enemy threatening Christian territory.[64]

Langmuir's theory about the relationship between doubt and irrational antisemitism in medieval Christendom, applied to Islamic-Jewish relations, deepens our understanding of the difference between the two societies. Because doubt played a substantial role in the intellectual life of medieval Muslims and their Jewish neighbors, the philosophical movement in Arabic culture, which began much earlier in Islam than in Christianity, concerned itself with dispelling skepticism. The numerous Arabic book titles beginning with, for example, the words "Guide of the Perplexed" are testimony to the potential corrosiveness of doubt in Islamic society. The Islamic religion, however, was relatively free of nonrational, nonempirical credos such as incarnation, the trinity, and transubstantiation—the very doubt-engendering beliefs that, according to Langmuir, Christians sought to repress with their irrational thoughts about the Jews.

The Response to Persecution

In Northern Christendom

The Jewish response to persecution differed markedly in Christian and Islamic lands. In northern Europe, Jews faced with the alternative of death or forced conversion (a choice often encountered during eruptions of anti-Jewish feeling), frequently chose a noble death—martyrdom, even by suicide.[65] A typical passage from one of the medieval Hebrew accounts of the massacre of the Jews during the First Crusade paints a moving picture of the typical Ashkenazic martyrdom:

> The women girded their loins . . . and slew their own sons and daughters, and then themselves. Many men also . . . slaughtered their wives and children and infants. The most gentle and tender of women slaughtered the child of her delight. They all arose . . . and slew one another. The young maidens, the brides, and the bridegrooms looked out through the windows and cried out in a great voice: "Look and behold, O Lord, what we are doing to sanctify Thy Great Name, in order not to exchange You for a crucified scion who was despised, abominated, and held in contempt in his own generation, a bastard son conceived by a menstruating and wanton mother."[66]

Martyrdom, rather than surrender to forced conversion, seems to have been a response to persecution introduced by Ashkenazic Jewry during the Middle Ages. It represents a substantial, generalized elaboration of the classic Jewish martyrdoms portrayed in the midrash.[67] Mass self-immolation by European Jews complemented a self-perception of standing up to a trial of faith imposed by God on an essentially holy and sinless generation and of reenacting on a human plane the sacrificial cult of the ancient Jerusalem Temple.[68]

Jacob Katz explains the northern European Jewish preference for martyrdom when faced with forced conversion. The Jews of Ashkenaz considered Christians theologically idolatrous and themselves obliged by the mishnaic ruling that a Jew must die rather than succumb to idolatry. Related to this was the Jews' revulsion at the sight of certain Christian symbols, notably the cross, which represented to Jews the inconceivable claim that Jesus had been both the Messiah and the son of God, crucified at the behest of the Jews.[69] In addition, the age-old Christian readiness to suffer martyrdom, to avoid apostasy and bear witness with one's life to the truth of Christianity, encouraged Jewish imitation. Jews held up *their* martyrdom to Christians as proof of the superiority of their faith and their God.[70] Gerson Cohen argues that the "messianic posture" of Ashkenazim, including an unquestioned belief in the dogma of resurrection, reinforced their willingness to suffer martyrdom.[71] Conversion to escape death occurred, and probably with greater frequency than the occasional allusions in the Hebrew accounts of persecution suggest. Approaching the late Middle Ages, especially the disastrous fourteenth century, one finds a significant increase in Jewish apostasy to Christianity, whether voluntary (to escape misery and antisemitism) or coaxed by the compulsory conversionary sermons of the newly invigorated Christian mission to the Jews.[72] Nonetheless, martyrdom remained the Ashkenazic ideal.

In Islamic Lands

By contrast, Jews in Islamic lands, when threatened with extinction unless they converted, typically accepted the religion of Islam rather than a martyr's death. Many factors contributed to determining this characteristically "Sephardic" response to violent persecution (which carried over to Christian Spain in the form of "marranism" beginning with the pogroms of 1391). In considering the "messianic posture" of Sephardim, Gerson Cohen pointed to the role of rationalism in undermining their faith, creating doubt about miracles such as the resurrection, and hence, discouraging the choice of death.[73]

In an essay on the forced converts in the Maghreb during the Almohad persecution, Menahem Ben-Sasson aptly observes that the Jews of the Arab world met the characteristic criteria for cultural Arabization, criteria that contemporary scholars believe made non-Muslims ripe candidates for Islamization.[74] Moreover, the Jews of Islam were not nearly as repelled by symbols of the dominant religion as were the Ashkenazic subjects of Katz's research. Nothing comparable to the invective and hatred characteristic of the Ashkenazic literary treatment of Christianity exists in the writings of the Jews of Islam, including the private letters of the Geniza, in which derogatory remarks about Muslims as a group might occasionally be expected but are not to be found.[75]

Then, too, martyrdom in the surrounding Muslim society was not as salient a concept as it was in Christianity. Muslims—particularly, Sunni Muslims—unlike the early Christians, did not have to suffer for their faith in the face of persecution by another dominant power such as Rome. In Islamic definition, the martyr was a warrior who died fighting in a holy war. Confronted by religious persecution, Muslims favored outward accommodation or dissimulation, in Arabic *taqiyya,* while inwardly maintaining belief in Islam. Rather than having a gentile model of martyrdom to emulate and even surpass, the Jews of Islam seem to have been influenced by the Islamic response to forced conversion in their own pattern of accommodation. Later on, this became the standard for persecuted Jews of Christian Spain, which was heavily influenced by the Islamic presence on Iberian soil for so many centuries.[76]

Another element is critical: Jews in Islamic countries followed the opinion of contemporary rabbinic teachers, who excluded Islam from the category of idolatry. They doubtless considered themselves exempt from the halakhic requirement to die rather than renounce Judaism for an idolatrous faith. Maimonides put the stamp of approval on this theological judgment. According to David Novak, Maimonides "not only regarded Islam as an unambiguously monotheistic religion, but he also saw certain Islamic practices as actually being mandated by Judaism"—for instance, circumcision.[77] He even allowed Jews to drink wine touched by Muslims, something forbidden in the case of idolaters because of the association with pagan libation.[78] Conversion to Islam could be accomplished by recitation of the inoffensive formula, called the *shahāda,* or "testimony," that "there is no God but God and Muhammad is his messenger." Jews could accept Islam outwardly, demonstrating their conversion by attending Friday prayer and avoiding acts disapproved of in Islam, while secretly adhering to Judaism in the privacy of their homes.

Equally important, while Islam, like Christianity, prohibits apostasy—that is, conversion from Islam to any other religion, on pain of death—in all three great persecutions of the classical period (al-Ḥākim's, the Almohads', and that in Yemen), Jews and Christians forced to accept Islam were allowed to revert to their original faith after the persecution had subsided. In the first of these persecutions, al-Ḥākim's son and successor, al-Ẓāhir, issued a reassuring decree in which he repeated the opposition of Islam to forced conversion and restated the Muslim obligation to protect the *dhimmī* population. The authorities required the *dhimmīs* to remit *jizya* retroactively.[79]

A tenth-century Muslim formulary from Spain includes model documents outlining the requirements for conversion, requirements that are more stringent than a simple recitation of the *shahāda.* Nonetheless, the manual stipulates that the person converted through compulsion be "permitted to return . . . his conversion to Islam is not binding, unless it becomes known for certain that he had gotten over the fear and compulsion and then converted to Islam, praying one *ṣalāt* and no more, in which case his conversion to Islam is binding."[80]

Jews knew the position of Islamic law on forced conversion. They were aware that it had been upheld in the past. They would have remembered from al-Ḥākim's persecution in Egypt that, with the relaxation of fanaticism, Jewish converts had been allowed to return to Judaism.[81] In addition to the reasons discussed above, it is likely that when North African and Andalusian Jews opted for life as nominal Muslims rather than for death as martyrs, they expected that their dissembling would be temporary, lasting only until the Islamic Holy Law opposing forced conversion was restored.[82]

Jewish History and Jewish Collective Memory

Collective memory—the memory preserved by a group of people—mirrors the perception of what was meaningful from that people's past, and, in turn, what is salient in the present.[83] Yosef Hayim Yerushalmi traces the Jewish tradition of writing history back to the Bible. Men examined the acts of individuals, Israel, and the nations in order to explicate God's covenant with Israel and his plan for their eternal existence as his holy people. Side by side with written history, biblical Israel preserved *memory*—with its inherent selectivity—in the form of ritual observance and recitation of past events, as in the Song of Deborah. The rabbis of the Talmud focused all their attention on the biblical account of the Jewish past. Indeed, they evidenced little interest in the history of postbiblical times.[84] Similarly, Bernard Lewis concludes that rabbinic preoccupation with legitimizing the oral law and their own authority to expound it contributed to the neglect of history.[85]

Yerushalmi and Lewis concur, too, that the store of Jewish historiographical works from the Middle Ages is paltry.[86] The popular medieval *Book of Yossipon* deals exclusively with Jewish history in antiquity. The most important vehicles for transmitting historical memory, they argue, were commemorative acts of ritual and liturgy.[87] In addition, Jews of the Middle Ages took inspiration from the biblical Book of Esther, the first and archetypal Jewish literary response to antisemitism, which relates the triumph of the Jews of Persia over their enemy, Haman, who had sought to destroy them. The book served as a model for medieval *megillot,* "scrolls" of deliverance—even "Second Purims," commemorating narrow escapes from catastrophic persecutions of local Jewish communities.[88] Only in the sixteenth century, Yerushalmi asserts, following the traumatic expulsion of the Jews from Christian Spain (1492), did the Jewish people begin to take historiography seriously. There appeared at that time a cluster of chronicles recounting the Jewish persecutions of the preceding centuries.[89]

Medieval Jewish Historiography and Collective Memory

What little there is that resembles genuine history writing in the Middle Ages comes mainly from the Ashkenazic world.[90] Attention has focused on a few "chronicles," describing acts of persecution by Christians and the Jewish response of self-immolation. Three of these chronicles depict the events of 1096, while a fourth recounts persecution during the Second Crusade (1146–47). I have quoted from one of these narratives in connection with Ashkenazic martyrdom. The compilers of these narratives relied in part on oral reports and circular letters.[91] Yerushalmi dismisses these writings as transmitters of Jewish memory, because "they describe something in the most recent past, be it the latest persecution or the latest deliverance," but, more importantly, because "historiography never served as a primary vehicle for Jewish memory in the Middle Ages."[92]

Yerushalmi is overly categorical in his statement of the case. In addition, he makes the distinction between collective memory and historiography too sharp. First, narratives of the Crusades are not the only medieval examples of this genre. A less well-known, but anonymous, Hebrew narrative relates how, in 992, the entire Jewish settlement in Le Mans, France, was placed in peril by the malevolent doings of a vagabond Jewish apostate to Christianity. The lost, final section of the manuscript of the text must have told about the divine deliverance foreshadowed in the fragment's opening passage:

> Writ of the community of Le Mans and book of the salvation from God, who acted on behalf of those who keep his covenant and guard his commands in the year nine hundred and twenty-four since the destruction of the Second Temple [traditionally dated 68 C.E.]. The book has been written to serve as an eternal remembrance [*zikkaron*] for the children of Israel, so that they may retell it to their children unto the final generation—children yet to be born—that they may become wise and know about the salvation from God and his strong hand: he who did not withhold his mercy from his servants who serve him in truth. He had compassion upon them in his mercy and left them a remnant in their exile, that they might fulfill his covenant with Abraham, Isaac, and Jacob. This is the content of the open book, which has been recorded truthfully.[93]

Another narrative relates the plight of the Jews in Rouen, France, in 1007. Responding to the anti-Jewish hue and cry of his Christian subjects, "King Robert of France" tried to convert the Jews by force. Many died renouncing Christianity before the rest were saved through the intercession of a prominent Jew with the pope.[94]

Obviously, these texts are concerned with the short term. They recount recent instances of persecutions. On the other hand, Ephraim of Bonn's *Book of Remembrance* (*Sefer zekhira*), which contains the last of the four Hebrew chronicles of the Crusades, is a historical remembrance of persecution written centuries before the Sephardic cluster from the sixteenth century. The *Book of Remembrance* is often, but imprecisely, characterized simply as a chronicle of the Second Crusade. True, the writer begins with the suffering of the Jews during that Crusade, but he goes on to recount, in sequence, seven other persecutions that occurred in France, Germany, and England during the second half of the twelfth century, starting with the first occurrence of the ritual murder accusation on the European continent —the case of Blois, France, in 1171.[95] The Blois narrative, with its martyrdoms, catches Yerushalmi's attention as an artifact of Jewish collective memory; the event produced *seliḥot* and, significantly, an annual fast day in memory of the victims that took hold in the Jewish calendar. In the seventeenth century, that fast assimilated a new element—the memory of the pogroms against the Jews of Poland and the Ukraine during the Cossack rebellion of 1648–49. These constitute some of the highly nonhistorical Jewish modes of memorialization Yerushalmi isolates as the vehicle of Jewish memory during the Middle Ages.[96]

In its literary form, Ephraim of Bonn's *Book of Remembrance* anticipates by several centuries the "chain-of-persecutions" chronicles that proliferated in the sixteenth century.[97] And there are others. An annalistic Hebrew narrative of Jewish travail in southern France (mostly from persecution), compiled near the end of the thirteenth century by a Provencal Jew named Shemtov Shanzolo, was borrowed in the sixteenth century by the Iberian refugee Joseph ibn Verga to serve as an appendix to his father Solomon's chronicle of persecution, *Shevet yehuda,* which Joseph published in 1554, in Turkey.[98] Another short chronicle, compiled between the middle of the fourteenth and the end of the fifteenth century, recounts a series of tribulations of Jewish communities and individuals from the days of the Merovingian king, Dagobert, to the Black Death.[99] There is also the lost *Remembrance of Persecutions* (*Zikhron ha-shemadot*) of the fourteenth-century Catalonian Jew, Profiat Duran ("Efodi"), known only from citation in a messianic work of the sixteenth century by a prominent exile from Christian Spain, Don Isaac Abravanel.[100]

This type of literature, anticipating by generations the Sephardic, post-Spanish expulsion chronicles singled out by Yerushalmi and serving to recount (and, often, sacralize) the suffering of European Jewry, is consistent with the collective memory of the Jews of Western lands under Christian rule. Viewed alongside a much larger harvest of liturgical poetry—elegies and dirges—they form the basis for a collective memory of suffering inflicted by Christians.[101] This, in turn, is linked with the older, biblical-rabbinical historical conception of persecution in exile (*galut*), usually viewed as punishment for past sins, eventually to be relieved by the Redemption. The "lachrymose conception" of Jewish history in Christendom had its origin in this medieval collective memory of tragic fate in the Christian world. It is a tradition that continues to live among European survivors of the Holocaust who have left individual or collective documents of memorialization.[102]

Collective Memory of Persecution among the Jews of Islam

Very little of the sorrowful memorialization of past oppression can be found among the writings of the Jews in Muslim lands during the classical centuries. This is not because episodes of persecution were not widely known to contemporaries. Writing from Fustat to Jerusalem not long after the death of his father (Shemarya b. Elḥanan, in 1011), Elḥanan b. Shemarya, his father's successor as leader of the Egyptian Jewish community, describes a recent wave of destruction of synagogues and other oppressive acts that can only refer to al-Ḥākim's persecution. In the characteristic flowery rhymed Hebrew prose of the period, he explains:

> Our debts [sins] increased and favor was removed on account of our many abominations [*toʿavot*]. [God's] anger was not delayed and fire descended. . . . Synagogues were destroyed, and signs came true. Torah scrolls were torn and spread about like seeds being sown. Pentateuch books were cast onto the streets. Churches [*ha-kenesiyot*] were destroyed and made desolate. We dressed in black and walked in darkness. Signs were placed on our loin and our houses became filled with cries. They suspended a piece of wood around our necks. We wearied, and none would leave us be. Fulfilled in us was the sages' midrash: "'The sacred gems are spilled' [Lamentations 4:1]—these are scholars who shall go into exile, their Torah scrolls having been plundered." Many turned away from their faith and abandoned their religions.[103]

Other Geniza letters refer to the traumatic events and the reconstruction that followed.[104] Given these facts, the apparent absence of any formal memorialization of the long reign of terror is puzzling—unless it is symptomatic of some aspect of Jewish collective memory under Islam that differed fundamentally from its counterpart in Christian lands.[105]

The massacre of 1066, in Granada, unequivocally anti-Jewish, had its memorialization in Arabic historiography; but it left hardly a literary trace among the Jews. It is mentioned briefly in Moses ibn Ezra's (b. 1055–60; d. after 1138) Arabic book on Hebrew prosody, where he speaks of Joseph ibn Nagrela in his biographical survey of poetic personalities;[106] it crops up in a passing notice in Abraham ibn Daud's *Book of Tradition,* composed ca. 1160, a source devoted to rabbinic history, not to Muslim-Jewish relations.

> R. Joseph ha-Levi the Nagid, succeeded to his [father's] post. Of all the fine qualities which his father possessed he lacked but one. Having been reared in wealth and never having had to bear a burden [of responsibility] in his youth, he lacked his father's humility. Indeed, he grew haughty—to his destruction. The Berber princes became so jealous of him that he was killed on the Sabbath day, the ninth of Tebet [4]827 [December 31, 1066], along with the commu-

nity of Granada and all those who had come from distant lands to see his learning and power. He was mourned in every city and in every town. (Indeed, a fast had been decreed for the ninth of Tebet as far back as the days of our ancient rabbis, who composed *Megillat Taʿanit;* but the reason had not been known. From this [incident] we see that they had pointed prophetically to this very day.)[107]

Two elegies on Joseph's death, by the contemporary Hebrew poet Isaac ibn Giyyat (1038–89), lack the faintest allusion to the gruesome circumstances surrounding his demise.[108]

The later report of the Almohad devastation in *Sefer ha-Qabbalah* is nearly as brief and low-keyed as Ibn Daud's report of the incident of 1066:

> After the demise of R. Joseph [ha-Levi ibn Megash] there were years of war, evil decrees and persecutions that overtook the Jews, who were compelled to wander from their homes, "such as were for death, to death; and such as were for the sword, to the sword; and such as were for famine, to the famine; and such as were for captivity, to captivity" [Jeremiah 15:2]. To Jeremiah's prophecy, there was now added "such as were [destined] to leave the faith." This happened in the wake of the sword of Ibn Tumart, which came into the world in [4]873, when he decreed apostasy on the Jews, saying: "Come, and let us cut them off from being a nation; that the name of Israel may be no more in remembrance."[109]

The casual treatment of the persecution in this passage, written a scant fifteen years after the event, when its consequences were still keenly felt, and by an author who apparently thought the persecution was a prelude to the imminent messianic event, is surprising.[110] Even though Ibn Daud's purpose was to trace the unbroken chain of rabbinical learning and authority—not a chain of persecutions—we are left wondering why neither he nor any other Andalusian Jew of his time left an account to memorialize the calamity.

There is contemporary memorialization of sorts, inter alia, in a letter written in Fustat in 1148, by one Solomon ha-Kohen al-Sijilmāsī (from a family that had originated in Sijilmasa, Morocco). Solomon, who had heard about the persecution from eyewitnesses, illustrates both how traumatic the events were and, like Elḥanan b. Shemarya, in his letter describing the al-Ḥākim persecution, that Jews had a capacity for literary memorialization no less developed than that of their contemporaries in Ashkenazic lands. Here is Goitein's translation of the relevant section:

> After [the Almohad leader, ʿAbd al-Mu'min] entered Sijilmāsa, he assembled the Jews and asked them to apostatize. Negotiations went on for seven months, during all of which they fasted and prayed. After this a new amīr arrived and demanded their conversion. They refused, and a hundred and fifty

> Jews were killed, sanctifying the name of God [*yiḥud ha-shem*]. . . . The others apostatized; the first of the apostates was Joseph b. ʿImrān, the judge of Sijilmāsa. "Because of this I lament and wail, etc." [Micah 1:8]. Before ʿAbd al-Mu'min entered Sijilmāsa, when the population rose against the Almoravids, a number of Jews, about two hundred, took refuge in the city's fortress. Among them were Mār Yaʿqūb and ʿAbbūd, my paternal uncles, Mār Judah b. Farḥūn, and. . . . They are now in Derʿā, after everything they had was taken from them. What happened to them afterward we do not know. Of all the countries of the Almoravids there remained in the hands of all dissenters [*khawārij*] only Derʿā and Miknāsa [Meknes]. As to the congregations of the West, because of [our] sins, they all perished . . . they either apostatized or were killed. And on the day I am writing this letter news has arrived that Bijāya has been taken and other matters. . . . At ʿAbd al-Mu'min's conquest of Fez 100,000 persons were killed and at that of Marrākesh 120,000. Take notice of this. This is not hearsay, but a report of people who were present at the events. Take notice.[111]

The portrayal in this letter is reminiscent of depictions in the Ashkenazic Hebrew chronicles of massacres during the First Crusade and the episodes chronicled by Ephraim of Bonn. Yet, unlike the situation in the Ashkenazic lands, epistolary reports like this one did not feed a literature of suffering in the Muslim world—not in the aftermath of the Almohad persecution nor following the earlier persecution of al-Ḥākim. Also worthy of note is that the North African Jew's letter is free of the invective toward the gentile oppressor that marks the accounts of European Jews.

Literary Responses to Almohad Persecutions

The two most important literary responses to the Almohad persecutions are the famous epistles of Maimonides and of his father, Maimon b. Joseph, known as "the Dayyan," or "judge." Unlike both the Ashkenazic "chain of persecution" chronicles and those of the sixteenth-century Sephardic refugees from Christian Spain, these epistles do not chronicle the events. They offer neither glorification of martyrdom nor a consolatory message of Jewish survival. Instead, they proffer rationalizations of the mass Jewish apostasy to Islam. The "Epistle of Consolation" of Maimon the Dayyan comforts those who had converted under Almohad pressure and exhorts them not to be plagued with guilt. He reassures them that Islam is not idolatrous. Those who converted to Islam can still retain their ties to Judaism—if they believe in God, Moses, and the Torah, if they clandestinely practice basic Jewish rituals, especially prayer, even in abbreviated form and even in Arabic, and if they feel penitent. God, whose will is immutable, has not ceased loving Israel. Inevitably Muslim fanaticism will relax and the nominal converts will be able to return to the open observance of their religion.[112]

Maimonides wrote his "Epistle on Apostasy" to refute the opinion of a rabbi who had ruled that Jews should martyr themselves rather than succumb to Islam and that converts who continued to observe Jewish precepts were compounding their transgression. Like his father, Maimonides condoned conversion accompanied by covert practice of Judaism, on the grounds that there was nothing objectionable in the Islamic confession of faith. And he, too, voiced the expectation that the persecution would pass. Nonetheless, he counseled forced converts to leave the place of religious oppression for one of religious freedom as soon as was feasible. This, indeed, is the course the Maimon family eventually took.[113]

In sharp contrast to the large output of Ashkenazic elegies (*qinot*) on persecution, among the thousands of Hebrew poems written during the classical Arab centuries, I know of only one clear-cut example of a poetical Jewish reaction to an outbreak of Islamic persecution.[114] That is Abraham ibn Ezra's famous contemporary eulogy for the Jewish communities in Spain and North Africa annihilated by the Almohad oppressor, "Aha yarad ʿal sefarad."[115] It begins: "O woe! Misfortune from heaven has fallen upon Sefarad [Spain] / My eyes, my eyes flow with tears!" Bemoaning, first, the loss of the learned community of Lucena, Ibn Ezra continues:

The Exile dwelt there blamelessly in safety
Without interruption for a thousand and seventy years.
But the day came when her people were banished and she became like a widow,
Without Torah study or biblical recitation, the Mishnah sealed shut,
The Talmud as though desolate, all its glory vanished.
With murderers and mourners this way and that,
The place of prayer and praise reduced to ill-repute.
That is why I weep and beat my hands, lament forever on my lips.[116]

It is true that poems about historical acts of persecution were not part of the literary tradition of the Jews of the East.[117] By the time of the Almohad invasion of Spain, Ibn Ezra had spent several years living among the Jewish communities of Christian lands; quite possibly, he was influenced in writing "Aha yarad ʿal sefarad" by the Ashkenazic model. On the other hand, similar poems may turn up as the vast corpus of medieval Hebrew poetry, much of it still unstudied, becomes better known.[118] Nonetheless, I believe that the apparent near absence of Jewish poetical memorialization of persecution under Islam in the classical centuries says something important about the difference between Jewish collective memory of suffering in the East and the West.[119] To my mind, the hypothesis is enhanced by the fact that, when we do find examples of Hebrew elegies about persecution from Andalusian poets, they refer to acts perpetrated by *Christians*.[120] Important, too, "Aha yarad ʿal sefarad" was not, as far as we know, incorporated into the liturgy of Andalusian or North African Jewry, at least not during the immediately succeeding period.[121] To the contrary, and consistent with the hypothesis that a vivid historical memory of persecution is more characteristic of the Jews of Christendom than of the Jews of Islam, Abraham ibn Ezra's lament over the Almohad destruction of Jewish communities in Andalusia was assimilated a century and a half later into a manuscript of Hebrew dirges written in the wake of the antisemitic pogroms in Christian Spain in 1391, the famous Lisbon Manuscript, ca. 1395, included in Simon Bernstein's anthology, *ʿAl naharot sefarad* (On the River Banks of Spain).[122]

The "Egyptian Scroll" of 1012

That we find virtually no memorialization of a major persecution in the classical centuries of Islam analogous to the chronicle and elegaic literature of the Jews of Ashkenaz and of Reconquista and post-expulsion Spain should not be taken to mean that the Jews of Islam were incapable of recollecting, mourning, or commemorating. Quite the contrary. For example, the Geniza contains the remains of manuscripts of a Hebrew "Egyptian Scroll" (*megilla*) of deliverance from persecution early in the year 1012, which is reminiscent of the genre discussed by Yerushalmi and others.[123] Composed by the Palestinian-born scholar and poet, Samuel b. Hoshaʿna, the scroll reports how, "on the 3rd of Shevat 4772 of the year since the creation of the world, which is the year 1323 since the cessation of prophecy and 943 since the destruction of the holy habitation [the Jerusalem Temple]" corresponding to December 31, 1011, a Muslim mob attacked a Jewish funeral procession on its way from Old Cairo to the cemetery outside the town.[124] Non-Muslim funeral corteges vexed Muslims because they violated the prohibition in the Pact of ʿUmar against public display of religious ceremonies. The Geniza documents, as well as Arabic historical sources, attest that this type of anti-*dhimmī* flare-up was not uncommon.[125]

The outbreak in question, which occurred at the height of the general anti-*dhimmī* persecution by al-Ḥākim, resulted in the arrest of twenty-three Jews. The victims were imprisoned and the community panicked. People hid in their homes, mourning, fasting, and weeping. On the third day, a group of Jews gathered outside the palace and beseeched the caliph to spare their captive brethren. Al-Ḥākim found wrongdoing on the part of the Muslims—false testimony, which Islam, in particular, condemns—and released the Jews. So great was the joy of the community that an annual fast was instituted to commemorate the deliverance. Samuel b. Hoshaʿna, who himself had been incarcerated, composed celebratory *piyyuṭim* and *seliḥot* to be recited during the fast.[126] These acts recall characteristic Ashkenazic responses to disaster. So does the rhetoric of "memory" in the *megilla*. Samuel urges his readers: "Remember this and place it before your eyes. Tell it to your children, your children to their children, and their children to another generation." The scroll, fulfilling the commandment to memorialize the miraculous deliverance, is also our only source about the terrifying incident itself.

In light of the document, it is all the more mystifying that we have no comparable contemporary response to the decade-long even more terrifying persecution of non-Muslims by the same caliph. This contrasts with the reaction of Egyptian Christians, who, to be sure, had a ready-made literary framework into which to fit the events. Pages of the official chronicle of the patriarchs of the Coptic church brim over with stories of the bizarre and evil acts that the caliph wrought against Christians during the nine years of affliction, "during which there was chastisement from the Lord."[127] In good Christian hagiographical tradition the recitation singles out incidents of martyrdom and expresses joy over the deliverance after the apparently deranged caliph rescinded all oppressive decrees and restored the Christians to their original faith.

Jacob Mann, the discoverer of the Hebrew celebratory scroll of 1012, surmises that the persecution, which began as early as 1004, must have affected only the Christians at first and must not have struck the Jews before 1012. Otherwise, there is no easy explanation for the warm words for the caliph.[128] This makes sense. Indeed, the letter of Elḥanan b. Shemarya from about the same time, depicting the ravages as a recent event, seems to support this hypothesis. But we are still left wondering why the Jews apparently did not leave behind some apposite literary response to the dreadful wave of persecution once it arrived.

The *megilla* of 1012 shows that the Jews of Islam were capable of reacting to distress in similar fashion to Jews in Ashkenazic lands, with typological acts of collective commemoration, although they seem not to have instituted a formal "Second Purim" to "remember" the deliverance of 1012 in some future ritual.[129] Moreover, it seems, Jews in Islamic lands were aware of the Ashkenazic-type of chronicle of persecution. Many must have read or at least heard about the engrossing narrative of the Norman-Christian proselyte from southern Italy, Johannes-Obadiah, numerous fragments of which were discovered in the Cairo Geniza. This fascinating individual appeared in the Near East at the turn of the twelfth century. There he composed an "autobiography" in Hebrew, highlighting the saga of his life and conversion to Judaism, in 1102. It included news of the persecution of the Jews in Europe in 1096, during the First Crusade, which Obadiah seems to have taken from an Aṣhkenazic source, as well as episodes of oppression of Jews in the Muslim lands that he had observed during his roamings in the Near East.[130]

Ibn ʿAqnīn's "Therapy of the Soul"

Like their Ashkenazic relatives in Europe, Near Eastern Jews related gentile persecution to some broader framework of Jewish suffering. The Barcelona-born Jewish philosopher Joseph b. Judah ibn ʿAqnīn devoted considerable attention to the Almohad tragedy in his "Therapy of the Soul."[131] The passage in question was first made available in print in Paul Fenton's partial translation, in Bat Ye'or's *The Dhimmi*.[132] It deals with the second wave of Almohad intolerance under the third Almohad ruler, Abū Yūsuf Yaʿqūb al-Manṣūr (1184–99). The Almohads directed their renewed persecution at the descendants of the first generation of forced Jewish converts, whom they suspected—rightly, it turns out—of sacred allegiance to Judaism.

Ibn ʿAqnīn's prose recalls the doleful tone of many Ashkenazic elegies, beginning with his chapter title: "On the explication of the trials and tribulations that have befallen us."[133] Just as Ibn ʿAqnīn blames the persecution on the earlier apostasy of the Jews in this chapter, so, too, elsewhere in "Therapy of the Soul," as well as in his commentary on the Song of Songs, he praises martyrdom as being preferable to forced abandonment of Judaism—in good "Ashkenazic" fashion.[134] In a tone reminiscent of Ashkenazic refrains, Ibn ʿAqnīn well summarizes the plight of the Jews during the Almohad oppression.[135] His chapter, however, is not part of a chronicle of persecution, but rather is used to illustrate the philosopher's broad ethical message about punishment for sins—here, the sin of apostasy, for which, he confesses, his generation had received its rightful due from God.

The Collective Memory of Muslim Persecution

The puzzling absence of a suitable literary commemoration of major persecutions of the Jews under Islam during the classical period suggests the nature of the collective memory of suffering among the Jews living in Islamic lands. Neither the murders of 1066, nor those in twelfth-century Spain and North Africa, constituted holy or noble acts worthy of memorialization for posterity.[136] When, on the other hand, an anti-Jewish episode fit the paradigm of persecution miraculously thwarted, the Jews reacted accordingly—as, for example, in the *megilla,* fast, and *piyyuṭ* celebrating the redemption from persecution at the turn of the year 1012. Letters and poems in the Geniza use the typology of Haman, enemy of the Jews, to describe local Jew-baiters and apply the title "Mordecai of Our Time" to Jewish victors over the evildoer's oppression.[137]

The hypothesis that the ingredients needed to produce a collective memory of persecution were present only among the Jews of Christendom is strengthened when we consider the apathetic reaction of the Jews of the East to the depredations that accompanied the Crusader conquest of Palestine in 1099. Goitein notes the remarkable absence of a historiographical literature in the East like that of the Ashkenazic Jews, describing Jewish suffering at the hands of the Christian armies. He relates this to the fact, deduced from contemporary Geniza documents, that the destruction of life and property was much less than that suggested by Christian chroniclers of the conquest of Palestine. Missing, too, is the entire cluster of theological factors rooted in the ancient Jewish-Christian conflict that underlay Jewish responses to persecution in Christendom proper. Equally important, it was not just Jews but Muslims as well, who were killed by Crusaders in the East.[138]

Intra-Jewish "Persecution" and Collective Memory

Remarkably, and furnishing more striking proof of the absence of a collective memory of persecution by Muslims, the Jews of Arab lands used the *megilla* genre to record and commemorate deliverance from *intra*-Jewish persecution. Again, the texts are found in the Geniza. A Palestinian scholar, Evyatar b. Solomon, dynastic successor to the gaonate (headship of the Palestinian yeshiva) wrote a *megilla* at the end of the eleventh century to tell his version of usurpation of the gaonate's authority between 1082 and 1094. The *megilla* culminates in the defeat of his evil rival in Egypt, with God's miraculous intervention.[139] In the next century, an Egyptian Jewish "historian" recounted a triumphal struggle between the legitimate holders of the office of head of Fatimid Jewry, among them Maimonides, and an evildoing usurping "Haman" pejoratively nicknamed "Zuṭa" (the Small) in a scroll consciously modeled on the *megilla* of Purim and expressly intended to memorialize the episode for future generations.[140]

The application to internal Jewish disputes of the model of the Scroll of Esther, the paradigmatic depiction of Jewish triumph over gentile victimization, would seem to reveal a Jewish perception of persecution as a general phenomenon, and not the monopoly of Muslims. While the Jews believed that salvation always came from God, they learned from their own communal, interpersonal disputes that self-righteous oppression of rivals and of the community-at-large was political in a worldly sense, even if it had religious underpinnings.[141] Going further, I believe that the dearth of literary sources devoted to persecution of Jews of the Islamic world during the classical centuries reflects a milieu in which there was much less of the kind of violent persecution of Jews *as* Jews than that which kindled the doleful literature and other memorializing traditions of Christian lands.

Memorializing Suffering in the Late Islamic Middle Ages

Only later, beginning in the sixteenth century, at the same time that Sephardim expelled from Christian Spain began to compose their chronicles of persecution, do we encounter Jewish literary texts from the Muslim world memorializing suffering and persecution at the hands of gentiles. From the year 1524 in Egypt comes a *megilla,* in Hebrew and Judeo-Arabic versions, echoing the Book of Esther and sprinkled with verses from it. The scroll describes the deliverance of the Jews of Cairo from a local persecutor, Aḥmad Pasha, the newly appointed governor of Egypt who rebelled against Ottoman overlordship.[142] The episode, which occurred two weeks after the holiday of Purim, was recorded in some of the Hebrew chronicles of the sixteenth and seventeenth centuries, including Ibn Verga's *Shevet yehuda.* Memorialized in the holiday cycle and liturgy of the Jews of Cairo as an "Egyptian Purim," it was observed as recently as the early 1950s.[143]

One example of the "chronicle of suffering" genre from the late Middle Ages of Islam is a work partly in Hebrew and partly in Judeo-Arabic.[144] The work consists of episodes recorded by members of a family of rabbis named Ibn Danan, descendants of Sephardic exiles who had lived in Morocco since their expulsion from Spain in 1492. The text was first redacted in 1724, but did not take final form until after 1879. It relates in disorderly annalistic fashion the afflictions of the Jews of Fez and other North African Jewish communities from the sixteenth to the nineteenth century.[145] In contrast to the Ashkenazic chronicles, it does not focus exclusively on persecution but, rather, interweaves accounts of mistreatment by Muslims with episodes of misfortune caused by natural catastrophes, especially drought and famine. The anecdotes themselves are replete with depictions of classic, Ashkenazic-like responses to suffering: fasting, prayer, and chronicling of events for posterity. The emergence of such a literary specimen in the late Islamic Middle Ages is suggestive, since it derives from a time when the position of the Jews had come more to resemble the plight of their brethren living in Christendom. This was especially true in Morocco, where, since the mid-twelfth century, the Jews had been the only infidels on the scene. (Jews had returned to their original faith at the end of the Almohad persecution, whereas Christians had not.) It casts into sharp relief my argument about the earlier, relatively secure period when the level of persecution was low and there was no significant Jewish collective memory of suffering at the hands of the gentiles.[146]

Persecution of Jews in Muslim Lands in the Sephardic Chronicles

Unnoticed, apparently, the historical portrait of suffering etched in the sixteenth-century chronicles of persecution written in the wake of the expulsion from Spain reveals Jewish awareness of the fundamentally different experiences of the Jews of Islam and those of Christendom. At the close of the Second Dialogue, in his *Consolation for the Tribulations of Israel,* Samuel Usque introduces his own historical account of persecutions. Ycabo, Usque's personification of the Jewish people, says: "I have received cruel punishments and pitiful wounds on my afflicted body—some from new nations who arose amongst those same Romans in the West after their heavy wheel had passed over my bones, and others at the hand of modern peoples in the East" (i.e., the Muslims).[147] But Usque and the other sixteenth-century Sephardic chroniclers drew their examples mainly from Christendom. The material from the Islamic world is lean: the pogrom in Granada in 1066, the Almohad persecution, and the persecution of the Jews of Yemen—in other words, those few events that are recorded in well-known literary texts from the classical Arabic period, Ibn Daud's *Sefer ha-Qabbalah* and Maimonides' *Epistle to Yemen.* The chroniclers also report the fascinating story of David Alroy, a twelfth-century messianic pretender whose activities endangered the Jews of Babylonia. But this tale had been told in the much read *Itinerary* of Benjamin of Tudela.[148] Most of the sixteenth-century chroniclers knew nothing of the al-Ḥākim terror, another indication that the Jews of Egypt left no enduring literary record of that ordeal. The only exception I know of is Abraham Zacuto's *Sefer yuḥasin.*[149] But this seems to be the exception that proves the rule, for the passage in question is part of Shulam's "additions" to Zacuto, including episodes from general Islamic history that the editor drew from Arabic chronicles.[150]

The French King, the Muslim Ambassador, and the Blood Libel

A fictitious story about a blood libel related in the sixteenth-century chronicle *Shevet yehuda,* by Solomon ibn Verga, illustrates a fundamental Jewish perception of the difference between Islamic and Christian attitudes toward the Jews.[151]

The tale (which Ibn Verga says he found in a chronicle from France) concerns two Christians who accused a Jew of killing a Christian "on the eve of their holiday"—Passover (when Jews were believed to reenact the crucifixion). The king, realizing its erroneous nature, vigorously dismissed the charge. Embarrassed, the Christian accusers enlisted the support of the commonfolk. Two witnesses came forth and reported that they had gone to the house of the Jew, "to borrow from him at interest"; there they "found the Jew coming out of the room with a blood-soaked knife in his hand."

Brought before the king, the Jew claimed that he had been using the knife to slaughter poultry according to Jewish ritual for the holiday. Nonetheless, at the king's command, he was subjected to judicial torture. Under duress, the Jew confessed to the murder, stating that fifty prominent Jews had conspired with him and joined in the deed. All were arrested, but the co-conspirators talked their way out of prosecution by reminding the king that his own law disallowed testimony about third parties that had been extracted by torture.

Present at court was a "Muslim ambassador,"[152] to whom the king posed the question: "Do things like this happen in your kingdom?" The Muslim ambassador replied:

> We have never heard nor seen this, thanks to our rulers, who will not be degraded by such childish matters that, moreover, have no basis either in rational thinking or in religion. How could a Jew dare to murder a Christian when he is subjugated to the latter's rule; certainly regarding such an abhorrent deed as performing a sacrifice with the blood of a human, concerning which we have never heard about any people on earth, even though they might be attracted to [other] irrational, abhorrent matters. This sort of thing would not occur to them, since it is completely foreign to human rationality. You adhere to in your land and heed in your courts—the courts of kings—things which one is forbidden to believe.
>
> The king became angry at this and said: "But the perpetrator confessed. According to the law, what else can I do? What does it matter if it is irrational, given that he confessed?"
>
> The Muslim replied: "In our realm, a confession extracted by torture will do as an excuse when it is accompanied by other inculpations, but it will not do [by itself] for pronouncing judgment."
>
> One of the Christians present then said to the Muslim: "Honored sir, if this does not exist in your realm, that is because the Jews have no gripe [*she'ela o to'ana*] against the Muslims. But they have one against the Christians on account of Jesus. That is why they take a Christian and give him the name Jesus and eat his blood to take vengeance upon him."

More deeply convinced of the prevarication, the Muslim questioned the logic of the Christians in the matter—for, according to their belief that the Jews killed Jesus ("whereas in our belief the Jews did not kill Jesus [see Sura 4:157], who, rather, ascended alive to heaven"), the Jews had already taken ample and cruel revenge on him. "Jesus ought to have asked his Father to take vengeance on the Jews! Praised be the Creator who separated us from such lies and cast our lot among the believers of truth."

The Christians replied: "You say that Jesus ought to have sought vengeance against the Jews. He already has! Real life circumstances prove it. Why would they be living in exile, cast aside, belittled, repressed, and having their hair torn out, if not to avenge the blood of Jesus?"

Responded the Muslim: "If the Father takes such vengeance on behalf of his son, should the Jews take vengeance yet again in order to exact a second payment? This is absurd. Moreover, if God exacts punishment against the Jews, why do you need to pursue separate justice? At any rate, I have not come to save the Jews, for they are not my coreligionists, nor do they come from my realm, nor do I love them, for I know what they did to some of the prophets. I came, however, to say the truth, since the king asked my opinion."

In the continuation of the story, the Christian commonfolk produce fresh "false witnesses" that the accused Jew and his alleged accomplices admitted their guilt in their earshot.[153] In the end, the alleged co-conspirators are saved by a divine miracle, and the Jew initially accused of the deed is saved from punishment when new Christian witnesses are found who testify that they had seen "so and so" (plainly, a Christian) throw the corpse into the Jew's house. The culprit is condemned to have his hands and feet cut off.

The view of Christian-Jewish and Islamic-Jewish relations underlying this fictional episode has deep significance for my argument in this book. Ibn Verga is aware of contrasting Christian and Muslim attitudes toward, and treatment of, the Jews. The Christians believe, irrationally, that Jews enact ritual murder, extracting the blood of the victim, representing Jesus—all in order to take revenge on him. Islam is different. Jews "have no gripe against the Muslims," as they do against the Christians on account of Jesus. Moreover, Islam, as represented by Ibn Verga's Muslim visitor to the court of the king of France, eschews irrational thinking about the Jews, whereas Christianity encourages it. And, while the Muslim insists that he has no love for the Jews,[154] he nonetheless attests that such things as the ritual murder accusation do not exist in the domain of Islam.

This unfavorable comparison between Christian and Islamic treatment of the Jews is not unique. The thirteenth-century Muslim polemicist against Christianity and Judaism, al-Qarāfī (d. 1285), wishing to demonstrate the depravity of Christianity, writes about the wanton violence unleashed against Jews in Europe:

> In the remainder of the cities of the Franks they have three days in the year [Good Friday through Easter Sunday] that are well known, when the bishops say to the commonfolk: "The Jews have stolen your religion and yet the Jews live with you in your land." Whereupon the commonfolk and the people of the town rush out together in search of Jews, and when they find one they kill him. Then they pillage any house that they can.[155]

This Muslim intellectual's disapproval of collective mob violence against Jews in Christian lands suggests a distinct preference for a "civilized" approach toward the "other" that, in the present study, we have found present somewhat more in medieval Islam than in medieval Christendom.

Galut—*Exclusion*

One of the Christian interlocutors of the Muslim ambassador in Ibn Verga's tale offers a classic Christian proof of the Jews' guilt for the deicide: They live "in exile [*galut*]—cast aside, belittled, repressed, and having their hair torn out." The biblical word *galut,* literally and originally, meant "exile," forced removal from homeland to a foreign place. It also denoted the place to which the Israelites had been exiled—hence, for example, *galut bavel,* "the Babylonian Exile."

By the Middle Ages the concept of *galut* embraced a semantic field that includes the state of being accompanying life in exile; hence, "the oppression of Exile." As Yitzhak Baer writes: "The word 'Galut' embraces a whole world of facts and ideas that have appeared with varying strength and clarity in every age of Jewish history. Political servitude and dispersion, the longing for liberation and reunion, sin and repentance and atonement: these are the larger elements that must go to make up the concept of Galut if the word is to retain any real meaning."[156]

This broadened conception of *galut* is exemplified in sources from the Islamic world during the period that forms the focus of this study. A Geniza fragment describing a persecution of the Jews in Baghdad in 1120–21 opens *in media res,* telling that the Jews had been afflicted by an act of government extortion. "They have been in this *galut* for a number of years."[157] Many a Hebrew poet, like his Jewish counterpart in Christian lands, wrote verse lamenting the hardship of *galut* and praying for its messianic end.

Jews from the outside—travelers from Christian lands in the late Middle Ages—readily observed the by then downtrodden circumstances of their oriental brethren. However, precisely at a time when the Jews of Christendom were experiencing the *galut* of Edom in all its gloomy connotations, some Jewish visitors to the East seem to have sensed something different about the quality of gentile-Jewish relations in the *galut* of Ishmael. Their observations are particularly germane to the subject here, for they shed light on the difference between Jewish-Christian and Jewish-Muslim relations even in this late period of decline in the East, and, a fortiori, in the earlier period.[158]

The first observation comes from the pen of Rabbi Obadiah of Bartinoro, a scholarly Italian rabbi who emigrated to Mamluk Palestine via Egypt in 1487 and rose to become the chief rabbi of Jerusalem. The regime of the Mamluk rulers of Egypt and Palestine had been oppressive, and for two centuries, Jews living in the Mamluk domains had suffered a serious decline in both welfare and status. One modern scholar, comparing their status to that of Jews elsewhere, even claimed that their experience "in many respects paralleled that of their brethren in medieval Christian Europe."[159] In Palestine, R. Obadiah did not fail to notice the discrimination against the Jews and their depressed condition. At the same time, he wrote the following curious passage about the impoverished Jewish community of Jerusalem in a letter home of 1488:

> In truth, the Jews do not experience *galut* from the Arabs at all in this place.[160] I have traveled the entire country . . . and no one says a negative word. Rather, they are very kind to the foreigner, especially to one who does not know the language. When they see many Jews together, they do not express any envy.[161]

Two other Western observers from about the same time use similar language to describe conditions of local Jewish life. Ibn Picho, a Sephardic Jew from a notable Spanish family, writes from Jerusalem to his relatives in Europe, apparently at the end of the fifteenth century or during the first half of the sixteenth. Ibn Picho encourages his kinfolk to leave their land of "upheaval" and come live in the Holy Land.[162] Among other advantages —spiritual and material—the writer adds inducements: "God be praised and thanked, we do not experience a very oppressive *galut* here, though it is inconceivable that there should be no *galut*. Nonetheless, it is not one-thousandth of what people claim for [Europe]."[163]

The third remark appears in a letter from an Italian Jewish merchant named David dei Rossi, in 1535, during the Ottoman revival. Having just settled in Safed, Palestine, Rossi writes home about the vibrant, robust local Jewish community as well as the flourishing commerce of the region. Comparing Jewish life under gentile rule in the East with that in his native Italy, dei Rossi writes, "Here there is not *galut* as there is in our homeland."[164] The enigmatic passage has been translated variously as, "Hatred of the Jews is, in contrast to our homeland, unknown here" and "The Exile here is not like in our homeland."[165]

The rendition of the word *galut* in these two cases misses an important nuance of perception in the mind of this and the other two Jewish visitors. The three letterwriters from the lands of Christendom, in their observation of Jewish life in Muslim Palestine, do not mean to say that the territory of Palestine, the homeland of the Jewish people, is not *galut*. It certainly was. As noted, *galut* connotes more than a place; it also means an oppressed state of being. One experienced this *galut* even in Palestine, where the Holy Land was still subject to gentile rule. The mass Jewish messianic movement that began in the Ottoman empire around the figure of Sabbatai Zevi in the mid-seventeenth century, a paroxysm of religious and social action to end the oppression of *galut*, flourished in Palestine as it did elsewhere in the Muslim and the Christian worlds.[166]

I believe, rather, that *galut* in the letters comes close to meaning *exclusion*. Three Jews from Christian Europe—where, by the end of the Middle

Ages, the Jews were substantially excluded from majority society—observed with considerable surprise that the indigenous Jews of Islam were not similarly excluded from the social order of their surroundings. Each sensed that Jews "here," in their relationship to gentiles, were less relegated to the "outside" than were Jews in Christian lands. Bartinoro and dei Rossi maintain this contrast in spite of the fact that they hailed from Renaissance Italy where, from a cultural point of view, the Jews were substantially more advanced (and embedded in their surroundings) than were the Jews of the East at the time. Both meanings of *galut,* the geographical and the psychological, appear side by side in Ibn Picho's paradoxical, if not nonsensical, statement referred to above (and in note 163).

If this lexical interpretation is correct, what we have expressed here is one of the most important differences between Christian-Jewish and Islamic-Jewish relations in the Middle Ages. In the West, Jews came to be excluded from the organic hierarchy of society: assaulted as aliens, persecuted collectively for alleged crimes against Christians and Christianity, increasingly isolated in their Jewish quarters, soon to be confined to legal ghettos, and all too often expelled from lands where they and their ancestors had lived for hundreds of years.

For all their marginality, Jews in the Orient remained, *marginal,* at least during the classical period; but they were not "excluded." Rabbi Obadiah (and, perhaps, also Ibn Picho) found this contrast even among the depressed Jewish communities of late Mamluk times.[167] David dei Rossi noticed it in Safed, the home of many exiles "excluded" from Christian Spain soon after the beginning of Ottoman rule. The dissimilarity between East and West was even greater during the classical period. Seen from the perspective presented in this book, the embeddedness of the Jews of Islam, the product of intertwining religious, legal, economic, and social factors, constitutes the most important reason for their relative freedom from violent persecution, and hence for a collective historical memory that was fundamentally different from that of the Jews of Christendom.

CONCLUSION

In this book, I have sought to explain why Jewish-Muslim and Jewish-Christian relations followed strikingly different courses in the Middle Ages. I have shown how, in the lands of Christendom, relations, favorable in the early Middle Ages, deteriorated beginning with the Crusades and especially in the thirteenth century, until one can speak of a "persecuting society."

In Islam, Jews and Christians, though protected as *dhimmīs,* were considered infidels and suffered humiliation and contemptuous treatment from the dominant group. This was in keeping with their religious inferiority and lowly rank in the hierarchy of Muslim society. Nonetheless, in day-to-day life, the Jews of Islam regularly crossed boundaries in the hierarchy to participate—however temporarily and, at times, tenuously—as virtual equals with Muslims of similar category. Though always at risk of incurring Muslim wrath and even persecution, Jews, nonetheless, enjoyed substantial security during the formative and classical periods of Islam.

According to the Islamic "law of the land," the *sharīʿa* [holy law], the *dhimmī* enjoyed a kind of citizenship, second class and unequal though it was.[1] The jurisdiction claimed by Islam over the Jewish and Christian communities—complementing the grant of internal autonomy (the right, inherited from pre-Islamic regimes in the Near East, "to live by their ancestral laws")—gave non-Muslims an aura of embeddedness in society. This was less true for Jews living in Latin Christian lands, where competing legal systems complicated their status and where the "law of utility" inexorably led to arbitrariness and eventually to isolation of the Jews into a special category of persons, legally possessed by this or that ruling authority.

In the economic sphere, the Jews of Islam apparently enjoyed parity with their counterparts belonging to the Islamic *umma.* Jewishness hardly impeded their integration into the nonconfessional Islamic marketplace, at both its local and international levels. Neither merchant status (which, in Islam, unlike Christendom, was a high status) nor Jewish credit activities carried the problematic associations that plagued the Jewish-Christian relationship in the West. The demand of Islamic law that *dhimmīs* remain subordinate in partnerships formed with Muslims was often ignored, as proved by the documents of the Cairo Geniza. Even when observed, the restriction may have represented little more than a minor irritant to the *dhimmī* partner.

Occupational integration and economic achievement were sometimes hazardous. Success tempted some Jews (and Christians) to feel so much at home outside the niche assigned them by their lowly religious rank that they frequently ignored the sumptuary restrictions of the *dhimma*. Seeming to acquiesce, many a Muslim ruler overlooked these flagrant violations of the stipulations of the Pact of ʿUmar. This combination of circumstances often created resentment in Muslims, exacerbating latent religious contempt and leading to acts of oppression.

The double-edged sword in Muslim-*dhimmī* relations is exemplified in the highest-status category in which Jews and Christians had visibility: government service. In this domain divergence between theory and practice was considerably more pronounced than in commerce. As *kātibs* (government clerks), not to speak of the higher-status position of chief minister, *dhimmīs* commanded authority over Muslims in a way that grossly flouted the rules of proper subordination.[2] Many of the most painful episodes of oppression and persecution Jews and Christians experienced were triggered by Muslim exasperation at their exploitation of the prerogatives of their category in a manner totally at variance with the limitations imposed by their religious rank.

In medicine, where *dhimmīs* were similarly prominent, this does not seem to have been so problematic, perhaps because the intrinsic benefits of medical healing overrode the (temporary) indignity of dependency upon the infidel. Similarly mitigating must have been the long tradition—pre-Islamic, in fact—of transmission of Greek medical knowledge by non-Muslim (particularly, Christian) physicians. In addition, Muslims, early on, lost whatever inferiority they might have felt toward non-Muslim transmitters of the Galenic corpus as they became their peers, thanks to newly translated Greek medical works. The contrast with northern Europe is stark. There, the general backwardness in medical knowledge in the early Middle Ages catapulted the Jewish physician to a place of superiority and made Christians jealous, often to the point of suspecting the Jewish doctor of inimical practices toward his Christian patient. Unfortunately, this damaging stereotype did not disappear after Christian medical knowledge improved, for by then the Jews as a group had come to be seen as allies of the Devil.

The situation of the Jewish infidel in Latin Christendom is set in bolder relief via the comparison drawn in this book. It was less equivocal and more threatened than that of the Jewish infidel in Islam. In the Latin West, Jewish activity in the economic realm, especially in the High and later Latin Middle Ages, intensified Christianity's inherent anti-Jewish feelings. The barriers against social interaction were raised higher and were less easily traversed. Also, deeply engrained theological hatred had a profoundly negative impact on law and policy that only grew over time.

The liberal Jewish privileges of the Carolingian era began to give way in the twelfth century to restriction on movement, to tightening of control over the Jews (the beginnings of "Jewish serfdom"), to unprecedented violence, and to incipient expulsions. The Christian polemical theme of divine rejection and Jewish inferiority assumed new momentum.

Writing at the end of twelfth century, a prominent north European rabbi registered his protest against one aspect of the deterioration in Jewish status, the restriction on movement. Commenting in one of the Tosafot (glosses on Rashi and the Talmud), part of a discussion of the third-century dictum that Jews must obey the "law of the kingdom," Rabbi Isaac b. Samuel of Dampierre (in Champagne) stated:

> This case is not in the nature of the "law of the kingdom" [which must be respected], but rather in that of the "robbery of the kingdom." *For we have seen in the countries around us that Jews have had the right to reside wherever they wished, like the nobles* [*kemo parashim,* the Hebrew word for horseback-riding fighters, hence "knights"], the law of the kingdom being that the ruler should not seize the property of Jews who left his town. This was indeed the practice in all of Burgundy. Therefore, if there is a regime which tries to alter the law and make a new law unto itself, this is not to be considered the "law of the kingdom," for this is not proper law at all.[3]

The Jews of Islam in the classical period seem not to have felt the need to protest oppression in the same way as R. Isaac of Dampierre. After all, they mingled more freely than their Ashkenazic brethren with merchants, courtiers, scholars, and physicians from the dominant religious group. They did not suffer restrictions on their freedom of movement. And they did not experience a degradation in legal status similar to the Jewish serfdom of Latin Europe. Rather, Jews seem to have accepted their lowly rank as the natural order of things. This was true, in part, because Islam devoted somewhat less polemical energy than did Christianity to the theme of divine rejection. It was true, partly, because the Jews shared their lowly religious rank with the numerically superior Christians. It resulted, too, from the circumstance that the Muslim social order permitted the Jews a certain degree of beneficial marginality: they sampled high status in government service, medicine, and commerce often enough to satisfy the human yearning to shake off the yoke of subordination. More important, the elite Jews of Islam enjoyed among themselves a truly aristocratic status and culture: the Judaeo-Arabic courtier society of Muslim Spain and other Arab lands, a calque of the Arabic-Islamic high society well known to them from firsthand experience.

To be sure, the agony of *galut* persisted for the Jews of Islam. The pain of *galut* came home anew to the Jews of Islam with each episode of persecution. These were few and far between in our period, however. The *galut* of

Ishmael, unlike that of Edom, stopped short of exclusion, which rendered it more bearable. Some, in fact (particularily in Muslim Spain before the Almohad invasion) found it quite bearable. When, around 1140, the celebrated Spanish Hebrew poet Judah ha-Levi abandoned his native land for the Holy Land—actualizing the theoretical verses of what moderns have called his "Zionide" poems—some of his Jewish friends were shocked, and we may imagine that his move challenged many to question their comfortable accommodation to the Arabic-Islamic world.[4] Ha-Levi's act of rejection of Andalusian Jewish complacency assumed terrifying corroboration less than a decade later, when the Almohads swept across the Straits of Gibraltar, forcing Jews and Christians in their path to choose between Islam and the sword.

Nonetheless, the Jews (those who were not killed or did not manage to escape to safer territory) responded to the persecution with dissembling acceptance of the Islamic religion while awaiting enforcement anew of the categorically strict law against forced conversion and the predictable restoration of the status quo ante. In the "persecuting society" of Christendom, to use R. I. Moore's term, the Jews resisted their dire fate with vigorous anti-Christian polemic and, when called on, with martyrdom. In Islam, less persecutory by circumstance if not in part by nature, the Jews assumed a more acquiescent posture toward their periodic difficulties.

This is not to say that the Jews of Islam abided oppression or that they accepted it with equanimity. They simply saw their oppression differently than the Jews of Christendom.[5] To take the point further, let us compare the statement of Rabbi Isaac b. Samuel of Dampierre with that of Maimonides, his contemporary in Egypt. The passage deserves our attention because it is a continuation of the crucial passage in which the great sage of Old Cairo writes, regarding "the nation of Ishmael": "no nation has ever done more harm to Israel. None has matched it in debasing, humiliating, and hating us." Ruminating on Islamic oppression and about the danger to the Jews of Yemen of following the local Jewish messianic pretender, he writes:

> Daniel, too has depicted our humiliation [*dhull*] and debasement [*iṣghār*] till we would become "like the dust in the threshing" [2 Kings 13:7]. He was describing none other than our condition under the rule of Ishmael—may it speedily be vanquished—when he said, "And some of the host and of the stars it cast down to the ground, and trampled upon them" [Daniel 8:10]. Although we have borne their imposed degradation, their lies, and absurdities, which are beyond human power to bear, and have become as in the words of the prophet [the Psalmist], "But I am as a deaf man, I hear not, and I am as a dumb man that opens not his mouth" [Psalm 38:14], and have done as our sages of blessed memory have instructed us, bearing the lies and absurdities of Ishmael, listening and remaining silent. . . . In spite of all this, we are not spared from the

> ferocity of their wickedness and their outbursts at any time. On the contrary, the more we suffer and choose to conciliate them, the more they choose to act belligerently toward us. Thus David depicted our plight: "I am at peace, but when I speak, they are for war" [Psalm 120:7]. How much worse it would be if we were to stir up a commotion and claim before them dominion [*mulk*], with ranting and raving. Then indeed we would be plunging ourselves into destruction.[6]

Maimonides' protest against oppression takes a different tack from that of Rabbi Isaac. However unrealistically, the French Tosafist seems to insist on a kind of entitlement to the privileges accorded nobles.[7] The Egyptian legist and philosopher acquiesces to the Jews' lowly place in society, the *dhimma* system, with its combination of humble rank and protection. What angers Maimonides is that, lately (in Almohad North Africa and Spain and now in Yemen), some Muslims had violated their own commitment to the bargain by their unwonted persecution. The present danger for the Jews of Yemen was that they might succumb to the blandishments of the local self-proclaimed Jewish messiah, and this inversion of the mutually accepted hierarchy of the social order in Islam would bring the axe down on them even more fiercely.

Physician to the Muslim ruling elite, intellectual equal and friend of many a Muslim scholar, head of the Jews of the Egypt—a position of high standing in the Islamic court—and illustrious leader of the aristocratic elite within the Jewish community, Maimonides sensed that times were changing, that the old, relatively comfortable operation of the *dhimma* system had entered a period of crisis.

People who live in periods of transition usually are ignorant of the change. It is historians who, with the benefit of hindsight, impose this construct on the past. Maimonides—who had witnessed the Almohad storm from close up, who knew about the oppression of Jews in nearby Yemen, and who probably observed that the Crusader advent to the Middle East had begun to shake the self-confidence of Islam—seems (we know this explicitly from other of his writings) to have intuited that one era was coming to a close and that another, this one less secure for the Jews, was beginning. It is this perception, too, that seems to have given rise—among Jewish refugees from Almohad persecution living in the, at that time, safer haven of the Christian kingdoms of northern Spain—to a new Jewish saying (a purposeful distortion of an ancient midrashic utterance): "Better [to live] under Edom [Christendom] than under Ishmael [Islam]."[8] The extent to which one can speak historically of deterioration in the Muslim world simulating if not rivaling the gloomy position of the Jews in medieval Christendom, and the degree to which one might justifiably apply the adjective *lachrymose* to the life and history of the Jews of Islam in recent centuries, are matters beyond the scope of this book.

NOTES

Preface

1. Chapter 10 presents evidence that supports this—the still regnant, though in recent years vigorously challenged—view.

2. "Islam and the Jews: Myth, Counter-Myth, History," *Jerusalem Quarterly,* no. 38 (1986), 125–37; repr. in *The Solomon Goldman Lectures,* ed. Byron L. Sherwin and Michael Carasik (Chicago, 1990), 5:20–32; trans. into Hebrew in *Zemanim: A Historical Quarterly* (Tel-Aviv University) 9, no. 36 (Winter 1990), 52–61; to appear in a revised and expanded version as a chapter in *Muslim Authors on Jews and Judaism* (Hebrew), ed. Hava Lazarus-Yafeh, The Zalman Shazar Center for Jewish History (Jerusalem), forthcoming.

3. "The Neo-Lachrymose Conception of Jewish-Arab History," *Tikkun* (May–June 1991), 55–60.

4. See, for instance, the apposite remarks of Juan R. I. Cole in the introductory paragraph of his "Of Crowds and Empires: Afro-Asian Riots and European Expansion, 1857–1882," *Comparative Studies in Society and History* 31 (1989), 106.

5. This book fills an important gap in the secondary literature. In many ways it complements the new, narrative history of Jewish life in medieval Latin Europe by Kenneth R. Stow, *Alienated Minority: The Jews of Medieval Latin Europe* (Cambridge, Mass., 1992), which does not, however, deal comparatively with its subject. Stow's book reached me some two months after I had submitted the manuscript of my own book to be considered for publication. I was pleased to find many of the ideas about medieval Jewish-Christian relations that I had developed as a result of my comparative research confirmed by this specialist in Jewish-Christian relations.

6. For further readings beyond works I cite in my notes, see my bibliographical essay, "The Jews under Islam: From the Rise of Islam to Sabbatai Zevi," which, since its original publication in *Bibliographical Essays in Medieval Jewish Studies* (New York, 1976), has been updated twice: *Princeton Near East Paper 32* (Princeton, N.J., Program in Near Eastern Studies, 1981); and in *Sephardic Studies in the University,* ed. Jane S. Gerber and Michel Abitbol (East Rutherford, N.J.: Fairleigh Dickinson University Press, forthcoming). For the Jews of Christendom, see the bibliographical essays by Ivan G. Marcus and by Kenneth Stow in *Bibliographical Essays in Medieval Jewish Studies,* and the more recent bibliography in Stow's *Alienated Minority.*

Introduction

1. Salo W. Baron, "Ghetto and Emancipation," *The Menorah Journal* 14, no. 6 (June 1928), 515–26, at the end: "Surely it is time to break with the lachrymose theory of pre-Revolutionary woe, and to adopt a view more in accord with historic truth." Essay repr. in *The Menorah Treasury,* ed. Leo W. Schwarz (Philadelphia,

1964), 50–63. In later writings, Baron called it "the lachrymose conception of Jewish history." The term *lachrymose school of Jewish history* (the coinage imprecisely attributed to Israeli historians who of late have begun to challenge this approach) recently achieved broad, popular exposure, thanks to an article in *Newsweek* magazine, "Rethinking Jewish History," May 18, 1992, 38; compare the corrective letter to the editor, ibid., June 22, 1992, 6, by Robert Liberles, who is writing a biography of Salo Baron.

In his classic history of Jewish persecutions, *Sefer ha-dema'ot* [Book of Tears] (Berlin, 1924–26), Simon Bernfeld was only able to fill a very few pages of the three volumes on the topic, "Muhammad and Islam" (1:114–34). Bernfeld's proclivity for finding persecution mainly under Christendom (and little under Islam) was consistent with the "lachrymose conception of Jewish history," as Salo Baron coined the term, but also in part a result of the availability of sources.

2. See Preface, note 3.

3. Moses ben Maimon, *The Epistle to Yemen,* trans. in Norman A. Stillman, *The Jews of Arab Lands: A History and Source Book* (Philadelphia, 1979), 241 (trans. slightly altered here). The translation in A. Halkin and D. Hartman, *Crisis and Leadership: Epistles of Maimonides* (Philadelphia, 1985), 126, varies a bit. For instance, the Arabic, *al-tafaqquh fī sharrinā,* is rendered "passed baneful and discriminatory legislation against us." Stillman's rendition is somewhat closer to the Arabic text, as is also the Hebrew translation of J. Kafiḥ, *Iggerot teiman,* in his *Iggerot le-rabbenu Moshe ben Maimon* (Jerusalem, 1972), 53.

4. *Encyclopaedia of Islam,* s.v. "Dhimma," 229.

5. Ibid., 230 (emphasis added).

6. H. H. Ben-Sasson, *Peraqim be-toledot ha-yehudim bi-mei ha-beinayim* [On Jewish History in the Middle Ages] (Tel Aviv, 1969), 36 (trans. mine).

7. Bernard Lewis, *The Jews of Islam* (Princeton, N.J., 1984), 85.

8. Ibid.; compare p. 19.

9. S. D. Goitein, *A Mediterranean Society: The Jewish Communities of the Arab World as Portrayed in the Documents of the Cairo Geniza,* 5 vols. (Berkeley and Los Angeles, 1967–88), 2:277–78.

10. Norman A. Stillman, "Antisemitism in the Contemporary Arab World," in *Antisemitism in the Contemporary World,* ed. Michael Curtis (Boulder, Colo., 1986), 73.

11. *Persecution and Toleration: Papers Read at the Twenty-Second Summer Meeting and the Twenty-Third Winter Meeting of the Ecclesiastical History Society,* ed. W. J. Sheils ([Oxford], 1984), xiii.

12. It is generally agreed among historians that beginning in the thirteenth century, the Islamic world entered a long period of political, economic, and cultural decline, and that Jewish fortunes ebbed along with the general tide. S. D. Goitein writes: "The abject economic and general conditions of the Jewish masses in most Arabic-speaking countries, which have impressed countless visitors in modern times, are the outcome of the *general* decline of these countries, and a corollary of the unfavorable socio-religious position of the non-Muslims" (*Jews and Arabs: Their Contact through the Ages* [New York, 1955], 72). Normal Stillman, echoing scholarly consensus, appropriately calls the era ushered in by the thirteenth century a "long twilight" (Stillman, *Jews of Arab Lands,* 64) following "the

best years," from 900 to 1200 (ibid., 40). The extended downturn was punctuated by a short intermission in Iraq and Iran during the second half of the thirteenth century, when a few Jewish courtiers flourished under the relatively tolerant rule of the pagan Mongol conquerors; this indulgence of non-Muslims ended abruptly with the Mongols' conversion to Islam in 1295. The other interruption was the brief but dramatic recovery during what some have called the "second Golden Age" in the orbit of Turkish rule in the sixteenth century. Here, too, characteristically, Jewish revival paralleled, even contributed to, an upswing in the general society.

13. Some suggestive lines of thinking about Polish Jewry that could be applied in such a comparative study are to be found, for instance, in Gershon Hundert's "An Advantage to Peculiarity? The Case of the Polish Commonwealth," *AJS Review* 6 (1981), 21–38.

14. William C. Jordan, *The French Monarchy and the Jews: From Philip Augustus to the Last Capetians* (Philadelphia, 1989), 110–12, cogently explains the reasons for the improved status of Midi Jewry.

Chapter One
Myth and Countermyth

1. A famous letter from Isaac Tzarfati—a Jew from France living in Turkey in the fifteenth century, encouraging his brethren back home to abandon Christian persecution for Islamic refuge—was surely but one of many means by which Ottoman largess became known to Jews in the West. There is an English translation of the letter in Franz Kobler, *Letters of Jews through the Ages* (Philadelphia, 1952), 1:283–85. The same favorable assessment of benevolent Ottoman rulers, as distinguished from persecutory Christians, appears in Ottoman rabbinic responsa (responses to questions on Jewish law) of the sixteenth century and, in turn, in the chronicle of the Egyptian Jewish historian Joseph Sambari in the seventeenth century. See also, Shimon Stober, "The Chronologies of the Muslim Kingdoms in Sambari's Chronicle *Divrei Yoseph*" (Hebrew), in *Exile and Diaspora: Studies in the History of the Jewish People Presented to Professor Haim Beinart on the Occasion of His Seventieth Birthday,* ed. A. Mirsky et al. (Jerusalem, 1988), 418–19.

2. See Franz Delitzsch, *Zur Geschichte der jüdischen Poësie vom Abschluss der heiligen Schriften Alten Bundes bis auf die neueste Zeit* (Leipzig, 1836), 44; and Ismar Schorsch, "The Myth of Sephardic Supremacy," in *Leo Baeck Institute Year Book* 34 (1989), 61.

3. Graetz, *A History of the Jews* (New York, 1894), 3:53. The translation was slightly revised here to add the words "in Christendom" found both in the German original, *Geschichte der Juden,* 3d ed. (Leipzig, 1895), 5:65, and in the popular German abridged edition, *Volkstümliche Geschichte der Juden von Heinrich Graetz* (1923; repr. Munich, 1985), 3:223. This passage is also cited by Jane S. Gerber in "Reconsiderations of Sephardic History: The Origin of the Image of the Golden Age of Muslim-Jewish Relations," in *The Solomon Goldman Lectures,* ed. Nathaniel Stampfer (Chicago, 1985), 4:90.

4. Graetz, *History of the Jews,* 3:236. I have restored in the translation some phrases deleted from *Geschichte der Juden,* 5:327. Ivan G. Marcus has dealt with "the

Sephardic mystique" and its left hand, the denigration of Ashkenazic culture, in "Beyond the Sephardic Mystique," *Orim: A Jewish Journal at Yale* 1 (1985), 35–53. See also, Schorsch, "Myth of Sephardic Supremacy," 47–66.

5. For instance, Ignaz Goldziher (1850–1921), a leading Jewish Orientalist, wrote in 1910: "It is undeniable that, in this earliest phase of the development of Islamic law, the spirit of tolerance permeated the instructions that Muslim conquerors were given for dealing with the subjugated adherents of other religions. What today resembles religious toleration in the constitutional practice of Islamic states—features in the public law of Islam often noted by eighteenth-century travelers—goes back to the principle of the free practice of religion by non-Muslim monotheists, stated in the first half of the seventh century." *Introduction to Islamic Theology and Law,* trans. Andras and Ruth Hamori (Princeton, N.J., 1981), 33 (German orig. *Vorlesungen über den Islam* [Heidelberg, 1910]). See also, Cohen, "Islam and the Jews: Myth, Counter-Myth, History," 127; and, idem, "The Neo-Lachrymose Conception of Jewish-Arab History," 55.

6. Bernard Lewis puts it succinctly when he writes that Jewish scholars of the nineteenth century used the myth of Spanish-Islamic tolerance "as a stick with which to beat their Christian neighbors." Lewis, *History: Remembered, Recovered, Invented* (Princeton, N.J., 1975), 77. In an earlier publication, Lewis writes that Jews used the myth "as a reproach to Christians." "The Pro-Islamic Jews," *Judaism* 17 (1968), 391–404; repr. in *Islam in History: Ideas, Men and Events in the Middle East* (London, 1973), 123–37. See also, more recently, Gerber, "Reconsiderations of Sephardic History."

7. Kayser, *The Life and Time of Jehudah Halevi,* trans. from the German by Frank Gaynor (New York, 1949), 50.

8. Eliyahu Ashtor, *Qorot he-yehudim bi-sefarad ha-muslimit* [History of the Jews in Muslim Spain], 2 vols. (Jerusalem, 1960–66); English trans., *The Jews of Moslem Spain,* trans. Aaron Klein and Jenny Machlowitz Klein, 3 vols. (Philadelphia, 1973–84).

9. André N. Chouraqui, *Between East and West: A History of the Jews of North Africa,* trans. Michael M. Bernet (Philadelphia, 1968; French orig., Paris, 1952), 53–54. Alfred Morabia, a native of Egypt, writes in a similar vein in his "About Relations between Judaism and Islam throughout History," *Alliance Review* 28, no. 48 (Fall 1978), 13–19; and 29, no. 49 (Fall 1980), 9–13.

10. Isacque Graeber and Steuart Henderson Britt, eds. (Westport, Conn., 1942). A bevy of scholars, including distinguished social scientists, set forth "the first attempt to utilize the findings of the various social scientists with respect to the practical issues that face both Jew and non-Jew." Graeber and Britt, p. v.

11. Graeber and Britt, 2. Compare the following observation of the sociologist J. O. Hertzler: "Whatever peace and happiness the Jews enjoyed in non-Christian lands, as in Spain under the Moors, was destroyed the very moment that Christianity conquered. As a notable example one need only mention an institution like the Inquisition." Graeber and Britt, 69.

12. Samuel Rosenblatt, "The Jews and Islam," in *Essays on Antisemitism,* ed. Koppel S. Pinson, 2d ed. (New York, 1946), 112–20. Rosenblatt quotes (120) A. de Gobineau: "If one separates religious doctrine from political necessity, which has often spoken and acted in its name, there is no religion more tolerant—one might

even say more indifferent, regarding the faith of men than Islam. . . . The religious factor is only invoked as a pretense but in reality remains outside."

13. Paul E. Grosser and Edwin G. Halperin, *The Causes and Effects of Anti-Semitism: The Dimensions of a Prejudice (An Analysis and Chronology of 1900 Years of Anti-Semitic Attitudes and Practices)* (New York, 1978), 365–89. As the compilers write in their introduction, they did so because, one, Muslim anti-Jewishness was "qualitatively and quantitatively distinct from the anti-Semitism of the Christian/Western World"; and, two, the Jew, "for the most part [was] protected by law from assault almost on a par with his neighbors" (7). In a note to the introduction, they add: "There is general agreement among historians that the golden age of the Islamic Empire was also a golden age for Jews living under Islamic rule. Jewish historians, Arab historians, historians specializing in Jewish or Arabic history and other general historians share this view" (12).

14. Antonius, *The Arab Awakening* (Philadelphia, 1939), 391–92, 409–10.

15. Emil Zaidan, a Christian Arab, published an essay in the Egyptian monthly, *Al-hilāl* 22, no. 4 (January 1914), 243–56, entitled *Al-yahūd fi'l-ta'rīkh* [The Jews in History]. The author contrasts the oppression and suffering of the Jews under Greek, Roman, and, particularly, Christian rule with the Jewish "Golden Age, especially in Muslim Spain" [*ʿaṣruhum al-dhahabī wa-lā siyyammā fi'l-andalus*]. His purpose (243f.) is to counteract the negative stereotype of the malevolent, child-murdering Jew prevalent among Christians—analogous, Zaidan says, to Christian prejudices against Islam and Muslim prejudices against Christianity. I suspect, too, that the author wished to praise Islam for providing a more comfortable home for the Jews than did Christendom, with a hoped-for continued Muslim toleration of Arab Christians in mind.

Less oblique in its purpose is the more recent multivolume work by the Christian Arab, Edmond Rabbath, *Les chrétiens dans l'Islam des premiers temps: Mahomet: Prophète arabe et fondateur d'état* (Beirut, 1981); *La conquête arabe sous les quatre premiers califes (11/632–40/661),* 2 vols. (Beirut, 1985). Rabbath chooses epigraphs from Voltaire's *Essai sur les moeurs et l'esprit des nations,* such as "Les arabes étaient les plus cléments de tous les conquérants de la terre" (epigraph to the first volume of *La conquête arabe*). The Christian-Arab, S. A. Aldeeb Abu-Sahlieh, in *L'impact de la religion sur l'ordre juridique: cas de l'Egypte: Non Musulmans en pays d'Islam* (Fribourg, 1979), pleads for the establishment of Western-style nation-states, with their separation of religion and politics, of obvious advantage to Christian citizens.

16. Merlin Swartz, "The Position of Jews in Arab Lands Following the Rise of Islam," *Muslim World* 60 (1970), 6–24. The final quotation is from 23 (italics in original).

17. Amir Hasan Siddiqi, *Non-Muslims under Muslim Rule and Muslims under Non-Muslim Rule* (Karachi, 1969), 158–74. Similarly, Ibrahim Amin Ghali's *Le monde arabe et les juifs* contrasts Islamic tolerance with Christian persecution (Paris, 1972), 210–14, esp. 212–14. A book by the journalist Marion Woolfson, *Prophets in Babylon: Jews in the Arab World* (London, 1980), characterizes Jewish history under Islam as a golden age and labels as a myth the claim that Jews from Arab countries suffered severe persecution in their homelands. Woolfson asserts that Oriental Jews were treated worse by the Ashkenazic ruling establishment in Israel after their mass immigration from Middle Eastern homelands. In *Islam versus Ahl al-Kitāb:*

Past and Present, an obscure publication from India, a Jewish convert to Islam who emigrated to Pakistan draws on the myth of the interfaith utopia to praise her adopted religion at the expense of the religion into which she was born. "The rise of the modern Zionist movement brought more than a thousand years of friendly Muslim-Jewish relationships to an abrupt end, with the result that since the days of the Holy Prophet never has Jewish hatred towards Muslims nor Muslim hatred for Jews been more bitter than at the present time." The author goes on to contrast relations between Muslims and Jews in the past with "the relation between Christendom and Jewry [which] was one of unremitting hostility, blackened by interminable chronicles of persecutions, massacres, [and] oppressive measures." Maryam Jameelah, *Islam Versus Ahl al-Kitāb: Past and Present* (Delhi, 1982), 11.

18. Following are some examples. Barakat Ahmad, *Muhammad and the Jews: A Reexamination* (New Delhi, 1979). W. N. Arafat, "New Light on the Story of Banū Qurayẓa and the Jews of Medina," *Journal of the Royal Asiatic Society of Great Britain and Ireland* (1976), 100–107: argues that the story originated among descendants of the Jewish Medinan tribes who wished to glorify their ancestors with a story of a Massada-like martyrdom. Tawfīq Sulṭān Yuzbakī, *Ta'rīkh ahl al-dhimma fi'l-ʿIrāq (12–247 A.H.)* [History of the Protected People in Iraq (12/633–247/861)] (Riyad, 1983), 69: mentions the expulsions but omits the massacre. Ḥussein Mu'nis, *ʿĀlam al-islām* [The World of Islam] (Cairo, 1989): refers to "the elimination" [*taṣfiya*] of the three main Jewish tribes (37) and to "the termination of the affair" [*intihā' sha'n*] without mentioning actions taken by the Prophet (161). For a discussion of the problem, see M. J. Kister, "The Massacre of the Banū Qurayẓa: A Re-examination of a Tradition," *Jerusalem Studies in Arabic and Islam* 8 (1986), 61–96.

19. Said Abdel Fattah Ashour, "Al-yahūd fi'l-ʿuṣūr al-wusṭā: dirāsa muqārina bayn al-sharq wa'l-gharb," *Kitāb al-mu'tamar al-rābiʿ li-majmaʿ al-buḥūth al-islāmiyya* ([Cairo], 1968), 2:349–61; *The Fourth Conference of the Academy of Islamic Research* (Cairo, 1970), 497–505.

20. English edition, 505. Some of the antisemitic sections from the beginning of this paper were published in a pamphlet containing photographically reproduced extracts from the English version of the proceedings of the Al-Azhar Conference of 1968 (*Arab Theologians on Jews and Israel*, ed. D. F. Green [pseudonym] [Geneva, 1971], 46–47). Through this pamphlet, also published in French and in German, the antisemitic tenor of that now infamous conference became widely known in Israel and elsewhere.

21. ʿAbd al-Karīm Zaydān, *Aḥkām al-dhimmīyyin wa'l-musta'minīn fī dār al-Islām* [The Laws Concerning the Protected People and Those Granted Safe Conduct] ([Baghdad], 1963), 77–80.

22. *Al-yahūd fī miṣr mundh al-fatḥ al-islāmī ḥatta al-ghazw al-ʿuthmānī* (Beirut, 1980).

23. Much of his book on the Jews was extracted from his earlier publication, *Ahl al-dhimma fī miṣr al-ʿuṣūr al-wusṭā* [The Protected People in Egypt during the Middle Ages], 2d ed. (Cairo, 1979), which aimed at documenting the general postulate that Islam tolerated all non-Muslim monotheists, both Jews and Christians.

24. *Al-islām wa-ahl al-dhimma* [Islam and the Protected People] (n.p., 1969).

25. Yūsuf al-Qaraḍāwī, *Ghair al-muslimīn fi'l-mujtamaʿ al-islāmī* [Non-Muslims in Islamic Society] (Cairo, 1977), highlights the theme of Islamic toleration of the *dhimmīs,* drawing, among other sources, from al-Kharbūṭlī. Qaraḍāwī devotes a chapter to refuting challenges to the notion of Muslim toleration, based on allegedly oppressive practices such as the poll tax and discriminatory differentiation in dress. A chapter at the end, entitled "Comparison," glorifies Islamic toleration by contrasting it with the *in*tolerance shown by other religions in the past and in our own time—for example, the oppression of Muslims in Christian countries and in the Soviet Union, the expulsion of the Jews from Spain, and the persecution of Christians by other Christians throughout history. Qaraḍāwī's book, which appeared in English translation, *Non-Muslims in the Islamic Society,* trans. Khalil Muhammad Hamad and Sayed Mahboob Ali Shah (Indianapolis, 1985), is aimed at "both Muslim and non-Muslim readers in order to introduce them to this important subject, which has been distorted and misrepresented by some non-Muslim writers" (from the introduction).

26. Other examples are: Yuzbakī, *Ta'rīkh ahl al-dhimma fi'l-ʿIrāq (12–247 A.H.):* "When the Arab conquest of Iraq and Persia took place, the Christians, Jews, and some of the Zoroastrians welcomed them because they rescued them from the harshness of their former rulers [the Sassanians]. For Islam tolerated [*samāḥa*] them by allowing them to enjoy religious freedom and relieved them of military service in exchange for payment of the poll tax [*jizya*]. This tolerance [*tasāmuḥ*] was a significant factor in the support given by the people of the conquered lands to the Muslim Arabs, and also in their acceptance of the Islamic religion with enthusiasm" (43).

Sallām S. M. Sallām, *Ahl al-dhimma fī Miṣr al-ʿaṣr al-fāṭimī al-thānī wa'l-ʿaṣr al-ayyūbī (467–648/1074–1250)* [The Protected People in Egypt during the Second Fatimid and Ayyubid Periods] (Cairo, 1982): "The Protected People in Egypt witnessed a golden age in all aspects of life in a society governed by a spirit of love and harmony, and they benefited from the wonderful principle of religious tolerance (*al-tasāmuḥ al-dīnī*) under the shelter of the regime of the caliphs of the second Fatimid period and of the Ayyubid sultans" (22).

Salwā ʿAlī Mīlād, *Wathā'iq ahl al-dhimma fi'l-ʿaṣr al-ʿuthmānī wa-ahammiyyatuhu al-ta'rīkhiyya* [Documents Concerning the Protected People during the Ottoman Period and Their Historical Importance] ([Cairo], 1983): "Islam spread by virtue of its special traits and benevolent teachings, just as Arab tolerance (*tasāmuḥ*) was one of the factors that helped it to spread. . . . The Arabs allowed the conquered people freedom of religion, just as the Muslims joined vigilance on behalf of their religion with a spirit of tolerance towards the adherents of other religions" (7).

Ḥussein Mu'nis, *ʿĀlam al-islām:* "They [the non-Muslims] were encompassed by Islam's tolerance [*tasāmuḥ*], tolerated by being safeguarded in their religion and in the continuity of their life within the Islamic community. . . . The Geniza documents confirm what we know, namely, that the Jews in Islamic-Arab lands lived in complete tolerance. . . . While they were experiencing harsh persecution in the West, compelled to live in quarters or 'the ghetto,' the Jews in Islamic lands lived in freedom, unfettered other than by the general system of regulations imposed upon them as 'Protected People' [*ahl al-dhimma*]" (249, 251–52).

27. A meritorious exception to Arabist devotion to the myth of the interfaith

utopia is *Toleranz im Islam* (Munich, 1980), by Adel Théodor Khoury, a Christian-Arab scholar who has written extensively on interreligious polemics between Christianity and Islam during the Middle Ages. Khoury wrote this book for the German series, "Entwicklung und Frieden" [Development and Peace], in response to Western concern over the radical militancy of Islamic fundamentalism. With its balanced objectivity, this volume forms a useful secondary source for information about one aspect of the problem under discussion in the present book.

28. This view is well established among scholars. See, for instance, Moshe Ma'oz, *The Image of the Jew in Official Arab Literature and Communications Media* (Jerusalem, 1976), 5–23; Norman Stillman, "New Attitudes toward the Jew in the Arab World," *Jewish Social Studies* 37 (1975), 198.

29. Harkabi, *Arab Attitudes to Israel* (Jerusalem, 1972; Hebrew orig.: Tel Aviv, 1968). Regarding the myth of the interfaith utopia, Harkabi writes: "It is true that the position of the Jews was much better in the Arab countries [than in Europe]. . . ." But, "[t]he position of the Jews . . . was not so idyllic as it is portrayed today by Arab spokesmen" (218–19). Writing several years later, Harkabi offered reasons for Israeli reluctance to acknowledge the extent and nature of Arab antisemitism: (1) because Arab antisemitism came from above, from governments or from the intellectual elite, rather than from below, as a social phenomenon; (2) because it was not Christian, "as if antisemitism can stem only from Christian sources"; (3) fear by "some Israelis . . . that broaching Arab antisemitism will provide an excuse for a hawkish Israeli position." Idem, "On Arab Antisemitism Once More," in *Antisemitism through the Ages,* ed. Shmuel Almog and trans. Nathan H. Reisner (Oxford, 1988), 227, 233, 238. The Hebrew original of this publication appeared in Jerusalem in 1980.

30. See Yehoshafat Harkabi, *The Indoctrination against Israel in U.A.R. Armed Forces* (Hebrew) (Tel Aviv, 1967). Harkabi includes a full Hebrew translation of an Arabic pamphlet, "The Problem of Palestine," which begins with a short historical survey comparing the suffering of the "misanthropic" Jews of Christendom with the freedom they enjoyed under a tolerant Islam (22).

31. In 1968, the Department of Information of the Israel Foreign Ministry published a pamphlet of representative extracts from Arab school texts, with illustrations, entitled "Hatred Is Sacred."

32. Reported, among other places, in the *New York Times,* April 26, 1972, 5, and in the Israeli news media.

33. Ronald L. Nettler, *Past Trials and Present Tribulations: A Muslim Fundamentalist's View of the Jews* (Oxford, 1987), 20–21.

34. *An Arrogant Oppressive Spirit: Anti-Zionism as Anti-Judaism in Egypt* (Oxford, 1989; Hebrew orig.: Jerusalem, 1988).

35. See the articles cited in the Preface. With the permission of the editor-publisher of *Tikkun,* portions of my "Neo-Lachrymose Conception of Jewish-Arab History" have been reused and expanded in the following section.

36. Published in the October 4, 1946, issue of the Zionist Organization of America's *New Palestine.* The essay appears on pages B17–B20 of the 1967 supplement to *Near East Report.* The supplement section later became institutionalized as a separate AIPAC publication, entitled *Myths and Facts: A Concise Record of the Arab-Israeli Conflict.* The nine issues that appeared, with massive distribution between

1970 and 1992, include sections refuting the myth of Arab toleration. In the 1990 issue of *Near East Report* itself, the editors excerpted the chapter, "Arab Treatment of the Jews," from *Myths and Facts* as expanded in the 1989 edition, including the comments of the French thinker Jacques Ellul, in his preface to the English edition of Bat Ye'or's "countermyth" book, *The Dhimmi* (see below). Roth's essay appeared concurrently, with a few editorial variants, in the British Zionist *Jewish Forum* (October 1946), 28–33—the version that is mentioned by S. D. Goitein in his *Jews and Arabs,* 66.

37. "The Myth of Arab Toleration," *Midstream* 16, no. 1 (January 1970), 56–59; expanded in the first chapter of Friedman's *Without Future: The Plight of Syrian Jewry* (New York, 1989). Compare Norman Stillman's unfavorable review in *MESA [Middle East Studies Association] Bulletin* 24, no. 2 (1990), 194.

38. Writing about "Arab-Jewish Bi-Nationalism" (*Jewish Frontier* [April 1976]), Saul Friedman again proclaims that "Arab hostility to Jews, which has been endemic to the Middle East since the time of Muhammad," confirms the impossibility of Arabs and Jews living in peace in a binational state. Two years later, in the same journal, Friedman explains how pro-Arab apologists invoke the "fabled Semitic fraternity which existed in the Middle East till recently" in order to cover up their intense antisemitism. "Universal Anti-Semitism," *Jewish Frontier* (August–September 1976), 14–18.

39. Lewis, "The Historical Jewish Presence in the Middle East," *Jewish Frontier* (January 1974), 13–16.

40. "Israel's Rights and Arab Propaganda," *Commentary* (August 1975), 38–43. In another contribution to countermyth revision of Jewish-Arab history, Rose Lewis debunks the "golden age" in Spain. Inspired by Bernard Lewis's statement in *History: Remembered, Recovered, Restored* ([Princeton, N.J., 1975], 77), that the "myth of Spanish Islamic tolerance," once used by Jewish scholars "as a stick with which to beat their Christian neighbors . . . has been taken up by Muslim scholars who use it for their own somewhat different purposes," Rose Lewis resolves to "take a harder look at the 'golden age' . . . with 20th century rather than 19th century eyes." She sets out to correct the record about Jewish florescence in Muslim Spain. By romanticizing that era, she complains, Jewish historians have provided ammunition for the Arab case against Israel. Her own version of the era features the "bloody pogrom" against the Jews of Granada, Spain, in 1066, and a contemporaneous Arabic poem filled with nasty invective about the Jews that is thought to have triggered the massacre. She writes: "This is Muslim anti-Semitism with deep native roots and a long historical tradition" ("Muslim Glamour and the Spanish Jews," *Midstream* [February 1977], 26–37). Lewis expatiates again on the theme of Jewish suffering at Arab hands in "Maimonides and the Muslims" (*Midstream* [November 1979], 16–22), in describing the fierce Almohad persecution of the twelfth century. Quoting the crucial passage from Maimonides' "Epistle to Yemen," she asserts that "[t]here can certainly be no doubt about what Moses Maimonides himself thought of Arab-Jewish relations during the alleged Golden Age he lived in" (22).

41. Albert Memmi, *Jews and Arabs,* trans. Eleanor Levieux (Chicago, 1975; French orig.: *Juifs et arabes* [Paris, 1974]), 11–12. There is a Hebrew translation, *Yehudim ve-ʿarvim,* trans. Aharon Amir (Tel Aviv, 1975).

42. Memmi, *Jews and Arabs,* 27 (emphasis in orig.). This chapter was also published as an essay in the French-Jewish magazine *L'Arche* in early 1974.

43. "The Jews of Islam: Golden Age or Ghetto?" *Jewish Chronicle Colour Magazine,* November 23, 1979, 56–60.

44. East Rutherford, N.J., 1985; French orig., Paris, 1980; Hebrew trans. Aharon Amir (Jerusalem, 1986). The book has also been translated into Russian. The subtitle of the French original, *Profil de l'oprimé en Orient et en Afrique du Nord depuis la conquête arabe,* better reflects the book's theme.

45. Bat Ye'or, *The Dhimmi,* 28. Bat Ye'or's newest contribution to the history of the *dhimmī, Les chrétientés d'orient entre Jihad et dhimmitude: VII*[e]*–XX*[e] *siècle* (Paris, 1991), also contains a preface by Ellul.

46. Joan Peters, *From Time Immemorial: The Origins of the Arab-Jewish Conflict over Palestine* (New York, 1984), 75. This book has been heavily criticized—by Israeli specialists, among others—for its flawed, tendentious methodology on the subject of Arab settlement in Palestine in the nineteenth and twentieth centuries. The book was published in a Hebrew translation under the title, *Me'az umi-tamid,* trans. Aharon Amir (Tel Aviv, 1988, 1990).

47. Moshe Gil, "The Constitution of Medina: A Reconsideration," *Israel Oriental Studies* 4 (1974), 44–66. Compare Uri Rubin, "The 'Constitution of Medina': Some Notes," *Studia Islamica* 62 (1985), 5–23.

48. Many more than the one essay on this topic in *Essays on Antisemitism,* published in the 1940s.

49. Haggai Ben-Shammai, "Jew-Hatred in the Islamic Tradition and the Koranic Exegesis," in *Antisemitism through the Ages,* 161–69; quotation from 168.

50. Avraham Grossman, "The Economic and Social Background of Hostile Attitudes toward the Jews in the Ninth and Tenth Century Muslim Caliphate," in *Antisemitism through the Ages,* 171–87. In a footnote, Grossman concedes that Maimonides was influenced by recent persecutions in Muslim Spain; ibid., 184, n. 3. Generally speaking, Grossman's thesis, that Muslim hatred of the Jews began in the ninth century in reaction to Jewish social and economic success, is not convincing. The hatred existed earlier, but, as I shall argue below, it was unrelated to economic factors (see Chap. 5 in this book). The other two essays in *Antisemitism through the Ages* on the premodern period do not have a countermyth objective: Jacob Barnai, "Blood Libels' in the Ottoman Empire of the Fifteenth to Nineteenth Centuries"; and Shalom Bar-Asher, "Antisemitism and Economic Influence: The Jews of Morocco (1672–1822)."

51. A pamphlet by Maurice Roumani in collaboration with Deborah Goldman and Helene Korn, "The Case of the Jews from Arab Countries: A Neglected Issue," vol. 1 (Jerusalem, 1975).

52. "Case of the Jews," 41–57.

53. Ibid., 48. The passage appears in italics in the chapter.

54. This situation seems to have begun to change with the Israeli elections of June 1992. See, for instance, Shlomo Deshen, "The Religiosity of Israeli Middle Easterners: Lay People, Rabbis and Faith" (Hebrew), to appear in *Alpayim* 9 (forthcoming). I am grateful to Professor Deshen for sharing the typescript of this article with me prior to its publication.

55. This view is expressed in, for instance, academic research that focuses on

instances of Arab persecution in past centuries; in attempts to show how European fascism, directly or indirectly, caused suffering to Jews in Arab lands before and during the Second World War; and in efforts to document a sometimes elusive indigenous Oriental Zionist response to Arab antisemitism.

56. Yossi Yonah, "How Right Wing Are the Sephardim?" *Tikkun* 5, no. 5 (May–June 1990), 38–39, 100–102.

57. Heskel M. Haddad, *Jews of Arab and Islamic Countries: History, Problems, Solutions* (New York, 1984), 20. Haddad dedicated his book to, among others, "my late father, who bore no hatred against Moslems and no grudge against Ashkenazim."

58. *New Outlook* (November–December 1991), 15. See also, Daniel Gavron, "Smashing the Stereotype," *Jerusalem Post Magazine,* July 8, 1983, 3–4.

59. For more of the "debate," see two responses to my own work: Bat Ye'or, "Islam and the *Dhimmis,*" *Jerusalem Quarterly,* no. 42 (1987), 83–88; and Norman A. Stillman, "Myth, Countermyth, Distortion," *Tikkun* (May–June 1991), 60–64, with "Letters to the Editor," ibid. (July–August 1991), 96 and rear cover. This latter exchange may be compared with Lawrence Rosen, "Muslim-Jewish Relations in a Moroccan City," *International Journal of Middle Eastern Studies* 3 (1972), 435–49, and the responses by Norman A. Stillman, "Muslims and Jews in Morocco," *Jerusalem Quarterly,* no. 5 (1977), 76–83, and "The Moroccan Jewish Experience: A Revisionist View," ibid., no. 9 (1978), 111–22 (cf. also, Moshe Shokeid, "Jewish Existence in a Berber Environment," in Shlomo Deshen and Walter Zenner, eds., *Jewish Societies in the Middle East: Community, Culture, and Authority* [Washington, D.C., 1982], 106–7).

Chapter Two
Religions in Conflict

1. Simon, *Verus Israel: A Study of the Relationship between Christians and Jews in the Roman Empire (135–425),* trans. H. McKeating (Oxford, 1986), 71–77.

2. Paul's "innovation" is sharply debated among experts on early Christianity. See John Gager, *The Origins of Anti-Semitism: Attitudes toward Judaism in Pagan and Christian Antiquity* (New York, 1983), 193ff. Regardless of Paul's true convictions in this matter, what is important here is that subsequent Christian thinkers understood Paul to have preached that the coming of Christ abrogated Jewish law, and that this became a salient feature of the Jewish-Christian conflict.

3. On the contrary, the Gospel (compare Matthew 5:17–19) puts into Jesus' mouth an unambiguous affirmation of the value of Jewish law: "Think not that I have come to abolish the law and the prophets; I have come not to abolish them but to fulfill them. . . . Whoever then relaxes one of the least of these commandments and teaches men so, shall be called least in the kingdom of heaven; but he who does them and teaches them shall be called great in the kingdom of heaven."

4. Simon, *Verus Israel,* 74.

5. Ibid., 78–80.

6. A. Lukyn Williams, *Adversus Judaeos* (Cambridge, 1935), 43–52. See also the survey in the chapter, "Das Alte Testament im Verständnis des Neuen Testaments und der Kirchenväter," in Heinz Schreckenberg, *Die christlichen Adversus-Judaeos*

Texte und ihr literarisches und historisches Umfeld (1.–11. Jh.), 2d rev. ed. (Frankfurt am Main, 1990 [first pub. 1982]), 58–73.

7. Much ink has been spilled trying to prove or disprove this allegation. See, for instance, James Parkes, *The Conflict of the Church and the Synagogue* (1934; repr., Cleveland, 1961), 121ff.

8. Simon, *Verus Israel,* 115–25. Even Rosemary Ruether, a staunch exculpator of the Jews in the Christian-Jewish conflict, concedes that, in the earliest stages, "it is possible to speak of Judaism as 'persecuting' Christians." *Faith and Fratricide: The Theological Roots of Anti-Semitism* (New York, 1974), 166.

9. Simon, *Verus Israel,* 286, 513. The quotation from Tertullian is the second page reference.

10. Ibid., 288, 290–91.

11. Gager, *Origins of Anti-Semitism,* 117ff.

12. Cited in Simon, *Verus Israel,* 316, 514.

13. From the first of eight "Homilies against the Jews," trans. Wayne A. Meeks and Robert L. Wilken, *Jews and Christians in Antioch in the First Four Centuries of the Common Era* ([Ann Arbor], 1978), 92, 98.

14. Simon, *Verus Israel,* 217, 220.

15. Ibid., 222; Gager, *Origins of Anti-Semitism,* 118–20.

16. Robert L. Wilken, *John Chrysostom and the Jews: Rhetoric and Reality in the Late 4th Century* (Berkeley and Los Angeles, 1983), 161–62.

17. St. Augustine, Sermon no. 201, in *The Fathers of the Church,* vol. 38, *Saint Augustine, Sermons on the Liturgical Seasons,* trans. Sister Mary Sarah Muldowney (New York, 1959), 70–71. See also, "Concerning Faith of Things Not Seen," in *A Select Library of the Nicene and Post-Nicene Fathers of the Christian Church,* ed. Philip Schaff (repr., Grand Rapids, Mich., 1980), 3:341–42; *The City of God against the Pagans* 18:46, in Loeb Classical Library, trans. William Chase Greene (London, 1960), 6:46–51; "In Answer to the Jews" [*Tractatus Adversus Judeos*], in *Fathers of the Church,* vol. 27, *Saint Augustine, Treatises on Marriage and Other Subjects,* ed. Roy J. Deferrari, trans. Sister Marie Liguori (New York, 1955). 403. See also, Bernhard Blumenkranz, *Die Judenpredigt Augustins: Ein Beitrag zur Geschichte der jüdisch-christlichen Beziehungen in den ersten Jahrhunderten* (Basel, 1946), 175–81; idem, "Augustin et les juifs, Augustin et le judaïsme," in *Recherches augustiniennes* (Paris, 1958), 1:225–41, repr. in Blumenkranz, *Juifs et chrétiens: Patristique et moyen age* (London, 1977).

18. Gedaliahu G. Strousma, "Early Christianity as Radical Religion: Context and Implications," *Israel Oriental Studies* 14 (1994), forthcoming. Professor Stroumsa presented this paper at Princeton University in February 1992.

19. The extent to which pagan anti-Judaism carried over into Christianity has been hotly debated in the scholarly literature. The view of M. Simon—that Christian anti-Judaism includes a theologized enhancement and expansion of the predominantly social "antisemitism" of pagan antiquity—seems to present the most reasonable balance between those who "blame" Christianity alone and those who would exculpate Christianity by casting all the blame on paganism. Simon's chapter on Christian antisemitism was selected by Jeremy Cohen for his collection, *Essential Papers on Judaism and Christianity in Conflict: From Late Antiquity to the Reformation* (New York, 1991), 131–73.

20. Ruether, *Faith and Fratricide,* 181. See also various responses to Ruether in

the symposium of Christian theologians, *Antisemitism and the Foundations of Christianity,* ed. Alan T. Davies (New York, 1979).

21. For some bibliography, see the sections "Jews in Arabia" and "Muhammad and the Jews," In Mark R. Cohen, "The Jews under Islam: From the Rise of Islam to Sabbatai Zevi," cited in the Preface, note 6. The most extravagant—hence, controversial—theory about the "Jewish origins" of Islam, based on external (non-Muslim) sources, sees it as a conscious adaptation of a marginal form of Judaism, originally focused on Palestine but later on Arabia. Patricia Crone and Michael Cook, *Hagarism: The Making of the Islamic World* (Cambridge, 1977); summarized in Cook, *Muhammad* (Oxford, 1983), esp. 73–76.

22. English trans. in Stillman, *Jews of Arab Lands,* 115–18. The revisionist suggestion by Moshe Gil about this passage would vocalize *dīn* (religion) as *dayn* (debt) and thereby eliminate from the document its statement of religious toleration. "Constitution of Medina," 63. But Uri Rubin convincingly upholds the dominant interpretation reflected in Stillman's translation. Rubin, "The 'Constitution of Medina,'" 160.

23. Ibn Qayyim al-Jawziyya, *Aḥkām ahl al-dhimma,* ed. Ṣubḥī Ṣāliḥ, part 1 (Beirut, 1983), 238ff.

24. William C. Jordan, "The Last Tormentor of Christ: An Image of the Jew in Ancient and Medieval Exegesis, Art, and Drama," *Jewish Quarterly Review,* n.s., 78 (1987), 21–47; idem, "the Erosion of the Stereotype of the Last Tormentor of Christ," *Jewish Quarterly Review,* n.s., 81 (1990), 13–14.

25. Stillman, *Jews of Arab Lands,* 129–30. As background to the expulsion of the Jewish tribe of the Banū Naḍīr from Medina, a story is told (in al-Wāqidī's *Kitāb al-maghāzī* [Book of the Military Campaigns (of the Prophet)]) about some Jews from the tribe who tried unsuccessfully to kill Muhammad by dropping a stone on him from the roof of a house, in hopes of putting an end to his religious movement. Although such attempts failed, it is noteworthy, by way of contrast with the Christian-Jewish religious conflict, that murderous intentions toward the founder of Islam did not play a major role in the Islamic polemic against the Jews.

26. Not surprisingly, the theme has salience in twentieth-century Arab anti-semitism.

27. Jeffrey Burton Russell, *A History of Medieval Christianity: Prophecy and Order* (New York, 1968), 27–31.

28. See Chap. 3.

29. Sura 3:65, 67, 68. In the translation by Mohammed Marmaduke Pickthall, *The Meaning of the Glorious Koran* (New York, n.d.), 67. Henceforth, all English citations from the Qur'an are from this edition.

30. James Kritzeck, *Sons of Abraham: Christians and Moslems* (Baltimore, 1965), 29.

31. Rudi Paret, "Toleranz und Intoleranz im Islam," *Saeculum* 21 (1970), 349–50.

32. Simon, *Verus Israel,* 80–82; Gager, *Origins of Anti-Semitism,* 217–20.

33. Discussed in Chap. 9.

34. Which was modeled on the Jewish fast of the Day of Atonement at the end of the Ten Days of Repentance following Rosh Hashanah, the celebration of the beginning of the Jewish New Year.

35. M. J. Kister, "Ḥaddithū 'an banī isrā'īla wa-lā ḥaraja: A Study of an Early

Tradition," *Israel Oriental Studies* 2 (1972), 215–39. Kister interprets the word *ʿan* to mean "about" or "concerning," rather than "from" or "in the name of," the more common sense of *ʿan* when used with the verb *ḥaddatha* (as pointed out to me by both Michael Cook and Haggai Ben-Shammai). For the present purpose, it makes no difference. See also, Georges Vajda, "Juifs et musulmans selon le ḥadīṯ," *Journal asiatique* 229 (1937), 115–20.

36. For similarities between Judaism and developed Islam, see E. I. J. Rosenthal, *Judaism and Islam* (London, 1961), part 1.

37. The very inappropriateness of this term speaks volumes about the difference between Islam and Christianity.

38. *Be-ḥuqqoteihem lo telekhu,* "do not follow their laws"; Leviticus 18:3.

39. Vajda, "Juifs et musulmans selon le ḥadīṯ," 62–63.

40. Ibn Taymiyya, *Kitāb iqtīdā' al-ṣirāt al-mustaqīm mukhālafat aṣḥāb al-jaḥīm,* ed. Aḥmad Ḥamdi Imām (Jaddah, 1980), 59; English trans. based on the 1950 Cairo edition, Muhammad Umar Memon, *Ibn Taimiya's Struggle against Popular Religion* (The Hague, 1976), 133.

41. Ibn Taymiyya, *Kitāb iqtidā' al-ṣirāt al-mustaqīm,* 206; English trans., 207.

42. According to church legislation as late as the fourteenth century, Christians sometimes attended and even assisted at Jewish celebrations, circumcisions, and funerals. Gilbert Dahan, *Les intellectuels chrétiens et les juifs au moyen age* (Paris, 1990), 178–79. This phenomenon, driven by curiosity rather than syncretistic impulses, is well known from the early modern period.

Chapter Three
The Legal Position of Jews in Christendom

1. Southern, *The Making of the Middle Ages* (New Haven, Conn., 1953), 75.

2. Kisch, *The Jews in Medieval Germany: A Study of Their Legal and Social Status,* 2d ed. (New York, 1970; first pub., 1949).

3. For a brief survey of law in medieval Christendom, see Norman Zacour, *An Introduction to Medieval Institutions* (Toronto, 1969), 136–52.

4. For pre-Christian Roman laws concerning the Jews, see *Ancient Roman Statutes,* trans. Alan Chester Johnson et al., ed. Clyde Pharr (Austin, Tex., 1961), index.

5. I am grateful to Amnon Linder for this clarification. See also, Schreckenberg, *Die christlichen Adversus-Judaeos Texte und ihr literarisches und historisches Umfeld (1.–11. Jh.),* 2d rev. ed., 216 (Tertullian, died after 220), 258 (Emperor Septimius Severus, r. 193–211).

6. See Menahem Stern, *Greek and Latin Authors on Jews and Judaism,* 3 vols. (Jerusalem, 1974–84), 3:index s.v. "anti-Semitism" for this material.

7. Preserved in Josephus' *Antiquities.* See *Ancient Roman Statutes,* 127. The edict goes on to state: ". . . their sacred offerings shall be inviolable and shall be sent to Jerusalem and shall be paid to the financial officials of Jerusalem; and . . . they shall not give sureties for appearance in court on the Sabbath or on the day of preparation before it after the ninth hour."

8. Historians are in dispute as to whether the Hadrianic decrees preceded or followed the short-lived Bar Kokhba revolt.

9. Shlomo Simonsohn, *The Apostolic See and the Jews: History* (Toronto, 1991), 94–95.

10. With reference to the Greeks, see Elias Bickerman, *From Ezra to the Last of the Maccabees* (New York, 1962), 20.

11. The laws, which date from the time of Emperor Constantine (312–37), are arranged chronologically by subject.

12. Linder, *The Jews in Roman Imperial Legislation* (Detroit, 1987; Hebrew original published in Jerusalem, 1983). In this book, I cite only the edition in English. Much of the discussion in this section follows Linder's exhaustive presentation. Quotations from the laws are taken from Clyde Pharr's English edition, *The Theodosian Code and Novels and the Simondian Constitutions* (Princeton, N.J., 1952), following the book, title, and section numbers in the Codex Theodosianus (CTh).

13. Due to repetition, the forty-five laws appear in sixty-eight citations. Many of them are dispersed among books on general subjects. For instance, Book 7, devoted to military affairs, decrees that synagogues must be protected from unauthorized quartering of soldiers (CTh 7.8.2, *Theodosian Code,* 165). A statute on court procedure, in Book 2, states the Roman position on Jewish judicial autonomy: matters that do not pertain to "their superstition" shall be adjudicated in Roman courts (hence, purely religious matters are left to Jewish judges). In civil cases, Jews may, by mutual consent, have their suits arbitrated by Jewish judges, whose decisions would be upheld by Roman tribunals (CTh 2.1.10, *Theodosian Code,* 39). In a more stringent restatement of this law, the Justinianic Code omitted the Latin word *non* ("not") in the clause relating to freedom of adjudication of purely religious matters, so that "tolerant" distinction was eliminated. See Linder, *Jews in Roman Imperial Legislation,* 206–7.

14. CTh 16.5.44, *Theodosian Code,* 458.

15. CTh 16.5.46, *Theodosian Code,* 458 (law of January 15, 409).

16. Linder, *Jews in Roman Imperial Legislation,* 62f.

17. Title 8 is entitled "On Jews, Caelicolists, and Samaritans." The Caelicolists ("Heaven-Fearers") were a group associated with the Jews but referred to elsewhere in the Theodosian Code as a sect "who hold assemblies of some unknown new dogma" and whose houses of worship, like those of the heretic, are to be "vindicated to the churches" (CTh 16.4.43, *Theodosian Code,* 458). See also, Linder *Jews in Roman Imperial Legislation,* 226–36.

18. CTh 16.8.9, *Theodosian Code,* 468.

19. CTh 16.8.20, *Theodosian Code,* 469.

20. CTh 16.8.12, *Theodosian Code,* 468.

21. CTh 16.8.21, *Theodosian Code,* 469. Linder, in *Jews in Roman Imperial Legislation,* 283–86, clears up the matter of the date.

22. "Wherefore once again I conjure you that, on the one hand, the Alexandrians show themselves forbearing and kindly toward the Jews, who for many years have dwelt in the same city, and dishonor none of the rights observed by them in the worship of their god but allow them to observe their customs as in the time of the deified Augustus, which customs I also, after hearing both sides, have confirmed. And, on the other hand, I explicitly order the Jews not to agitate for more privileges than they formerly possessed." Naphtali Lewis and Meyer Reinhold, eds., *Roman Civilization. Sourcebook II: The Empire* (New York, 1966), 368;

trans. from the Loeb Classical Library edition, *Select Papyri,* trans. A. S. Hunt and C. C. Edgar (Cambridge, 1934), 2:87. I owe the notion of this possible Claudian antecedent of Christian-Roman Jewry law to my teacher, the late Gerson D. Cohen. I have not seen the suggestion in print elsewhere.

23. CTh 16.8.26, *Theodosian Code,* 470–71. Compare Linder, *Jews in Roman Imperial Legislation,* 289–91.

24. Jeremy Cohen suggested many years ago, in anti-lachrymose, revisionist fashion, that the restrictive legislation itself was not an innovation of Christian-Roman law, but was almost wholly derived from Roman precedents. See his "Roman Imperial Policy toward the Jews from Constantine until the End of the Palestinian Patriarchate (ca. 429)," *Byzantine Studies* 3 (1976), 1–29. But see Simonsohn, *Apostolic See and the Jews: History,* 6 and n. 19.

25. CTh 16.8.14, *Theodosian Code,* 468.

26. CTh 16.8.22, *Theodosian Code,* 470; Linder, *Jews in Roman Imperial Legislation,* 269, renders *in solitudine* as "in deserted places," which differs from Pharr's less precise "in desert places."

27. CTh 16.8.25, *Theodosian Code,* 470. Compare Linder, *Jews in Roman Imperial Legislation,* 267–70.

28. Novella of Theodosius 3.1.3, *Theodosian Code,* 489 (emphasis added).

29. Linder, *Jews in Roman Imperial Legislation,* 55ff.

30. CTh 9.7.5 and 3.7.2, *Theodosian Code,* 232, 70. Adultery was punishable by death perhaps as early as pre-Christian Roman law. Compare Linder, *Jews in Roman Imperial Legislation,* 181, n. 4.

31. CTh 16.8.16, 24, *Theodosian Code,* 469, 470.

32. CTh 16.8.24, *Theodosian Code,* 470.

33. Theodosius gave as justification the fear that the Jews might gain power over Christians: "For we consider it impious, that the enemies of the Supreme Majesty and of the Roman laws shall be considered as avengers of our laws by seizing stolen jurisdiction, and armed with the authority of an ill-gotten dignity shall have the power to judge and pronounce sentence against Christians, very often even against priests of the sacred religion, to the insult of our faith." NTh 3.2, in Linder, *Jews in Roman Imperial Legislation,* 328.

34. Ben Zion Wacholder, "The Halakah and the Proselyting of Slaves during the Gaonic Era," *Historia Judaica* 18 (1956), 90.

35. Linder, *Jews in Roman Imperial Legislation,* 99–102, 117–20.

36. CTh 16.9.1, *Theodosian Code,* 471.

37. CTh 16.9.4., *Theodosian Code,* 472.

38. Walter Pakter, *Medieval Canon Law and the Jews* (Ebelsbach, 1988), 84ff., "The Jew and His Servants," discusses the subject in detail.

39. Linder, *Jews in Roman Imperial Legislation,* 48.

40. Ibid., 381–87.

41. There is still uncertainty about the meaning of *deuterosis.* Linder (see ref. in next note) takes it to mean Mishnah. Other suggestions include midrashic homilies or Targum, the Aramaic translation of the Hebrew Bible.

42. Linder, *Jews in Roman Imperial Legislation,* 402–11.

43. Article, "Corpus Iuris Civilis," *DMA* (*Dictionary of the Middle Ages*) 3:609 (Kenneth Pennington); Linder, *Jews in Roman Imperial Legislation,* 46–50.

44. Linder, *Jews in Roman Imperial Legislation,* 33.

45. Ibid.

46. Under the canons, there was to be no intermarriage between Christians and Jews (Elvira, ca. 300, often repeated in Spain and elsewhere); Christians might not share feasts with Jews (Laodicea, 360); Jews were not to work on Sunday (Narbonne, 589); Christian slaves must not be sold to Jews (Toledo, 656, often reiterated in Spain and other countries); Jews might not serve as judges or tax collectors (Macon, 581); Jews "dare [not] . . . ask the Prince for any authority over Christians or to exercise it" (Paris, 614; quoted in J. N. Hillgarth, ed., *Christianity and Paganism, 350–750: The Conversion of Western Europe* [Philadelphia, 1986], 115); Christians might not eat unleavened bread of Jews, nor employ Jews as physicians or bathe with them (Constantinople [Quini-Sext, or Trullan Council], 692). A law prohibiting compulsory baptism of Jews (Toledo, 633) consistent with the Catholic church's conviction that an insincere conversion is worse than none at all, soon lost is force in Spain during the latter part of the seventh century as the intolerance of the Visigothic rules reached fever pitch. Bernard Bachrach, "A Reassessment of Visigothic Jewish Policy, 589–711," *American Historical Review* 78 (1973), 11–34, and *Early Medieval Jewish Policy in Western Europe* (Minneapolis, 1977), 3–26, while providing food for thought about the "lachrymose conception of Jewish history," goes too far in reinterpreting the evidence (or lack thereof) to document Jewish power and well-being in Visigothic Spain. See the rebuttal of Bat-Sheva Albert, "Un nouvel examen de la politique anti-juive wisigothique: A propos d'un article récent," *Révue des études juives* 135 (1976), 3–29.

The "Jewish" canons of church councils from 300 to 800 are conveniently listed and briefly described by James Parkes, *Conflict of the Church and the Synagogue,* app. 1. The texts and discussions of the councils can be found in English translation or paraphrase (sometimes accompanied by the original Greek or Latin) in Charles J. Hefele, *A History of the Councils of the Church,* trans. from the German by William R. Clark, 5 vols. (1883–96; repr., New York, 1972). See also, Solomon Grayzel, "Jews and the Ecumenical Councils," in *The Seventy-fifth Anniversary Volume of the* Jewish Quarterly Review, ed. A. A. Neuman and S. Zeitlin (Philadelphia, 1967), 287–91.

47. Solomon Katz, "Pope Gregory the Great and the Jews," *Jewish Quarterly Review,* n.s., 24 (1933–34), 113–36; Simonsohn, *Apostolic See and the Jews: History,* 40. The Latin texts are consolidated in Simonsohn, *Apostolic See and the Jews, Documents: 492–1404* (Toronto, 1988), 3–24 (nos. 3–28).

48. Cited in English translation in Solomon Grayzel, *The Church and the Jews in the XIIIth Century,* rev. ed. (New York, 1966), 9. Latin text in Simonsohn, *Apostolic See and the Jews, Documents: 492–1404,* 15 (no. 19, June 598, addressed to Victor, bishop of Palermo): "Sicut Iudaeis non debet esse licentia quicquam in synagogis suis ultra quam permissum est lege praesumere, ita in his quae eis concessa sunt nullum debent praeiudicium sustinere"; repeated in no. 20, 16–17 (October 598, in a follow-up letter to Palermo), with somewhat different wording, but referencing the earlier formulation in the phrase "ut et ipsi prius scripsimus" ("and, as we have written earlier"). The second letter to Palermo has been translated in Bernard S. Bachrach, *Jews in Barbarian Europe* (Lawrence, Kans., 1977), 55 (no. 7).

49. Textual connection between Gregory the Great's formulation and Theodo-

sian Code 16.8.18 and 20 (or 22) has been suggested by Kenneth R. Stow, *Catholic Thought and Papal Jewry Policy, 1555–93* (New York, 1977), xix; idem, "The Approach of the Jews to the Papacy and the Papal Doctrine of Protection of the Jews, 1063–1147" (Hebrew), in *Studies in the History of the Jewish People and the Land of Israel* 5 (1980), 187; idem, *The "1007 Anonymous" and Papal Sovereignty: Jewish Perceptions of the Papacy and Papal Policy in the High Middle Ages* (Cincinnati, 1984), 13; and most recently in Stow's *Alienated Minority,* 267. The law in CTh 16.8.21, guaranteeing protection for the Jews' persons and synagogues, seems an even closer parallel: "But just as it is Our will that the foregoing provision shall be made for the persons of the Jews, so we decree that the Jews also shall be admonished that they perchance shall not become insolent and, elated by their own security, commit any rash act in disrespect of the Christian religion ("Sed ut hoc Iudaeorum personis volumus esse provisum, ita illud quoque monendum esse censemus ne Iudaei forsitan insolescant elatique sui securitae quicquam praeceps in Christianae reveraentiam cultionis admittant"); *Theodosian Code,* 470; Linder, *Jews in Roman Imperial Legislation,* 284. On the possible connection between Claudius's letter to the Alexandrians and the *Sicut* formula, see note 22 in this chapter.

50. Solomon Grayzel, "The Papal Bull *Sicut Judeis,*" in *Studies and Essays in Honor of Abraham A. Neuman,* ed. Meir Ben-Horin et al. (Leiden, 1962), 243–80. See also, Simonsohn, *Apostolic See and the Jews: History,* 42–45; the notes cross-reference the Latin texts in *Apostolic See and the Jews, Documents: 492–1404.*

51. See Robert Chazan, ed., *Church, State, and Jew in the Middle Ages* (New York, 1980), 31–32.

52. Grayzel, *Church and the Jews,* 274 (no. 118). Compare 261–62 (no. 111). See also, Simonsohn, *Apostolic See and the Jews: History,* 52–54, and doc. no. 183 in *Apostolic See and the Jews, Documents: 492–1404,* 192–93.

53. Grayzel, *Church and the Jews,* 93, 95; Simonsohn, *Apostolic See and the Jews, Documents: 492–1404,* 74–75 (no. 71).

54. Grayzel, *Church and the Jews,* 311.

55. Simonsohn, *Apostolic See and the Jews: History,* 147–54; Pakter, *Medieval Canon Law and the Jews,* 221ff.

56. Grayzel, *Church and the Jews,* 309; Guido Kisch, "The Yellow Badge in History," in Kisch, *Forschungen zur Rechts-, Wirtschafts- und Sozialgeschichte der Juden* (Sigmaringen, 1979), 2:115–64.

57. Grayzel, *Church and the Jews,* 140–41; Simonsohn, *Apostolic See and the Jews, Documents: 492–1404,* 99 (no. 94).

58. Grayzel, *Church and the Jews,* 311.

59. Ibid., 307.

60. Chazan, *Church, State, and Jew,* 34–35, 30.

61. This is the major theme of the posthumously published second volume of Grayzel's *The Church and the Jews in the XIIIth Century, Vol. 2: 1254–1314,* ed. Kenneth R. Stow (New York, 1989), which reprints as its introduction Grayzel's article, "Popes, Jews, and Inquisition: From 'Sicut' to 'Turbato'" (originally published in *Essays on the Occasion of the Seventieth Anniversary of Dropsie University,* ed. Abraham I. Katsh and Leon Nemoy [Philadelphia, 1979], 151–88).

62. Jordan, *French Monarchy and the Jews,* 137–40.

63. Grayzel, *Church and the Jews,* 240–41; Simonsohn, *Apostolic See and the Jews Documents: 492–1404,* 172–73 (no. 163).

64. Benjamin Z. Kedar, "Canon Law and the Burning of the Talmud," *Bulletin of Medieval Canon Law* 9 (1979), 79–82; James Muldoon, *Popes, Lawyers, and Infidels: The Church and the Non-Christian World, 1250–1550* (Philadelphia, 1979), 10–11, 30–31; Pakter, *Medieval Canon Law and the Jews,* 73–76.

65. Grayzel, "Popes, Jews, and Inquisition: From 'Sicut' to 'Turbato.'"

66. Edward Synan, *The Popes and the Jews in the Middle Ages* (New York, 1965).

67. Allan Harris Cutler and Helen Elmquist Cutler, *The Jew as Ally of the Muslim: Medieval Roots of Anti-Semitism* (Notre Dame, Ind., 1986); see the review by G. Dahan, in the *Jewish Quarterly Review,* n.s., 79 (1989), 370–77.

68. Kenneth R. Stow, "Hatred of the Jews or Love of the Church: Papal Policy toward the Jews in the Middle Ages," in *Antisemitism through the Ages,* 71–89.

69. Kenneth R. Stow, "Papal and Royal Attitudes toward Jewish Lending in the Thirteenth Century," *AJS Review* 6 (1981), 161–84; *The "1007 Anonymous" and Papal Sovereignty,* 273–80.

70. Simonsohn, *Apostolic See and the Jews: History,* 39–93.

71. John Gilchrist, "The Perception of Jews in the Canon Law in the Period of the First Two Crusades," *Jewish History* 3, no. 1 (Spring 1988), 9–24.

72. Ibid.

73. Pakter, *Medieval Canon Law and the Jews.*

74. Ibid., chap. 5: "Family Law."

75. Ibid., 321–30.

76. Ibid., chap. 4: "Jews in Public Office."

77. Ibid., 82–83.

78. Ibid., 40–83, charts the development of canonical jurisdiction over the Jews. Compare also, Simonsohn, *Apostolic See and the Jews: History,* 110.

79. Kisch, *Jews in Medieval Germany,* 353.

80. Kisch, "Yellow Badge," 147–48. "Tables" means the tablets of the Law.

81. Salo W. Baron, *A Social and Religious History of the Jews,* 2d ed., 18 vols. (New York and Philadelphia, 1952–83), 11:96ff.

82. Jeremy Cohen, *The Friars and the Jews: The Evolution of Medieval Anti-Judaism* (Ithaca, N.Y., 1982).

83. Robert J. Burns, "Anti-Semitism and Anti-Judaism in Christian History: A Revisionist Thesis" (review article), *Catholic Historical Review* 70 (1984), 90–93. Cohen's thesis is disputed by Robert Chazan, *Daggers of Faith: Thirteenth-Century Christian Missionizing and the Jewish Response* (Berkeley and Los Angeles, 1989), esp. 170ff. Chazan sees an intensification of prior trends, rather than a fundamental reversal of doctrine.

84. Simonsohn, *Apostolic See and the Jews: History,* 34, 38, 39; and on Cohen, specifically, 26, n. 92.

85. For example, James Parkes, *The Jew in the Medieval Community,* 2d ed. (New York, 1976), 101ff.

86. Alfredo M. Rabello, *He-yehudim bi-sefarad lifnei ha-kibbush ha-ʿaravi bi-re'i ha-ḥaqiqa* [The Jews in Visigothic Spain in the Light of the Legislation] (Jerusalem, 1983), 26, 95–106.

87. Rabello, *Jews in Visigothic Spain,* 33; Linder, *Jews in Roman Imperial Legislation,* 44–46, noting that the relatively scant selectivity of the Breviary of Alaric concerning Jewry law should probably be attributed to a reaction of the Arian editors against the religious nature of the Theodosian Code, especially in Book 16.

Sectarian Arianism is somewhat simplistically thought to be more warmly disposed toward the Jews than Roman Catholicism because it is more "monotheistic" (rejecting the divinity of Jesus). For a more nuanced explanation of the sympathetic attitude of Germanic Christianity, in general, and of the Visigothic case, in particular, where conversion from Arianism to Nicaean Catholicism more or less coincided with the onset of a harsher policy toward the Jews, see Gavin I. Langmuir, *Toward a Definition of Antisemitism* (Berkeley and Los Angeles, 1990), 75–83. For an excellent survey of the legal situation of the Jews under the Visigoths, see Jean Juster, *The Legal Condition of the Jews under the Visigothic Kings, Brought up to Date by A. M. Rabello* (Jerusalem, 1976; orig. published as a series of three articles in *Israel Law Review* 11 [1976]).

88. Rabello, *Jews in Visigothic Spain,* 64–67.

89. *The Visigothic Code (Forum Judicum),* trans. and ed. S. P. Scott (Boston, 1910), Book 12, titles 2 and 3, 362–409 (including the prohibition of observance of circumcision, Passover, the dietary regulations, and the Sabbath and other festivals: 12.2.7; 12.2.8; 12.3.4; 12.3.5; 12.3.7).

90. For general background on law in the lands conquered by Germanic tribes, here and below, I have relied in part on the succinct summary in *DMA,* s.v. "Law, German, Early Germanic Codes" 7:468b–477a (Theodore John Rivers).

91. Margaret Deansley, *A History of Early Medieval Europe: From 476 to 911,* 2d ed. (London, 1960), 62–63.

92. Compare Jacques Le Goff: "In a barbarian kingdom it was not the case that every man was subject to a single law valid for all the inhabitants of a territory: he was judged according to the judicial custom of the ethnic group to which he belonged. . . ." *Medieval Civilization 400–1500,* trans. Julia Barrow (Oxford, 1988), 30. Also compare Bernhard Blumenkranz, *Juifs et chrétiens dans le monde occidental 430–1096* (Paris, 1960), 375; and Bachrach, *Early Medieval Jewish Policy in Western Europe,* 66, 137.

93. Hillgarth, *Christianity and Paganism,* 113.

94. These Latin charters, three of which are actually sample texts in a medieval collection of formularies (published in *Monumenta Germaniae Historica: Formulae Merowingici et Karolini Aevi,* ed. Karolus [Karl] Zeumer [Hanover, 1886], 309–11, 325) are discussed in virtually every work dealing with the status of the Jews in the early Middle Ages. They are available in English translation in Bachrach, *Jews in Barbarian Europe,* 68–91, along with the fourth charter, ibid., 73 (Latin text: M. Bouquet, ed., *Recueil des historiens des Gaules et de la France,* rev. ed. [Paris, 1870], vol. 6, no. 232). Bachrach's discussion of the charters is useful; see his *Early Medieval Jewish Policy in Western Europe,* 90–94.

95. The Latin texts of the Speyer and Worms charters are printed in full and synoptically in R. Hoeniger, "Zur Geschichte der Juden Deutschlands im Mittlelater," *Zeitschrift für die Geschichte der Juden in Deutschland* 1 (1887), 137ff. They can be found in English translation, one after the other, in Chazan, *Church, State, and Jew,* 60–66.

96. Chazan, *Church, State, and Jew,* 63–66.

97. Julius Aronius, *Regesten zur Geschichte der Juden im fränkischen und deutschen Reiche bis zum Jahre 1273* (repr., New York, 1970), 74–77 (no. 171); Kisch, *Jews in Medieval Germany,* 138; and J. A. Watt seem to take for granted that the clause *ad*

cameram nostram attineant was already present in the earlier Worms charter. But Stow, *Alienated Minority,* 275–76, makes a strong case that is consistent with the view presented here. For Watt's article, see below, note 110.

98. Where, rather, it is the Jews named in the charter who petition Henry "that we take and hold them under our protection" (*sub tuicionem nostram*).

99. Parkes, *Jew in the Medieval Community,* 101–54.

100. See Marc Bloch, *Feudal Society,* trans. L. A. Manyon (Chicago, 1961) 1:256; Le Goff, *Medieval Civilization 400–1500,* 288–89.

101. I use the term *feudal* in awareness of the fact that some medievalists dealing with England prefer the more specific word *manorial,* relating to estates and fiefs.

102. Baron, *Social and Religious History,* 11:4–13, 18–22; and his "Medieval Nationalism and Jewish Serfdom," in *Studies and Essays in Honor of Abraham A. Neuman,* ed. Meir Ben-Horin et al. (Leiden, 1962), esp. 42–48.

103. Cecil Roth, *A History of the Jews in England,* 3d ed. (Oxford, 1964), 96–104.

104. William C. Jordan, *From Servitude to Freedom: Manumission in the Sénonais in the Thirteenth Century* (Philadelphia, 1986), 99; his critical appraisal of the revisionist "Toronto School" appears on 9–10.

105. Southern, *Making of the Middle Ages,* 106–7.

106. Ibid., 108.

107. Kisch, *Jews in Medieval Germany,* 129–53.

108. Compare also, Simonsohn, *Apostolic See and the Jews: History,* 94–102, esp. 99, on the theological doctrine of servitude which reinforced the "special 'Jewish status' . . . a mixture of protection and dependency, of discrimination in favour of and against the Jews . . . that paved the way for the almost total elimination of the Jews from Christian society."

109. Lotter, "The Scope and Effectiveness of Imperial Jewry Law in the High Middle Ages," *Jewish History* 4, no. 1 (Spring 1989), 31–58. The Salians were the Frankish dynasty that ruled Germany from 1024 to 1138.

110. This formulation needs to be modified in light of J. A. Watt, "The Jews, the Law, and the Church: The Concept of Jewish Serfdom in Thirteenth-Century England," in *The Church and Sovereignty c. 590–1918: Essays in Honour of Michael Wilks,* ed. Diana Wood (Oxford, 1991), 153–72, who shows that the "Statute for Jewry" passed by Parliament in 1275, outlawing Jewish usury and demanding that Jews switch to more productive occupations, refers (in French) to the Jews as the king's "serfs" three times.

111. Gavin I. Langmuir, "*Tanquam servi:* The Change in Jewish Status in French Law about 1200," in *Les juifs dans l'histoire de France, première Colloque international de Haïfa,* ed. Myriam Yardeni (Leiden, 1980), 24–54; and his earlier article, "'Judei nostri' and the Beginning of Capetian Legislation," *Traditio* 16 (1960), 203–9 (both essays are printed in his *Toward a Definition of Antisemitism*). See also, Jordan, *French Monarchy and the Jews,* 131–33. An English translation of the French ordinance is found in Chazan, *Church, State, and Jew,* 213–14. See also, Gilbert Dahan's summary in *Les intellectuels chrétiens,* 66–68.

112. On the king's "takings" from Jews in royal France, see Jordan, *French Monarchy and the Jews,* index, s.v. *captiones.* For the regime of taxation of the Jews in the feudal domain of Champagne (not absorbed into royal France until the end of the thirteenth century), see Emily Taitz, "The Jews of Champagne from the First

Settlement until the Expulsion of 1306" (Ph.D. diss., Jewish Theologial Seminary of America, 1992), 149, 201–10, 227.

113. Langmuir, *History, Religion, and Antisemitism* (Berkeley and Los Angeles, 1990), 295.

114. On "arbitrariness" of monarchs as a principal reason for Jewish insecurity (as opposed to the supposedly consistent lawfulness of the popes), see Kenneth Stow, "The Church and Neutral Historiography" (Hebrew), in *'Iyyunim be-historiografiya* (Jerusalem, 1988), 110.

115. Kisch, *Jews in Medieval Germany,* 235, 343–44.

116. Ibid., 191–97.

117. Parkes, *Jew in the Medieval Community,* 199–204.

118. Susan Reynolds, *Kingdoms and Communities in Western Europe, 900–1300* (Oxford, 1984), 184.

119. Kisch, *Jews in Medieval Germany,* 344–46.

120. Baron, *Social and Religious History of the Jews,* 11:15.

121. Jordan, *French Monarchy and the Jews,* 153.

Chapter Four
The Legal Position of Jews in Islam

1. Jurists sum this up in the phrase *iltizām ḥukm* (or *aḥkām*) *al-islām* (subjection to Islamic jurisdiction or authority). The most important secondary work on the legal position of the Christians and Jews of Islam is *Le statut légal des non-Musulmans en pays d'Islam,* by the Christian-Arab jurist Antoine Fattal (Beirut, 1958). Fattal is not superseded by the recent book by Ḥassān al-Zayn, *Al-awḍāʿ al-qānūniyya li'l-naṣārā wa'l-yahūd fi'l-diyār al-islāmiyya ḥattā al-fatḥ al-ʿuthmānī* [The Legal Condition of the Christians and Jews in Islamic Lands up to the Ottoman Conquest] (Beirut, 1988), which is rather apologetic in its excessive emphasis on the toleration and freedom granted to non-Muslims.

2. The *dhimmīs* were also known as *ahl al-dhimma,* or "protected people."

3. For the example of Hinduism, see Yohanan Friedmann, "The Temple of Multān: A Note on Early Muslim Attitudes to Idolatry," *Israel Oriental Studies* 2 (1972), 176–82; idem, "Medieval Muslim Views of Indian Religions," *Journal of the American Oriental Society* 95 (1975), 214–21.

4. This provision is taken from the Visigothic Council of Agde (506).

5. *Patrologia Latina,* ed. J.-P. Migne (Paris, 1880), 140:col. 742: "De judaeis, quomodo ante baptismum examinari debeant. Judaei quorum perfidia frequenter ad fomitem redit, si ad legem catholicam venire voluerint. . . ." For the original canon, see Parkes, *Conflict of the Church and the Synagogue,* 319–20.

6. Bernard Blumenkranz, "The Roman Church and the Jews," in *The World History of the Jewish People: The Dark Ages, Jews in Christian Europe, 711–1096,* ed. Cecil Roth (Ramat Gan, 1966), 79; idem, *Juifs et chrétiens,* 304–6. Book 13 contains laws about theft, usury, greed, drunkenness, and other sins.

7. Sometimes broadened as "Concerning the Jews, Saracens, and Their Servants" (in Christian Spain, of course, the issue was a combined "Jewish-Muslim question"). See also, Pakter, *Medieval Canon Law and the Jews,* 34–35; Muldoon, *Popes, Lawyers, and Infidels,* 4.

8. So claims the modern editor of this collection. Ibn al-Qayyim, *Aḥkām ahl al-dhimma,* part 1, intro., 6. Discussion of some of the laws of the *dhimma* can be found in the administrative treatise, *Sirāj al-mulūk,* by al-Ṭurṭūshī (d. 1126), in the chapter that begins with the Pact of ʿUmar (see below, note 16). The Shafiʿite jurist and *qāḍī,* Badr al-Dīn ibn Jamāʿa (1241–1333), included a broader summary of the rights and obligations of the *dhimmīs* (including a version of the Pact of ʿUmar as the final chapter of his administrative treatise, *Taḥrīr al-aḥkām fī tadbīr ahl al-islām,* ed. and trans. into German by Hans Kofler, "Handbuch des islamischen Staats- und Verwaltungsrechtes von Badr-ad-Dīn Ibn Ǧamā ʿah," *Islamica* 7 (1935), 27–34; the translation of the chapter appears in the next, and final, issue of *Islamica,* which was published in *Abhandlungen für die Kunde des Morgenlandes,* 23, no. 6 (1938), 118–28.

9. Ibn Abī Shayba, *Muṣannaf fī'l-aḥādīth wa'l-āthār,* ed. Saʿīd al-Laḥḥām (Beirut, 1989).

10. One of the four equally orthodox canonical Islamic law schools, or *madhhabs.*

11. *Bāb nikāḥ ahl al-dhimma,* chap. on *Dhimmī* Marriage. Sarakhsī, *Al-mabsūṭ* ([Cairo], 1906–13), 5:38–48.

12. Sarakhsī, *Al-mabsūṭ,* 13:130–39.

13. Ibid., 9:195.

14. F. E. Peters, *Children of Abraham: Judaism, Christianity, Islam* (Princeton, N.J., 1982), 62.

15. Kenneth Stow ("Hatred of the Jews or Love of the Church: Papal Policy toward the Jews in the Middle Ages," 80–81) suggests that the papacy had a similar, bilateral contact with the Jews especially dating from the Bull *Sicut Judeis* issued by Innocent III in 1199, appending a clause, Stow claims, borrowed "almost verbatim" from the Pact of ʿUmar. This hypothesis—especially the part about textual borrowing from Arabic into Latin—is, to my mind, doubtful.

16. The most characteristic version of the document is found in a "Mirror for Kings" treatise by the twelfth-century writer, al-Ṭurṭūshī, *Sirāj al-mulūk* (Cairo, 1872), 229–30, (Cairo, 1935), 252–53; English trans. in Bernard Lewis, *Islam: From the Prophet Muhammed to the Capture of Constantinople* (New York, 1974), 2:217–19; and Stillman, *Jews of Arab Lands,* 157–58.

17. Antoine Fattal draws attention to parallels between Islamic and Christian law throughout *Le statut légal des non-Musulmans en pays d'Islam,* often in order to show that Christianity was also discriminatory toward *its* infidels.

18. Sura 2:256.

19. Rudi Paret, "Sura 2, 256: lā ikrāha fī d-dīni. Toleranz oder Resignation?" *Der Islam* 45 (1969), 299–300. Compare Lewis, *Jews of Islam,* 13.

20. See Chap. 2.

21. An excellent summary of the encounter between Muhammad and the Jews is found in Stillman, *Jews of Arab Lands,* 3–21.

22. Bukhārī, *Ṣaḥīḥ,* Kitāb al-Jihād, Arabic text with English translation (partly revised here), in Muḥammad Muḥsin Khān, *The Translation of the Meanings of Ṣaḥīḥ al-Bukhārī,* 6th rev. ed. (Lahore, 1983), 4:182. The chapter title preceding this statement—"One Should Fight on Behalf of the Protected People and They Should Not Be Enslaved"—well expresses the position of early Islam on Jews and Christians.

23. CJ 1.9.14 (= CTh 16.8.21), Linder, *Jews in Roman Imperial Legislation,* no. 46; CJ 1.11.6 (= CTh 16.8.27; 16.10.24), Linder, *Jews in Roman Imperial Legislation,* no. 49.

24. The verse in full reads: "Fight against those who have been given the Scripture as believe not in Allah nor the Last Day, and forbid not that which Allah hath forbidden by his Messenger, and follow not the religion of truth, until they pay the *jizya ʿan yadin wa-hum ṣāghirūn*" (roughly and uncertainly rendered: "Pay the *jizya* out of hand while being in a lowly state").

25. ʿAbd al-Razzāq al-Ṣanʿānī, *Al-muṣannaf,* ed. Ḥabīburraḥmān al-Aʿẓamī (Beirut, 1972), 6:89–90.

26. Most modern scholars understand the linguistically problematic Qur'anic prescription to lack the element of ceremonial humiliation altogether, preferring medieval explanations that follow that more benign line of thinking. (1) One view holds that the verse simply prescribes that the *dhimmī* acknowledge his inferiority and submission. (2) Another scholar translates the four last words of the verse in accord with the medieval interpretation of *ʿan yadin,* as "out of ability and sufficient means, they (nevertheless) being inferior." (3) The explanation of a third Orientalist leads him to translate the entire expression—in keeping with pre-Islamic Arab legal conceptions and parallel linguistic usage: "reward (*jizya*) due for a benefaction (*ʿan yadin*) (namely, the sparing of the life of the defeated non-Muslim in battle), while they (the defeated non-Muslims) are ignominious (*wa-hum ṣāghirūn*) (for not having fought unto death)." The fascinating debate over the original meaning of the phrase appeared in a series of exchanges in the journal *Arabica* between 1962 and 1967. To the Arabic linguistic evidence summoned by Meir M. Bravmann (*Arabica* 10 [1963], 94–95; 13 [1966], 307–14; 14 [1967], 90–91, 326–27) in favor of the third interpretation and in opposition to the views of Claude Cahen (*Arabica* 9 [1962], 76–79; 10 [1963], 95); and M. J. Kister (*Arabica* 11 [1964], 272–78), the proponents of the first and second, respectively, we may add that, in the Hebrew Bible, *yad* appears in a similar sense of benefaction, for instance, in 1 Kings 10:13, ". . . in addition to what King Solomon gave [to the Queen of Sheba] *out of his royal bounty* [*ke-yad ha-melekh*]," and in Nehemiah 2:8, ". . . thanks to my God's *benevolent care* [*ke-yad elohay ha-tova*] for me," and elsewhere (the new JPS translation, which I have quoted here, captures the meaning that the Arabic parallel reciprocally confirms).

27. Some sort of poll tax was in effect in most of the territories annexed by Islam, where it had been collected from the populace in general, although the privileged classes were often exempted. See Daniel C. Dennett, *Conversion and the Poll Tax in Early Islam* (Cambridge, Mass., 1950), 5, 28, 32–33, 54, 68; and David Goodblatt, "The Poll Tax in Sassanian Babylonia: The Talmudic Evidence," *Journal of the Economic and Social History of the Orient* 22 (1979), 233–95.

28. Fattal, *Le statut,* 18–60. A sampling of conquest treaties in English translation can be conveniently found in Lewis, *Islam,* 1:228–41.

29. The document is discussed at length in two standard works: A. S. Tritton, *The Caliphs and Their Non-Muslim Subjects: A Critical Study of the Covenant of ʿUmar* (1930; repr., London, 1970); and Fattal, *Le statut.*

30. *Amān,* here with the meaning, "safe conduct."

31. "It is not usual for a conquered people to decide the terms on which they

shall be admitted to alliance with the victors." Tritton, *Caliphs and Their Non-Muslim Subjects,* 8.

32. Tritton found no real resemblance between the Pact of ʿUmar and the many considerably shorter and less complex conquest treaties recorded in Arabic chronicles.

33. Noth, "Abgrenzungsprobleme zwischen Muslimen und Nicht-Muslimen: Die 'Bedingungen ʿUmars (*aš-šurūṭ al-ʿumariyya*') unter einem anderen Aspekt gelesen," *Jerusalem Studies in Arabic and Islam* 9 (1987), 290–315.

34. The most important research on the petition and the decree forms in Islam are the studies of S. M. Stern, "Three Petitions of the Fatimid Period," *Oriens* 15 (1962), 172–209; "Petitions from the Ayyubid Period," *Bulletin of the School of Oriental and African Studies* 27 (1964), 1–32; "Petitions from the Mamluk Period (Notes on the Mamluk Documents from Sinai)," ibid., 29 (1966), 233–76; and *Fatimid Decrees* (London, 1964).

35. Stern speculates that the petitions of the early Islamic centuries were "simply in the form of letters." Stern, "Three Petitions of the Fatimid Period," 189. Geoffrey Khan notes that "the earliest surviving Arabic document . . . that can be identified as a petition"—from Sogdiana at the beginning of the eighth century—has a structure that corresponds closely to the usual form of Umayyad letters written in Egypt and preserved in Arabic papyrus collections." See his "Historical Development of the Structure of Medieval Arabic Petitions," *Bulletin of the School of Oriental and African Studies* 53 (1990), 8. The argument compressed into this paragraph will be detailed in a paper I am preparing on the Pact of ʿUmar.

36. Specifically, "Christians" may not build "monasteries, churches, convents, [or] monks' cells." See Fattal, *Le statut,* 174ff.

37. Fattal, *Le statut,* 180ff.

38. Ibid., 185ff.

39. Ibn Qayyim al-Jawziyya devotes a long chapter to the subject in his extensive analytical commentary on the text of the Pact of ʿUmar. See his *Aḥkām ahl al-dhimma,* part 2, 665–713.

40. Seth Ward, "Construction and Repair of Churches and Synagogues in Islamic Law: A Treatise by Taqī al-Dīn ʿAlī b. ʿAbd al-Kāfī al-Subkī" (Ph.D. diss., Yale University, 1984); idem, "Taqī al-Dīn al-Subkī on Construction, Continuance and Repair of Churches and Synagogues in Islamic Law," in *Studies in Islamic and Judaic Traditions II,* ed. William S. Brinner and Steven Ricks (Atlanta, Ga., 1989), 169–88.

41. Moshe Perlmann, ed. and trans., *Shaykh Damanhūrī on the Churches of Cairo (1739)* (Berkeley and Los Angeles, 1975), 18–23.

42. Perlmann, *Shaykh Damanhūrī,* 25–26.

43. Cairo was founded in 969.

44. Ward, "Construction and Repair of Churches and Synagogues."

45. Richard Gottheil, "An Eleventh-Century Document Concerning a Cairo Synagogue," *Jewish Quarterly Review,* o.s., 19 (1906–7), 467–539. The document is also translated in Stillman, *Jews of Arab Lands,* 189–91.

46. Two died from their wounds, and one, or, possibly, two others converted to Islam.

47. Mark R. Cohen, "Jews in the Mamlūk Environment: The Crisis of 1442 (A

Geniza Study)," *Bulletin of the School of Oriental and African Studies* 47 (1984), 425–48.

48. "Display of the cross is like displaying idols. . . . Therefore it is not permitted to them to put crosses on the doors of their churches outside of their walls, but they should not be interfered with when they sculpt them indoors." Ibn al-Qayyim, *Aḥkām ahl al-dhimma,* part 2, 719.

49. Fattal, *Le statut,* 205–11.

50. Goitein, *A Mediterranean Society,* 2:285. See also, Chap. 10 in this book.

51. CTh 16.8.18, *Theodosian Code,* 469. Haman is the antisemitic villain of the Book of Esther whose plan to kill all the Jews of Persia backfired, resulting in his death and that of his ten sons on the gallows. Christians mistook the gallows and the effigy at Purim time for "setting fire to and burning a simulated appearance of the holy cross, in contempt of the Christian faith and with sacrilegious mind." Hence the Theodosian Code barred alleged anti-Christian abuses in the ritual.

52. Simonsohn, *Apostolic See and the Jews: History,* 467.

53. See Chap. 6.

54. CTh 16.8.5, *Theodosian Code,* 467.

55. Riding a horse was considered a sign of honor.

56. Canon 68.

57. In the following discussion, I have condensed the contents of a paper I have written on the distinctive dress of non-Muslims, which will be published in *The Byzantine and Early Islamic Near East II* (Studies in Late Antiquity and Early Islam II), ed. Lawrence I. Conrad. Previous literature on the dress regulations in Islam includes Ilse Lichtenstadter, "The Distinctive Dress of Non-Muslims in Islamic Countries," *Historia Judaica* 5 (1943), 35–52; Tritton, *Caliphs and Their Non-Muslim Subjects,* chap. 8; Fattal, *Le statut,* 96–112; and the overlooked, but important, article by Habib Zayat, "The Distinctive Signs of the Christians and Jews in Islam" (Arabic), *Al-Machriq* 43:2 (1949), 161–252. I am grateful to my student, Hassan Khalilieh, for bringing this article to my attention. Fattal does not seem to have referred to it.

The idea of differentiating privileged from unprivileged classes via dress already existed in ancient Rome. Augustus imposed distinctive dress on noncitizens and assigned them separate places at public spectacles, in order to distinguish them from citizens. Citizens wore a white toga (the *plebs togata;* also mentioned is a piece of headgear, the *plebs pileata*). Noncitizens wore colored garments and were referred to as *pullati* ("those wearing black"). Augustus also decreed a penalty for citizens who did not appear in public in their togas, whereas the wearing of the toga was forbidden to those who did not have citizenship or who had lost it through some punishment. This ordinance was reissued until the late empire. See Denis Van Berchem, *Les distributions de blé et d'argent a la plèbe romaine sous l'empire* (Geneva, 1939), 61.

58. Tritton, *Caliphs and Their Non-Muslim Subjects,* 115.

59. Lichtenstadter's claim that the "main reason for which ʿUmar allegedly introduced the dress regulations was to render non-Muslims easily distinguishable from Muslims in order to prevent inter-marriage and free intercourse [sexual?] between Muhammedans and Unbelievers" (Lichtenstadter, "Distinctive Dress," 43) has no basis in Muslim sources. The author seems to have been influenced by the rationale of the Fourth Lateran Council.

60. Tritton, *Caliphs and Their Non-Muslim Subjects,* 116; also, Fattal, *Le statut,* 97–98.

61. G. Liddell and R. Scott, *A Greek-English Lexicon,* rev. and augmented by H. J. Jones (Oxford, 1968), 759. *Zōnarion* is a diminutive of the classical Greek word *zōnē;* it came into Latin as *zona* and is synonymous with the Latin *cingulum.*

62. Noth, "Abgrenzungsprobleme," 304–5. To "turn Muslim," a modern historian of Nestorian Christianity explains, is often expressed in medieval sources by the expression "to remove the *zunnār*"; J. M. Fiey, *Chrétiens syriaques sous les abbasides: surtout à Bagdad (749–1258)* (Louvain, 1980), 88, n. 24.

63. In *Caliphs and Their Non-Muslim Subjects,* 117; and in *Encyclopaedia of Islam,* 1st ed., s.v. "*Zunnār.*" Noth does not mention the Syriac connection.

64. *Chronique de Seért (Histoire Nestorienne),* in *Patriologia Orientalis* (Paris, 1919), 13:630: *wa-kāna awwal man amara al-iskalānīyyin bi-shadd al-zanānīr fī awsāṭihim li-yatamayyazū bi-dhalika min ghairihim* (the accompanying French translation glosses the last words, "from others," "des autres jeunes gens"). According to the footnote, one source places Mar Emmeh's consecration as Catholicos in the first year of ʿUthmān's caliphate. Passage also cited in Zayat, "The Distinctive Signs of the Christians and Jews in Islam," 201–2, and in Tritton's article, "*Zunnār.*"

65. Iohannis Ephesini (John of Ephesus), *Historiae Ecclesiasticae, Pars Tertia,* ed. and trans. into Latin E. W. Brooks (1935; repr., Louvain, 1952), Syriac text, 165, Latin trans., 2:122–23 (chap. 33), English trans. by R. Payne Smith, *The Third Part of the Ecclesiastical History of John Bishop of Ephesus* (Oxford, 1860), 223.

66. See my article cited in note 57.

67. On the self-defensive purpose of the Pact of ʿUmar stipulations, see Noth, "Abgrenzungsprobleme," 307–13.

68. See Chap. 2.

69. Plus the *ṭaylasān* (a kind of hood) and the *qalansuwa* (a conical cap). Fattal, *Le statut,* 101–2; Lewis, *Islam,* 2:224 (no. 77). See also Chap. 10 in this book.

70. Casual evidence comes from Saadya Gaon (d. 942), the eminent scholar and head of the Babylonian yeshiva. In his Arabic commentary on the talmudic tractate of Berakhot, in the section dealing with the morning blessings (*birkhot ha-shaḥar*), Saadya uses the Syriac-like form *zunāra* and the devised Arabic verb *tazannara* (*yatazannarū al-zunāra*) to explain the talmudic prescription that one should recite the invocation "Blessed is He who girds Israel with might" (*ozer yisrael bi-gevura*) when fastening one's girdle (the Aramaic word in the talmudic passage is *himyana*). See *Perush R. Saadya Gaon le-masekhet berakhot,* in *Ginzei yerushalayim* (Ginzei Jerusalem), ed. Abraham J. Wertheimer (Jerusalem, 1981), 241. I am grateful to Professor Michael Sokoloff for bringing this publication to my attention.

Similarly, in his prayerbook, in the directions for reciting the morning blessings (*birkhot ha-shaḥar*), Saadya writes, without special comment: "At the moment of (fastening) the *zunnār,* say [the blessing ending with 'God], who girds Israel with greatness.'" *Siddur R. Saadja Gaon,* ed. I. Davidson et al. (Jerusalem, 1970), 88, line 17. While Geniza documents apparently make little mention of the *zunnār,* these passages from Saadya regarding everyday liturgical practice suggest that it was fairly commonly worn by Iraqi Jewry.

71. Fattal, *Le statut,* 102–10. See also the chronological survey of decrees (807–1364), including repromulgation of the dress regulation, in Zayat, "The Distinctive Signs of the Christians and Jews in Islam," 213–15.

72. Goitein, *A Mediterranean Society,* 2:286, 288.

73. I am grateful to Michael Cook for bringing this to my attention. See his "Magian Cheese: An Archaic Problem in Islamic Law," *Bulletin of the School of Oriental and African Studies* 47 (1984), esp. 451–54.

74. See Chap. 6.

75. See Chap. 3.

76. Fattal, *Le statut,* 38 (treaty with Hira, 633 C.E.).

77. In *ḥadīth,* one finds considerable discussion of slaves in *dhimmī* possession. For instance, an unbeliever might not enslave a Muslim. A *dhimmī*'s slave who converted to Islam must be sold off, at a price determined by evaluating the monetary worth of the slave, even against the will of the owner. A Christian servant girl (*ama*) who converted to Islam after bearing the child of her Christian master must be set free unless the father followed her into Islam, in which case she might remain his slave. ʿAbd al-Razzāq al-Ṣanʿānī, *Al-muṣannaf,* 6:43ff.

78. Ibn al-Qayyim, *Aḥkām ahl al-dhimma,* part 2, 730ff. The form the clause takes in one version of the Pact (the one preserved by Badr al-Dīn ibn Jamāʿa; see note 8 in this chapter) incorporates this meaning: "They shall not purchase any of our captives." Kofler, "Handbuch des islamischen Staats und Verwaltungsrechtes von Badr-ad-Dīn Ibn Ǧamāʿah," 30.

79. ʿAbd al-Razzāq al-Sanʿānī, *Al-muṣannaf,* 6:46–47.

80. It should be noted that Ibn al-Qayyim relied on a version of the Pact of ʿUmar in which the slave clause comes sandwiched between two stipulations which normally come together much earlier, and with no intervening clause. One forbids *dhimmīs* from proselytizing, while the other forbids them from preventing a coreligionist from adopting Islam. Ibn al-Qayyim, *Aḥkām ahl al-dhimma,* part 2, 657–61.

81. See Chap. 3.

82. Pakter, *Medieval Canon Law and the Jews,* 132–37.

83. Goitein, *A Mediterranean Society,* 1:130–37.

84. Fattal, *Le statut,* 240. Ibn Qayyim al-Jawziyya's long section on the prohibition of employing *dhimmīs* in positions of authority (*wilāya*) over Muslims is filled with anecdotes in which Muslims acknowledge, however regrettably, the indispensability of these infidel *kātibs* (government clerks). Ibn al-Qayyim, *Aḥkām ahl al-dhimma,* part 1, 208–38.

85. Fattal, *Le statut,* 236–37; Ibn al-Qayyim, *Aḥkām ahl al-dhimma,* section cited in n. 84.

86. This appears several times in Ibn al-Qayyim's chapter, already mentioned.

87. Fattal, *Le statut,* 240–52. Ibn Qayyim al-Jawziyya (section cited in n. 84) provides a historical survey of caliphal attempts to stamp out the practice, beginning with ʿUmar ibn ʿAbd al-ʿAzīz and extending over centuries.

88. Lewis, *Islam,* 2:225 (no. 77). In other anthologies—e.g., Stillman, *Jews of Arab Lands,* 167–68; and Bat Ye'or, *The Dhimmi,* 186.

89. Lewis, *Islam* 2:225 (no. 78).

90. Fattal, *Le statut,* 252ff.

91. The story of Jewish achievements in Muslim government in Andalusia can be followed in Ashtor's *Jews of Moslem Spain.*

92. Goitein, *A Mediterranean Society,* 2:374–80.

93. Richard Gottheil, "Fragments from an Arabic Common-Place Book," *Bulletin de l'Institut Française d'Archéologie Orientale* 34 (1934), 103–28; compare Mark R. Cohen, "Correspondence and Social Control in the Jewish Communities of the Islamic World: A Letter of the Nagid Joshua Maimonides," *Jewish History* 1, no. 2 (1986), 40.

94. Often cited in books about the period and in Lewis, *Islam,* 2:227 (no. 80). For more on Abū Saʿd and his family, see Chap. 5 in this book.

95. Claude Cahen, "Histoires coptes d'un cadi médiéval," *Bulletin de l'Institut Française d'Archéologie Orientale* 59 (1960), 141–42; other sources cited in Fattal, *Le statut,* 259; Goitein, *A Mediterranean Society,* 2:281; Mark R. Cohen, *Jewish Self-Government in Medieval Egypt: The Origins of the Office of Head of the Jews, ca. 1065–1126* (Princeton, N.J., 1980), 284–85.

96. Lewis, *Islam,* 2:228–29 (no. 83).

97. Ibid., 2:229–32; Bat Ye'or, *The Dhimmi,* 192–94.

98. For an example of an attempt by *dhimmīs* to pay a sum of money to minimize the potential danger from the distinctive dress requirement, see Lichtenstadter, "Distinctive Dress," 51.

99. Fattal, *Le statut,* 262. See also, Donald P. Little, "Coptic Converts to Islam during the Baḥrī Mamluk Period," in *Conversion and Continuity: Indigenous Christian Communities in Islamic Lands Eighth to Eighteenth Centuries,* ed. M. Gervers and R. J. Bikhazi (Toronto, 1990), 263–88.

100. E. Strauss (Ashtor), "L'inquisition dans l'état mamlouk," *Rivista degli Studi Orientali* 25 (1950), 11–26. Ashtor points out that trials of Jews were far less frequent than trials of Christians, because, he surmises, of the Jews' perceived weakness, their small numbers, and their inability to count on support from European states—all of which made the Jews more cautious, and hence, less likely to be prosecuted than were Christians.

101. See, for instance, Claude Cahen, "Histoires coptes d'un cadi médiéval," 133–50. Compare J. Sadan, "Some Literary Problems Concerning Judaism and Jewry in Medieval Arabic Sources," in *Studies in Islamic History and Civilization in Honour of Professor David Ayalon,* ed. M. Sharon (Jerusalem, 1986), 365–70. Cahen did not publish the chapter on the Jews. Moshe Perlmann, "Asnawi's Tract against Christian Officials," in *Ignace Goldziher Memorial Volume, Part II,* ed. Samuel Löwinger et al. (Jerusalem, 1958), 172–208; idem, "Notes on Anti-Christian Propaganda in the Mamlūk Empire," *Bulletin of the School of Oriental and African Studies* 10 (1940–42), 843–61; Richard Gottheil, "An Answer to the Dhimmis," *Journal of the American Oriental Society* (1921), 383–457; anon., *Minhāj al-sawāb fī qabḥ istiktāb ahl al-kitāb* (Beirut, 1982; a treatise against employing *dhimmīs* in public service, written in the fourteenth century); D. S. Richards, "The Coptic Bureaucracy under the Mamluks," in *Colloque International sur L'histoire du Caire* (Cairo [ca. 1970]), 373–81.

102. Ibn Taymiyya wrote an entire book on the subject of blasphemy in Islam. See also, Ibn al-Qayyim, *Aḥkām ahl al-dhimma,* part 2, 795–96, and n. 130 in this chapter.

103. Fattal covers the *jizya* in his *Le statut.* See 264ff.

104. Abū Yūsuf lived from 731 to 798. Hārūn al-Rashīd ruled from 786 to 809.

105. Abū Yūsuf, *Kitāb al-kharāj* (Bulaq, 1302/1885), 122–26 (*jizya*), 127–28

(distinctive dress), 138–49 (houses of worship, *dhimmī* obligations, and further discussion of peace terms during the conquest).

106. Al-Shāfiʿī, *Kitāb al-umm* (Bulaq, 1903–4), 4:118–19; trans. in Lewis, *Islam,* 2:219–23.

107. Ibid., 4:125–26: *Taḥdīd al-imām mā ya'khudh min ahl al-dhimma fi'l-amṣār;* and 127: *Ma yuʿṭihum al-imām min al-manʿ min al-ʿadūw.*

108. Ibn al-Qayyim, *Aḥkām ahl al-dhimma,* part 1, 1.

109. Ibid., 15ff., 22ff.

110. Fattal, *Le statut,* 324.

111. Abū Dā'ūd, *Sunan,* ed. ʿAzīz ʿUbayd Ri'as (Hims, 1972), 3:433–34, no. 3045; English trans. in Abū Dā'ūd, *Sunan,* trans. Aḥmad Ḥasan (Lahore, 1984), 2:865. The *ḥadīth* occurs often elsewhere (in a variant, the victim of the torment is called *nabaṭ,* "a Nabatean" [Ibn al-Qayyim, *Aḥkām ahl al-dhimma,* part 1, 34]). Compare also, Fattal, *Le statut,* 288.

112. Quoted from *Kitāb al-kharāj,* in Lewis, *Islam,* 2:224.

113. Quoted from A. Ben-Shemesh, *Taxation in Islam* (Leiden, 1969), 3:85.

114. Ibn al-Qayyim, *Aḥkām ahl al-dhimma,* part 1, 155.

115. Moshe Gil, "Religion and Realities in Islamic Taxation," *Israel Oriental Studies* 10 (1980), 24–26.

116. Goitein, *A Mediterranean Society,* 2:380ff.

117. Fattal, *Le statut,* 289–90.

118. Goitein, *A Mediterranean Society,* 2:384.

119. Fattal, *Le statut,* 281–83.

120. For instance, Yuzbakī, *Ta'rīkh ahl al-dhimma fi'l-ʿIrāq (12–247 A.H.),* 77–80.

121. This point is made by Rabbath, *Les chrétiens dans l'Islam des premiers temps: La conquête arabe sous les quatre premiers califes (11/632–40/661),* 1:245, stressing *jizya*'s original function as tribute or ransom in return for safeguards.

122. First published by A. Harkavy, "Netira und seine Söhne: Eine angesehene jüdische Familie in Bagdad am Anfang des X. Jahrhunderts," in *Festschrift zum siebzigsten Geburtstage A. Berliner's* (Hebrew part) (Frankfurt am Main, 1903), 1:34–43. The whereabouts of the Harkavy manuscript remains unknown. Another fragment—this one in the Taylor Schechter Collection of manuscripts from the Cairo Geniza (TS Misc. Box 10, fol. 252)—parallels the important passage translated below; unfortunately it is torn precisely where the text contains the greatest difficulties. See also, Walter J. Fischel, *Jews in the Economic and Political Life of Mediaeval Islam* (1937; repr., New York, 1969), 34ff.

123. Harkavy, "Netira und seine Söhne," 36. In translating the passage I have found useful the emendations to and plausible explanation of the problematic first part of this passage by S. Friedlaender, *Jewish Quarterly Review,* o.s., 17 (1904–5), 387–88. Additional emendations: for *ytqn,* read *yḥqn,* hence *yaḥqin dammahu,* "spares his life" (courtesy of Professor Moshe Gil); for *yṭ'lim,* read *yṭ'lbw,* hence *yuṭālabū,* "will be demanded" (courtesy of Professor Joshua Blau). I lectured on this passage at the Sixth International Conference of the Society for Judaeo-Arabic Studies (Bar-Ilan University, June 1993) and benefited from comments on the text from colleagues. That paper will be published in the conference proceedings (in Hebrew), ed. David Doron. Compare Raphael Patai, *The Seed of Abraham: Jews and*

Arabs in Contact and Conflict (Salt Lake City, Utah, 1986), 44; and Nissim Rejwan, *The Jews of Iraq: 3000 Years of History and Culture* (Boulder, Colo., 1985), 88–90, who misconstrues some details of the conversation between Neṭira and the caliph regarding the *jizya*.

124. Compare Baron, *Social and Religious History of the Jews*, 3:153. For a gloomier interpretation of this "episode," see Avraham Grossman, "The Economic and Social Background of Hostile Attitudes toward the Jews in the Ninth and Tenth Century Muslim Caliphate," 175–86. The author acknowledges that "neither in this source nor in any other contemporary ones do we find evidence of violent mob outbreaks against the Jews as a result of this jealousy [of the powerful Jewish banker-courtier, Neṭira]."

125. S. D. Goitein, "A Report of Messianic Troubles in Baghdad in 1120–21," *Jewish Quarterly Review*, n.s., 43 (1952), 75 (bottom).

126. John O. Hunwick, ed., *Sharīʿa in Songhay: The Replies of al-Maghīlī to the Questions of Askia al-Ḥājj Muḥammad* (Oxford, 1985), 30–37. Also, idem, "Al-Mahīlī [*sic*] and the Jews of Tuwāt: The Demise of a Community," *Studia Islamica* 61 (1985), 155–83.

127. Kisch, *Jews in Medieval Germany*, 167–68.

128. I heard this idea long ago in lectures in graduate school on medieval Jewish history by my teacher, Professor Gerson D. Cohen. I have never seen it mentioned in print elsewhere. The verb form does not appear in Menahem Moreshet, *Leqsiqon ha-poʿal she-nitḥadesh bi-leshon ha-tannaim* [A Lexicon of New Verbs in Tannaitic Hebrew] (Ramat Gan, 1980). I am grateful to Professor Moshe Greenberg for bringing this reference book to my attention. I located one attestation of the verbal usage in a Tannaitic passage in the Talmud (Babylonian Talmud Berakhot 28b): R. Yoḥanan b. Zakkai, on his sickbed, compares an earthly king to God, only the former of whom he can appease and "bribe with money" (*le-shaḥdo be-mammon*).

129. In al-Jāḥiẓ, *Kitāb al-bayān wa'l-tabyīn* (Cairo, 1311H./1893), 1:168; quoted in Levy, *The Social Structure of Islam* (Cambridge, 1957), 55; and, from there, in Patai, *Seed of Abraham*, 51.

130. Abridged by the editor of *Aḥkām ahl al-dhimma* from Ibn Taymiyya's *Kitāb al-ṣārim al-maslūk ʿalā shātim al-rasūl* (214–15, 243–45, 252–53) and included as an appendix (*Aḥkām*, part 2, 891–93). Ibn al-Qayyim himself explains that ʿUmar's promulgation was incumbent upon the *dhimmīs* "forever" (ibid., 7–14). Compare also, ibid., 795, where Ibn al-Qayyim introduces the final part of his *Aḥkām*, dealing with acts by the *dhimmī* that cause the Pact to be canceled, especially blasphemy toward the Prophet.

131. Kisch, *Jews in Medieval Germany*, 154–647.

132. In 1301: al-Maqrīzī, *Kitāb al-sulūk li-maʿrifat duwal al-mulūk*, ed. M. M. Ziyāda et al. (Cairo, 1939), 1:909–13; trans. in Lewis, *Islam*, 2:229ff., esp. 231. In 1354: al-Qalqashandī, *Ṣubḥ al-aʿshā'* (Cairo, 1918), 13:378–79; trans. in Lewis, *Islam*, 2:234–35. In ca. 1442: Cohen, "Jews in the Mamlūk Environment: The Crisis of 1442 (A Geniza Study)," 429, where the Jewish, Samaritan, and Christian community heads "professed to have no knowledge of it," either because they wished to avoid responsibility or perhaps precisely because an actual ceremony of repromulgation had never before taken place in their time. The contents of the stipulations of ʿUmar were, of course, well known to them.

133. Isma'īl ibn 'Umar ibn Kathīr, *Al-bidāya wa'l-nihāya,* 14 vols. (Cairo, 1932–39/40), 11:339.

134. Al-Sarakhsī, *Al-mabsūṭ,* 5:39. Compare, also, the statement in al-Shāfi'ī's juristic compilation of the rights and obligations to be written by the Imam into the contract for the *dhimmīs:* "If one of you or any other unbeliever applies to us for judgment, we shall adjudicate according to the law of Islam. But if he does not come to us, *we shall not intervene among you*" (*lam nu'riḍ lakum fīmā baynakum wa-baynahu*)"; *Kitāb al-umm* 4:118; trans. in Lewis, *Islam,* 2:219–23.

135. Ibn al-Qayyim, *Aḥkām ahl al-dhimma,* part 2, 809.

Chapter Five
The Economic Factor

1. Baldwin, *The Medieval Theories of the Just Price: Romanists, Canonists, and Theologians in the Twelfth and Thirteenth Centuries, Transactions of the American Philosophical Society* (Philadelphia, 1959), 12, 13; monograph repr. in *The Evolution of Capitalism. Pre-Capitalist Economic Thought: Three Modern Interpretations* (New York, 1972).

2. "The outbursts against possession of great wealth, which occurred frequently in the writings of the Church Fathers, undoubtedly were prompted primarily by the New Testament teachings about wealth and especially by the account of the rich young ruler." Baldwin, *Medieval Theories,* 13.

3. Baldwin, *Medieval Theories,* 15. J. Gilchrist adds: "Tertullian spoke of trade as avarice; St. John Chrysostom considered merchants to be men who 'wish to become rich at any price. . . .' Jerome treated trade as fraud; for Augustine it was a pursuit that turned men's minds away from true rest. . . . [Pope] Leo I's conclusion that 'it is difficult for buyers and sellers not to fall into sin' became common opinion in the Church and set the stage, for the theory, that is, for the next six centuries." Gilchrist, *The Church and Economic Activity in the Middle Ages* (London, 1969), 51.

4. Zacour, *Introduction to Medieval Institutions,* 54–55. For a similar view, see Henri Pirenne, *Medieval Cities: Their Origins and the Revival of Trade,* trans. Frank D. Halsey (Garden City, N.Y., 1956), 86–87.

5. Simmel, *The Sociology of Georg Simmel,* trans. and ed. Kurt H. Wolff (Glencoe, Ill., 1950), 403–4; emphasis added.

6. Gil, "The Rādhānite Merchants and the Land of Rādhān," *Journal of the Economic and Social History of the Orient* 17 (1974), 299–328. See also the more recent article by Charles Verlinden, "Les Radaniya et Verdun: a propos de la traite des esclaves slaves vers l'Espagne musulmane aux IXe et Xe sièlces," in *Estudios en homenaje a Don Claudio Sanchez Albornoz en sus 90 años* (Buenos Aires, 1983), 2:105–32, which unfortunately, while surveying the earlier literature, overlooks Gil's indispensable contribution.

7. Le Goff, *Medieval Civilization 400–1500,* 26. On the prominence of Jews in long-distance international trade of early medieval Europe, see Robert-Henri Bautier, *The Economic Development of Medieval Europe,* trans. Heather Karolyi (London, 1971), 77–78; Robert S. Lopez, *The Commercial Revolution of the Middle Ages, 950–*

1350 (Cambridge, 1976), 60–61; Charles Verlinden, "A propos de la place des juifs dans l'économie de l'Europe occidentale aux IXe et Xe siècles: Agobard de Lyon et l'historiographie arabe," in *Storiografia e Storia; Studi in onore de Eugenio Depré Theseider* (Rome, 1974), 21–37, and the same author's "Les Radaniya et Verdun." The disappearance of the Syrians from the East-West trade, and its consequences for the Jews, is explained by Robert Lopez as follows: "The Arab invasion did not end all relations between East and West, but opened to Syrian merchants wider Asiatic markets toward which they turned. . . . Thus the Jews alone were left to provide a link, however tenuous, between Catholic Europe and the more advanced countries beyond it: the Islamic world, the Byzantine Empire, even India and China. Lopez, *Commercial Revolution,* 60.

Another explanation—hypothetical, yet reasonable, and not mutually exclusive with Lopez—is that Syrian Christians would have felt, or have been made to feel, uncomfortable traversing the Muslim-Christian frontier. Muslims might have suspected them of conveying intelligence to the Christian enemy in the Domain of War. For their part, the Syrians might have risked forfeiting their *dhimmī* status for the less favorable status of *musta'min.*

8. Baldwin, *Medieval Theories,* 31–34.

9. Avraham Grossman, *Ḥakhmei ashkenaz ha-rishonim* [The Early Sages of Ashkenaz: Their Lives, Leadership, and Works (900–1096)] (Jerusalem, 1981), 29–35, 39–41.

10. Blumenkranz, *Juifs et chrétiens,* 12–33.

11. Jews are frequently referred to in Latin by such phrases as "mercatores, id est Judei at ceteri mercatores" [merchants, that is, Jews and other merchants]; Aronius, *Regesten,* 52 (no. 122, dated ca. 906); also 55 (no. 129): "ne vel Judei vel ceteri ibi [in urbe Magadaburg] manentes negotiatores" (nor Jews nor other merchants remaining [in Magdeburg]).

12. The role of medieval urbanism in Jewish fate in Christendom and in Islam is treated at some length in Chap. 7 of this book.

13. Chazan, *Church, State, and Jew,* 58–59; Aronius, *Regesten,* 69–70 (no. 168).

14. Gilchrist, *Church and Economic Activity,* 53–56. Compare Le Goff, *Medieval Civilization 400–1500:* "During the period of the eleventh and twelfth centuries . . . [t]he Church protected the merchant and helped him to conquer the prejudice which made the inactive seigneurial class despise him" (82).

15. Gilchrist, *Church and Economic Activity,* 58–62.

16. Ibid., 62–70; *DMA,* s.v. "Usury." This standard was also applied to the Jews by the thirteenth-century papacy.

17. Wilhelm Roscher, a nineteenth-century historian whose theory about the role of the Jews in medieval economic life still has merit, wrote:

> In those days the Jews satisfied a great economic need, something which, for a long time, could not be done by anyone else, namely, the need for carrying on a professional trade. Mediaeval policy toward the Jews may be said to have followed a direction almost inverse to the general economic trend. As soon as peoples became mature enough to perform that function themselves, they try to emancipate themselves from such guardianship over their trade, often in bitter conflict. The persecutions of the Jews in the later Middle

> Ages are thus, to a great extent, a product of commercial jealousy. They are connected with the rise of a national merchant class.

English translation by Guido Kisch in his tribute to Roscher, "The Jews' Function in the Evolution of Mediaeval Economic Life," in Kisch, *Forschungen zur Rechts-, Wirtschafts- und Sozialgeschichte der Juden,* 2:109 (orig. published in *Historia Judaica* 6 [1944] and later in Kisch's *Jews in Medieval Germany,* 316ff.).

18. Judah Rosenthal, "The Law of Usury Relating to Non-Jews" (Hebrew), *Talpioth* 5 (1952), 479–82.

19. Ibid., 484–85.

20. *Dialogue of a Philosopher,* trans. P. J. Payer (Toronto, 1979), 33.

21. Kisch, *Jews in Medieval Germany,* 329.

22. Jordan, "Jews on Top: Women and the Availability of Consumption Loans in Northern France in the Mid-Thirteenth Century," *Journal of Jewish Studies* 29 (1978), esp. 47, 50–52, 55–56.

23. Jenks, "Judenverschuldung und Verfolgung der Juden im 14. Jahrhundert: Franken bis 1349," *Vierteljahrschrift für Sozial- und Wirtschaftsgeschichte* 65 (1978), 309–56.

24. William Jordan notes the essential legality of pawnbrokering in medieval times, which explains why it left "virtually no evidence." Jordan, *French Monarchy and the Jews,* 87. Jenks points out that Würzburg was exceptional by virtue of the occupational differentiation of its Jews and by the atypically close and congenial contact with their Christian neighbors. Jenks, "Judenverschuldung und Verfolgung der Juden," 348–50.

25. Cecil Roth, *A History of the Jews in England,* 3d ed. (Oxford, 1964), 18–24.

26. Dobson, *The Jews of Medieval York and the Massacre of March 1190* (York, 1974). In York, the author argues, nobles who besieged and killed Jews acted out of resentment toward the king by taking revenge on his agents. They recognized that the Jews were pawns of the king, who supported Jewish usury in order to exact revenues from his subjects in the form of profits from oppressive Jewish moneylending.

27. *DMA,* s.v. "Banking, European," col. 76a, and "Lombards"; Gilchrist, *Church and Economic Activity,* 110; Kurt Grunwald, "Lombards, Cahorsins, and Jews," *Journal of European Economic History* 4 (1975), 393–98.

28. See Grayzel, *Church and the Jews,* 86–87, 132–33, for two examples among many (= Simonsohn, *Apostolic See and the Jews, Documents: 492–1404,* 71 [no. 67] and 94–95 [no. 89]).

29. Grayzel, *Church and the Jews,* 307; Simonsohn, *Apostolic See and the Jews: History,* 190–95.

30. Roth, *History of the Jews in England,* 70–73.

31. H. G. Richardson, *The English Jewry under Angevin Kings* (London, 1960), 213–33.

32. Stow, "Papal and Royal Attitudes toward Jewish Lending in the Thirteenth Century," 161–84.

33. Jordan, *French Monarchy and the Jews,* chaps. 8–13.

34. Ibid., 45; Joshua Trachtenberg, *The Devil and the Jews: The Medieval Conception of the Jew and Its Relation to Modern Antisemitism* (Cleveland, 1961), 188–95;

Kisch, *Jews in Medieval Germany,* 192; Rosenthal, "Law of Usury," 134; S. Stein, "A Disputation on Moneylending between Jews and Gentiles in Me'ir b. Simeon's Milḥemeth Miṣwah (Narbonne, 13th century)," *Journal of Jewish Studies* 10 (1959), 45–61.

35. Shatzmiller, *Shylock Reconsidered: Jews, Moneylending, and Medieval Society* (Berkeley and Los Angeles, 1990), 46–47.

36. Ibid., 99–103 (quotation on 103).

37. "A Letter [Polemic] of R. Jacob of Venice" (Hebrew), *Jeschurun: Zeitschrift für die Wissenschaft des Judenthums,* ed. Joseph Kobak 6 (1868), 16; also quoted in David B. Ruderman, *The World of a Renaissance Jew: The Life and Thought of Abraham ben Mordecai Farissol* (Cincinnati, 1981), 87, 210, n. 8. See Kenneth R. Stow, "Jacob of Venice and the Jewish Settlement in Venice in the Thirteenth Century," in *Community and Culture: Essays in Jewish Studies in Honor of the Nineteenth Anniversary of the Founding of Gratz College 1895–1985,* ed. Nahum M. Waldman (Philadelphia, 1987), 221–32.

38. *DMA,* s.v. "Muhammad," col. 522a.

39. Maxime Rodinson, *Islam and Capitalism,* trans. Brian Pearce (Austin, Tex., 1978), 13–15 (quotation on 14).

40. Cited and translated from al-Muttaqī, *Kanz al-ʿummāl,* in Lewis, *Islam,* 2:125–27.

41. See the article by Goitein cited in note 45.

42. Abdul Azim Islahi, *Economic Concepts of Ibn Taimiyah* (London, 1988), 179.

43. Ibid., 181.

44. Rodinson, *Islam and Capitalism,* 103, 108.

45. In an influential article by that title, published in the *Journal of World History* 3 (1957), 583, 604; repr. in Goitein's *Studies in Islamic History and Institutions* (Leiden, 1968), 217–41.

46. Fischel, *Jews in the Economic and Political Life of Mediaeval Islam,* 1–44.

47. Eliyahu Ashtor, "Migrations de l'Irak vers les pays méditerranéens dans le haut Moyen Age," *Annales: économies, sociétés, civilisations* 27 (1972), 185–214.

48. On the *wakīl tujjār,* see Goitein, *A Mediterranean Society,* 1:186–92.

49. See Mark R. Cohen and Sasson Somekh, "In the Court of Yaʿqūb ibn Killis: A Fragment from the Cairo Geniza," *Jewish Quarterly Review,* n.s., 80 (1989–90), 283–314.

50. Fischel, *Jews in the Economic and Political Life of Mediaeval Islam,* 68–69; Moshe Gil, *Ha-tustarim: ha-mishpaḥa veha-kat* [The Tustaris: The Family and the Sect] (Tel Aviv, 1981).

51. A. L. Udovitch, *Partnership and Profit in Medieval Islam* (Princeton, N.J., 1970), esp. 256–59; and numerous articles.

52. Islahi, *Economic Concepts of Ibn Taimiyah,* 136–37.

53. *Responsa of the Geonim* (Hebrew), ed. Abraham E. Harkabi (Berlin, 1887), 216 (no. 423). For a discussion of the *suftaja* as it appears in the Geniza, see Goitein, *A Mediterranean Society,* 1:242–45. On this particular Geonic responsum, see ibid., 2:328.

54. S. M. Stern, "The Constitution of the Islamic City," in A. H. Hourani and S. M. Stern, ed., *The Islamic City: A Colloquium* (Oxford, 1970), 36–47.

55. Goitein, *A Mediterranean Society,* 2:276, 401–2.

56. *Responsa of the Geonim,* ed. Harkabi, 140 (no. 278); cited by Gideon Libson, "Between Jewish Law and Muslim Law: The Preference Given Neighbors of Differing Religions in Acquiring Neighboring Property" (Hebrew), *Peʿamim* 45 (1990), 85, n. 44, as evidence of Geonic confidence in the Muslim judiciary.

57. Ibid., 85 (text in S. Abramson, "Five Sections of Rabbi Hai Gaon's 'Sefer Hamekach'" [Hebrew], in *Jubilee Volume in Honor of Moreinu Hagaon Rabbi Joseph B. Soloveitchik,* ed. Shaul Israeli et al. [Jerusalem, 1984], 2:1350).

58. Guido Kisch, "Relations between Jewish and Christian Courts in the Middle Ages," in Kisch's *Forschungen zur Rechts-, Wirtschafts- und Sozialgeschichte der Juden,* 2:78–105.

59. Louis Finkelstein, *Jewish Self-Government in the Middle Ages,* 2d printing (New York, 1964), 150–60.

60. Gideon Libson, "The Custom to Supplement to the *Ketuba* Based on 'Appropriate *Mohar*' for a Wife Who Has Lost Her *Ketuba*" (Hebrew), *Sefunot,* n.s., 5 (20), 71–94 (Proceedings of the Second Conference of the Society for Judaeo-Arabic Studies); idem, "Between Jewish Law and Muslim Law," 71–88; and a book, tentatively titled *Studies in Comparative Jewish and Islamic Law: Gaonic Practice and Islamic Law,* to be published by the Faculty of Laws, Hebrew University.

61. In the Muslim world, the gentile (Hebrew: *goy*) par excellence was the Muslim; Christians were usually called *ʿarelim* (uncircumcised) in Hebrew.

62. Louis Ginzberg, *Geonica,* vol. 2, *Genizah Studies,* 2d ed. (New York, 1968), 194 (cf. 186–87). Other responsa on the same theme include two in *Teshuvot hageonim,* ed. Jacob Musafia (Lyck, 1864), 25–26 (nos. 67–68).

63. Ginzberg, *Geonica,* vol. 2, *Genizah Studies,* 186–87, 194–96.

64. *Responsa of Maimonides* (Hebrew), ed. J. Blau (Jerusalem, 1958), 2:360 (no. 204); Goitein, *A Mediterranean Society,* 2:296. Goitein translates: "the crafts exercised are in one case goldsmithing; in another the making of glass."

65. Udovitch, *Partnership and Profit in Medieval Islam,* 227–29; Ibn al-Qayyim, *Aḥkām ahl al-dhimma,* part 1, 270–74 (273: "becoming partners with them leads to intermingling [*mukhālaṭa*], and that, in turn, to friendship [*mawadda*]"); part 2, 776–77.

66. *Responsa of Maimonides,* ed. Blau, 1:170 (no. 101); compare Goitein, *A Mediterranean Society,* 1:199.

67. Udovitch, *Partnership and Profit in Medieval Islam,* 77–80.

68. Quoted, ibid., 79.

69. *Responsa of Maimonides,* ed. Blau, 1:89 (no. 53); Goitein, *A Mediterranean Society,* 1:197.

70. Libson, "Between Jewish Law and Muslim Law," 85.

71. Goitein, *A Mediterranean Society,* 1:256–57.

72. *Responsa of Maimonides,* ed. Blau, 1:122 (no. 79).

73. Fischel, *Jews in the Economic and Political Life of Mediaeval Islam,* 12–25.

74. Goitein, *A Mediterranean Society,* 1:258.

75. Gottheil, "An Answer to the Dhimmis," 457 (English), 415 (Arabic).

76. Goitein, *A Mediterranean Society,* 1:362–67, 87.

77. Ibid., 116–27.

78. See above, p. 80.

79. Clifford Geertz, "Suq: The Bazaar Economy in Sefrou," in Cliffort Geertz, Hildred Geertz, and Lawrence Rosen, *Meaning and Order in Moroccan Society: Three Essays in Cultural Analysis* (Cambridge, 1979), 165.

80. Ibid. 169.

81. Lawrence Rosen, *Bargaining for Reality: The Construction of Social Relations in a Muslim Community* (Chicago, 1984), 154–55.

82. Daniel Schroeter, "Trade as a Mediator in Muslim-Jewish Relations: Southwestern Morocco in the Nineteenth Century," in *Jews among Arabs: Contacts and Boundaries,* ed. M. R. Cohen and A. L. Udovitch (Princeton, N.J., 1989), 115. Schroeter's book, *Merchants of Essaouira: Urban Society and Imperialism in Southwestern Morocco, 1844–1886* (Cambridge, 1988), deals with the subject in a broader context.

83. Schroeter, "Trade as a Mediator," 117.

84. S. D. Goitein, *Letters of Medieval Jewish Traders* (Princeton, N.J., 1973), 76–78.

85. Ibid., 199–200.

86. An exception to this view is that of Maurice Kriegel. In his "Un trait de psychologie sociale dans les pays méditerranéens du Bas Moyen Age: le juif comme intouchable" (*Annales: économies, sociétés, civilisations,* 31 [1976], 326–30), and more comprehensively in *Les Juifs à la fin du moyen âge dans l'Europe méditerranéene* (Paris, 1979), Kriegel argues—against received wisdom—that the attitude toward the Jew in southern Europe was just as hostile as it was in the north. Noël Coulet has challenged this revisionist thesis in "'Juif intouchable' et interdits alimentaires," in *Exclus et systèmes d'exclusion dans la littérature et la civilisation médiévales* (Aix-en-Provence, 1978), 207–21. See also, Coulet, "Les Juifs en Provence au bas moyen âge: Les limites d'une marginalité," in *Minorites et marginaux en Espagne et dans le Midi de la France VIIe–XVIIIe siècles)* (Paris, 1986), 203–19.

87. Y. Dossat, "Les Juifs à Toulouse: un demi-siècle d'histoire communautaire," in *Juifs et judaïsme de Languedoc xiiie siècle–début xive siècle,* ed. Marie-Humbert Vicaire and Bernhard Blumenkranz (Toulouse, 1977), 132–35.

88. Gerard Nahon, "Condition fiscale et économique des juifs," in *Juifs et judaïsme de Languedoc xiiie siècle–début xive siècle,* 63–72, following Saige, Luce, Régné, among others.

89. Shatzmiller, *Shylock Reconsidered,* 123.

90. See William C. Jordan's review, *Jewish Quarterly Review,* n.s., 82 (1991), 221–23.

Chapter Six
Hierarchy, Marginality, and Ethnicity

1. Dumont, *Homo Hierarchicus: The Caste System and its Implications,* complete rev. Eng. edition, trans. Sainsbury, Dumont, and Galiati (Chicago, 1980). For a discussion of the controversial reception given this book, see Dumont's "Preface to the Complete English Edition."

2. Ibid., 66; the entire passage appears in italics in the original.

3. Ibid., 243, in the author's "Postface: Toward a Theory of Hierarchy."

4. Ibid., 191.

5. Duby, *The Three Orders: Feudal Society Imagined,* trans. Arthur Goldhammer (Chicago and London, 1980), 3–4.

6. Russell, *A History of Medieval Christianity: Prophecy and Order,* 86. Compare Le Goff, *Medieval Civilization 400–1500:* "Freedom meant a guaranteed status: it was, according to Gerd Tellenbach's definition, 'one's legitimate place before God and men.' It meant belonging to society" (280). The seminal contribution of Tellenbach to the elaboration of the related notions of hierarchy, "right order," and "*libertas*" in the Middle Ages can be found in Tellenbach's *Church, State and Christian Society at the Time of the Investiture Contest,* trans. R. F. Bennett (Oxford, 1959). See, for instance, the chapter "The Medieval Conception of the Hierarchy": "[Hierarchy] is one of the forms in which human thought about the problems of the world has always found expression, though it has never been so thoroughly exploited as it was during the middle ages" (38).

7. Dominique Sourdel, *Medieval Islam,* trans. J. Montgomery Watt (London, 1983), 135.

8. I draw upon H. F. Dickie-Clark, *The Marginal Situation: A Sociological Study of a Coloured Group* (London, 1966); and Noel P. Gist and Roy Dean Wright, *Marginality and Identity: Anglo-Indians as a Racially Mixed Minority in India* (Leiden, 1973). The passage quoted is from Gist and Wright, *Marginality,* 21.

9. Dickie-Clark, *Marginal Situation,* 32–33.

10. *Marginality,* as used here, differs from the way in which it is employed in the work of Maurice Kriegel, who, in turn, was influenced by the model of the caste system of India. Writing about the Jews of Mediterranean Europe at the end of the Middle Ages, Kriegel uses *marginality* more or less synonymously with *exclusion.* He views the various moves to segregate Christians from Jews as acts to avoid contamination by Jewish "impurity," as in a caste system requiring strict avoidance of those considered "untouchable." Kriegel, *Les Juifs à la fin du moyen âge,* esp. chap. 2. This approach has the disadvantage of obscuring the search for a subtler understanding of majority-minority relations regarding the Jews, one that makes it possible to account for or partially explain the differences between Christian-Jewish and Muslim-Jewish relations in the Middle Ages and to steer away from the polarity of "marginality-integration" that seems to underlie the critique of Kriegel by Noël Coulet, "Les Juifs en Provence au bas moyen-âge: Les limites d'une marginalité."

11. Dickie-Clark, *Marginal Situation,* 21–22.

12. Ibid., 37–38, where this is referred to as "status inconsistency."

13. Blumenkranz, *Juifs et chrétiens.* In English, Blumenkranz condensed his book into a pair of essays appearing in Roth, ed., *Dark Ages,* 69–99, 162–74. In the chapter "The Roman Church and the Jews," Blumenkranz writes: "The Jews were part of medieval society, and not merely a group on the fringes" (18). But, like Kriegel, he equates "on the fringes" with the shift to "exclusion" that began, he says, in the eleventh century.

14. Simonsohn, *Apostolic See and the Jews, Documents: 492–1404,* 33 (no. 34). See also, Roth, ed., *Dark Ages,* 74–75, 81, 118, 167.

15. Aronius, *Regesten,* 61 (no. 144).

16. On the expulsion of 1012 and Wecelin's conversion to Judaism and his

postconversion polemical treatise in defense of Judaism against Christianity, see Aronius's discussion, *Regesten;* Roth, ed., *Dark Ages,* 84, 87–88, 93, 96, 149, 172–74; and Robert Chazan, "1007–1012: Initial Crisis for Northern European Jewry," *Proceedings of the American Academy for Jewish Research,* 38–39 (1970–71), 101–18.

17. Pakter, *Medieval Canon Law and the Jews,* 47 (emphasis added). Paul's statement, in I Corinthians 5:12, was aimed at immoral Christians.

18. Kisch, *Jews in Medieval Germany,* 246.

19. Ibid., 248–49.

20. Le Goff, *Medieval Civilization 400–1500,* 316, 320–21.

21. Dahan, *Les intellectuels chrétiens,* 174.

22. Robert I. Moore, "Anti-Semitism and the Birth of Europe," in *Christianity and Judaism,* vol. 29 of *Studies in Church History,* ed. Diana Wood (Oxford, 1992), 49–50, citing Noël Coulet, "De l'intégration a l'exclusion: la place des juifs dans les cérémonies d'entrée solonnelle au Moyen Age," *Annales: économies, sociétés, civilisations* 34 (1979), 672–83.

23. Le Goff, *Medieval Civilization 400–1500,* 152, 261–64.

24. *Amān;* the person becomes a *musta'min.*

25. Khoury, *Toleranz im Islam,* 116.

26. Muḥammad ibn Aḥmad al-Sarakhsī, *Sharḥ kitāb al-siyar al-kabīr,* ed. ʿAbd al-ʿAzīz Aḥmad (n.p., 1972), 5:2045 (the book is a commentary on the work of Shaybānī [d. 803], a student of Abū Ḥanīfa [d. 767], the founder of the Hanafite school). See also, 2163: "*li 'annahu min ahli dārinā wa-yajrī ʿalayhi ḥukmunā fa-kāna bi-manzilat al-muslim* [for he belongs to our Domain and our law applies to him, and (in this matter) he has the status of a Muslim]." Compare the editor's introduction to Ibn al-Qayyim, *Aḥkām ahl al-dhimma,* part 1, 12–13.

27. Sarakhsī, *Al-mabsūṭ,* 9:195.

28. The line of thinking in the following discussion of *ṣaghār* and *ghiyār* partly owes its inspiration to an unpublished paper on the *dhimma* system by A. L. Udovitch.

29. Ibn al-Qayyim, *Aḥkām ahl al-dhimma,* part 1, 23–24.

30. Ibn Ḥazm, *Kitāb al-muḥallā* (Cairo, 1349 H.), 7:346.

31. Also *taghyīr,* from the root, *gh-y-r,* meaning "to be or make dissimilar."

32. Zayat, "Distinctive Signs," 235–40, esp. 235–36.

33. Mottahedeh, *Loyalty and Leadership in an Early Islamic Society* (Princeton, N.J., 1980), 108–15.

34. Shaun E. Marmon, *Eunuchs and Sacred Boundaries in Islamic Society* (New York: Oxford University Press, forthcoming), chap. 3: "The word *ṭā'ifa* is one of the most common designations in medieval Arabic for any kind of human category or sub-category."

35. Mottahadeh, *Loyalty and Leadership,* 149, 150, 159, 165.

36. See David Wasserstein, *The Rise and Fall of the Party-Kings: Politics and Society in Islamic Spain, 1002–1086* (Princeton, N.J., 1985), chap. 4.

37. Richard Gottheil, "An Eleventh-Century Document Concerning a Cairo Synagogue," 474; English, 485. A new English translation is in Stillman, *Jews of Arab Lands,* 189.

38. *Siddur R. Saadja Gaon,* ed. I. Davidson et al. (Jerusalem, 1970). *Sharīʿa:* 2, line 1, while a few lines above, page 1, line 6, he writes *tawrīya* and elsewhere (13,

line 9) *tawrāt,* using the Qur'anic (perhaps pre-Islamic Jewish-Arabic) form of the Hebrew *torah; qibla:* 20, lines 10–11; *imām:* 41, lines 10, 15; and frequently elsewhere in the *Siddur.* Similarly, in Saadya's commentary on the Bible, see Yehuda Ratzaby, ed., *Otzar ha-lashon ha-ʿaravit be-tafsir R. Saadya Gaon* [A Dictionary of Judaeo-Arabic in R. Saadya's Tafsir] (Ramat-Gan, 1985), s.v. "*imām*" (translating the word *kohen,* "priest"), *qibla, qur'ān.*

39. Rippin, "Saʿadya Gaon and Genesis 22: Aspects of Jewish-Muslim Interaction and Polemic," in *Studies in Islamic and Judaic Traditions,* ed. Brinner and Ricks, 36–38, 42.

40. I. Goldziher, "Über eine Formel in der jüdischen Responsen-litteratur und in den muhammedanischen Fetwâs," *Zeitschrift der Deutschen Morgenländischen Gesellschaft* 53 (1899), 645–52. A random inspection of Blau's edition of Maimonides' responsa (3 vols., Jerusalem, 1958–61) illustrates this phenomenon.

41. Goitein, *A Mediterranean Society,* 2:325–26.

42. Coon, *Caravan: The Story of the Middle East,* rev. ed. (New York, 1958).

43. Dale F. Eickelman, *The Middle East: An Anthropological Approach* (Englewood Cliffs, N.J., 1981), 49–51; Daniel G. Bates and Amal Rassam, *Peoples and Cultures of the Middle East* (Englewood Cliffs, N.J., 1983), 83–84.

44. Coon, *Caravan,* 153, 167.

45. Barth, ed., *Ethnic Groups and Boundaries* (Bergen-Oslo, 1969), 9–10, 16, 18.

46. A. L. Udovitch and Lucette Valensi, *The Last Arab Jews: The Communities of Jerba, Tunisia* (Chur, Switzerland, 1984), 3.

47. Ibid., 101.

48. Ibid., 118 (emphasis added).

49. Geertz, "Suq: The Bazaar Economy in Sefrou," 141.

50. Ibid., 164.

51. Langmuir puts it differently, emphasizing the role of religion: "Germanic monotheistic religiosity seems to have preserved some of the polytheistic tolerance that expected each people to have its own gods and rituals." Langmuir, *Toward a Definition of Antisemitism,* 78.

Chapter Seven
The Jew as Townsman

1. Edith Ennen, *The Medieval Town,* trans. Natalie Fryde (Amsterdam, 1979), 33, 45.

2. Kathryn L. Reyerson gives a concise, up-to-date summary of urban history in this area: "Urbanism, Western European," *DMA,* 12:311–20.

3. This process is described, mainly with reference to Germany, in Fritz Rörig, *The Medieval Town* (Berkeley and Los Angeles, 1967), 22–29, 48ff.

4. Susan Reynolds, *An Introduction to the History of English Medieval Towns* (Oxford, 1977), esp. chap. "The Growth of Independence," 91–117.

5. Le Goff, *Medieval Civilization 400–1500,* 293, 295.

6. Ennen, *Medieval Town,* 111, 113.

7. Baron, *Social and Religious History of the Jews,* 11:206.

8. Kisch, *Jews of Medieval Germany,* 345; Baron, *Social and Religious History of the Jews,* 11:14ff.; Pirenne, *Medieval Cities,* 143.

9. Le Goff, *Medieval Civilization 400–1500,* 318.

10. Dahan, *Les intellectuels chrétiens,* 176–78; Simonsohn, *Apostolic See and the Jews: History,* 139–41.

11. Baron, *Social and Religious History of the Jews,* 11:21.

12. Ibid., 76 (emphasis in original).

13. Stow, "The Jewish Community in the Middle Ages Was Not a Corporation" (Hebrew) in *Kehuna u-melukha* (Jerusalem, 1987), 146–48.

14. Kisch, *Jews in Medieval Germany,* 348–49.

15. Pakter, *Medieval Canon Law and the Jews,* 20–23.

16. On the perseverance of collective responsibility in medieval Christendom, see Le Goff, *Medieval Civilization 400–1500,* 174. Here is one example from England: In a Pipe Roll (no. 31) from the reign of Henry I, for the year 1130, we read, "The Jews of London render account of £2000 for the infirm man whom they slew." Excerpt with the relevant passage in Carl Stephenson and Frederick George Marcham, eds., *Sources of English Constitutional History* (New York), 1:54. I am grateful to William Jordan for directing me to this reference.

17. See the assemblage of examples of English "tallages levied on the Jewish communities at large." Pakter, *Medieval Canon Law and the Jews,* 22.

18. Reynolds writes about the contrast between southern Europe—where "a good many people lived in towns although they worked in the country"—and the English case, where the separation of town and country was more marked. *Introduction,* 87.

19. Y. Dossat, "Les Juifs à Toulouse: un demisiècle d'histoire communautaire," 127–28.

20. Coulet, "Les Juifs en Provence au bas moyen-âge: Les limites d'une marginalité," 203–6.

21. Pakter, *Medieval Canon Law and the Jews,* 20–25. Among reasons historians give for "the relative tolerance of southern society in respect to the Jews," as summarized by William Jordan, is the fact that "the Jewish communities of the Midi were an organic part of the cities and towns of the south. Jews had lived here since the period of Roman domination, and they had never lost the semblance of protection under Roman law." Jordan, *French Monarchy and the Jews,* 110–11.

22. Gerard Nahon, "Condition fiscale et économique des juifs," 63–72.

23. Recent scholarship on Islamic urbanism is summed up in "Urbanism, Islamic," *DMA,* 12:307–11 (A. L. Udovitch).

24. Ira M. Lapidus, "Muslim Cities and Islamic Societies," in *Middle Eastern Cities: A Symposium on Ancient, Islamic, and Contemporary Middle Eastern Urbanism,* ed. Lapidus (Berkeley and Los Angeles, 1969), 51.

25. Salo Baron writes: "Of course there was a difference between self-imposed or incidental segregation, particularly characteristic of all ethnically and religiously mixed regions in the ancient and medieval Near East, and a Jewish quarter in a Western land within an otherwise more or less homogeneous population. . . . Certainly, a Jewish quarter in ancient Alexandria or Sardes, a medieval Cairo or Cordova, carried no connotation of second-class citizenship." *Social and Religious History of the Jews,* 11:88. "The fact of the existence of special Jewish or Christian quarters all over the Arab Muslim world had nothing humiliating in it," writes Goitein, *Jews and Arabs,* 74.

26. Goitein, *A Mediterranean Society,* 2:289–93.

27. Yuzbakī, *Ta'rīkh ahl al-dhimma fi'l-ʿIrāq (12–247 A.H.),* 92.

28. Ibn al-Qayyim, *Aḥkām ahl al-dhimma,* part 1, 284f.

29. This is the main reason why ethnic and religious groups preferred segregated living.

30. Goitein, *A Mediterranean Society,* 2:295.

31. Jacob Katz, *Exclusiveness and Tolerance: Studies in Jewish-Gentile Relations in Medieval and Modern Times* (Oxford, 1991), 55–63; Goitein, *A Mediterranean Society,* 2:297.

32. Stern, "Constitution of the Islamic City," 25–50.

Chapter Eight

Sociability

1. An example from the Carolingian period was the Council of Metz, in 888; see Aronius, *Regesten,* 51–52 (no. 119).

2. *Agobardi Lugdunensis Archiepiscopi Epistolae,* ed. E. Duemmler, in *Monumenta Germaniae Historica, Epistolae Karolina Aevi* (Berlin, 1899), 3:182–85, 190ff. An abridged English translation of Agobard's letters was published by Kenneth R. Stow, in *Conservative Judaism* 29, no. 1 (Fall 1974), esp. 63, 65.

3. Grayzel, *Church and the Jews,* 309.

4. Possibly as early as 339 C.E., by Emperor Constantius in connection with a specific circumstance. In 388, it was stated explicitly by Emperor Theodosius I. CTh 16.8.6, *Theodosian Code,* 467; and CTh 3.7.2, *Theodosian Code,* 70; Linder, *Jews in Roman Imperial Legislation,* 149–50, nn. 9–10, 178–82.

5. Baron, *Social and Religious History of the Jews,* 11:77ff.

6. Brundage, "Intermarriage between Christians and Jews in Medieval Canon Law," *Jewish History* 3, no.1 (Spring 1988), 29, 31.

7. In the words of the compiler of a recent critical edition, translation, and commentary on the chapter devoted to Jewish-Christian relations (part 7, chap. 24). Dwayne E. Carpenter, *Alfonso X and the Jews: An Edition of and Commentary on* Siete Partidas *7.24 "De los judíos"* (Berkeley and Los Angeles, 1986), 104.

8. See article by Kenneth Pennington, "Law Codes: 1000–1500," *DMA,* 7:430.

9. Carpenter, *Alfonso X and the Jews,* 34.

10. Ibid., 85–87. The prohibition against communal bathing was incorporated into Gratian's *Decretum,* ca. 1140; ibid., 126, n. 15. The source seems to be a conciliar decree of the Quini-Sext, or Trullan Council, in Constantinople, in 692; see *A Select Library of Nicene and Post-Nicene Fathers of the Christian Church, Second Series, The Seven Ecumenical Councils,* ed. Schaff and Wace (repr., Edinburgh, 1988), 14:370 (canon no. 11). See also, Chap. 3, n. 46.

11. Carpenter, *Alfonso X and the Jews,* 36.

12. Ibid., 28.

13. Jordan, *French Monarchy and the Jews,* 253–57; and Moore, "Anti-Semitism and the Birth of Europe," 45.

14. Ibn al-Qayyim, *Aḥkām ahl al-dhimma,* part 1, 191, 199.

15. Muslim, *Ṣaḥīḥ,* trans. ʿAbdul Ḥamid Ṣiddīqī (Lahore, 1973), 3:1183–85. Vajda, "Juifs et musulmans selon le ḥadīṯ," 87–89.

16. In addition to the examples cited below, see Tritton, *Caliphs and Their Non-Muslim Subjects,* 137–54.

17. Fattal, *Le statut,* 97: Ghāzī al-Wāsiṭī reports this as the doing of Caliph ʿUmar ibn ʿAbd al-ʿAzīz; Richard Gottheil, "An Answer to the Dhimmis," 392 (Arabic), 424 (English).

18. Dahan, *Les intellectuels chrétiens,* 168–69. In one version of Abbasid Caliph al-Mutawakkil's severe anti-*dhimmī* decree of 850, he is said to have required that non-Muslims be provided with separate baths "whose attendants are *dhimmīs*" (Ibn al-Qayyim, part 1, 222); but no rationale beyond physical separation is given for this measure.

19. Ibn al-Qayyim, *Aḥkām ahl al-dhimma,* part 1, 200–201.

20. Ibid., 205–6. Mishnah Avodah Zarah ("Idolatry"), esp. chap. 1, which can be read in English in the translation by Herbert Danby (*The Mishnah* [Oxford, 1933]), beginning on 437. For medieval understandings of this tractate and its application to Christians, see the north European commentaries of Rashi and the Tosafists in the standard printed editions of the Babylonian Talmud; and Katz, *Exclusiveness and Tolerance,* 26–31.

21. The Islamic marketplace did not just serve "as a place for economic exchange. . . . It was also the place of meeting and interaction for individuals from the different quarters of the city and for people of varying ethnic, religious, and geographic backgrounds." Article, "Urbanism, Islamic," *DMA,* 12:310 (A. L. Udovitch).

22. Especially the taking of interest or the purchase of wine or pork.

23. Ibn al-Qayyim, *Aḥkām ahl al-dhimma,* part 1, 270–74; the passage is found on 273.

24. Ibn Taymiyya, *Kitāb iqtiḍā' al-ṣirāṭ al-mustaqīm mukhālafat aṣḥāb al-jaḥīm,* 122; English trans. (based on the 1950 Cairo edition) in *Ibn Taimiya's Struggle against Popular Religion,* 169.

25. Ibn al-Qayyim, *Aḥkām ahl al-dhimma,* part 1, 244–45, 270.

26. Sura 5:50. See Ibn al-ʿAṭṭār, *Kitāb al-wathā'iq wa'l-sijillāt,* ed. P. Chalmeta and F. Corriente (Madrid, 1983), 410. In the discussion of the formulary for a document attesting to the conversion of a Jew to Islam, he records that the convert is permitted to keep his Jewish (or Christian) wife, since a Muslim is allowed to marry a Jewish or Christian woman.

27. Ibn al-Qayyim, *Aḥkām ahl al-dhimma,* part 2, 441.

28. Ibid., 437–39.

29. Ibid., 436–37.

30. Vera B. Moreen, *Iranian Jewry's Hour of Peril and Heroism: A Study of Bābāī Ibn Luṭf's Chronicle (1617–1662)* (New York, 1987), 66.

31. Beryl Smalley, *The Study of the Bible in the Middle Ages* (Notre Dame, Ind., 1964), 149–72; Roth, ed., *Dark Ages,* 168–69; Dahan, *Les intellectuels chrétiens,* esp. part 3, "La rencontre."

32. Ibn ʿAqnīn in Stillman, *Jews of Arab Lands,* 226–28; Avicenna, in Lewis, *Islam,* 2:177–81.

33. Dahan, *Les intellectuels chrétiens,* 311–22.

34. Kraemer, *Humanism in the Renaissance of Islam: The Cultural Revival during the Buyid Age* (Leiden, 1986), includes a section on the involvement of the non-Muslim minority groups in Baghdad's intellectual life (75–86).

35. Gardet, *Les hommes de l'Islam: Approche des mentalités* (Paris, 1977), 130, 134–36.

36. *'Uyūn al-anbā' fī ṭabaqāt al-aṭibbā'* (Beirut, 1965), 583. See also, the praise of Jewish savants by Ṣā'id al-Andalusī (11th c.), rendered into English in Patai, *Seed of Abraham,* 101–4. On the medical profession as reflected in the Geniza, see Goitein, *A Mediterranean Society,* 2:240–61.

37. See Mark R. Cohen, "The Burdensome Life of a Jewish Physician and Communal Leader: A Geniza Fragment from the Alliance Israélite Universelle Collection," *Jerusalem Studies in Arabic and Islam* 16 (1993), 125–36 (Joshua Blau Festschrift).

38. Goitein, *A Mediterranean Society,* 2:288. On Europe, see Tractenberg, *Devil and the Jews,* 93–95, 97–98; Dahan, *Les intellectuels chrétiens,* 169–72. For an example from late antiquity, see the sixth-century *La vie ancienne de Saint Syméon Stylite le jeune (521–592),* ed. and trans. Paul Van den Ven (Brussels, 1970), 2:205 (sec. 208).

39. Harvey Goldberg, "The Mimuna and the Minority Status of Moroccan Jews," *Ethnology* 17 (1978), 75–87.

40. Tritton, *Caliphs and Their Non-Muslim Subjects,* 108–9.

41. Benjamin of Tudela, *The Itinerary of Benjamin of Tudela,* ed. and trans. Marcus N. Adler (London, 1907), 43–45 (Hebrew), 43–45 (English, slightly altered here).

42. Ibid., 48–49 (Hebrew), 51 (English).

43. *Sibbuv R. Petachiah* [The Tour of Rabbi Petaḥiah of Regensburg], ed. L. Grünhut (Frankfurt am Main, 1905), 13–15.

44. Ibid., 17f., 20.

45. Meshullam of Volterra, *Massa' Meshullam mi-voltera,* ed. A. Yaari (Jerusalem, 1948), 69 (tomb of the Patriarchs at Hebron), 71 (Rachel's tomb), 73 (Absalom's tomb), 75 (burial caves of mishnaic sages around Jerusalem); English trans. in Elkan Nathan Adler, *Jewish Travellers* (repr., New York, 1966), 185, 188–89, 191–92, 193f.

Chapter Nine
Interreligious Polemics

1. Blumenkranz, "Augustin et les juifs, Augustin et le judaïsme," 231–32; Amos Funkenstein, "Anti-Jewish Propaganda: Pagan, Christian and Modern," *Jerusalem Quarterly,* no. 19 (Spring 1981), 63–64; and the sources cited in Chap. 2, n. 17 of this book.

2. Langmuir, *Toward a Definition of Antisemitism,* 58; Ruether, *Faith and Fratricide,* 181.

3. Williams, *Adversus Judaeos.* For a survey of the most important themes of this polemic, see Ruether, *Faith and Fratricide,* 117–65.

4. Schreckenberg, *Die christlichen Adversus-Judaeos Texte und ihr literarisches und historisches Umfeld (1.–11. Jh.); Die christlichen Adversus-Judaeos Texte (11.–13. Jh.), mit einer Ikonographie des Judenthemas bis zum 4. Laterankonzil* (Frankfurt am Main, 1988).

5. Williams, *Adversus Judaeos,* 3–13.

6. St. Augustine, "In Answer to the Jews," 392–93.

7. David Berger, *The Jewish-Christian Debate in the High Middle Ages* (Philadelphia, 1979), 11.

8. On this subject, see Gerson D. Cohen, "Esau as Symbol in Early Medieval Thought," in *Jewish Medieval and Renaissance Studies,* ed. Alexander Altmann (Cambridge, Mass., 1967), 19–48.

9. Ruether, *Faith and Fratricide,* 167–69, gives examples from the early period of Christian-Jewish conflict.

10. Shlomo Eidelberg, trans. and ed., *The Jews and the Crusaders: The Hebrew Chronicles of the First and Second Crusades* (Madison, Wis., 1977), 99. On Christianity as idolatry, see Katz, *Exclusiveness and Tolerance,* 33, 37.

11. Blumenkranz, *Juifs et chrétiens,* 169–71, 258–59.

12. Ch. Merchavia, *Ha-talmud be-re'i ha-natzrut* [The Church versus Talmudic and Midrashic Literature (500–1248)] (Jerusalem, 1970).

13. Erwin I. J. Rosenthal, "Anti-Christian Polemic in Medieval Bible Commentaries," *Journal of Jewish Studies* 11 (1960), 115, 134; and most recently, Avraham Grossman, "The Jewish-Christian Polemic and Jewish Biblical Exegesis in Twelfth-Century France (On the Attitude of R. Joseph Qara to Polemic)" (Hebrew), *Zion* 51 (1986), 29–60, which cites other important studies (aside from that of Rosenthal), including E. Touitou, "The Exegetical Method of Rashbam in the Light of the Historical Reality of His Time" (Hebrew), in *'Iyyunim be-sifrut ḥazal ba-miqra uve-toledot yisrael* [Studies in Rabbinic Literature, Bible, and Jewish History], ed. Y. D. Gilat et al. (Ramat-Gan, 1982), 48–74; Sarah Kamin, "The Polemic against Allegory in the Commentary of R. Joseph Bekhor Shor" (Hebrew), in *Meḥqerei yerushalayim be-maḥshevet yisrael* [Jerusalem Studies in Jewish Thought] 3 (1983–84), 367–92; and, idem, "Rashi's Commentary on the Song of Songs and Jewish-Christian Polemic" (Hebrew), in *Shenaton la-miqra ule-ḥeqer ha-mizraḥ ha-qadmon* 7–8 (1983–84), 218–48.

14. Judah Rosenthal, "Anti-Christian Polemic in Rashi's Bible Commentary" (Hebrew), in *Meḥqarim u-meqorot* (Jerusalem, 1967), 1:106, 108; and the second article by Sarah Kamin cited in the preceding note.

15. Daniel J. Lasker, *Jewish Philosophical Polemics against Christianity in the Middle Ages* (New York, 1977), 13–20.

16. Joseph Kimḥi, *The Book of the Covenant,* trans. Frank Talmage (Toronto, 1972), 43–45.

17. Ibid., 36–37.

18. Ibid., 33–35.

19. Jacob ben Reuven, *Milḥamot ha-shem,* ed. J. Rosenthal (Jerusalem, 1963), 141. Jacob singled out the Gospel of Matthew.

20. Berger, *Jewish-Christian Debate,* 36.

21. Ibid., 89–90.

22. This is a goal of both the Christian and the Jew in the Latin disputation written by Gilbert Crispin, Abbot of Westminster, at the end of the eleventh century. *Gisleberti Crispini disputation iudei et christiani,* ed. B. Blumenkranz, *Stromata Patristica et Mediaevalia* (Utrecht, 1956), vol. 3; compare Blumenkranz, *Juifs et chrétiens,* index s.v.; and his English essay, "The Roman Church and the Jews," in Roth, ed., *Dark Ages,* 89–94, 97.

23. Blumenkranz, *Juifs et chrétiens,* esp. part 3, "La polémique judéo-chrétienne."

24. Ibid., 239.

25. Dahan, *Les intellectuels chrétiens,* esp. part 3, "La rencontre."

26. Ibid., part 4, "La affrontement"; Cohen, *The Friars and the Jews;* Chazan, *Daggers of Faith.* Although Chazan disagrees with Cohen on the latter's fundamental thesis (that the thirteenth century brought a reversal of the Augustinian recognition of the legitimacy of Judaism's existence within Christendom), he is consistent with Cohen in seeing an escalation of Christian assault on Judaism in the thirteenth century.

27. Amos Funkenstein, "Changes in the Pattern of Christian anti-Jewish Polemic in the Twelfth Century" (Hebrew), *Zion* 33 (1968), 137–41; idem, "Basic Types of Christian Anti-Jewish Polemics," *Viator* 2 (1971), 379–81; Jeremy Cohen, "Scholarship and Intolerance in the Medieval Academy: The Study and Evaluation of Judaism in European Christendom," *American Historical Review* 91 (1986), 599–613 (Cohen's article repr. in his *Essential Papers,* 310ff.); Merchavia, *Ha-talmud be-re'i ha-natzrut.*

28. For an introduction to, and translated excerpts from, the three, see Hyam Maccoby, ed. and trans., *Judaism on Trial: Jewish-Christian Disputations in the Middle Ages* (East Rutherford, N.J., 1982).

29. Moshe Perlmann, "The Medieval Polemics between Islam and Judaism," in *Religion in a Religious Age,* ed. S. D. Goitein (Cambridge, Mass., 1974), 103–38, contains a survey of Islamic polemics against Judaism. An older study, focusing on Islamic treatment of the Bible, is Hartwig Hirchfeld, "Mohammedan Criticism of the Bible, *Jewish Quarterly Revew,* o.s., 13 (1900–1901), 222–40. The still standard bibliographical introduction to the subject is Moritz Steinschneider, *Polemische und apologetische Literatur in arabischer Sprache zwischen Muslimen, Christen und Juden* (Leipzig, 1877). See also, Hava Lazarus-Yafeh, *Intertwined Worlds: Medieval Islam and Bible Criticism* (Princeton, N.J., 1992).

These works do not present the comparative perspective attempted in the present chapter. An essay that does so, concisely and suggestively, is Amos Funkenstein's "Juden, Christen und Muslime: Religiöse Polemik im Mittelalter," in *Die Juden in der europäischen Geschichte* (Munich, 1992), 33–49, which came into my hands while I was working on the copyedited manuscript of my book. Funkenstein makes observations that are consistent with ideas that I had developed when researching and writing Chap. 9.

30. Sura 5:82. The verse is treated variously by different scholars, reflecting the myth-countermyth debate. For instance, Norman Stillman writes regarding the first part of the verse: "The Jews had come to be considered the number-one opponents of the early Muslim community along with the pagans who until now had been the sole enemy. The adversary relationship was, so to speak, enshrined for all time in holy writ"; Norman A. Stillman, "Traditional Islamic Attitudes toward Jews and Judaism," in *The Solomon Goldman Lectures,* ed. Nathaniel Stampfer (Chicago, 1985), 4:78. Tawfīq Sulṭān Yuzbakī adduces the *second* part of Sura 5:82 to show Islam's friendship toward the Christians, but he conveniently omits the *first,* condemning the Jews; Yuzbakī, *Ta'rīkh ahl al-dhimma fi'l-ʿIrāq (12–247 A.H.),* 110. James Kritzeck observes that the Christians' initial advantage over

Judaism, expressed in Sura 5:82, "was short-lived. No symbiosis of the Jewish-Moslem type was possible so long as the most powerful resistance on the frontiers of what the Moslems termed the 'territory of warfare' . . . came from Christians, and that situation was never to change. Moreover, the Islamic conquest had been more disastrous to Christendom than to Judaism in that immense numbers of Christians had become Moslems. Indeed the lines following the passage [i.e., verse 83] . . . suggest that Christians were viewed more kindly than Jews or pagans because so many of them apostatized more readily"; Kritzeck, *Sons of Abraham: Jews, Christians and Moslems,* 57–58. Verse 83 of Sura 5 continues: "When they listen to that which hath been revealed unto the messenger, thou seest their eyes overflow with tears because of their recognition of the Truth. They say: Our Lord, we believe. Inscribe us among the witnesses." For some twentieth-century Islamic fundamentalists, Sura 5:82 serves as a favorite prooftext of allegedly eternal Jewish (and Zionist) enmity toward Islam, which, in turn, is considered part of a general, Western anti-Islamic antipathy; Reuven Paz, "The Stance of the Radical Islamic Movement on the Jews and Zionism in Our Time" (Hebrew), in *Islam ve-shalom: gishot islamiyyot le-shalom ba-ʿolam ha-ʿaravi ben zemaneinu* [Islam and Peace: Islamic Approaches to Peace in the Contemporary Arab World] (Givat Haviva, 1992), 48.

31. "And lo! there is a party of them who distort the Scripture with their tongues, that ye may think what they say is from the Scripture, when it is not from the Scripture. And they say: It is from Allah, when it is not from Allah; and they speak a lie concerning Allah knowingly."

32. The largely interchangeable Arabic terms are *taḥrīf, taqhyīr,* and *tabdīl.*

33. See Lazarus-Yafeh, *Intertwined Worlds,* chap. 3, on the metamorphosis of the polemical motif regarding Ezra.

34. Ibid., 19–35.

35. The very term *Old Testament* is inappropriate in the Muslim context.

36. William Adler, "The Jews as Falsifiers: Charges of Tendentious Emendation in Anti-Jewish Christian Polemic," in *Translation of Scripture,* Proceedings of a Conference at the Annenberg Research Institute, May 15–16, 1989 (*Jewish Quarterly Review* suppl.) (Philadelphia, 1990), 1–27. I am grateful to Martha Himmelfarb for bringing this article to my attention.

37. Ibid., 16f.

38. Despite its promising title, the article, "Forgery and Abrogation of the Torah: A Theme in Muslim and Christian Polemic in Spain" by Norman Roth (*Proceedings of the American Academy for Jewish Research* 54 [1987], 203–36) does not delve deeply into the comparison.

39. The theme continues in 15:26: "But when your Advocate has come, whom I will send you from the Father . . . he will bear witness to me." The translation "Advocate" for the enigmatic word *paraklētos* is in *The New English Bible.*

40. Ibn Qayyim al-Jawziyya, *Hidāyat al-ḥayārā fī ajwibat al-yahūd wa'l-naṣārā,* ed. Aḥmad Ḥijāzī Aḥmad Al-Saqqā (Cairo, 1979), 118, 119. Compare Lazarus-Yafeh, *Intertwined Worlds,* 77–78.

41. ʿAlī ibn Rabban al-Ṭabarī, *The Book of Religion and Empire,* trans. A. Mingana (Manchester, 1922), 3; Arabic: *Kitāb al-dīn wa'l-dawla* (Tunis, [1973]), 12–13.

42. *Book of Religion and Empire,* 15–18; *Kitāb al-dīn wa'l-dawla,* 23.

43. Wadi Z. Haddad, "Continuity and Change in Religious Adherence: Ninth-

Century Baghdad," in *Conversion and Continuity: Indigenous Christian Communities in Islamic Lands, Eighth to Eighteenth Centuries,* ed. Gervers and Bikhazi, 47–48.

44. "It would seem that to a very great, decisive measure, Islamic polemic directed against Jews and Judaism originated from and was fed by Christian sources, partly pre-Islamic, flowing into the Islamic milieu with the mass conversion of Christians." Perlmann, "Medieval Polemics," 106; compare Lewis, *Jews of Islam,* p. 86. For a discussion of other pre- and non-Islamic sources of Islamic polemics against Judaism and Christianity, see Lazarus-Yafeh, *Intertwined Worlds,* 130–35.

45. Ibn al-Qayyim, *Hidayāt al-ḥayārā,* 114.

46. Reuven Firestone, *Journeys in Holy Lands: The Evolution of the Abraham-Ishmael Legends in Islamic Exegesis* (Albany, N.Y., 1990), 76–79. Compare Aviva Schussman, "Abraham's Visits to Ishmael: The Jewish Origin and Orientation" (Hebrew), *Tarbiz* 49 (1980), 325–45. A close parallel appears in chap. 30 of the eighth-century midrash *Pirkei de Rabbi Eliezer.* See *Pirke de Rabbi Eliezer,* trans. Gerald Friedlander (1916; repr., New York, 1970), 218–19.

47. ʿAlī Ṭabarī, *Book of Religion and Empire,* 80–83 (excerpt found on 82–83); *Kitāb al-dīn wa'l-dawla,* 76–77.

48. Ibn al-Qayyim, *Hidāyat al-ḥayārā,* 115.

49. Samau'al al-Maghribī, *Ifḥām al-yahūd,* ed. and trans. Moshe Perlmann, *Proceedings of the American Academy for Jewish Research* 32 (1964), 46–47.

50. Hava Lazarus-Yafeh, "The Contribution of a Jewish Convert from Morocco to the Muslim Polemic against the Jews and Judaism" (Hebrew), *Peʿamim* 42 (1990), 86–87; E. Strauss, "Methods of Islamic Polemics" (Hebrew), in *Sefer ha-zikkaron le-veit ha-midrash la-rabbanim be-vina* [Memorial Volume for the Vienna Rabbinical Seminary] (Jerusalem, 1946), 189ff.

51. ʿAlī Ṭabarī, *Book of Religion and Empire,* 140–41; *Kitāb al-dīn wa'l-dawla,* 125.

52. Ibn al-Qayyim, *Hidāyat al-ḥayārā,* 109–12.

53. Aḥmad ibn Idrīs al-Qarāfī, *Al-ajwiba al-fākhira ʿan al-as'ila al-fājira,* printed in the margins of ʿAbd al-Raḥman Bachajī Zādeh, *Al-fāriq bayn al-makhlūq wa'l-khāliq* (Cairo, n.d.), 238–39.

54. ʿAlī Ṭabarī, *Book of Religion and Empire,* 86–87; *Kitāb al-dīn wa'l-dawla,* 81.

55. Firestone, *Journeys in Holy Lands.*

56. The same fourteenth-century scholar whose *Aḥkām ahl al-dhimma* is frequently cited in this book.

57. Ibn al-Qayyim, *Hidāyat al-ḥayārā,* 249–59 (Judaism), 260–99 (Christianity).

58. Moshe Perlmann, "Ibn Qayyim and Samau'al al-Maghribī," *Journal of Jewish Bibliography* 3 (1942), 71–74.

59. Ibn al-Qayyim, *Hidāyat al-ḥayārā,* 260.

60. Ibid., 263.

61. See Sidney H. Griffith, "Anastasios of Sinai, the *Hodegos,* and the Muslims," *Greek Orthodox Theological Review* 32 (1987), 341–58, apparently the first Christian writer—about a half-century before the better-known Christian apologist against Islam, John of Damascus (d. 749?)—to respond polemically (albeit in passing) to Muslim critique of Christianity. See also, *Anti-Christian Polemic in Early Islam: Abū ʿĪsā al-Warrāq's "Against the Trinity,"* ed. and trans. David Thomas (Cambridge, 1992), a text by an early ninth-century Shiite scholar. On John of

Damascus and his critique of Islam, see Daniel J. Sahas, *John of Damascus: The "Heresy of the Ishmaelites"* (Leiden, 1972).

62. Sidney H. Griffith, "Theodore Abū Qurrah's Arabic Tract on the Christian Practice of Venerating Images," *Journal of the American Oriental Society* 105 (1985), 53–73; idem, "Theodore Abū Qurrah: The Intellectual Profile of an Arab Christian Writer of the First Abbasid Century," Annual Lecture of the Irene Holmos Chair of Arabic Literature, Tel Aviv University (Tel Aviv, 1992), with much useful bibliography on the general subject of Muslim-Christian interreligious polemics.

63. Wadi Z. Haddad, "Continuity and Change in Religious Adherence: Ninth-Century Baghdad," 35–47.

64. Thomas F. Michel, ed. and trans., *A Muslim Theologian's Response to Christianity: Ibn Taymiyya's* Al-Jawāb al-Ṣaḥīḥ, 143 in the translation.

65. A fragment from a previously unknown Judaeo-Arabic apologetic work found in the Geniza tells of a tense encounter between Jews and Muslims at one of the weekly *majlises* (interconfessional discussions of religion) at the court of the ex-Jewish Fatimid Vizier, Yaʿqūb ibn Killis (d. 991). See Cohen and Somekh, "In the Court of Yaʿqūb ibn Killis: A Fragment from the Cairo Geniza." If and when additional folios from this book are found, it may be possible to reconstruct a relatively early exemplum of Jewish-Muslim disputation. For now, see Sasson Somekh, "Fragments of a Polemical Work from the Cairo Geniza" (Hebrew), in *Sefer Shivṭiel: Meḥqarim ba-lashon ha-ʿivrit uve-masorot ha-ʿedot* [Shivtiel Book: Studies in the Hebrew Language and in the Linguistic Traditions of the Jewish Communities], ed. Isaac Gluska and Tzemah Kessar (Ramat Gan and Tel Aviv, 1992), 141–59, which appends a fragment unknown to us when the above-mentioned article was written.

66. "Timothy's Apology for Christianity," trans. A. Mingana, *Woodbrooke Studies* (Cambridge, 1928), 2:27–29; compare Hans Putman, *L'Église et l'Islam sous Timothée I* (780–823) (Beirut, 1975), 231–32.

67. Lewis, *Jews of Islam,* 85–86.

68. Kraemer, *Humanism in the Renaissance of Islam,* 55–60.

69. Aryeh Grabois, "The *Hebraica Veritas* and Jewish-Christian Intellectual Relations in the Twelfth Century," *Speculum* 50 (1975), 613–34.

70. Compare Ivan G. Marcus, "Hierarchies, Religious Boundaries and Jewish Spirituality in Medieval Germany," *Jewish History* 1 (1986), 7. Marcus applies the work of Natalie Zemon Davis to the Jewish case. See Davis, "The Rites of Violence," in her *Society and Culture in Early Modern France* (Stanford, Calif., 1975), 152–87.

71. Katz, *Exclusiveness and Tolerance,* 90.

72. Daniel J. Lasker, "The Jewish Critique of Christianity under Islam in the Middle Ages," *Proceedings of the American Academy for Jewish Research* 57 (1990–91), 121–49.

73. Ora Limor, "Religious Disputation in Mediterranean Ports" (Hebrew), *Peʿamim* 45 (Autumn 1990), 32–44. Limor's evidence is for the twelfth century and afterward.

74. Steinschneider, *Polemische und apologetische Literatur,* 302–3.

75. Jews punned on the word *Qur'an,* calling it in Hebrew "the book of *qalon* [disgrace]."

76. In the "shorter commentary" (*perush qatzar*) on Exodus, *Sefer Ibn Ezra . . . le-sefer shemot,* ed. Judah Fleischer (Vienna, 1926), 2. "As for those who say, concerning the king of Ishmael, that the numerical value of *bi-me'od me'od* is the same as his name, what do they have to say about the current verse, which refers to Israel? Moreover, far be it for the prophet [Moses] to speak in numerical code [*gemaṭron*] or in allusions [*remizot*]." I am grateful to Hava Lazarus-Yafeh for bringing this reference to my attention. The comment of Ibn Ezra on Exodus 3:7 does not appear in the standard editions of the *Miqra'ot gedolot,* nor in A. Weiser's edition of Ibn Ezra's Torah commentary (Jerusalem, 1974).

77. "The Lord came from Sinai, He shone upon them from Seir, He appeared from Mount Paran."

78. They were disqualified from accepting the Torah when God offered it, for the Torah commands, "Thou shall not steal." Sifre on Deuteronomy, para. 343, ed. L. Finkelstein (repr., New York, 1969), 395–96.

79. It is noteworthy that the treatment of Ishmael in rabbinic literature is not entirely negative, unlike the rabbis' hostile stance against "evil" Edom/Rome/Christendom. See David J. Zucker, "Conflicting Conclusions: The Hatred of Isaac and Ishmael," *Judaism* 39, no. 1 (Winter 1990), 37–46.

80. See Saadya Gaon's and Ibn Ezra's commentaries on Daniel 7 in the standard Hebrew Bible with commentaries [*Miqra'ot gedolot*]. Compare also, Yisrael Levin, *Avraham ibn Ezra: ḥayyav ve-shirato* [Abraham ibn Ezra: His Life and Poetry] (Tel Aviv, 1969), 33–34.

81. "From Sinai" is exactly like "at Sinai," as is "from Seir."

82. Hebrew (*Sinai*), Latin (*Seir,* another name for Edom or for Rome), Arabic (*Paran*), and Aramaic (*Ribeboth Qodesh*).

83. Genesis 21:12. Moshe Zucker, ed., *Saadya's Commentary on Genesis* (Hebrew) (New York, 1984), 156 (Arabic), 412–22 (Hebrew trans.).

84. Morris Goldstein, *Jesus in the Jewish Tradition* (New York, 1950), 177–82.

85. "Saadya Gaon on Islam and Christianity," paper presented at "The Jews of Medieval Islam," a conference at University College, London, June 24–25, 1992. Lasker takes issue with Eliezer Schlossberg, "Concepts and Methods in the Commentary of R. Saadya Gaon on the Book of Daniel" (Hebrew) (Ph.D. diss., Bar-Ilan University, 1988), which deals with the polemic against Islam in Saadya's writings (see idem, "R. Saadia Gaon's Attitude toward Islam" [Hebrew], *Daat: A Journal of Jewish Philosophy and Kabbalah* 25 [1990], 21–51). Schlossberg finds polemical pronouncements on Islam in many of the Gaon's writings but principally in *Beliefs and Opinions,* and not in the Book of Daniel itself. Lasker proposes three possible reasons for Saadya's prioritization: (1) circumspection—fear that Jewish apostates to Islam might inform on him; (2) the differentiation between Judaism and Christianity was greater than that between Judaism and Islam; (3) Jewish feeling of "being at home" among Muslims removed the motive to attack Islam.

86. Hava Lazarus-Yafeh takes this for granted. *Intertwined Worlds,* 37.

87. Saadia Gaon, *The Book of Beliefs and Opinions,* trans. Samuel Rosenblatt (New Haven, Conn., 1948), 157–73; Haggai Ben-Shammai, "The Attitude of Some Early Karaites towards Islam," in *Studies in Medieval Jewish History and Literature II,* ed. I. Twersky (Cambridge, Mass., 1984), 7–8; Rippin, "Sa'adya Gaon and Genesis 22: Aspects of Jewish-Muslim Interaction and Polemic," 40–42;

Schlossberg, "Concepts and Methods in the Commentary of R. Saadia Gaon on the Book of Daniel," chap. 6.

88. Ben-Shammai, "Attitude of Some Early Karaites," 3–40.

89. For instance, determining the date of the new moon by actual sighting, barefooted ambulation of the synagogue, and Islamic-like prostrations during prayer.

90. *Kuzari,* part 2, sec. 14. Critical edition of the Judaeo-Arabic text, *Kitāb al-radd wa'l-dalīl fī'l-dīn al-dhalīl,* ed. D. S. Baneth and H. Ben-Shammai (Jerusalem, 1977); English trans. by Hartwig Hirschfeld, *Book of Kuzari* (New York, 1946).

91. The ninth of the thirteen articles, which appear in the introduction to the chapter known as *Ḥeleq,* chap. 10 of tractate Sanhedrin. Compare Eliezer Schlossberg, "The Attitude of Maimonides toward Islam" (Hebrew), *Peʿamim* 42 (1990), 50ff. I leave aside the subject of Maimonides as first formulator of a Jewish dogma, about which there are good studies—for instance, by Arthur Hyman, "Maimonides' 'Thirteen Principles,'" in *Jewish Medieval and Renaissance Studies,* ed. Alexander Altmann (Cambridge, Mass., 1967), 119–44; and by Menachem Kellner, *Dogma in Medieval Jewish Thought from Maimonides to Abravanel* (Oxford, 1986), chap. 1.

92. See Reuben Ahroni, "From *Bustān al-ʿuqūl* to *Qiṣat al-baṭūl:* Some Aspects of Jewish-Muslim Religious Polemics in Yemen," *Hebrew Union College Annual* 52 (1981), 311–30. For discussion of Maimonides' work and its context, see Chap. 10 in this book.

93. Moses ben Maimon, *Iggerot,* ed. and trans. into Hebrew by Kafiḥ, 32, 36–37; English trans., Halkin, *Crisis and Leadership: Epistles of Maimonides,* 107, 110–12. The Halkin translation (111) spells the name, "Omar." Michael Cook called to my attention that it must be ʿAmr (comprised of the same three consonants as ʿUmar), the name traditionally paired with Zeid (Zayd) in Islamic *fatwās.* They are analogous to "Reuben and Simeon," who, in Jewish responsa, replace the real names of the parties (like "A and B" in English legal texts). See also the note of Kafiḥ, p. 36, n. 92. In Arabic, ʿUmar and ʿAmr are distinguished orthographically by an enclitic *waw* at the end of the consonants *ʿ-m-r,* but in a Judaeo-Arabic manuscript, as Michael Cook observes, this could easily have been omitted or dropped.

94. Moses ben Maimon, *Iggerot,* ed. and trans. into Hebrew by Kafiḥ, 53; English trans. by Halkin, *Crisis and Leadership: Epistles of Maimonides,* 126. On the marginal role of messianism in Islam, see Hava Lazarus-Yafeh, *Some Religious Aspects of Islam* (Leiden, 1981), chap. 4, "Is There a Concept of Redemption in Islam?" Maimonides singles out for ridicule the Christian trinitarian reading of Deuteronomy 6:4, "Hear O Israel, the Lord is our God, the Lord is one," at the beginning of his "Essay on Resurrection," written in 1191 (Halkin trans., 211).

95. Abraham's discussion of the birth of Ishmael (chap. 17) is not available, since that section of his commentary on Genesis has not been found.

96. Abraham ben Moses ben Maimon, *Commentary on Genesis and Exodus,* ed. and trans. into Hebrew by E. Wiesenberg (London, 1959), 42–43.

97. Ibid., 42–45.

98. Ibid., 64–65.

99. Ibid., 202–5.

100. See Baron, *Social and Religious History of the Jews,* 5:275–83; Gerson D. Cohen, ed. and trans., *Sefer ha-Qabbalah* [The Book of Tradition] (Philadelphia, 1967), xliii–l (in twelfth-century Spain); Samuel A. Poznanski, "The Anti-Karaite Writings of Saadiah Gaon," repr. in Philip Birnbaum, ed., *Karaite Studies* (New York, 1971), 89–127 (orig. pub. 1898 in *Jewish Quarterly Review*); Jacob Mann, "A Polemical Work against Karaite and Other Sectaries," *Jewish Quarterly Review* 12 (1921–22), 123–50.

101. Discovered in a manuscript and given the title *Ma'amar ʿal yishmaʿel* by Joseph Perles when publishing it in the appendix to his *R. Salomo b. Abraham b. Adereth: Sein Leben und seine Schriften* (Breslau, 1863).

102. Simon b. Tzemaḥ Duran, *Qeshet u-magen* (photographic reproduction of Livorno, 1763 ed.; Jerusalem, 1970), fols. 2a–3b.

103. Ibid., fols. 13b–14a.

104. Ibid., fol. 19a.

105. For other explanations of the comparative lack of Jewish response to Islamic polemics, see Lazarus-Yafeh, *Intertwined Worlds,* 7–8.

Chapter Ten
Persecution, Response, and Collective Memory

1. Elton, in *Persecution and Toleration: Papers Read at the Twenty-Second Summer Meeting and the Twenty-Third Winter Meeting of the Ecclesiastical History Society,* xiii.

2. For instance, the Christian ritual murder accusation and related blood libel.

3. The literature on Jewish persecution in Christendom is vast. In this chapter, I will devote more attention to the less well-known story of persecution of Jews in Islamic lands—and response to persecution—comparing these to the situation in Christian lands.

4. *Encyclopaedia of Islam,* 2d ed., s.v. "Dhimma," 229.

5. A chapter of Tritton's *Caliphs and Their Non-Muslim Subjects,* 127–36.

6. Goitein, *A Mediterranean Society,* 2:278–83 (quotation appears on 283).

7. They were:

When a pious ruler enforced the "proper subordination of the unbeliever" as part of a general effort to restore orthodoxy in the Islamic community.

When a messianic, zealous Muslim regime, such as the Almohads, during a time of upheaval, extended its campaign against deviation to forcing the *dhimmīs,* against the rule of the *sharīʿa,* to choose between Islam and the sword.

When a ruler, in need of money, tightened the regimen of "humiliation" in expectation that the non-Muslims would pay to have it relaxed.

When non-Muslims were oppressed on suspicion of colluding with some external enemy of Islam, especially in the period beginning with the Crusades and the Mongol invasions.

When, particularly in the late Middle Ages, one non-Muslim minority tried to turn an Ottoman ruler against another non-Muslim group.

See Lewis, *Jews of Islam,* 45–57.

8. Ibid., 53. This is well expressed in an anecdote included in Ibn Qayyim al-Jawziyya's compilation of the laws of the *dhimma,* in the chapter on the exclusion of *dhimmīs* from positions of authority over Muslims. Caliph ʿUmar ibn ʿAbd al-ʿAzīz

(717–20) writes to his provincial governors: "Put them into the place of lowliness [*dhull*] and humiliation [*ṣaghār*] assigned to them by God." Ibn al-Qayyim, *Aḥkām ahl al-dhimma,* part 1, 213.

9. This passage from Arabic chronicles is cited in many anthologies, for example, Stillman, *Jews of Arab Lands,* 167–68, from which the present citation is taken. See also, Lewis, *Jews of Islam,* 2:224–26.

10. The ban on holding office, not in the Pact of ʿUmar, as noted in Chap. 4, is thought to have been introduced by Caliph ʿUmar ibn ʿAbd al-ʿAzīz.

11. Lewis, *Jews of Islam,* 49. Some Christian sources relate Mutawakkil's stern decree and other persecutory acts against the Christians of the time to the fall from grace of the caliph's Christian court physician, Bukhtīshūʿ. See Fiey, *Chrétiens syriaques sous les abbasides,* 93–94, who notes, however, that Muslim sources date Bukhtīshūʿ's fall somewhat later than 850.

12. Raoul (Radulphus) Glaber (ca. 985–ca. 1047), a contemporaneous Latin historian, reports that, in France and Italy, Jews were blamed for instigating al-Ḥākim's anti-Christian act and that many were expelled, killed, or forcibly converted, and some committed suicide. Blumenkranz, *Juifs et chrétiens,* 380–81.

13. A representative account by a medieval chronicler is translated in Lewis, *Islam,* 1:46–59: "It is said that he was afflicted with a dryness in his brain and that this was the cause of his many contradictions" (59). On the al-Ḥākim episode, see Goitein, *A Mediterranean Society,* index s.v. "al-Ḥākim," and Moshe Gil, *A History of Palestine, 634–1099,* trans. Ethel Broido (Cambridge, 1992), 370–81 (hereafter, Gil, *Palestine* [English]).

14. Joseph ibn Nagrela was accused of betraying the state.

15. An English translation of the long passage appears in Lewis, *Islam,* 1:123–34. The passage cited here is found on 133–34.

16. Bernard Lewis, "An Anti-Jewish Ode: The Qasida of Abu Ishaq against Joseph ibn Nagrella," in *Salo Wittmayer Baron Jubilee Volume,* ed. Saul Lieberman in association with Arthur Hyman (Jerusalem, 1975), English section, 657–68; Moshe Perlmann, "Eleventh-Century Andalusian Authors on the Jews of Granada," *Proceedings of the American Academy for Jewish Research* 19 (1948–49), 269–90; Stillman, *Jews of Arab Lands,* 214–16, repr. trans. by Bernard Lewis.

17. Lewis, *Jews of Islam,* 45: "[I]n striking contrast to the anti-Semitism of Christendom, Abū Isḥāq [the poet's name] even in his outrage does not refuse Jews the right to life, livelihood, and the practice of their religion. As a jurist he is aware that these rights are guaranteed by the Holy Law and incorporated in the *dhimma,* which is a binding legal contract."

18. H. Z. Hirschberg, *A History of the Jews in North Africa* (Leiden, 1974), 1:108; also cited in Bat Ye'or, *The Dhimmi,* 61.

19. Tritton, *Caliphs and Their Non-Muslim Subjects,* 56. See also, Baron, *Social and Religious History of the Jews,* 3:136 (with some inaccuracies, inc. date, given by Tritton as 573 A.H./1177–78).

20. An anti-Jewish riot that I have not seen mentioned in the secondary literature about the Jews of Islam occurred in the year 1135, in Cordova, during the Almoravid period in Spain, when warfare between Islam and militant, crusading Christendom raised fears and passions in the beleagured Muslim population. The sentence is in Ibn al-Qaṭṭān's (mid-thirteenth-century) historical account of the

Almoravid-Almohade period, in an entry for the year 529 (1134–35): "A Jew killed a Muslim, whereupon the Muslims overcame the Jews, plundering their possessions and destroying their residences." Ibn al-Qaṭṭān, *Juz' min kitāb naẓm al-jumān,* ed. Maḥmūd ʿAlī Makkī (Rabat, n.d.), 217. A parallel elaborates somewhat: "In that year, during Rajab [April 17–May 16, 1135], also in Cordova, a mob attacked the Jews—God curse them—when a dead body was found in their midst. They stormed their houses, plundered their possessions, and killed a number of them." Ibn ʿIdhārī [d. ca. 1312], *Al-bayān al-mughrib fī akhbār al-andalus wa'l-maghrib.* A. Huici-Miranda, "Un fragmento inédito de Ibn ʿIḍārī sobre los almorávides," *Hespéris Tamuda* 2 (1961), 101.

21. The Almohad persecution is covered in detail in Hirschberg, *A History of the Jews in North Africa,* 1:123–39.

22. The Almohads professed, for example, the absolute unity of God and a morality based on scriptural sources of Islamic law.

23. David Corcos-Abulafia, "The Attitude of the Almohade Rulers toward the Jews" (Hebrew), *Zion* 32 (1967), 137–60; repr. in his *Studies in the History of the Jews of Morocco* (Jerusalem, 1976), 319–42. Also see the comments of Menahem Ben-Sasson, "On the Jewish Identity of Forced Converts: A Study of Forced Conversion in the Almohad Period" (Hebrew), *Peʿamim* 42 (1990), 19, n. 5.

24. Another wave of persecution and forced conversion in Yemen at the end of the twelfth century—this time under the dominant Shiite rulers—evidently is described in certain Geniza letters discovered by Goitein, *Letters of Medieval Jewish Traders,* 212, although Goitein was inclined to connect the persecution with the events that underlay Maimonides' "Epistle to Yemen."

25. "You write of the affair of the rebel leader in Yemen, who decreed forced apostasy of the Jews, and compelled all the Jewish inhabitants in all the places he had subdued to desert their religion, just as the Berbers had obliged them to do in the Maghreb [North Africa]. This report has broken our backs. . . . Indeed our hearts are weakened, our minds are confused, and our strength wanes because of the dire misfortunes that have come upon us in the form of the religious persecution in the two ends of the world, East and West." Moses ben Maimon, *Iggerot,* ed. and trans. into Hebrew by Kafiḥ, 17–18; English trans. by Halkin, *Crisis and Leadership: Epistles of Maimonides,* 95.

26. Lewis, *Jews of Islam,* 102–3.

27. Shalom b. Saʿadya Gamliel, *Pequdei teiman* [The Jizya-Poll Tax in Yemen], ed. Mishael Maswari Caspi (Jerusalem, 1982), 34.

28. Sometimes stated in the secondary literature, this is unfounded. Ibn Daud's statement that Jews were "compelled to wander from their homes" does not refer to expulsion. *Sefer ha-Qabbalah,* 87–88 (English). The Hebrew, *ve-yatze'u be-galut mi-mekomotam* (literally, "they went into exile from their homes [or localities]"), misrepresented in the English edition of Hirschberg's *A History of the Jews in North Africa* 1:125 ("they were exiled from their localities"), clearly means voluntary departure to escape death or forced conversion. This is precisely what Maimonides urges as the desirable strategy for besieged Jews in his "Epistle on Apostasy," a recommendation that is incomprehensible if the Jews had been expelled by decree.

29. Fattal, *Le statut,* 83. See also, Seth Ward, "A Fragment from an Unknown Work by al-Ṭabarī on the Tradition 'Expel the Jews and Christians from the

Arabian Peninsula [and the Lands of Islam],'" *Bulletin of the School of Oriental and African Studies,* 53 (1990), 407–20. (Ward notes that the ascription to al-Ṭabarī is uncertain.) And the section in Ibn al-Qayyim, *Aḥkām ahl al-dhimma,* part 1, 175–91, on "places which the *dhimmīs* are forbidden to enter or remain therein," including the extravagant view of Abū Ḥanīfa that they are permitted to enter the holy shrine of the Kaʿba in Mecca (188).

30. Baron, *Social and Religious History of the Jews,* 11:chap. 50; and Baron's "Medieval Nationalism and Jewish Serfdom."

31. Especially in the case of the Norman and Anglo-Saxon populations of England.

32. "Attempts by European rulers to develop homogeneous populations have resulted in the persecution and the mass expulsion of minority groups." Tamotsu Shibutani and Kian M. Kwan, *Ethnic Stratification: A Comparative Approach* (New York, 1965), 325–26.

33. Vociferously, for example, by Guido Kisch, *Jews in Medieval Germany,* 307–16, 335–41. Kisch prefers to explain the deterioration of Jewish life in Christendom primarily in terms of religious hostility. On the other hand, independently of Baron, Robert S. Lopez, referring to the repression of "nonconformists" in medieval society—namely, heretics and Jews—writes: "[T]he most basic cause of intolerance is probably the one of which people are least conscious—incipient nationalism. It is less strong with the intellectuals, but it asserts itself both at the top of the social hierarchy and at the bottom of the scale." *The Birth of Europe* (New York, 1967), 353.

34. Although, by "nationalism," Baron does not mean the nationalism characteristic of the nineteenth century.

35. Lewis, *Jews of Islam,* 121–25; Joseph Hacker, "Ottoman Policy toward the Jews and Jewish Attitudes toward the Ottomans during the Fifteenth Century, in *Christians and Jews in the Ottoman Empire: The Functioning of a Plural Society,* ed. Benjamin Braude and Bernard Lewis (New York, 1982), 1:120–21.

36. Moreen, *Iranian Jewry's Hour of Peril and Heroism,* 108–14.

37. Gamliel, *Pequdei teiman,* 45; Yehuda Ratzaby, "The Exile of Mawzaʿ: A Chapter of Yemenite Jewish History" (Hebrew), *Sefunot* 5 (1961), 337–95; idem, "An Expulsion of Jews in the Yemen" (Hebrew), *Zion* 37 (1972), 197–215. Reuben Ahroni, *Yemenite Jewry: Origins, Culture and Literature* (Bloomington, Ind., 1986), 121–35.

38. Philip Ziegler, *The Black Death* (New York, 1969), 96–109; Norman Cohn, *The Pursuit of the Millennium,* rev. expanded ed. (New York, 1970), 138–39.

39. Michael W. Dols, *The Black Death in the Middle East* (Princeton, N.J., 1977), 293–301. The quotation is from 300.

40. Baron, *Social and Religious History of the Jews,* 17:169.

41. R. I. Moore, *The Formation of a Persecuting Society: Power and Deviance in Western Europe, 950–1250* (Oxford, 1987); the quotation is from 88. Moore adds: "Since Jews were in fact better educated, more cultivated and more skillful than their Christian counterparts legend must reduce them below the level of common humanity, filthy in their person and debased in their passions, menacing Christian society from below, requiring the help of the powers of darkness to work evil far beyond their own contemptible capacities" (*Formation,* 151–52). He reiterates this

argument in his "Anti-Semitism and the Birth of Europe." I am not persuaded that this is a satisfactory explanation, especially for northern Europe; for the thesis requires evidence of close-knit relationships between Christians and of highly skilled Jews in the bureaucracies of the state and the church. As Moore concedes, the evidence for Jewish involvement in government in northern Europe is sparse ("Anti-Semitism and the Birth of Europe," 51–52).

42. See Carlo Ginzburg's study, *Ecstasies: Deciphering the Witches' Sabbath,* trans. Raymond Rosenthal, ed. Gregory Elliott (London, 1990), 33–62.

43. Lewis, *Jews of Islam,* 53–54; idem, "Some Observations on the Significance of Heresy in the History of Islam," *Studia Islamica* 1 (1953), 43–63; rev. version, idem, *Islam in History* (New York, 1973), 217–36.

44. Lewis, *Jews of Islam,* 103–4.

45. Louis I. Newman, *Jewish Influence on Christian Reform Movements* (New York, 1925), 303–59.

46. See, for instance, Hillgarth, *Christianity and Paganism,* 12–14, passim.

47. Robert Bonfil, "The Devil and the Jews in the Christian Consciousness of the Middle Ages," in *Antisemitism through the Ages,* 91–92.

48. Quoted in Simon, *Verus Israel,* 216.

49. Quoted in Parkes, *Conflict of the Church and the Synagogue,* 299–300.

50. Bishop Caesarius of Arles, later a saint, lived from 470 to 543. Hillgarth, *Christianity and Paganism,* 37–38 (on the *Life* and the bishop, see 20–21).

51. *Agobardi Lugdunensis Archiepiscopi Epistolae,* ed. E. Duemmler, 185, 196. For the second reference, compare Kenneth Stow, "Agobard of Lyons and the Medieval Concept of the Jew," *Conservative Judaism* 29, no. 1 (1974), 65.

52. Such as the belief that Jews stabbed the eucharistic Host in order to reenact the crucifixion of Christ, or that they murdered Christian children, to withdraw their blood for magical and medicinal purposes. Characteristically, southern France saw little of the blood libel. See Gavin I. Langmuir, "L'absence d'accusation de meurte rituel à l'ouest du Rhône," in *Juifs et judaïsme de Languedoc xiiie–début xive siècle,* 235–49.

53. Trachtenberg, *Devil and the Jews,* 170–87.

54. Roth, "The Mediaeval Conception of the Jew: A New Interpretation," in *Essays and Studies in Memory of Linda R. Miller,* ed. Israel Davidson (New York, 1938), 171–90; the quotation is from 188–89. This essay was selected by Jeremy Cohen for his collection, *Essential Papers on Judaism and Christianity in Conflict: From Late Antiquity to the Reformation,* 298–309.

55. Most recently, in his *History, Religion, and Antisemitism* and *Toward a Definition of Antisemitism.*

56. Langmuir, *History, Religion, and Antisemitism,* 302–3.

57. Langmuir, "Doubt in Christendom," in his *Toward a Definition of Antisemitism,* 100–133; and *History, Religion, and Antisemitism,* chaps. 12, 13. The conviction that the Jews constitute "the great symbol of hidden menaces of all kinds within Christendom" (*History, Religion, and Antisemitism,* 303) did not die out with the massive de-Christianization of Europe that occurred in the nineteenth century. It exhibited itself especially in what Langmuir calls "physiocentric" (as distinguished from "psychocentric") religions. Historically, the worst manifestation of this phenomenon is Nazism, with its irrational Aryan myth ascribing to the Jews

hidden evil characteristics, biological inferiority, and a conspiracy to destroy Western non-Jewish civilization, necessitating and justifying the "Final Solution" (345–46).

58. Called *Shayṭān* or *Iblīs* in Arabic.

59. A Qur'anic passage (58:19) refers to an unnamed people who are the object of God's anger as "the party of Satan" (*ḥizb al-shayṭān*)—taken by commentators as meaning the Jews. The passage says in Arabic: *qaum ghaḍaba allāh ʿalayhim,* "a people with whom God is angry." Jews are regularly called *al-maghḍūb ʿalayhim,* "those who earn God's anger" (based on the first Sura of the Qur'an). Ibn Qayyim al-Jawziyya, *Hidāyat al-ḥayārā,* 32–33.

60. Lewis, *Islam,* 2:165; and Ibn al-Qayyim, *Aḥkām ahl al-dhimma,* part 1, 212.

61. Ibn al-Qayyim, *Aḥkām ahl al-dhimma,* part 2, 744–46. The purpose—consistent with the distinctive dress regulation of the Pact of ʿUmar—was, Ibn al-Qayyim states, to distinguish the inferior non-Muslims from their Muslim superiors. Along the same lines, some versions of the harsh anti-*dhimmī* decree of al-Mutawakkil (850) stipulate that the non-Muslims must affix wooden images of the devil (Shayṭān) to their doors "in order," so explains the tenth-century historian al-Ṭabarī, "to distinguish their houses from those of the Muslims" (Lewis, *Islam,* 2:225 [no. 77]).

62. This, notwithstanding the presence of a Qur'anic motif, that of the "accursed ape" (Sura 2:65 et al.)—apparently derived from pre-Islamic folklore and merged in Christian iconography with the figure of the Devil—which, in post-Qur'anic commentary, became associated with the Jews (and so appears in the inflammatory anti-Jewish poem of 1066 cited above). See Ilse Lichtenstadter, "'And Become Ye Accursed Apes,'" *Jerusalem Studies in Arabic and Islam* 14 (1991), 153–75. Another folkloric theme in Arabic sources depicts the Jews as engaging in witchcraft to harm the Prophet or other members of the nascent Muslim community. Michael Lecker, "The Bewitching of the Prophet Muḥammad by the Jews: A Note a propos ʿAbd al-Malik b. Ḥabīb's *Mukhtaṣar fīl-ṭibb,*" *Al-Qanṭara* 13 (1992), 561–68. But this theme did not have the damaging consequences for Muslim-Jewish relations that its counterpart had in Christendom.

63. Ibn al-Qayyim, *Aḥkām ahl al-dhimma,* part 1, 242–43.

64. The argument by Cutler and Cutler, that Christianity persecuted the Jews of Europe principally because they believed the Jews were allies of the Muslims, fails to convince. See their *Jew as Ally of the Muslim: Medieval Roots of Anti-Semitism.*

65. Martyrdom is rendered *qiddush ha-shem,* "sanctification of the divine name." Suicide might, on occasion, include taking the lives of other family members, lest they fall victim to forced baptism.

66. From the English translation by Shlomo Eidelberg, *The Jews and the Crusaders,* 32. The Hebrew text is available in A. M. Habermann, ed., *Sefer gezerot ashkenaz ve-tzarfat* [Persecution of the Jews in Germany and France] ([1945], repr., Jerusalem, 1971), 31.

67. Such as the story of ten martyrs executed by the Romans after the abortive Bar Kokhba rebellion. Alan Mintz, *Ḥurban: Responses to Catastrophe in Hebrew Literature* (New York, 1984), 84–105.

68. Shalom Spiegel, *The Last Trial: On the Legends and Lore of the Command to Abraham to Offer Isaac as a Sacrifice: The Akedah,* trans. with intro. by Judah Goldin

(New York, 1967); Ivan Marcus, "From Politics to Martyrdom: Shifting Paradigms of the Hebrew Narratives of the 1096 Crusade Riots," *Prooftexts* 2 (1982), 40–52; Mintz, *Ḥurban,* 95–97.

69. Katz, *Exclusiveness and Tolerance,* 22–23.

70. Ibid., 92.

71. Cohen, "Messianic Postures of Ashkenazim and Sephardim (Prior to Sabbethai Zevi)," in *Studies of the Leo Baeck Institute,* ed. Max Kreutzberger (New York, 1967), 115–56, reprinted in Cohen's *Studies in the Variety of Rabbinic Cultures* (Philadelphia, 1991), esp. 289ff.

72. Simonsohn, *Apostolic See and the Jews: History,* 257–62.

73. Cohen, "Messianic Postures of Ashkenazim and Sephardim," in *Studies,* esp. 289ff. See also, Haym Soloveitchik, "Between Islam and Christendom" (Hebrew), in *Qedushat ha-ḥayyim ve-ḥeruf ha-nefesh* [Sanctity of Life and Martyrdom: Studies in Memory of Amir Yekutiel], ed. Isaiah M. Gafni and Aviezer Ravitzky (Jerusalem, 1992), 149–52.

74. Ben-Sasson, "On the Jewish Identity of Forced Converts: A Study of Forced Conversion in the Almohade Period," 20.

75. Goitein, *A Mediterranean Society,* 2:276.

76. Lewis, *Jews of Islam,* 82–84; Hava Lazarus-Yafeh, "Queen Esther: A Forced Convert?" (Hebrew), *Tarbiz* 57 (1988), 121–22. On the possible role of Shiite *taqiyya* in influencing Jews to prefer conversion to martyrdom in late medieval Iran, see Moreen, *Iranian Jewry's Hour of Peril and Heroism,* 163.

77. Novak, "The Treatment of Islam and Muslims in the Legal Writings of Maimonides," in *Studies in Islamic and Judaic Traditions,* ed. Brinner and Ricks, 233–50 (quotation from 240). Eliezer Schlossberg finds a distinction in Maimonides' views as between his halakhic judgment and his theoretical assessment, which was more negative. See his "Attitude of Maimonides towards Islam."

78. Novak, "Treatment of Islam and Muslims," 237.

79. Yaakov Lev, "Conversion and Converts in Medieval Egypt" (Hebrew), *Peʿamim* 42 (1990), 79. See also, Lev, "Persecutions and Conversions to Islam in Eleventh-Century Egypt," *Asian and African Studies* 22 (1988), 87.

80. Ibn al-ʿAṭṭār, *Kitāb al-wathā'iq wa'l-sijillāt,* 407–8. Compare Monserrat Abumalham, "La conversión segun formularios notariales andalusíes: valoración de la legalidad de la conversión de Maimónides," *Miscelanea de estudios arabes y hebraicos* (Universidad de Granada), 24 (1985), 71–84.

81. Goitein, *A Mediterranean Society,* 2:299–300.

82. Ibid., 300. I do not touch here on the well-documented phenomenon of voluntary conversion, out of apparent religious or intellectual conviction, among Jews in the medieval Islamic world, some attracted through philosophy, others through Sufism (Islamic mysticism). For a recent contribution to this subject, see Joel L. Kraemer, "The Andalusian Mystic Ibn Hūd and the Conversion of the Jews," *Israel Oriental Studies* 12 (1992), 59–73.

83. Collective memory also reflects, even if on an unconscious level, the actual historical experience of their ancestors. The study of Jewish collective memory is still in its infancy. Yerushalmi's eloquent *Zakhor: Jewish History and Jewish Memory* is the best-known work on this subject, although Bernard Lewis's *History: Remembered, Recovered, Invented,* which examines Jewish evidence as part of a broader,

comparative inquiry using Middle Eastern examples, preceded it and anticipated many of its conclusions. Two smaller studies applying anthropology to history, one by Lucette Valensi and the other by Nathan Wachtel, bear on this subject as well, as does their joint effort, *Mémoires juives* (English, *Jewish Memories*). In a major essay, Ivan G. Marcus brings the anthropological approach to bear on medieval Jewish history and collective memory with respect to Ashkenazic culture.

In his classic work on collective memory, Maurice Halbwachs, speaking of the tension between history and collective memory, writes: "Collective memory . . . retains from the past only what still lives or is capable of living in the consciousness of the groups keeping the memory alive." Unlike history, which deals with change—which, in turn, is unitary and which means to be "objective and impartial"—collective memory is not universal but selective. The selection is determined by the self-perception of the group in the present. "History is a record of changes. . . . The collective memory is a record of resemblances and, naturally, is convinced that the group remains the same, because it focuses attention on the group, whereas what has changed are the group's relations or contacts with other groups." Halbwachs, *The Collective Memory,* trans. Francis J. Ditter and Vida Yazdi Ditter (New York, 1980; orig. in French [Paris, 1950]), 78–87. I have found this formulation helpful in organizing my own approach to the subject. But I feel that the dichotomy between history (written) and memory, as far as medieval Jewry is concerned, may not be so absolute. For instance, I believe there exists somewhat more "history" from the Ashkenazic Middle Ages than usually is recognized, and that these texts convey the same kind of thematics of Jewish collective memory that Yerushalmi's *Zakhor* finds in the premodern period only in nonhistoriographical formats. Said another way, historical texts themselves are inexorably intertwined with the commemorative acts of ritual and liturgy that mark the principal vehicles of Jewish collective memory in the premodern Jewish world.

Other citations above are: *Zakhor: Jewish History and Jewish Memory* (Seattle, Wash., 1983); Lewis, *History: Remembered, Recovered, Invented* (Princeton, N.J., 1975); Valensi, "From Sacred History to Historical Memory and Back: The Jewish Past," *History and Anthropology* 2 (1986), 283–305; Wachtel, "Remember and Never Forget," ibid., 307–35; Valensi and Wachtel, *Mémoires juives* (Paris, 1986), *Jewish Memories,* trans. Barbara Harshav (Berkeley and Los Angeles, 1991); Marcus, "History, Story, and Collective Memory: Narrativity in Early Ashkenazic Culture," *Prooftexts* 10 (1990), 365–88 (see also his "Medieval Jewish Studies: Toward an Anthropological History of the Jews," in *The State of Jewish Studies,* ed. Shaye Cohen and Edward Greenstein [Detroit, 1990], 113–27).

84. Yerushalmi, *Zakhor,* 8ff.

85. Lewis, *History,* 14ff.

86. The most recent book on this subject, Reuven Michael, *Ha-ketiva ha-historit ha-yehudit meha-renasan ʿad ha-ʿet ha-ḥadasha* [Jewish Historiography: From the Renaissance to the Modern Time] (Jerusalem, 1993), echoes the conviction that no significant Jewish historical writing existed in the Middle Ages (see the Introduction to the book).

87. Yerushalmi, *Zakhor,* 40–52; Lewis, *History,* 23, 45–48.

88. Yerushalmi, *Zakhor,* 46–48. Zvi Malachi discusses, and republishes some

of, the medieval *megilla* literature in *Sugyot ba-sifrut ha-ʿivrit shel yemei ha-beinaym* [Studies in Medieval Hebrew Literature] (Tel Aviv, 1971), vol. 1.

89. Yerushalmi, *Zakhor,* 53–75. Compare Lewis, *History,* 26–28. On the issue of how "new" the historical outlook of the sixteenth-century chroniclers was, see Robert Bonfil, "How Golden Was the Age of the Renaissance in Jewish Historiography?" *History and Theory* 27 (1988), 78–102. For a critique of Yerushalmi's assumption that the expulsion of 1492 was a watershed in Jewish history, and thus giving rise to the histories of the sixteenth century, see Ivan G. Marcus, "Beyond the Sephardic Mystique."

90. See Marcus, "History, Story, and Collective Memory," 365–88.

91. Robert Chazan, "The Blois Incident of 1171: A Study in Jewish Intercommunal Organization," *Proceedings of the American Academy for Jewish Research* 36 (1968), 17–21.

92. Yerushalmi, *Zakhor,* 34, 37–39. Yerushalmi observes that the "single most important religious and literary response to historical catastrophe in the Middle Ages was not a chronicle of the event but the composition of *seliḥot,* penitential prayers, and their insertion in the liturgy of the synagogue"; ibid., 45.

93. Text in Habermann, *Sefer gezerot ashkenaz ve-tzarfat,* 11–15. Compare Robert Chazan, "The Persecution of 992," *Revue des études juives* 129 (1970), 217–21; idem, *Medieval Jewry in Northern France: A Political and Social History* (Baltimore, 1973), 10–12.

94. Text in Habermann, *Sefer gezerot ashkenaz ve-tzarfat,* 19–21. Compare Chazan, "1007–1012: Initial Crisis for Northern-European Jewry"; idem, *Medieval Jewry in Northern France,* 12–15. See also note 100 below.

95. Ephraim of Bonn's chronicle, *Sefer zekhira,* in Habermann, *Sefer gezerot ashkenaz ve-tzarfat,* 115–32. The first part of Ephraim's chronicle, dealing with the persecutions during the Second Crusade, is translated in Eidelberg, *The Jews and the Crusaders,* 121–33. The part about Blois is translated in Jacob R. Marcus, *The Jews in the Medieval World: A Source Book, 315–1791* (Cincinnati, 1938), 127–30. On the Blois persecution, see Chazan, "Blois Incident of 1171," 13–31. On the "chronicle" as a work of historiography, see idem, "R. Ephraim of Bonn's *Sefer Zechirah,*" *Revue des études juives* 132 (1973), 119–26.

96. Yerushalmi, *Zakhor,* 48–52.

97. Ephraim took material from letters contemporary with the event in Blois. The text of the letters has been published in Habermann, *Sefer gezerot ashkenaz ve-tzarfat,* 142–46. A partial English translation appears in Chazan, *Church, State, and Jew,* 300–304; idem, "Blois Incident of 1171," 17–21. At some time (probably not long after the event), the text of the letters was tacked onto the end of the longest of the three Hebrew chronicles of the First Crusade.

98. Solomon ibn Verga, *Shevet yehuda,* ed. A. Shohat and Y. Baer (Jerusalem, 1947), 146–49. Joseph Shatzmiller, "Provençal Chronography in the Lost Pamphlet by Shemtov Schanzolo" (Hebrew), *Proceedings of the American Academy for Jewish Research* 52 (1985), 43–61.

99. A. David, "Stories Concerning Persecutions in Germany in the Middle Ages" (Hebrew), in *Papers on Medieval Hebrew Literature Presented to A. M. Habermann,* ed. Zvi Malachi (Jerusalem, 1977), 69–83. The account was copied in 1485, at the end of a manuscript containing astronomical and astrological texts.

100. Mentioned in Fritz (Yitzhak) Baer, *Untersuchungen über Quellen und Komposition des Schebet Jehuda* (Berlin, 1936), 2. In his monograph, *The "1007 Anonymous" and Papal Sovereignty: Jewish Perceptions of the Papacy and Papal Policy in the High Middle Ages,* Kenneth Stow argues that the Hebrew account of an episode of persecution at Rouen in 1007, during the reign of King Robert of France, assumes background that makes it necessary to date its composition in the thirteenth century, rather than in the eleventh. It fits with what Stow calls a realistic Jewish awareness that the papacy was their most dependable protector, a conviction, he says, that first emerged in the post-Gregorian reform period, grew during the period of the Crusades, and became firm during the thirteenth century. If this revisionist interpretation gains acceptance, it will mean that the "chronicle" constitutes yet another exception to Yerushalmi's rule that medieval Hebrew chronicles "dwell either on the distant, ancient past, up to the destruction of the Second Temple [i.e., *Yossipon*], or they describe something in the most recent past, be it the latest persecution or the latest deliverance."

101. On the liturgical poetry, see, for instance, Mintz, *Ḥurban,* 89–105; and, for numerous examples in the original Hebrew, Bernfeld, *Sefer ha-dema*ʿ*ot,* vols. 1–2.

102. The latter, Nathan Wachtel observes, "recount, basically the same trials: uprooting, migrations, persecutions, impossibility of mourning"; Wachtel, "Remember and Never Forget," 333.

103. The best edition is Moshe Gil, *Eretz yisrael ba-tequfa ha-muslimit ha-rishona (634–1099)* [Palestine during the First Muslim Period (634–1099)] (Tel Aviv, 1983), 2:41–43 (no. 26) [hereafter, Gil, *Palestine* (Hebrew)]; compare Gil, *Palestine* (English), 377. The Babylonian Gaon Samuel b. Ḥofni (d. 1013), learning about the suffering of the Jews of Fez, Morocco, during some local disturbance, wrote to them: "When we heard the news from you, our heart trembled. . . . Our eyes and hearts wept over the destruction of our sanctuary [probably: synagogues] and over the deaths of our people and the evil done to our young men. We ask God to kill those who killed them, and afflict and smite with pestilence those who smote them." Hirschberg, *A History of the Jews in North Africa,* 1:106 (my English translation differs slightly from Hirschberg's); the editor of this text, A. Cowley, "Bodleian Geniza Fragments," *Jewish Quarterly Review,* o.s., 18 (1905–6), 403–4, incorrectly surmised (ibid., 400) that the Gaon was referring to the al-Ḥākim persecutions.

104. Gil, *Palestine* (English), 378.

105. A dirge by the Spanish-Hebrew poet, Joseph b. Isaac ibn Abitur, begins, "Weep, my brothers, and lament / over Zion with great commotion." The dirge originally was taken to have been composed on the occasion of the persecutions by Caliph al-Ḥākim in 1012. See Hayyim Schirmann, "Elegies on Persecutions in Palestine, Africa, Spain, Germany, and France" (Hebrew), *Kobez al Jad,* 3 (13) (1939), 27–29; idem, *Ha-shira ha-*ʿ*ivrit bi-sefarad uve-provans* [Hebrew Poetry in Spain and Provence] (Jerusalem, 1954), 1:64–65.

As Goitein argues in an article first published in 1964, Ibn Abitur mourns Jews who died as a result of the atrocities committed against the populace when rebellious Bedouin tribes overran Fatimid Palestine in 1024 and 1025. (Geniza letters, similarly, depict Jewish suffering during this time of troubles in Palestine.) See Goitein, *A Mediterranean Society,* 5:58–59. On the events, see Gil, *Palestine* (English), 385–97. Goitein's theory has been confirmed by Ezra Fleischer's discovery of a Hebrew quasi-liturgical poem from about the same time by an otherwise unknown poet, who, however, dwells on the general depredations, not on Jewish suffering. See "A Historical Poem Describing Some Military Events in Syria and Erez Israel in the Early 11th Century" (Hebrew), *Zion* 52 (1987), 417–26.

106. Moses ibn Ezra, *Kitāb al-muḥāḍara wa'l-mudhākara,* ed. A. S. Halkin (Jerusalem, 1975), 66–67.

107. Ibn Daud, *Sefer ha-Qabbalah,* 75–76 (English).

108. Yonah David, ed., *Shirei Yitzḥak ibn Giyyat 1038–1089* [The Poems of Rabbi Isaac Ibn Ghiyyat Lucena 1038–Cordoba 1089] (Jerusalem, 1987), 165 (no. 84) and 219–20 (no. 120).

109. Ibn Daud, *Sefer ha-Qabbalah,* 87–88 (English). On the possibly symbolic meaning of the incorrect date of 4873 (1112–13), see Cohen's supplementary note, ibid., 141ff. A few pages later in the book, Ibn Daud returns to the Almohad persecutions in order to describe how God, "who prepares the remedy before afflictions," had previously arranged for the installation of the Jewish notable, Judah b. Ezra, in the good graces of King Alfonso, so that the Jews fleeing Almohad terror could find refuge in the Christian North (*Sefer ha-Qabbalah,* 96–97).

110. Ibn Daud, *Sefer ha-Qabbalah,* 219–20.

111. Goitein, *A Mediterranean Society,* 5:59–61.

112. L. M. Simmons, "The Letter of Consolation of Maimun ben Joseph," *Jewish Quarterly Review,* o.s., 2 (1890), 62–101 (the Arabic text lies between pages 335 and 369). See also, Eliezer Schlossberg, "The Attitude of R. Maimon, the Father of Maimonides, to Islam and Muslim Persecutions" (Hebrew), *Sefunot,* n.s., 5 (20), 95–107 [Proceedings of the Second Conference of the Society for Judaeo-Arabic Studies].

113. Moses ben Maimon, *Iggerot,* ed. and trans. into Hebrew by Kafiḥ, 107–20; English trans. by Halkin, *Crisis and Leadership: Epistles of Maimonides,* 13–45.

114. In thinking through the next section, I consulted several scholars of medieval Hebrew poetry and would like to thank them for their bibliographical assistance and comments. They are Professors Ross Brann, Ezra Fleischer, Ephraim Hazzan, Raymond Scheindlin, Yosef Yahalom, and Masha Yitzhaki. I am also grateful to Professor Sasson Somekh for his helpful criticism of the argument.

115. Discussed, among other places, in Hirschberg, *A History of the Jews in North Africa,* 1:123–25 (compare also, the Hebrew edition, *Toledot ha-yehudim be-afriqa ha-tzefonit* [Jerusalem, 1965], 1:90–91); and in Yisrael Levin, *Avraham ibn Ezra: ḥayyav ve-shirato,* 18–20, 344, n. 58, where Levin discusses evidence for the single authorship of both "Aha yarad ʿal sefarad" and another, imitative eulogy beginning "Eikh neḥerav ha-maʿarav" ("O how the Maghreb has been destroyed"), found in the Geniza among some leaves containing lamentations on the destruction of the Temple (Dropsie College, now Annenberg Institute MS 316), and excerpted by Schirmann for his article, "Elegies on Persecutions in Palestine, Africa, Spain, Germany, and France," 31–35. See also, Dan Pagis, "Dirges on the Persecutions of 1391 in Spain" (Hebrew), *Tarbiz* 37 (1968), 357 and n. 19, where Pagis expresses his opinion that the Geniza version is from the pen of Ibn Ezra.

116. I am grateful to Professor Ross Brann for allowing me to read his article, "Power and Poetry: Constructions of Exile in Hispano-Hebrew and Hispano-

Arabic Elegies," and to use his translation of parts of Ibn Ezra's poem. The article will appear in the Yisrael Levin Festschrift, ed. R. Tsur and T. Rosen, Tel Aviv University Press.

117. The tradition developed in Italy and passed to the Ashkenazic lands of northern Europe, as Professor Fleischer commented.

118. Or when the questions raised by the present analysis are asked of the known material in a systematic fashion.

Professor Fleischer kindly showed me several *piyyuṭim* from the Cairo Geniza by Shlomo Sulaymān ibn ʿAmr al-Sinjārī (whose floruit Fleischer has convincingly dated to the second half of the ninth century), which Fleischer is planning to publish in a forthcoming article in *Zion*. Extremely hostile toward Muslims (called *meshuggaʿim* [on this polemical term, see Chap. 9 in this book]), these poems contain allusions to specific acts of oppression (being forced to wear "colored" items; plundering of "tents and dwellings"; taxes). Possibly the verses allude to the oppressive decree of Caliph al-Mutawakkil in 850 (see above) and/or to some other general violence during the ninth century from which Jews suffered. On the poet Shlomo Sulaymān al-Sanjārī, see Ezra Fleischer, *Ha-yotzerot be-hithavutam ve-hitpatḥutam* [The Yoẓer: Its Emergence and Development] (Jerusalem, 1984), 191–93; and, idem, "Piyyuṭ and Prayer in *Maḥzor Eretz Israel*" (Hebrew), *Kiryat Sefer* 63 (1990–91), 257. For some Jewish reactions to the early Islamic conquests in poetry and prose, see Yosef Yahalom, "The Transition of Kingdom in Eretz Israel (Palestine) as Conceived by Poets and Homilists" (Hebrew), *Shalem* 6 (1992), 1–22.

119. Regarding the dirge of Joseph ibn Abitur, once thought to have been dedicated to the al-Ḥākim persecution, see above, note 105.

A dirge by Judah ha-Levi, included in Sephardic and Yemenite collections of lamentations for the Ninth of Av (also published in Schirmann *Ha-shira ha-ʿivrit bi-sefarad uve-provans*, 2:325–26) and formerly incorrectly ascribed to Isaac ibn Giyyat and believed to refer to the destruction of the Jerusalem Temple, actually relates atrocities suffered by the Jewish community of Majorca when it was ruled by or in the name of the Muslim Almoravides. See Wasserstein, *The Rise and Fall of the Party Kings*, 89. The historical background of this elegy has not yet been investigated. See also, Fleischer, "Materials and Observations towards a Future Edition of the Poems of R. Judah ha-Levi" (Hebrew), *Asufot: Annual for Jewish Studies* 5 (1991), 111.

120. The eleventh-century Hebrew poet of Muslim Spain, Solomon ibn Gabirol, penned two elegies, each about the brutal murder by Christians ("Edomites") of possibly one and the same friend (the method of death, by stabbing, and other details occur in both poems). H. Brody and H. Schirmann, eds., *Shlomo ibn Gevirol: shirei ḥol* [Solomon ibn Gabirol: Secular Poems] (Jerusalem, 1974), 122–24 (no. 198), 164–66 (no. 248). Two lamentations by an unidentified poet, found in the Geniza, bemoan the murder of a Jew that took place in Guadalajara, in Christian Spain. H. Schirmann, *Shirim ḥadashim min ha-geniza* [New Hebrew Poems from the Genizah] (Jerusalem, 1965), 446–50.

A *seliḥa* (penitential poem) for the Day of Atonement by the Saragossan Hebrew poet Levi ibn al-Tabbān describes anti-Jewish persecutions thought to have occurred at the time of the sacking of the city by King Alfonso VI of Castille and Leon (ca. 1090) or on the Christian reconquest of the city from the Muslims by King

Alfonso I of Aragon, in 1118; Dan Pagis, ed., *Shirei Levi ibn Tabban* (Jerusalem, 1968), 68–72 and 6 in the editor's introduction.

Two elegies on a local persecution written by Judah ha-Levi pertain, it seems, to an outbreak of violence in Christian Toledo (one of the poems mentions Toledo in the rubric, and E. Fleischer assumes that the other refers to the same event); Fleischer, "Materials and Observations towards a Future Edition of the Poems of R. Judah ha-Levi," 121–30. See also, Y. Levin, "Suffering in the Poetry of Judah ha-Levi from the Time of the Crisis of the Reconquista" (Hebrew), *Otzar yehudei sefarad (Tesoro de los judíos sefardíes)* 7 (1964), 49–64.

121. Dr. Masha Yitzhaki kindly informed me that "Aha yarad ʿal sefarad" is contained in a Yemenite collection of lamentations (*qinot*) for the Ninth of Av, dating from the beginning of the seventeenth century (MS Paris Heb. 1332, fol. 60a) as well as in a manuscript of diverse Hebrew poems copied at the end of the eighteenth century by a certain Rabbi Abraham Ḥalfon, who lived in Tripoli, Libya (D. Cazés, "Antiquités judaïques en Tripolitaine," *Revue des études juives* 20 [1890], 83–87). The version "Eikh neḥerav ha-maʿarav" found in the Geniza is contained among poems of lamentation by Ibn Ezra on the destruction of the Jerusalem Temple. Possibly some Jews used these pages during the *qinot* of the Ninth of Av. Many other liturgical poems (*piyyuṭim*) by Ibn Ezra can be found in the good company of those by other famous Andalusian poets in Sephardic prayer-books. For instance, the *Sefardi Maḥzor for Yom Kippur from the Year 1481,* MS Parma De Rossi 1377, facsimile edition by Makor (Jerusalem, 1973), folios 24a, 77b, 96b, 102a. Hirschberg writes regarding the main phase of Almohad oppression in North Africa during the reign of ʿAbd al-Mu'min, that "Moroccan-Jewish popular tradition preserves no memory of these events"; *A History of the Jews in North Africa,* 1:138.

122. Simon Bernstein, ed., *ʿAl naharot sefarad* (Tel Aviv, 1956), 243–44 (as truncated in the manuscript), 114–19 (repr. according to the full version in the Diwan of Abraham ibn Ezra, ed. Jacob Egers in 1886). Egers's Yemenite manuscript places the poem in a section on dirges "for the Ninth of Av, the Exile, the Destruction [namely, of the Jerusalem Temple], and for the persecution [literally, 'forced apostasy,' Hebrew *shemad*] in North Africa and Andalusia" (66–69 in the Egers edition).

Bernstein also reprints (112–13, 241–43), from the Sephardic Maḥzor printed in Venice in 1524, another dirge ascribed to "Abraham [ibn Ezra]," beginning *Yom nilḥemu vi yaḥad shekhenai,* "On the day my [gentile] neighbors did battle against me." This poem does not, however, appear in the Lisbon Manuscript nor in any of the printed editions of Abraham ibn Ezra's works. Professor Fleischer kindly gave me his opinion (private communication, February 11, 1992) that, despite the poem's inclusion in Y. Levin's critical edition of the sacred poetry of Ibn Ezra, *Shirei ha-qodesh shel Avraham ibn Ezra* (Jerusalem, 1980), 2:297–99, the authorship of the poem remains doubtful.

123. Jacob Mann, *The Jews in Egypt and in Palestine under the Fāṭimid Caliphs,* 2 vols. (1920–22; repr. as 2 vols. in 1, New York, 1970), 1:30–32; 2:31–37; idem, "A Second Supplement to 'The Jews in Egypt and in Palestine under the Fāṭimid Caliphs,'" *Hebrew Union College Annual* 3 (1926), 258–63 (passage quoted on 261); Goitein, *A Mediterranean Society,* 2:28–29; Gil, *Palestine* (English), 376–77.

Yerushalmi says (imprecisely; *Zakhor* 119, n. 37) that the Scroll "refers to deliverance from the persecution of the Caliph Al-Hakim in 1012." The text is also discussed briefly in Malalchi, *Sugyot,* 25–26 and reprinted there, 34–39.

124. Some years earlier, Samuel composed a similar prose/poetic account of deliverance from a different "persecution." Two individuals, one in Palestine and the other in Egypt, had attempted to harm the Jews by leveling accusations against them before Christian clerks in the Fatimid government, but were seized and punished by the authorities before they could effectuate their evil designs. This occurred under the rule of the same Caliph al-Ḥākim of the infamous persecutions. See Benjamin Z. Kedar, "Notes on the History of the Jews of Palestine in the Middle Ages" (Hebrew), *Tarbiz* 42 (1972–73), 401–5. Kedar gives this text the nickname "Megillat Shenei Ha-Soṭenim," or "The Scroll of the Two Fiends."

125. Goitein, *A Mediterranean Society,* 2:285; Tritton, *Caliphs and Their Non-Muslim Subjects,* 109.

126. M. Zulay, "Liturgical Poems on Various Historical Events" (Hebrew), *Yediʿot ha-makhon le-ḥeqer ha-shira ha-ʿivrit* 3 (1936), 163–75.

127. Sāwīrūs ibn al-Muqaffaʿ, *Ta'rīkh baṭārikat al-kanīsa al-miṣriyya,* 2:part 2, ed. and trans. Aziz Suryal Atiya et al., 183–209 (English trans.), quote from 204.

128. Mann, *Jews in Egypt,* 1:34.

129. Samuel the Nagid ibn Nagrela's call for a "Second Purim" at the end of his triumphal poem, "Eloha ʿoz" (Mighty God), celebrating the victory of his Granadan troops over the army of the "party kingdom" of Almeria in 1038, memorializes a deliverance from harm that Samuel feared would have come to himself and his Jewish community had he lost the battle. Fascinating in the poem are: (1) the application of the typology of the Book of Esther to what was essentially a "cover" for a human victory; (2) the poet's prideful command that his (and God's) local victory be commemorated throughout the Arabic-speaking Jewish communities of Ifriqiya (Tunisia), Egypt, Palestine, and Babylonia (Iraq) with a special Purim; and (3) his call that it be recorded "in their books" so that the event would be "remembered forever after and by generation after generation." Unlike the instance of the "Egyptian Purim" of 1524 (discussed below), however, I know of no evidence that the anticipated deliverance from danger in 1038 entered the collective historical memory of the Jews, even in Spain itself. See *Divan Shmuel Hanagid,* ed. Dov Jarden (Jerusalem, 1966), 1:4–14; and the discussion by Yerushalmi, *Zakhor,* 46–47.

130. See Malachi, *Sugyot,* 61–97.

131. Judah ibn ʿAqnīn was a crypto-Jew of the early Almohad period who lived in Fez, Morocco, where he met Maimonides.

132. *Dhimmi,* 346–51. It comes from Part 6 of Ibn ʿAqnīn's unpublished Judaeo-Arabic ethical treatise, *Ṭibb al-nufūs* [Therapy of the Soul]. See Oxford MS Huntington 517 (Neubauer *Catalogue,* 1273), beginning at fol. 138v, lines 27–28. I consulted the manuscript on microfilm at the Jewish Theological Seminary and the Bodleian Library. Compare Abraham S. Halkin, "On the History of the Almohad Persecution" (Hebrew), in *The Joshua Starr Memorial Volume* (New York, 1953), 101–10. I am grateful to Saul Zucker for sharing some of his knowledge of the book with me.

133. "Trials and tribulations" is rendered *al-imtiḥānat wa'l-ḍayqāt.*

134. In Part 3 of the manuscript of *Ṭibb al-nufūs,* Ibn ʿAqnīn mentions the Jews of the "community of Fez, of Sijilmasa, of Darʿa, and of other places, all of which, together, have singular standing in that they martyred themselves [in Hebrew, *qiddeshu et ha-shem*]." Compare Joseph ben Judah ibn ʿAqnīn, *Inkishāf al-asrār wa-ẓuhūr al-anwār* [The Divulgence of Mysteries and the Appearance of Lights], ed. and trans. into Hebrew by A. S. Halkin (Jerusalem, 1964), 308, referring to forced conversion and *qiddush ha-shem* (martyrdom).

135. The following excerpts from "Therapy of the Soul" are taken from Bat Ye'or's anthology:

> Our hearts are disquieted and our souls are affrighted at every moment that passes, for we have no security or stability. On account of our numerous sins it was said of us, "And among these notations shalt thou find no ease" (Deuteronomy 28:65). . . . Past persecutions and former decrees were directed against those who remained faithful to the law of Israel. . . . But in the present persecutions, on the contrary, however much we appear to obey their instructions to embrace their religion and forsake our own, they burden our yoke and render our travail more arduous.
>
> If we were to consider the persecutions that have befallen us in recent years, we would not find anything comparable recorded by our ancestors in their annals.
>
> Then a new decree was issued, more bitter than the first, which annulled our right to inheritance and to the custody of our children, placing them in the hands of the Muslims.
>
> We were prohibited to practice commerce, which is our livelihood.
>
> Then they imposed upon us distinctive garments. . . . The purpose of these distinctive garments is to differentiate us from among them so that we should be recognized in our dealings with them without any doubt, in order that they might treat us with disparagement and humiliation. . . . Moreover it allows our blood to be spilled with impunity.
>
> It is clear from what I have explained that we have deserved all these persecutions that we have suffered, for they bare [reveal] not even a fraction of the sins that we have committed against God and the great punishment we deserve for having sinned whether deliberately or unwittingly when we were forced to forsake our faith. For of a truth, we should have suffered martyrdom rather than convert, since our law requires that if the sin demanded of us is not for the benefit of our enemy . . . but only to convert us, then we must die rather than transgress.

136. Nor, certainly, was this true of the apostasies in Egypt and Palestine under al-Ḥākim, in North Africa and Spain under the Almohads, or in the Yemen.

137. "Mordecai of Our Time" = *mordechai ha-zeman,* alluding to Mordecai, the Jew who defeated Haman. Mann, *Jews in Egypt,* 1:212–14, 2:257–63; Cohen, *Jewish Self-Government,* 279–80.

138. See my review of Goitein's collected Hebrew essays, *Palestinian Jewry in Early Islamic and Crusader Times,* in *Tarbiz* 53 (1983–84), 153–54.

139. The best edition is Gil, *Palestine* (Hebrew), 3:391–413 (no. 559). Compare

Gil, *Palestine* (English), 750–74. The *megilla* and the episode are also treated in my *Jewish Self-Government,* 178–226.

140. See the edition by A. Kahana, "The Scroll of Zuta the Evil-doer" (Hebrew), *Haschiloach* 15 (1905), 175–184; repr. in Malachi, *Sugyot,* 41–51.

141. My *Jewish Self-Government* is devoted to the subjects of administration, politics, and political conflict within a Jewish community of the Islamic High Middle Ages.

142. Aḥmad Pasha is called the "well-known Satan" in several Hebrew versions of the story. Muslim sources called him *al-khā'in,* or "the traitor."

143. See the study, with edited texts, linguistic analysis, and English translation, by Benjamin Hary, *Multiglossia in Judeo-Arabic* (Leiden, 1992), with discussion of all earlier bibliography on this source. For a literary discussion, see Malachi, *Sugyot,* 53–60. Compare also, Yerushalmi, *Zakhor,* 48.

144. The work has been described and translated into French by Georges Vajda and later published in the original by David Ovadia. Georges Vajda, *Un recueil de textes historiques judéo-marocains* (Paris, 1951). See also David Ovadia, ed., *Fas va-ḥakhamekha* [Fez and Its Scholars] (Jerusalem, 1979), 1:1–63, and Vajda's translation, included as an appendix.

145. Vajda reorders the episodes chronologically.

146. Two other "chronicles," from late medieval Iran, written in Judeo-Persian, recite the disastrous persecution and forced conversion of Jews by the Shiite regime of the Safavids. One of them, composed by Bābāī ibn Luṭf, covers periodic persecutions between 1617 and 1662. The other, by Bābāī ibn Farhād, the grandson of Bābāī ibn Luṭf, relates the oppression that led to the mass conversion of the Jewish community of Kāshān around 1729. Moreen's publications on these two sources have made it feasible for students of Jewish collective memory in Europe to compare the well-known Ashkenazic and Sephardic chronicles with Oriental counterparts from a period of great oppression. Moreen, *Iranian Jewry's Hour of Peril and Heroism;* and *Iranian Jewry during the Afghan Invasion:* The Kitāb-i Sar Guzasht-i Kāshan *of Bābāī b. Farhād* (Stuttgart, 1990).

147. Samuel Usque, *Consolation for the Tribulations of Israel,* trans. Martin A. Cohen (Philadelphia, 1964), 163.

148. Benjamin of Tudela, *Itinerary,* 54–56 (English trans.).

149. *Book of Genealogies,* first published in 1566, in Constantinople by the Egyptian Jew, Samuel Shulam.

150. I consulted the Cracow edition of 1600, fol. 146v. Dinur, *Yisrael ba-gola,* 2d ed. (Tel Aviv, n.d.), 1:102, excerpts the passage from the first edition (1566; part 5, fol. 148r). On Zacuto, see Yerushalmi, *Zakhor,* 57. A longer account—which begins in the same way as that in *Sefer yuḥasin* and which reproduces additional elements found in Arab chronicles—appears in the seventeenth-century Egyptian Jewish historian Joseph Sambari's *Divrei yosef,* MS Paris Alliance Israélite Universelle Collection H 130 A, facsimile ed. by S. Shtober (Jerusalem, 1981), fols. 26v–27r. Sambari borrowed heavily from Muslim Arabic sources through the medium of Shulam's "additions" to Zacuto's *Sefer yuḥasin* (see Shtober, "The Chronologies of the Muslim Kingdoms in Sambari's Chronicle, *Divrei Yoseph,*" 424–29). For the passage on al-Ḥākim in Sambari, see also, Mann, *Jews in Egypt,* 1:33–34, n. 3. Al-Ḥākim is characterized as "fickle-minded and malicious" (*hafakhpakh ve-ish*

tekhakhim) and credited with the forced conversion of 10,000 Jews and Christians, whom he, a week later, allowed to return to their original faiths, as well as with the "burning" of 12,000 Jews in their quarter in Fustat.

151. Solomon ibn Verga, *Shevet yehuda,* 63–66. Baer has little to say about this story in his *Untersuchungen über Quellen und Komposition des Schebet Jehuda,* beyond confirming Isidore Loeb's observation that the story is factually impossible. See Baer's work, 63; for Loeb's, see "Le folk-lore juif dans la chronique du Schébet Iehuda d'Ibn Verga," *Revue des études juives* 24 (1892), 27. See also M. Wiener, *Das Buch Schevet Jehuda* (Hannover, 1856), 78–84. I have not found the passage discussed at any significant length in the literature on *Shevet yehuda.*

152. *Sar eḥad mi-sarei yishmaʿel asher baʾ ʿim sheliḥut.*

153. The Muslim ambassador finds this quite unbelievable.

154. Perhaps a veiled jab at Christianity, which professes to love its enemies but persecutes the Jews.

155. Al-Qarāfī, *Al-ajwiba al-fākhira ʿan al-asʾila al-fājira,* 4.

156. Yitzhak F. Baer, *Galut,* trans. Robert Warshow (New York, 1947), 9.

157. See S. D. Goitein, "A Report on Messianic Troubles in Baghdad in 1120–21," *Jewish Quarterly Review,* n.s., 43 (1952), 57–76 (text begins on 73). Here, *galut* means something like "state of persecution or oppression."

158. Passages from letters from three European Jewish visitors to the Middle East in the late Middle Ages, characterizing the local Jewish condition for Jews "back home," are offered below. Provisionally, I shall leave the word *galut* untranslated in each case.

159. Stillman, *Jews of Arab Lands,* 75. Compare Eli Strauss (Ashtor), "The Social Isolation of Ahl Adh-Dhimma," in *Essais orientaliques: Livre d'hommage à la mémoire du P. Hirschler,* ed. O. Komlós (Budapest, 1950), 73–94.

160. *Ve-omnam min ha-yishmaʿelim ein galut la-yehudim klal ba-maqom ha-ze.*

161. A. Yaari, ed., *Letters from the Land of Israel* (Hebrew) (repr., Ramat-Gan, 1971), 128.

162. The word used for "upheaval" is *hafekha;* compare Genesis 19:29.

163. *Ein kol kakh galut daḥuq be-khaʾn af ʿal pi shelo yittakhen bilti galut.* Yaari, ed. *Letters from Israel,* 181.

164. Ibid., 186–87 (*po ein galut kemo be-artzenu veha-togarmim mekhabbedim ha-yehudim ha-nikhbadim*). The second part means, "and the Turks hold the respectable Jews in esteem."

165. Kobler, *Letters of Jews through the Ages,* 2:339; Stillman, *Jews of Arab Lands,* 291.

166. Gershom Scholem, *Sabbatai Sevi: The Mystical Messiah* (Princeton, N.J., 1973), chap. 3: "The Movement in Palestine (1665)."

167. Jews were more excluded in Morocco, where, since late Almohad times, they constituted the sole *dhimmī* community. In Fez, in 1438, for example, the first more or less compulsory Jewish quarter in the Muslim world was established, although initially for the Jews' own protection, and not as punishment. This soon came to be called *mellaḥ,* a word often rendered imprecisely as "ghetto." See Stillman, *Jews of Arab Lands,* 79–80; and his "Moroccan Jewish Experience: A Revisionist View," 116.

Noteworthy in the present context is the text Stillman cites from Jacob

Toledano, *Ner ha-maʿarav: hu toledot yisrael be-morocco* [The Western Lamp: History of the Jews in Morocco] (Jerusalem, 1911), 44. Citing unnamed chroniclers (*kotevei zikhronot* [literally, "writers of remembrances"; the reader will recall Ephraim of Bonn's *Sefer zekhira,* or Book of Remembrance]), Toledano explains that the Jews themselves viewed their confinement as a "sudden and bitter exile" [*galut mar ve-nimhar*], indeed, an "expulsion" [*gerush,* from the Old City of Fez, where they had long lived, to a location outside, reserved for the Jews].

Conclusion

1. "Second-class citizenship, though second-class, is a kind of citizenship," writes Bernard Lewis, *Jews of Islam,* 62.

2. Jews rarely held the position of chief minister. The Andalusians Samuel the Nagid ibn Nagrela and his son Joseph, and the Egyptian merchant Abū Saʿd al-Tustarī are notable exceptions.

3. Babylonian Talmud, Bava Kama, 58a, s.v. "*inammi*" (near the bottom), trans. Salo Baron, in *Social and Religious History of the Jews,* 4:63–64 (emphasis added). Baron interprets Rabbi Isaac's statement as an early Jewish protest against the rescindment of former liberties of movement. See also, Baron, *Social and Religious History,* 11:18ff., where the author shows how Rabbi Isaac's doctrine caught on among later rabbis.

4. See H. Schirmann, "The Life of Jehuda ha-Levi" (Hebrew), *Tarbiz* 9 (1938), 239.

5. See the discussion of collective memory in Chap. 10.

6. Moses ben Maimon, *The Epistle to Yemen,* trans. Stillman, *Jews of Arab Lands,* 241–42 (slightly altered here). Stillman's rendition is somewhat closer to the Arabic text than the translation in Halkin and Hartman, *Crisis and Leadership: Epistles of Maimonides,* 126–27, as is the Hebrew translation of J. Kafiḥ, in his *Iggerot,* 54.

7. In a recent study of the Jews in medieval Champagne, Emily Taitz builds on the statement of Rabbi Isaac of Dampierre, arguing that some Jews of northern Christendom maintained a pretense of noble status and that this persisted even as their legal and social position declined in the thirteenth century. Taitz, "The Jews of Champagne from the First Settlement until the Expulsion of 1306" (Ph.D. diss., Jewish Theological Seminary of America, 1992), 154, 318–19. I am grateful to Dr. Taitz for allowing me to obtain a copy of her thesis, which stimulated me to think comparatively about the equally celebrated Maimonidean passage.

8. Bernard Septimus, "Better under Edom than under Ishmael: The History of a Saying" (Hebrew), *Zion* 47 (1962), 103–11; compare the source quoted in Bat Ye'or, *The Dhimmi,* 352–54.

INDEX